THE

SPY

WHO

SEDUCED

AMERICA

Lies and Betrayal in

the Heat of the Cold War

The Judith Coplon Story

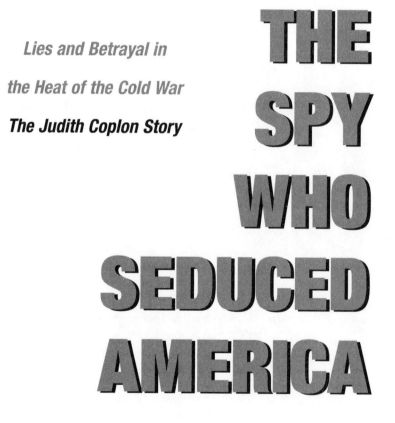

THE SPY WHO SEDUCED AMERICA

Marcia and Thomas Mitchell

Invisible Cities Press • Montpelier, Vermont

Invisible Cities Press
50 State Street
Montpelier, VT 05602
www.invisiblecitiespress.com

The Library of Congress has catalogued this book as follows:

Mitchell, Marcia.
The spy who seduced America : lies and betrayal in the heat of the Cold War :
the Judith Coplon story / Marcia and Thomas Mitchell.
p. cm.
Includes bibliographical references and index.
ISBN 1-931229-22-8 (cloth : alk. paper)
1. Coplon, Judith. 2. Spies—United States—Biography. 3. Espionage, Soviet—
United States—History. I. Mitchell, Thomas. II. Title.

UB271.R92 C675 2002
327.1247073'092—dc21
2002024295

Book design by Peter Holm, Sterling Hill Productions

SECOND PRINTING

He was of the old school, of the days when the FBI's Quantico was a single three-story building with a basement, when high-tech was no-tech. He was bright, dedicated, visionary. For all he gave to us, for all he told us, this book is lovingly dedicated to Robert Lamphere, who died during our final editing stage. For Robert, like others who worked on this case, its star was the enigmatic "spy who seduced an entire country."

CONTENTS

AUTHORS' NOTES

Fact or Fiction?

The Spy Who Seduced America is not based on a true story; it *is* a true story, true according to the available record. Very little between these covers can be attributed to discretionary or whimsical poetic license. The writers' sources included more than fifteen thousand pages of trial transcripts and nearly two thousand published news reports; court filings, dockets, evidentiary exhibits, and related documents. Significant sources were people who kindly granted interviews, including retired FBI agents who played major roles in the story, and former KGB officers who knew the other side of it. If there is poetic license involved, madcap attorney Archibald Palmer is the principal licensee, author of perhaps the most colorful, convoluted and confusing language ever uttered in a courtroom. Palmer's unorthodox literary and oratorical flights of expression, his savaged syntax and dazzling dialogue, appear here as delivered. Appropriately outrageous, they belong within, and are part and parcel of, the context of this bizarre tale of Justice on a wild theme-park holiday.

When fiction entered the story, it often did so masquerading as fact, parading in different patchwork costumes in two mind-boggling courtroom trials. The fact of Justice became fiction, depicted in a New York *Mirror* cartoon as cross-eyed, holding a grievously unbalanced scale. Underneath, Supreme Court Justices comment on the case: "The whosis of the howsis is the cause of the whysis." The fact of a government complying with its own laws was fictionalized in a deceptive web of its own spinning. The fiction of a spy as being irretrievably valueless and terminally unprincipled was considered fact. In a very real sense, fact and fiction need redefining here, an exercise left to the reader.

Another exercise in definition is left to the reader sorting through the fact/fiction issue. Who, or what, was the protagonist of the story? The authors have learned that the controversy about her, begun so many years ago, surprisingly continues today in certain erudite circles.

Sources

In nearly all cases, with the exception of some personal interviews and letters, more than one source supports what is written here. To have used traditional methods of citation would have resulted in a volume twice this size and a distressingly disruptive flow to the narrative. For example, quotations and courtroom scenarios are reported or recorded, in much the same language, in numerous sources—often partly in one and partly in another. The same information may be found in original stenographic notes and other court documents, as well as in several media sources; it may as well have come from more than one personal interview. Had this been a textbook, voluminous, extensive citing would have been required. But it is not. The book is intended for a general audience and thus the problem of supporting what appears here was addressed by providing key source documentation in the appendices.

Readers wishing to go to original sources for this story will find in the appendices information on specific testimonies and their archival locations, as well as the location of relevant court documents. It should be noted that, for the most part, only the original documents are available in the archives and record center, placed there in the days before mirofiche and computer capabilities facilitated research. They can be accessed by personal visit—an extraordinary experience, particularly when one finds a historic, formerly secret document someone failed to destroy as directed.

Other key information is from the joint NSA/CIA Venona monographs and reports, and case-related published writings. Citations for the relevant documents appear in the appendices. Finally, there is a notation on one recently declassified document from KGB files, acquired by the authors during an exhilarating moment of revelation in Moscow.

Access to FBI reports and records on the Coplon case is limited to those that were made a part of the public record; fortunately, certain key FBI surveillance reports were found in court files and are cited here with their court, rather than Bureau, identification.

Given the amount of material reviewed, collected and copied over more than a decade, the authors can only imagine, with gnawing desire, what is still kept secret in the Hoover Building on Pennsylvania Avenue.

PROLOGUE

Views from Different Windows

There was something terribly wrong about the case. FBI agents lied in court, one after another committing perjury on the stand. A young government lawyer who would later be a part of the prosecution team was the defendant's lover until the day of her arrest. Not one of the dozens of agents on twenty-four-hour-a-day surveillance ever saw the accused pass secrets to the enemy, or heard an incriminating word on their wiretaps and bugs. A mysterious "confidential informant" who supposedly set the government on her trail never existed. There was not a single shred of evidence presented in either of her trials that proved she had spied against her country. And, of course, there never should have been two trials, two arrests, two indictments. For good reason, J. Edgar Hoover was set against even one arrest, and never wanted to prosecute her.

She was Judith Coplon, a brilliant graduate student and a Washington, D.C., employee of the U.S. Department of Justice who had received numerous commendations for exemplary performance on the job. She had grown up in a loving Jewish American family, a family known to be impeccably honest, decent, and respected. Records from elementary school through college showed not only excellent scholarship but also outstanding citizenship—and patriotism. Her arrest shocked the nation. It simply did not fit into the picture of someone friends and neighbors thought of as "the all-American girl" and "the typical girl next door."

Judith Coplon, twenty-seven, enchanted and mesmerized the country. She became an immediate media phenomenon, with reporters and photographers following her every move, paparazzi without the name their successors would earn. More than any film star, for nearly two years she made the headlines, gossip columns, radio newscasts. To some, she was a victim of excesses born of a Red-hating group fantasy. To others, she was "Mata Hari in Bobby Sox," and deserved the death penalty.

As for me, I believed she was innocent when I set out to learn the truth more than a decade ago. My husband did not, although it was his business to believe she was guilty. After all, he was part of the agency that pursued her.

Through years of research, I became very fond of the woman who was the subject of perhaps the most bizarre legal case in American jurisprudence. It is a strange sort of caring. We send greetings through her husband, attorney Albert Socolov, whom my husband and I have come to know and treasure. On one occasion, Albert thought Judy might join us for dinner, but he came alone. For decades, Judith has remained firm in her resolve not to grant interviews, not to talk to any writer. The past has been her bottled genie.

Al's insistence upon his wife's innocence matches her own. Still deeply in love, he has told us amazing things about Judith's "second" life, which began in 1967, when her eighteen-year legal ordeal finally ended. We have decided to speak in generalities about that life, wishing to impose as little as possible on matters belonging to the family and not to history.

Judith's husband was set against publication of her story. "It happened so long ago, and her grandchildren don't know," he said. Unwilling to inflict pain on this woman, we decided to put the story aside, to forget about finishing this book. But then, between 1995 and 1997, the National Security and Central Intelligence Agencies released to the public certain Cold War information held secret for more than four decades. Some of the information I already had collected through other sources, but now all of it is available to anyone interested. The genie, it seems, is emerging from the bottle.

Following release of the Cold War data, the picture changed significantly for Judith Coplon, and for us. Someone was bound to write about this incredible case and its amazing aftermath. I could not live with the thought that the someone might be someone else. The project moved back on track, with my ex-G-man husband agreeing to coauthor the book.

In the summer of 1997, curiously enough, we found the final pieces of the Judith Coplon puzzle in Moscow, Russia, and near Moscow, Idaho. In Russia we met with former KGB officers; in Idaho with the retired American FBI counterespionage supervisor who orchestrated the Coplon case from its beginning in December 1948.

Here, then, is the completed picture, put together from thousands of pages of court transcripts and documents; federal agency evidence and records, some held secret for nearly half a century; surveillance logs; thousands of press clippings; and personal interviews, here and abroad. The puzzle, with all the pieces finally in place, appears to answer the question: Victim or spy? Or, perhaps, both?

MARCIA MITCHELL

It became an immediate and unrelenting obsession from the moment she first heard the story. "She" was my wife, whose career had gone from journalism to public broadcasting to, now, the world of film. "What a movie," she said, "what a book."

It began as we drove from Washington, D.C., down to Virginia Beach through a pounding rainstorm, with her at the wheel. Not complaining, but matter-of-factly, she observed that it only poured rain when it was her turn to drive. "Pull over where it's safe, and I'll drive," I offered.

"No, I'd rather," she answered. "But entertain me. Tell me a story. An FBI story, one from the years when you were on counterespionage. I like that era best."

And so I told her about Judith Coplon, the first Cold War spy arrested and tried in this country. In my opinion, the case had all the elements of a fiction writer's dream of the ideal espionage script: a beautiful but innocent-looking female subject; the international intrigue of a mysterious informant; possible compromise of the government's most sensitive counterespionage information; and sophisticated (for that period) technical surveillance of the subject's most personal conversations and activities leading up to the night of her arrest, a night when I was on duty in the secret nerve center of our technical surveillance operations. It was a night when all agents were operating under explicit instructions: Don't lose her, and don't get "made." They did, and they were.

To me, this was only the first phase of a fascinating story. The trials were to come, trials in which Archie Palmer, a relatively unknown attorney, inexperienced in criminal law, outwardly bumbling and unorthodox in his courtroom tactics, completely befuddled the top legal experts of the U.S. Department of Justice and caused experienced, competent FBI agents to embarrass the Bureau. Embarrassing the Bureau was a mortal sin in the eyes of its director, J. Edgar Hoover.

Other major espionage cases were to follow, some in which I had a more prominent role, but none (thank God) had the high drama, desperation, confusion, and, yes, madness of the Coplon case.

In my mind, Judith was unquestionably guilty of espionage, a Soviet agent who escaped federal prison through the antics of a zany attorney. There was never a doubt in my mind. I was there at the time, and I knew all the players. My belief in her guilt was based on the suspicious nature of her behavior while under surveillance, and on the evidence found in her purse the night of March 4. And I believed what I believed because, one night two weeks later, I heard the voice of guilt—her voice.

And so the obsession to find the truth, along with our constant arguing about the case, began that rainy day along Interstates 95 and 64. It took us back and forth and up and down this country and to another country halfway around the world. It took us on searches through musty boxes of court records that had not been touched in fifty years. On one occasion, it took us to Manhattan at Christmastime, where we sat in a small Chinese restaurant with Judith's husband, talking quietly about the case, life afterward, about his family and ours. Al produced a picture of Judith, taken on a recent trip to China.

"Look at her," Marcia wept, "she looks just the same. After all these years, so much like the news shots, with that same wonderful smile."

"You," Al told her kindly, "are a softie."

Which is why it has taken so long to finish the story. But for us, finally, it has come to an end. Sadly, for Al and Judith and their family, it never will.

Tom Mitchell

PART ONE

FROM **BROADWAY** TO **CONSTITUTION AVENUE**

March 4, 1949

The stalker's eyes, frosty, intense, never left the woman. His brain, carefully trained for the process, recorded her every step, her every movement and gesture as he moved expertly through the early-evening crowd in Manhattan's Pennsylvania Station. At one point, a heavyset woman with a child attached to each side of her shabby winter coat stopped directly in front of him, momentarily blocking his view, and he roughly shoved her out of his way. She turned to give him a withering look, but he was gone.

If the object of his pursuit was aware of the danger the stalker presented, she did not show it in her expression, which remained calm and confident. But her movements suggested that she at least suspected his presence. Both of them, the man and the woman, were aware of the possibilities tonight. One could win and one could lose. Her loss could be her freedom or, even, her life.

At first glance, nothing about the attractive young woman who had stepped off the train from Washington, D.C., would seem unusual. But only at first glance. Wearing a fitted black wool coat and a black beret cocked fashionably over her left brow, she moved briskly, like a mechanical doll with a short circuit, going first one direction and then another, up one flight of stairs and down a different flight; moving forward, turning, retracing steps. She entered the two-story women's room on the lower level and seconds later emerged through the upper-level door. A silent signal from the stalker alerted another follower, a woman, who went into the rest room.

A casual observer might have conjectured that the subject of their interest, whom they called "the package," was lost or bewildered by the five-thirty crunch of commuters rushing by, but the self-assured way in which she walked, in whichever direction, belied that conclusion. She did, however, seem to be looking for someone in the crowd, even as she thumbed through a magazine at a newsstand. Finally, after a last glance over her shoulder, she left the station and went out into the chilly Manhattan night, using the busy 34th Street exit. At that moment, they were now three, but that would soon change.

At New York City's Foley Square headquarters of the Federal Bureau of Investigation, Al Belmont, the assistant special agent in charge, was monitoring an extensive surveillance operation, puffing on the ever-present cigar clenched between his teeth. Remarkably, Ed Scheidt, special agent in charge of the New York City FBI office, and Robert Granville, chief of the Espionage Section, were both "on the street," supported by two dozen agents. It was an extraordinary level of Bureau activity, even for New York.

In Washington, D.C., J. Edgar Hoover sat in his office, waiting. When he received word, he would place a call to President Harry Truman. Hoover was not happy about what was happening in Manhattan at the moment, had not been happy about any of it from the beginning. His had been a different solution to the problem, but, uncharacteristically, he had allowed himself to be talked into a distasteful, risky operation. The chief of the world's top intelligence agency waited now in the smaller of his two private offices, a single Acco-bound folder resting on his highly polished desk. The file was new, numbered 65-58365. The first two numerals identified the nature of the case: espionage.

Although his position often required him to play a waiting game, J. Edgar Hoover never did so with any measure of patience. In this case, the director of the Federal Bureau of Investigation was particularly impatient.

At ten minutes after six o'clock, forty minutes after her arrival in Manhattan, the young woman in black boarded a crowded Eighth Avenue northbound train, clutching a large leather handbag to her chest, shoving into standing space where she remained until, many blocks later, she found a seat. At the 181st Street station she left the train, moving along with the crowd toward the 181st Street exit. Suddenly, she reversed her direction and walked, alone, toward the northernmost exit, one leading to 184th Street.

Outside the station, she stood looking about her. On Broadway she walked past 187th Street, then continued to 193rd. The evening was growing colder, with the temperature just above freezing. With black-gloved hands she pulled the lapels of her coat closer, then stopped and walked into a small, brightly lighted coffee shop. One would assume her purpose was to order something warm to drink, but she was out on the street again within two minutes, hardly time enough. Continuing north on Broadway, she crossed to the east side of the street and stood in front of a drugstore. After some seven minutes of standing and pacing, she left the corner and walked south.

The unmarked black Ford sedans winding through the streets of Manhattan had radio contact with headquarters but not with each other, which meant the man in the cigar cloud and his radio operator, Flo Bachrach, had their hands full controlling a street operation of this magnitude.

In Brooklyn, at 178 Ocean Parkway, an older Jewish couple waited for their only daughter, a bright, successful young government worker in Washington, who had telephoned a few days earlier to say that she would spend the night with them. She was faithful about coming to New York to see them whenever possible; usually, like today, on a Friday. Their daughter was a source of enormous pride to both parents. A cum laude Barnard graduate, she was in the process of completing a brilliant master's degree program at American University.

• • ● • •

Entering a cigar store on the corner of Broadway and 193rd Street, the young woman inquired of the proprietor where she might find a rest room. And not one in a tavern, she said. She did not want to go to a tavern.

"Well, there's Bickford's. It's a nice restaurant," he offered.

At exactly the time the woman disappeared into the cigar store, a short, stocky, fair-haired man left the tunnel leading from the 191st Street station of the Seventh Avenue subway. Hurriedly he walked north on the east side of Broadway and made his way to a drugstore on the southeast corner of 193rd Street, diagonally across from the coffee shop the young woman had entered earlier. A few minutes later he left the store carrying a small package and stood on the street, waiting. After five minutes, he went one block down to 192nd Street, crossed over, and stood at a bus stop. Twenty minutes passed; then, after having ignored several southbound buses, he boarded one going that direction, twice glancing over his shoulder as he climbed the steps.

At FBI headquarters in New York, Raymond Whearty, now an assistant U.S. attorney and former head of the Foreign Agents Registration Section of the Department of Justice in Washington, D.C., was another who waited impatiently. Down the hall, a matron sat idly waiting. Bob Granville had asked her to stay tonight because they were bringing in a woman; normally, she would have been home by now.

The women's room at Bickford's was clean and well appointed. After a few minutes, the young woman emerged from the restaurant and was back out on Broadway, where she turned and went north. Immediately, the stocky, fair-haired man came into view, walking toward her. For a moment, it looked as if he were going to greet her, but some gesture, some signal, must have put him off and he continued walking in the opposite direction, passing her in the process. They went on this way for half a block, when he whirled, retraced his steps, and caught up with her. Neither spoke, and they walked side by side for several steps before he pulled away and rushed to a bus stop at the corner of Elmwood and Broadway. And she, meanwhile, walked leisurely to the next corner and turned left for one block, up an empty, unlighted street. She turned again and went back to Broadway, where she caught the Seventh Avenue subway.

There was desperation in the radio room. One of subjects was now on a bus and the other on a subway. What if they didn't get together? What if she didn't make the transfer? If it didn't work tonight, would it ever work? Would the pair take the risk if they were aware of being tailed? The question of "another time" was burning into Granville's brain. This was a cat-and-mouse game of the first order. No doubt the mice knew the cats were out tonight, knew they were closing in. If it didn't happen tonight, the mice might never come out of their holes again. Granville listened to the latest report on his radio. "They never touched," he complained to Scheidt. "Nothing transferred."

Leaving the subway at Times Square, the young woman once again stood outside a cigar store for several minutes, this one on the northwest corner of Seventh Avenue and 42nd Street, before walking west. As if from nowhere, the fair-haired man suddenly appeared about fifteen feet behind her. For more than two blocks he kept precisely the same distance between them; then, without apparent warning, he took off running, dashing across Ninth Avenue, where he boarded a bus. The young woman broke into a run and, at the last possible second, hopped on board the same bus.

The couple left behind more than one surprised surveillance agent. But two agents in one of the black Fords had not been left behind; they pulled alongside the bus, where the man and woman were clearly in view, seated several rows apart. At 14th Street, the couple left the bus and walked briskly to Eighth Avenue, where they entered the BMT subway station.

The Ford pulled to a stop in a loading zone directly in front of the station and its occupants hurried inside, their quarry still in sight. The man and woman were walking together toward a train; the agents followed, closely, but not too closely. If the surveillance subjects were aware of two men who boarded their train at the last minute, they did nothing to show it. The followers settled into separate seats at the rear of the car, caught their breath, relaxed their muscles ever so slightly, and went about the business of locked-on watching. Moments later, both men visibly tensed as the nearly empty car ground to a noisy stop at the next station. No one moved, not until the final second before the door slammed shut. And in that final second, the mysterious couple bolted from their seats and were out of the train and running across the platform. The agents made a desperate dive for the door, but were not in time. They watched in dismay as the car pulled from the station, with them inside.

Belmont, his ever-present foggy halo overhead, slammed down the telephone. Bachrach immediately began directing all cars to the area where the suspects had left the train.

The chase that so interested Mr. Truman and Mr. Hoover in Washington continued on in America's sweetheart city, in wild, vibrant Manhattan. By now it had gone from Penn Station to uptown, uptown to midtown, downtown, crosstown to Times Square, through the chilly neon-lighted night. It was a deadly game played out to the cacophony of impatient taxicab horns and elevated trains and the nighttime people noises that make Manhattan unique.

Granville was thinking about this city, about the possibility of losing the suspects altogether in its labyrinthine possibilities, when he came to a conclusion. If they were found again, here in Manhattan on this noisy March night, he would arrest them. From the beginning, the decision to arrest or not had been his. And now he made it. There would be no waiting to make certain that documents had changed hands. There was no worry about not having an arrest warrant; after all, Granville assured himself, the law provided for an arrest without warrant under these circumstances.

At that very moment, the news burst through the static. The subjects had been spotted. Together. Down on 15th Street and Third Avenue.

"Let's go!" Granville yelled, shoving the accelerator to the floor and turning on the siren. With the wail of the siren and the high-pitched squeal of the car's noisy fan belt, a giveaway trademark of the Bureau's black Fords, they raced downtown from Broadway and 180th Street. Careening onto 14th Street, the siren was silenced by design, and the car slowed by traffic. They dodged taxicabs and ignored red lights, nearly clipping the coattails of pedestrians taking too long to cross intersections.

The woman in black and the fair-haired man stood watching, rooted to the sidewalk as Granville whirled the car around a post supporting the Third Avenue el and brought it to a screeching halt at the curb. He leaped from the car and grabbed Judith Coplon's arm.

"FBI! I'm Special Agent Robert Granville. You're under arrest," he told her.

March 4–5, 1949

FBI headquarters occupied several floors in the Federal Courthouse Building at Foley Square. The Espionage Section was on the twenty-ninth floor, with various Bureau offices on the sixth floor and the court itself on the first. In the basement of the building, behind an FBI firing range, were two holding cells. It was to a sixth-floor office that Judith Coplon, a political analyst at the U.S. Department of Justice in Washington, was taken immediately following her arrest. Waiting for her, among others, were Sappho Manos, a Bureau secretary, and Genevieve Charos, a nurse. The man who had been arrested with her, Valentin Gubitchev, an engineer with the Soviet UN delegation, was taken to an office down the hall.

The three women, Coplon, Manos, and Charos, went into a private office, where Manos held Judith while Charos stripped and searched her. "I need my glasses from my pocketbook," Judy told them. "Could you get my pocketbook for me?"

"Are you kidding me?" Manos asked.

In another office, Granville watched as FBI Agent T. Scott "Scotty" Miller dumped the contents of Judith's purse on the table. A cursory examination horrified them. What they had expected to find on the Russian was there; it had never passed from the woman to Gubitchev. Not a single thing.

Granville paled, realizing they had to break this unfortunate bit of news to the old man. "Scotty, you make the call. He's waiting." At the moment, Granville had other matters to attend to, which did not include listening to J. Edgar Hoover rant and rave for thirty minutes. He turned to the crestfallen Miller. "Listen, we've still got a case. Not as good, but a case. Remind him of that." Both Granville and Scheidt left the office. With a trembling hand, Miller reached for the telephone.

In the room where Judith had been searched, she asked about calling her parents. They were expecting her, she explained. They were not well; they would be frightened. There was no response.

The office to which she was taken was large, with Miller and two other agents waiting. They introduced themselves as Agents Robinson and Wilson. Miss Charos and Miss Manos took two of the remaining chairs, and Robinson pulled up a chair for Judy.

"Sit down," he said, not unkindly.

From this point on, until approximately three o'clock in the morning, there are two very different versions of what took place in that office on the sixth floor. According to Judith, the following occurred after she was seated:

"Please, I need to have my parents notified," she asked. "They're both ill and I know they're worried. Will you have someone call them?"

"Later," Miller responded.

"Well, may *I* call my parents? Now?"

"Later."

"What about an attorney? Are we in the United States or not?"

"Yes, young lady, we're in the United States. Of course you have a right to call an attorney. You've already been told that."

"Fine. Then let me call a lawyer!"

"We'll get to that later. Now," he pulled his chair directly in front of hers, "you know what we're holding you for, don't you? You know what you were arrested for?"

"Absolutely not! Why was I arrested? What are you charging me with, for God's sake?"

She was not given an answer. Nurse Charos rose from her chair, reached into the pocket of her white uniform, removed several capsules, and handed them to Judith. "Ammonia," she said crisply. "In case you feel faint."

Miller began the questioning. "Judy, you had a meeting in New York tonight with Valentin Gubitchev. Do you know who he is?"

"No comment."

The questions were repeated over and over again. How many times had she met Gubitchev? Where? When? For what reason? Was he her controller? Had she intended to give the contents of her purse to Gubitchev? And more. To each she answered, "No comment."

The interrogation went on for more than five hours, the same questions asked over and over again. Angry, exhausted, Judy finally cried, "I have no comment. I won't have until I talk to a lawyer."

"Say, I've got a lawyer for you and he's close by," Robinson laughed at one point, gesturing toward Miller. "Scotty's a lawyer. How about him? No? Well, we've got a lot of other agents who are lawyers and several of them are in the building right now. You can take your choice."

Seldom were all five of the FBI staff in the room at the same time. One or another would leave, then return and beckon someone else into the hallway. Judy could hear excited whispering from time to time and could catch phrases such as, "The Russian said . . ." or "and he said that the papers"—that sort of thing. She clearly heard the loudly whispered words "a dirty spy" come from outside the open door. Then Manos disappeared and reappeared about thirty minutes later with a typewritten draft several pages long, which she showed to the three men.

The accused looked at her watch. It was after two-thirty in the morning. The morning of March 5. "How much longer is this going to go on?" she asked. "It should be obvious that I'm not going to answer any questions until I have a lawyer and until my parents have been notified." And then, realizing the hour, she added hastily, "Wait, don't call my parents." It was too late; a call would terrify them.

At about three-fifteen, physically and emotionally drained, Judith was alone in the room with Robinson. "Can I go somewhere to sleep for a while?" she asked.

"Sure. You probably need some rest."

"Where? Where can I lie down?"

"Fall asleep in your chair," he suggested.

Scott Miller's recall was different:

Judy was told about 10 P.M. that she could have an attorney, "the first time. And shortly after 11 P.M., the second time," and still later, at 2:05 A.M. She never asked for one, although, Miller said, "I told her she was entitled to the services of an attorney. She didn't ask for one when I told her that."

As for Judy's asking him to get in touch with her parents and let them know her whereabouts, Miller insisted, "She never asked me that."

From 10 P.M. until after 2 A.M., Miller was Judy's principal interrogator, during which time she was completely uncooperative, refusing to answer questions or make any statements, with the exception of saying, at one point, "I would prefer to talk with an attorney." Despite Judy's refusal to answer questions, the examination continued until federal attorney Raymond Whearty came into the room and said, "You'd better stop questioning her and tell Miss

Coplon that we have called a judge . . . when she is brought before the judge she can make any request that she desires."

Miller would assert over and over again that Judy had not asked for an attorney until after two o'clock on the morning of March 5, and that not once had she asked anyone to call her parents or her brother, Bertram Coplon. He did not, he would later claim, ever "call her names" or treat her in an insulting manner. There was no dispute over the length of time spent questioning Judy or with regard to her refusal to answer questions. The interrogation ceased when Miller left the room to prepare a complaint for Judith's arrest. In the normal course of events, a complaint would have been filed before an arrest was made. These were not normal circumstances.

Judge Simon H. Rifkind was sleeping soundly when the call came asking him to go to the federal courthouse in the wee hours of the morning to arraign two alleged spies. A few minutes before four o'clock, Judith Coplon and Valentin Gubitchev were led separately into the first-floor courtroom to appear before Rifkind. In the hallway outside the courtroom, Raymond Whearty, former friend, former supervisor at the Justice Department, approached Judith and coldly handed her a subpoena. "Here, Judy, here's a subpoena," he said. Nothing more. She was stunned.

The defendants were without counsel. Judy told the judge she had requested, and had been denied, access to an attorney. "I had decided I wanted to call Mr. Levin," she said. Levin, an attorney friend, lived in New York and would, she felt certain, come to the courthouse as soon as possible. Rifkind immediately announced a new time for the arraignment, seven o'clock, when he would expect counsel for both defendants to be present.

Levin, shocked and horrified, hurried to Foley Square and stood beside his friend for the scheduled arraignment. No, he told the judge, he was not prepared to represent Judy and asked for a delay until eleven o'clock, at which time he would return with another attorney, a friend, Bertram Adams. Adams, he explained, had experience in criminal law. And so, for a second time, arraignment of the first Cold War spies arrested in the United States was postponed, and the prisoners were led again, separately, downstairs to the holding cells behind the firing range.

By midnight Friday, in the house at 178 Ocean Parkway, Rebecca and Samuel Coplon were frantic, certain that something terrible had happened to their daughter. It was so unlike Judy not to have called, not to have explained why her plans to return home "about ten, after dinner with a friend," had changed. Although Al Socolov, the man Judith would later marry, insists that Samuel was too ill to be aware of what was happening at the time, Rebecca said of that night that a troubled Samuel kept asking, "Where is Judy?"

After a sleepless night, at 6:50 in the morning, a representative of the Associated Press called Mrs. Coplon to tell her that her daughter, Judith, had been arrested on a charge of giving official information to a representative of the Soviets and was being held in custody. Screaming, "It's not true, it's not true," Rebecca dropped the telephone. Confused and frightened, Judy's Aunt Emma picked it up and nervously explained that Judy had been expected home last night, but had not arrived.

Ten minutes later, Bertram Coplon called. Yes, he told his hysterical mother, his beloved sister, Judy, had been arrested and charged with passing papers to the Russians. The whole matter, he thought, had to deal with her work in the Department of Justice. The next call was from *New York Times* reporter Randy Cunningham.

"It's not true!" she repeated in response to his news. "We are all good Americans. We were born here!" Later, she would tell reporters, "I screamed and screamed when I finally learned the truth."

Bert Coplon, six years Judy's senior, was an attractive, intelligent man. Readers who saw his photograph in the newspapers in the days to follow were reminded of a favorite film star of the day, Tyrone Power. This morning, distraught, burdened with the role his father would have held not that many years ago, he hurried to the Ocean Parkway apartment, where he tried to comfort his mother and aunt, check on his ailing father, and decide what he should do first. He had been told of Judy's arraignment and planned to be there, but without his mother. Rebecca and Emma would stay with Samuel.

Shirley Seidman Coplon, Bert's wife, listened to her husband telling her, over the telephone, that the charge against his sister was very serious. How many times, Shirley asked, did Bertram think Judith had passed papers to Russia? Bert was furious. In a second conversation, Shirley asked if Bert thought there was a foundation for the charges against Judy. Yes, Bert said, he thought there was. He worried that she had been used as "a tool."

Shirley's father, banker J. A. Seidman, suggested that Bert get in touch with attorney Archibald Palmer, whom Mr. Seidman said was "well connected in Washington." Seidman also knew a Mr. Keenan, identified as "the man who tried the criminals in Japan." Seidman wanted to be helpful, but before the week was out, there would be an effort to distance him from his son-in-law's family. As vice president of the Kings Highway Savings Bank in Brooklyn, the connection might cost him his job.

Rebecca Coplon experienced the first day of what would be a period of profound, unrelenting misery. It was, from the outset, beyond her belief that anyone could say such terrible, impossible things about her daughter. "Judy is so sweet, so gentle, so kind. Just like her father," she told friends who called this Saturday morning. Later, she said, "I think my heart will break . . . when they tell about arresting her and then taking her down to their headquarters and disrobing her. How dare people do such things to a child?"

Outwardly calm, Bert Coplon watched his younger sister enter the courtroom at precisely eleven o'clock. The man walking behind her, the Russian engineer, was handcuffed; she was not.

Judith Coplon and Valentin Gubitchev were seated at separate tables in front of the bench. Judge Rifkind first called the Coplon case, indicating that the young woman should stand before him.

"Did you expect to have counsel here?" he asked. She turned and looked around the courtroom. "My counsel does not seem to be here."

"Please be seated," he told her. He called Gubitchev's case and the Russian reluctantly rose and went forward. "Are you represented by counsel?" Rifkind asked.

"Yes sir," Gubitchev answered in English, "but I don't see him in court. I expect him later." Irritated, Judge Rifkind instructed the waiting U.S. attorneys to locate missing defense counsel, and to do so in a hurry. Levin and Adams appeared moments later.

Another attorney was present, Oscar Schachter, a member of UN secretary general Trygve Lie's staff. Schachter explained to the court that he was not representing Gubitchev, who was a UN employee, but instead was representing the United Nations itself.

Charges against Judith and the Russian were read:

"Conspiracy to commit espionage, conspiracy to remove government documents relating to the national defense, and conspiracy to defraud the government of the impartial services of Miss Coplon." These were only technical charges supporting the arrest, the judge explained, merely "arraignment charges." In going before the grand jury, the government could, and most likely would, seek indictments under other sections of the federal law that carried more severe sentences. The arraignment charges carried maximum penalties of ten thousand dollars in fines and five years in prison. Judge Rifkind, of course, did not mention to the accused that the United States, some four years after hostilities with Japan had ended, was still technically at war. More serious charges could mean the death penalty.

Adams waived examination for his client, which allowed the court to hold Judy for the grand jury. Raymond Whearty immediately rose to his feet. "Your Honor, the government asks that bail for Miss Coplon be set at $50,000," he said.

"Fifty thousand!" shouted Adams. "That's totally out of line! The data allegedly found on Miss Coplon's person are not of an important nature, and she certainly isn't going anywhere."

"We do not know whether she intends to flee," Whearty argued, "but it would be hard to apprehend her if she did."

"Hard?" Adams challenged hotly. "This young woman's family is here; her parents, parents who are quite ill. Where would she go?" He turned and gestured toward a silent, intent Judy. "Further, my client's record in Washington is unblemished and she is far, far from a sinister type." Adams's voice softened. "Your Honor, we must allay the prevailing hysteria in connection with such charges as these, hysteria that might make it difficult for my client to have a bonding agency write her bail. We ask $5,000 bail."

"I certainly don't find myself involved in any hysteria," Rifkind responded evenly, denying the request. "The charge is of maximum gravity because of the nature of the possible penalties. It is a charge of conspiracy with an agent of a foreign government involving defense materials." A pause, then, "Bail is set for Miss Coplon at $20,000," an announcement that satisfied neither Adams nor a visibly angry Whearty.

Judy, who stood to hear the judge's decision, looked composed, almost indifferent. She was still clad in the same clothes she had worn when arrested, a black wool skirt, matching sweater, and the black wool coat. Her tam was not in evidence. She wore a strand of pearls as her only jewelry. Judith's thick auburn hair was neatly parted in the middle and waved loosely above her shoulders. She might have been going out to lunch with friends.

The Coplon toy manufacturing business, now directed by Bert, adequately supported his parents and his own young family, but did not provide sufficient reserves for contingencies such as a sister in jail for high crime. He had been worried about raising five thousand dollars. Now he needed to find four times that amount.

Whearty requested one hundred thousand dollars' bail for Gubitchev, who continued to insist that he had diplomatic immunity and was therefore being held contrary to international law. Because no attorney appeared to speak for the Russian, Judge Rifkind addressed all of his remarks directly to Gubitchev, taking pains to ensure that he clearly understood what was taking place. From time to time, Gubitchev would say, "I don't know what that means," and the judge would painstakingly repeat and rephrase.

During a brief recess, reporters asked Schachter for his opinion on the immunity question.

"Immunity applies only to an official function," he answered. "Anything in the nature of personal or private acts, outside of diplomatic service, does not have immunity." His answer settled nothing. It was not a part of the court procedure and was only the first shot in a bitter diplomatic battle about to take place over the Russian's status.

With the court back in session, Whearty reiterated his request for high bail. "Mr. Gubitchev even now has permission to return home in June. The government feels that he is the chief offender in this case."

Chief offender. The government's position on culpability, favorable to Judith, would soon change. For now, it offered some relief to Bertram Adams and Bert Coplon. As for Judith, she seemed not to notice, now appearing distant, unmoved. When it was all over, she moved almost dreamily down the aisle, her arm held by a marshal. Her brother went to her and caught her in his arms; the officer, kindly, stepped back and allowed the embrace. Bert let her go, turned quickly, and headed for a telephone, dialing his home number. Shirley was not helpful; she said Judy "knew what she was doing all along."

Reporters and photographers had a field day. An attractive young woman, a government worker at that, was the most exciting alleged spy since the ill-fated Mata Hari. Outside, as Judy was taken to a federal women's detention center, the gray spring midday was suddenly splashed with a brilliant, silvery, meteor shower of flashguns.

It had only just begun.

Judith

Who was Judith Coplon? The country was immediately, insatiably, curious, wanting to know everything about her. The initial story of her arrest carried little background information, but each subsequent piece revealed additional details about the alleged spy and her life before March 4, 1949. The American public soon learned that, according to her neighbors, Judy was a quiet, respectable "girl," who sometimes went bicycling with a dark-haired young man. She was described at first as beautiful, attractive, petite; later, as sultry-eyed, vivacious, and glamorous. She had a "flashing" smile and stylish shoulder-length hair in a deep brown that matched her "lovely eyes." And always she was described as a girl, never a woman. Except for the young man on the bicycle, there were no reports of romantic activity.

Forty-two years later, Curt Gentry, writing in *J. Edgar Hoover: The Man and the Secrets*, would paint a totally different picture of Judith Coplon. She was, Gentry insists, a woman of loose morals, one who routinely entertained men in her apartment, who brazenly had sex with the drapes left open, whose behavior titillated the FBI agents who had her under surveillance. Her adventures, he reports, were known to them as "The Punch and Judy Show." Differing with this view, along with the early media interviews with her neighbors, are two FBI agents who were on the case in 1949. "I would have heard about this if it were true," one says. "Not so," says the other. A third surveilling agent told the authors that Judy openly flirted with the men following her. Still, reports of Judy's college lifestyle suggest that the possibility of a wild, exhibitionist sex life seems totally out of character for her.

In the United States and abroad, the Coplon story was mesmeric from the beginning. An ardent public studied pictures of a smiling, wholesome-appearing young woman, and read about her family and a background atypical only in her outstanding scholarship and selfless service to others. She looked so American, so decent, so proper. People were confused.

Did spies look like this?

Many thought not. A debate ensued almost immediately. Questions flew. Wasn't it possible that Judith Coplon was as innocent as she appeared? That the arrest was based on a tragic misunderstanding? Worse, there was speculation that this whole business was an insidious figment of ultra-right-wing imagination gone out of control. Clearly, certain politicians and their supporters were extremely gratified to find an alleged spy in Harry Truman's government. It was a brouhaha of enormous proportion, with the ingredients for the McCarthy era already simmering away in the national cauldron.

Newspapers and radio broadcasts reported to their readers and audiences that Judith was an accomplished young woman who had been not only a Barnard College honor student, but also an honorable student. Judy had chaired the college war board, a patriotic campus organization supporting the war effort. She was a giving, caring student, the media learned and reported, who actively participated in a dozen student organizations, including the honor society, Arista. Teachers and administrators who had known Judith were quoted praising Judith's accomplishments. In an amazing summary of her attributes, Barnard's Placement Bureau said she was "in the top category in the following qualities—natural ability, application, originality, integrity, straightforwardness, modesty, fair play, public spirit, enthusiasm, leadership, good breeding."

Did spies begin like this?

Adding to the public bewilderment and fascination during those first days after the arrest, particularly for people living in New York State, was the revelation that Judith Coplon was the daughter of the "real" Santa Claus so many of them loved.

For nearly three decades, Samuel Coplon, Jewish, a onetime traveling toy salesman and later a successful toy manufacturer, spent the Christmas holidays delivering thousands of toys to poor children in six upstate New York counties. He was widely known in New York and, in fact, throughout the East as the "Santa Claus of the Adirondacks." As a wounded Spanish-

American War veteran recuperating in the Adirondacks, Samuel had been moved by the plight of poor children running through the snow with only flour sacks to protect their feet. Years later, Samuel was playing Santa to children who, without his generosity, would have had no Christmas. Each holiday season, Samuel's family participated through their enthusiastic support of his annual trek. It made the holidays happier not only for "Santa," which generations of grateful mountain children and their parents called him, but also for Mrs. Santa and Santa's own children, Judith and Bertram.

Did spies come from families like this?

Little was written about the younger Judith Coplon, the obedient child brought up in Brooklyn's East Flatbush section in a modest, middle-class household filled with love. Mother and father were patriotic, highly respected citizens; brother and sister were model children who adored each other. Judy Coplon was a bright and well-behaved student from her earliest school days. Her teachers delighted in her, and her grades and deportment always were excellent. At James Madison High School, she joined the staff of the school's magazine, *The Highwayman*, and began an interest in writing and publishing that would last a lifetime.

A scholarship awarded for scoring an impressive 97 on her state college placement examinations launched Judy's college career. She was a day student, a member of that part of Barnard's student body that did not participate in the more active social life of those who resided in dormitories. There was a very definite distinction between the two; dorm students went to fraternity dances, dated Columbia boys, socialized on campus. Day students went home. Judith's circle was mainly Jewish, all exceptionally bright, survivors of tough competition for the limited number of day enrollments available. Political interests provided an opportunity to get together. Discussion and focus on Russia, on international politics, on communism, provided a social outlet. Having a cause was a reason to meet people, to socialize, to be involved. And Judith was involved, deeply, an involvement that soon became an obsession.

Clues to this increasingly obsessive interest in all things Soviet can be found in the mercurial fortunes of communism in America during Judith's most impressionable years. Both she and the Communist Party (by that name) celebrated their eighteenth birthdays in May 1939. At the time, there was cause for celebration for both honorees—Judith's scholarship and acceptance at Barnard, and the Party's then-favorable political position in the United States, one based on cooperative and commodious relations between the Communists and President Franklin Roosevelt. Ostensibly shed of its threatening revolutionary image, the Communist Party had moved into and taken over a number of legitimate and well-respected organizations, some of which were youth oriented. Even First Lady Eleanor Roosevelt, a model for young American women, supported the Communist-driven American Youth Congress. Of special interest to the young, and to Mrs. Roosevelt, was the Party's advocacy of basic American ideals. In fact, from time to time, it was the most vocal movement exhibiting concern about economic inequities so evident in tenements and factories, about sexual and racial discrimination, about fairness and justice, about American youth. Along with non-Communists, it railed against war and, especially, against Fascism.

There was no question that the antiwar, anti-Fascist, antidiscrimination mentality that prevailed became a natural mind-place for many of the nation's more thoughtful, more serious young people. It welcomed bright young students, Judith Coplon among them, as explorers of its ideological premises. Add to the mix that Judith was Jewish, living in New York. During the New Deal era, the Communist Party's membership, although by this time more nationwide in its profile than in earlier years, was still dominated by New Yorkers. And its ethnic strength was among the Jews, whose anti-Fascist outrage and pro-Communist leanings grew with each new report of Nazi persecution abroad. Russian propaganda coupled with such horrifying revelations gave communism an understandable appeal.

Nowhere in the country was communism debated as hotly and, often, as sympathetically as on New York college campuses.

It was into this world that Judith entered in September 1939, when many of the most influential, most popular intellectuals of the day, whom she would study, were Communists or sympathizers. Earlier, and from a blue-collared, collective perspective, the Communists avoided American intellectuals because of their annoying penchant for independent thinking and their unforgivably bourgeois backgrounds. Now, however, the Communists found themselves welcoming the writers and thinkers whose works influenced Americans, who provided new inroads to the masses—especially to the young. Intellectuals dialed into the caring, humanitarian Communist Party line—some just listening in, some becoming long-term subscribers. In the mid-1930s, a number grouped around the existing John Reed clubs, cultural organizations founded earlier to attract intellectuals and named after the young Party founder who died in Moscow in the late 1920s. Among them were John Dos Passos, Kenneth Burke, Langston Hughes, Erskine Caldwell, William Saroyan, and more. However long their tenure on the Party line, they did precisely what the Communists wanted: They influenced the young, including Judith Coplon, who most likely read them all.

These were exciting, stimulating, challenging times on the nation's campuses, where the brightest of the bright daily discussed politics, war, popular writers, and, of course, communism. Among Judith's new classmates were two extremely intelligent young women eager to talk about such matters, Flora Don Wovschin and Marion Davis Berdecio. Both were excellent students, but there was something quite unique about tall, red-haired Flora Don.

Miss Wovschin already was a messianic recruiter of spies for Soviet Russia.

By her senior year at Barnard, Judith's interest in Russia and its economic and social structure was all-consuming. An editor of the Barnard weekly *Bulletin*, her writings were openly and strongly favorable to Russia. She complained bitterly that the Allies were not doing enough to support the brave Russians in their heroic struggle against the Nazi invaders. Why hadn't the Allies opened a second front? she asked, demanding that they do so. Delay, she speculated, came from political motivation, from an interest in ensuring that the Russians were substantially weakened before the war ended. If they were stronger, they could represent a postwar threat to the West.

Lend-lease, America's pipeline of goods to Russia, was another subject of great interest to Judith. "We must realize that Russia is at this moment the heart of the war and that our obligation is to keep that heart beating," she wrote, insisting that the United States was shortchanging the Soviets.

Within days of her graduation from Barnard, Judith went to work in New York City at the Economic Warfare Section of the War Division of the U.S. Department of Justice. A background check at the time of her employment noted her intense interest in and writings about Soviet Russia. No yellow lights flashed. She worked there until early in 1945, when she was transferred to the Foreign Agents Registration Section of the Department of Justice in Washington, D.C. In her new job, Judith would research and collect information about political trends, about various foreign organizations and individuals in the United States. She would help determine who among these were required by law to register as "foreign agents." Her role as a political analyst would allow access to secret FBI files containing information about whom, and what organizations, the Bureau was watching.

Routinely, Judith's job performance evaluations were excellent. One of her commendations for outstanding performance came from Raymond Whearty, who would later prosecute her for espionage. From Attorney General Tom Clark came praise when she received a civil service promotion. "Dear Miss Judith," he wrote, "P-3 is really an accomplishment and I congratulate you on it." He asked her to "keep up the good work." Judith was known to take work home and to stay at her typewriter until late into the night. From time to time, neighbors complained about the incessant tapping.

Judith Coplon stayed in her intelligence-sensitive job until March 4, 1949, when the red light flashed. For good.

The public already was forgetting that, during Judith's college years and for a time thereafter, being a Communist was both socially and politically acceptable. The picture that emerged later of clandestine, scruffy malcontents was far from accurate. Then, in 1945, when Judith was moving into her new job in Washington, D.C., the ambience of acceptability vanished; prorevolutionary garb was once again taken from the closet and worn publicly, and capitalism was decried. The relationship between official Washington and the Communists soured, and Americans who supported the Communist cause experienced untold despair and confusion. Russia, former lover, was now the estranged enchantress.

By 1948, the year Judith Coplon claimed to have met Valentin Gubitchev at an art exhibit, the Communist Party found itself on the legal defensive with the indictment of twelve members of its national board. Charged under the 1940 Smith Act prohibiting conspiracy to overthrow the U.S. government by force or violence, trial of eleven of the twelve initially indicted dragged on throughout most of 1949.

In May 1949, Judith and the Party both turned twenty-eight. There was little cause for celebration; both were on trial for their lives.

There is little question that Judith was a Communist, even during her student days. At the time of her trial, however, there was no evidence of Party membership presented and, in fact, Judith denied under oath that she was or ever had been a Communist. Former special agent of the FBI Robert Lamphere, who orchestrated Judith's capture, has no doubt. "She was a member of a Communist youth group. Unquestionably, she was a Communist." Robert Granville, who arrested her, agrees. Given her sociopolitical background and interests, Judith fit the Party profile as neatly as one could. But Lamphere's sister-in-law Phyllis, a college classmate of Judith's, fifty years later notes that strong interest in Russia and communism at Barnard was not all that unusual, not enough to set Judith apart.

"There was a lot of sympathy for Russia at the time," she says. "And not everyone who fit the profile was a Communist. Judith was like so many others."

What is significant throughout is that being a Communist was not tantamount to being a spy—although by 1949 the distinction frequently escaped notice and the terms were considered synonymous.

Looking back years after the Coplon case was closed, Judith's chief Washington prosecutor, successful, distinguished John M. Kelley Jr., said he was absolutely convinced that Judith Coplon, onetime government employee, graduated from college as a full-fledged Soviet agent. There was not a shred of doubt in his mind.

Kelley was wrong.

March 5–6, 1949

Saturday morning's newspapers were filled with details of Judith's arrest. Once early-morning deadlines were past, reporters in Washington scrambled for background stories and for news updates. It was a fabulous, frenzied day for the press.

That morning, Walter Trohan of the *Chicago Daily Tribune* called on one of the country's most outspoken anti-Communists, Congressman Richard Nixon. The journalist had a specific question in mind: What did Nixon think about a 1946 report, just surfaced, that claimed Judith Coplon had Communist leanings—that her government office was, in fact, "pro-Russian"?

Nixon seemed unfamiliar with the report, so Trohan obligingly clarified: A Wayne University professor who worked in Coplon's office for a time during the war had reported to the Department of Justice and the House Committee on Un-American Activities (HUAC) that the Justice Department's Foreign Agents Registration Section was "being submarined by Communists." Further, manning the torpedoes, according to the would-be whistle-blower, was Judith Coplon, along with three other staff members. No one, apparently, had listened at the time.

By afternoon, an admittedly shocked and horrified Richard Nixon was speaking his mind not only to Trohan but also to other members of the press. He could do no less, given the terrifying ramifications of the inexcusably belated discovery of a traitor in the Department of Justice, a few short blocks from his own office on Capitol Hill. A discovery, given the 1946 report, that was long overdue. Shaking his head in disbelief, Nixon blasted the department where Judith Coplon had worked until Friday afternoon.

"I demand a full scale investigation of this shocking laxity on the part of the Justice Department in screening its own employees for loyalty," Nixon thundered. "In my opinion, this case shows why the Justice Department may be unfit and unqualified to carry out the responsibility of protecting the national security against Communist infiltration."

There was more. This same report showed that Miss Coplon's section was responsible for keeping four Communist fronts from registering under the Foreign Agents Act. More importantly, she had access to every counterespionage activity of the FBI, to the most secret of secret files.

Republican Nixon went on to note, forcefully, that Judith Coplon's arrest proved America's worst fears. Espionage was rampant in government. Mr. Truman's Democratic government. Finally, he called for immediate response from HUAC, of which he was a member. A gruff farewell to the press, and the newly armed representative from California was off to the legislative battleground.

Sunday's newspapers identified Judith Coplon as Santa's daughter. They focused on her as the subject of Nixon's outrage and as the reason for unprecedented activity on the parts of other members of Congress, who pledged to be at their desks all weekend working on new anti-Communist legislation. A dozen or so were in their offices, surrounded by staff, feverishly drafting language that would protect upstanding American citizens from the Red Menace and the influence of undesirable aliens.

Among them was South Dakota senator Karl Mundt, to whom *Washington Post* reporter Seymour Friedin went that afternoon to follow up on a rumor circulating around the Capitol that a large number of government employees associated with Coplon would be rounded up immediately and arrested for espionage activity. The city was breathless with anticipation. Judy was only the tiniest tip of a clandestine iceberg on which the nation could well have foundered, save for FBI spycatchers who now, rumor had it, were ready to spring a giant trap. Mundt, an initiator of frequent, if unsuccessful, anti-Communist legislation, was ready for Friedin.

"It is unquestionably true that espionage systems run through many of our government agencies," the senator said, in acknowledging that the arrest rumor was "substantially correct."

"This pair, Coplon and Gubitchev, are just a couple of tentacles of existing spy rings inside the government," Mundt told Friedin, to whom the news that spy rings had tentacles must have come as something of a surprise.

"My new bill, the one I'm working on right now," the South Dakota senator explained, "will sharpen the teeth and expand the bite of my proposed anti-Communist legislation that died last year. Among its provisions, my new bill, co-authored by Richard Nixon, will prohibit any Communist from holding a government job. Previous spy rings uncovered were given a pat on the wrist and let go. My legislation, mine and Congressman Nixon's, will change all of that."

"What spy rings?"

Mundt ignored the question, instead offering the reporter news of what he planned to say in introducing his new anti-Communist legislation. President Truman, he reminded, had called HUAC's Red hearings "red herrings."

"I'll say, 'One of the famous red herrings has been found in the personal pantry of the Department of Justice itself.'" These words, the congressman observed, would make it clear to Truman that his only course of action would be to support the new Mundt-Nixon bill.

Saturday's call for immediate HUAC action had been answered, the press reported on Sunday. And thus, the recently lethargic body was back in business, much to the dismay of President Truman, who had become increasingly uncomfortable with its loose-cannon behavior and who had fervently sought a quieting of the national emotion. Now America's fever was rising once again because of young Judith Coplon.

HUAC, the bumbling, awkward congressional child born in 1938 and destined for a single year of life; the child reborn year after year of the same ambivalent parents, the precocious, precious child would once again be dragged on stage to entertain. This was the same child who, in one of its more temperamental moments, had accused another youngster, nine-year-old Shirley Temple, of being an "unwitting dupe of the Communists," a designation that tickled the funnybones of nearly everyone but HUAC's founder, Representative Martin Dies, and certain of his colleagues.

HUAC, in one of its more reasonable moods, had responded the year before to Truman's concern about the rising level of anti-Communist hysteria by pursuing its mission in quieter, less inflammatory ways. But when, in the fall, word was leaked to committee members that a grand jury had suppressed the delicious spy-and-tell confession of Elizabeth Bentley, HUAC leaped back into action. It called Bentley to repeat the revelations given to the grand jury about spies in high places; it called Whittaker Chambers as well, and asked him to repeat his allegations against Alger Hiss.

Truman was furious. He complained angrily throughout the highly publicized committee hearings, ears burned by implications that the testimony of Bentley and Chambers proved Communist spies, giant Red termites, were destroying his administration from within.

For a time, Americans thrilled to the excitement of hearing about dozens of subversives in government. "Red Spy Queen" Bentley became the world's new Mata Hari. But once the committee, and the country, became bored with Bentley's claims and moderately content with Hiss's trial for perjury, the scene, and HUAC (much to Truman's relief), settled down to routine investigations of organizations. And then Judith Coplon, a professional employee of the Department of Justice, *his* Department of Justice, had been arrested in the company of a suspicious Soviet national. Once again, Harry Truman lost his composure; Judith Coplon had reignited the fire. As for the colorless Elizabeth, she lost her title.

In enthusiastic response to Nixon's demand, an emergency session of HUAC was scheduled for the following evening, March 7; its purpose, to look into the Justice Department's failure to root out spies within its own organization. Mr. Nixon, along with his eager colleagues, quieted.

But only until they learned, later this same day, some additional shocking news.

Robert C. Alexander, assistant director of the State Department's Visa Section, claimed to have known all along that Judith's partner in crime, Valentin Gubitchev, was one of fifteen "iron curtain UN aides actively engaged in espionage today." Not only that, but Alexander had shared this information with an unresponsive State Department.

It seems that five months before Coplon and Gubitchev were arrested, Alexander nearly lost his State Department job after alleging that the UN was a "hotbed of spying," and listing the names of 263 people he considered to be suspicious characters. Of those, Alexander insisted, fifteen were definitely spies, including Valentin Gubitchev; Alexander had his own doubts about the other 248. He had presented his report to a Senate subcommittee and received an official reprimand from State for his trouble. Tomorrow, the American public, along with its political leaders, would find, printed on page one, lists of names from Alexander's previously excoriated report. Accompanying the story would be the smug State Department official's claim that Gubitchev's arrest with Coplon had vindicated him.

By late Sunday afternoon, House and Senate leaders were voicing criticism of the State Department for failing to set tougher regulations for iron-curtain aliens entering the country via the UN. New calls came to HUAC chairman John Wood, who painted another ring on the committee's investigative target to be unveiled the following night. HUAC, he decided, would investigate not only the Departments of Justice and State, but also the entire United Nations.

For the Republican members of the controversial committee, there was one especially satisfying aspect of the recent turn of events. In a pique over endless unproven allegations about Communists on the government payroll, Attorney General Tom Clark six months earlier had angrily challenged HUAC to "name one Communist now employed by the government." The committee could not. Now, because of Judith's downfall, members of the committee, contacted by Wood, announced that they would immediately present Clark with a list of at least twenty-five "known Reds" whose paychecks were signed by that soft-on-communism Democrat, Uncle Sam.

Before the events of March 4, they did not dare respond to Clark without proof. But now, who needed actual evidence of betrayal?

Everyone in Washington, it seemed, was working this Sunday.

Out of the spotlight, Harold Shapiro, a dark-haired young Justice Department lawyer, observed the madness with a paralyzing fear. He knew they would come for him before long, and wondered if he should make the first move. What was beginning to gnaw at his insides was the knowledge that, sooner or later, it would likely come down to saving his life or hers.

This same Sunday afternoon in Washington, in various unnaturally quiet homes, a small number of highly concerned people wondered whether their own spy apparatuses were about to be uncovered, wondered if Judith Coplon's alleged theft of government documents might, somehow, lead to their own downfall. A small number. In the minds of certain others who suspected the existence of these people, their numbers were not small but legion, their chosen destiny to destroy the American way of life.

The cause of it all, Judith Coplon, was calm and confident in her Manhattan jail cell, even cheerful. She visited with Bert, who appeared far more distressed than she. Bert later called a business friend and said the "strangest part" of what had happened in the courtroom Saturday morning was that he didn't know whether his sister was guilty or had been unwittingly used by someone else. Of one thing Bert was certain: Judy was not and had never been a Communist.

Meanwhile, Judy's good humor at the detention center clearly was irritating her matron, who found her prisoner's behavior "unnatural."

"She hasn't cried," the matron complained. "She isn't normal. There's something wrong with her."

March 7–8, 1949

On the evening of March 7, Bertram Coplon told his wife, Shirley, that he intended to move into the family home, putting a cot in the bedroom with his sister when she was released from the Women's Detention Center. He intended to stay there, he said, until the "present matter is cleared up."

While Judith Coplon remained calm in her cell at the detention center, Valentin Gubitchev stormed and raged in his cell at the Federal House of Detention at 427 West Street.

Lev S. Tolokonnikov, first secretary of the Soviet embassy in Washington, and Leonid Morozov, first secretary of the Soviets' UN delegation, arrived for a meeting on March 8 with the unhappy prisoner, its purpose to brief him on the status of his claim of diplomatic immunity. An irate Gubitchev greeted them.

"They have me associating with common criminals," he complained. "There are two of them in my cell. Common! I think they are income tax evaders!" Further, he insisted that he had been "kidnapped."

Attempts to assure the Russian engineer that he would be saved through a successful claim of diplomatic immunity began with a review of the various Soviet legal actions undertaken on his behalf. His visitors reported that on Saturday night, Ambassador Panyuishkin had met with the American undersecretary of state, Mr. Webb, to demand a release based on the grounds of diplomatic immunity. Undersecretary Webb had promised to consider the demand carefully and to confer with Secretary Acheson, who would confer with Mr. Truman if necessary. It was only a matter of time. Everything that could be done was being done. Gubitchev, Tolokonnikov explained today, would simply have to wait.

If Gubitchev was distraught, his wife surely must have been more so. A quiet, unassuming native of Orel, Russia, she was frightened and alone in their apartment, afraid as much of the Soviets now as she was of the Americans. Representatives from the Soviet UN delegation had been in touch with her, but she knew that a man with a problem like Valentin's was now a Soviet liability.

Lidjida Gubitchev no doubt knew then what KGB general Oleg Kalugin would observe to the authors many years later: "Russian intelligence officers seldom live long." She knew that diplomatic immunity or no, her husband's chances for survival, and perhaps hers as well, were grim. She was at least thankful that Violetta, their thirteen-year-old daughter, had gone home to Russia to study this school year.

The Gubitchevs, along with four other Russian families, lived in a six-story, forty-two-family building between Amsterdam and Manhattan

Avenues. They occupied a four-room flat on the fifth floor, for which they paid an impressive $63.25 monthly. The Russian families had moved to the building when their consulate had closed its doors and its school the year before following an unfortunate incident. One in which Mme. Kasenkina, a teacher in the consulate school, mysteriously leaped from one of the building's windows. There were no explanations, and the move was made quietly and efficiently.

Before coming to America, Valentin Gubitchev was a high-ranking engineer in his native country and was, at one time, deputy chief of the Ural Construction Technical Department in Chalybinsk. It was in 1946, three years before, that the prominent engineer was named to his UN post by the Soviet foreign office. Well educated and successful, he never expected to find himself in a setting so common as that which now surrounded him.

At home, his wife was left alone to think terrible, unthinkable thoughts, including, perhaps, about Mme. Kasenkina.

At the detention center, Bert Coplon was leaving after another visit with his sister, and telling waiting reporters that she looked "very well and cheerful."

"What do you think, Mr. Coplon? How's it going?" a reporter stationed outside the apartment asked.

"I am definitely convinced of her innocence," Bert responded. "And the more I see and talk to her, the more I am convinced of it." He added that he hoped to be able to post bond later in the day.

Nearby, Judge Simon Rifkind was busy with a different case. A distinguished, sixty-five-year old New Yorker, William Rosen, had earlier refused to testify before the Alger Hiss grand jury. He now repeated his refusal to Judge Rifkind. He would not provide testimony regarding his alleged receipt thirteen years ago, in 1936, of an auto once owned by Alger Hiss. It was nobody's business about the car, Rosen held. The court felt differently and cited him for contempt, making him only one of 150 cited for refusing to tell the grand jury about such matters.

Judge Rifkind gave Rosen six months in jail. He also denied application for bail.

It was the way the wind was blowing.

Igor, Elizabeth, and Alger

Three people from the world of Cold War espionage never knew each other or Judith Coplon, at least to anyone's knowledge. But regardless of any personal or professional connection between Judith and the espionage ensemble, Igor Gouzenko, Elizabeth Bentley, and Alger Hiss helped set the stage in 1945 and 1946 for what happened to Judith Coplon following her arrest in 1949.

Had Gouzenko known Bentley—both were confessed Soviet spies—he could have warned her about the most critical aspect of giving up the spy game and naming names. It is imperative, Igor knew, to collect incriminating evidence against those one accuses of espionage. When the GRU cipher clerk, stationed in the Russian embassy in Canada, decided to defect in September 1945, he had the foresight to steal incriminating cables and hide them in his shirt. Bentley, an American businesswoman, had no such foresight. Her knitting bag, which for several years carried secret U.S. government documents to her Russian controllers, was empty the fateful day she walked into the FBI field office in New Haven, Connecticut, not long after Gouzenko's defection.

It took Gouzenko several days to convince the cautious Canadians that he was a legitimate defector, but once he'd done so, he had the proof to send more than a dozen Canadians, some of them in prominent government positions, to prison. Without the stolen documents, who would have believed that McGill University professor Raymond Boyer (code name THE PROFESSOR) would betray his country? Or that Canadian affairs editor David Gordon Lunan (code name BACK) would organize a local spy ring, or that seemingly legitimate, loyal Canadians working in government could become espionage agents?

In the United States, the situation was more difficult. When Elizabeth Bentley found herself totally disillusioned with the espionage business (and most likely frightened for her life), when she went to the FBI to confess her years of recruiting and courier activities for the Soviets, a lack of evidence created enormous problems for the FBI and, ultimately, for Elizabeth as well. Trying to prove her shocking allegations was a frustrating and, ultimately, unsuccessful task.

The table of contents of an FBI memo lists individuals Elizabeth named as spies in 1945; some would later surface in the Coplon case. The list includes thirteen members of a Washington, D.C., Soviet spy ring led by U.S. Department of Agriculture employee Nathan Gregory Silvermaster and his wife, Helen. It lists eleven members of a second Soviet spy ring operating in Washington, which included Harry Dexter White, then assistant secretary of the treasury and subsequent Truman appointee as U.S. executive director on the International Monetary Fund; and Mary Price, the beautiful secretary to columnist Walter Lippmann, a woman the Russians desperately wanted to use for the purpose of luring federal officials into bed and betrayal. It also included fifteen accused under the heading of "Miscellaneous Figures in Washington, D.C. and Vicinity." Judith Coplon was not among the accused named and known by Bentley, but Alger Hiss was.

State Department official Alger Hiss would later be publicly accused of espionage by Whittaker Chambers in one of the most colorful and controversial spy dramas in the nation's history. He was not only named by Bentley, but also later identified as the unnamed U.S. assistant secretary of state on Gouzenko's list.

Whether Hiss secretly knew Judith Coplon was a question never answered, although Representative Francis E. Walter of Pennsylvania believed they likely were connected and sought to use the suspected collaboration as a means of bringing new charges against Hiss and putting Judith behind bars. Immediately after Judith's arrest, Walter searched for a link between Judith and the State Department employee, then under indictment for perjury. Spies in the Departments of State and Justice surely would know each other, he surmised. Speculation about a connection fueled interest for a short time, but eventually fizzled, and the government went back to the messy business of trying to bring charges more serious than perjury against the troublesome Hiss and trying to build a case against Judith.

There is no doubt that Igor, Elizabeth, and Alger dressed the set for the appearance of Santa's daughter in the role of the newest Mati Hari. Elizabeth, a *Mayflower* descendant, showed that an intelligent, extremely well-educated American woman, a hardworking professional with an impeccable family background, could betray her country. In a sense, she made Judith Coplon, Santa's-daughter-turned-spy, believable to at least some of the American public. Igor made believable the notion that there were indeed Soviet spy rings circling here and there in key branches of Western governments, such as in the U.S. Department of Justice, where Judith worked. As for Alger, uncovered in just such a place, he was proof of Igor's pudding, as it were, and, despite Representative Walter's failure to connect Hiss to Coplon, there were those who continued to believe that such a connection existed.

There is more of significance about Igor's and Elizabeth's influence on the Coplon case. They provided U.S. counterintelligence officers with firsthand information about how Soviet Cold War spies recruited others into their spy apparatuses, information helpful to the Coplon prosecution. Elizabeth described in detail the modus operandi of her apparatus. Included was the exact cat-and-mouse scenario Judith Coplon and Valentin Gubitchev used when they met. Among other details, Igor described specific Soviet requirements for background sketches on potential recruits. Similar sketches found in Judith's possession when she was arrested could have been models from the Gouzenko textbook. Between them, Igor and Elizabeth gave the U.S. government exactly what it needed to support Judith Coplon's arrest and prosecution.

March 10, 1949

In a brightly lighted meeting room at the Federal Courthouse Building in Manhattan's Foley Square, the grand jury considering the Coplon-Gubitchev case listened intently to the last of the FBI agents to testify before them.

Presiding as jury foreman was John Brunini, editor of *Spirit* magazine. There is little doubt that Brunini was more interested in the case than were the other members of the panel, and not simply because of his responsibilities as foreman. There is also little doubt that he believed himself more knowledgeable about this sordid business than did his fellow grand jurors. All of which, for Brunini, added up to a significant risk. If anyone knew what was going on in his life outside the jury room, he would find himself dismissed and sent packing. Or worse.

Agent Scott Miller was the fourth and last witness to testify in this second day of the jury's sitting. The agents who preceded Miller testified to the circuitous, convoluted route Judith Coplon had taken to meet Valentin Gubitchev on Broadway and 193rd Street on the night of March 4. Miller, however, addressed a more interesting topic: the contents of Judith's purse the night she was arrested.

In addition to thirty-two FBI data slips—summaries of raw, unverified FBI reports gathered from both reliable and unreliable sources—agents had found a statement of the defendant's efforts to obtain access to a secret report of the FBI, a handwritten note regarding use of scientific instruments, a brief statement of her postgraduate educational status (considered to be a résumé of the sort spies routinely gave their controllers), and three background statements suspiciously like those Igor Gouzenko said were used for recruiting espionage agents.

By eleven forty-five in the morning, under Brunini's leadership, indictments were returned against Judith Coplon and Valentin Gubitchev. The jury's charge was delivered to Judge Rifkind—a four-count indictment that could lead to a maximum jail sentence for Coplon of thirty-five years and for Gubitchev, fifteen. Or death, at least for one of them. It was made clear that this option remained open to the government because of the legal technicality continuing the country's state of war. As for the difference in length of possible jail terms, it was also clear that the mantle of "chief offender" had passed from the stocky Russian engineer to the petite American political analyst.

The first count charged both of the accused with conspiring "between themselves and other unknown persona" to defraud the United States by obstructing the lawful functions of the Justice Department and the FBI. It also concerned the right of the government to the "honest, conscientious and faithful services" of Judith Coplon. This, the conspiracy count, alleged the existence of three overt acts in which she and Gubitchev "did meet and confer."

The second count charged Judith with unlawfully having secret documents that she "did willfully attempt to communicate and transmit . . . to Valentin A. Gubitchev, who was then and there a person not entitled to receive the same."

Gubitchev alone was charged in the third count, with unlawfully attempting to obtain national defense secrets from Judith. And she was charged alone in the fourth, which held that she attempted to deliver to Gubitchev "information relating to the national defense, to wit, documents, writings, and notes containing intelligence reports relating to espionage and counter-espionage activities in the United States."

Attorney General Tom Clark announced the indictments later in the day, along with the scheduled time of arraignment on the new charges. At ten-thirty the following morning, March 11, Judy and Gubitchev would once again be taken before Judge Rifkind.

Surely satisfied with the day's outcome, Jury Foreman Brunini went back to work. Perhaps to the magazine, or perhaps to a highly secret job of editing a manuscript for Elizabeth Bentley, titled *Out of Bondage*. Brunini and Bentley were deeply involved in a literary project certain to have greater value if Judith Coplon were indicted. Women spies were big business at the moment. Years later, the authors found a document in Bentley's FBI file describing Brunini's fear that the FBI would learn of his involvement with Bentley during this sensitive time. She absolutely must not tell, he warned Bentley. Not a word to anyone about his involvement, especially not to the FBI. He could be in *very* serious trouble.

She told the FBI, of course, but long after the Coplon indictment, long after it mattered.

This same day in Washington, Congressman Richard Nixon of California and Congressman Francis Walter of Pennsylvania urged the FBI to make a deal with Judith Coplon. "Let's go after the big fish," they suggested. Get her to tell what she knows about Soviet spy operations and promise that in return she will be treated leniently. The more she tells, the lighter the punishment. Nixon added a caveat. The deal should be weighed carefully on the basis of "how big a fish may be caught."

For all the talk of weighing fish and making deals, the FBI had no intention of taking such a step. It needed no other fish to fry; its skillet was full as it was, and perilously close to the fire.

March 11–12, 1949

On March 11, Bert Coplon carried four checks in his pocket: one for ten thousand dollars and another for twenty-five hundred, both from the

Williamsburg Savings Bank of Brooklyn; one for twenty-five hundred dollars drawn on the Corn Exchange Bank; and, surprisingly, one for five thousand dollars drawn on his father-in-law's Kings Highway Savings Bank. Twenty thousand dollars, a small fortune. He had been trying to raise the money for more than a week.

"How'd you get the dough?" a reporter called to him as he mounted the steps to the federal courthouse at Foley Square.

"God only knows," Bert replied.

His sister arrived at the courthouse minutes later, clad in a gray plaid skirt and black sweater, in obvious good cheer, smiling and waving at the reporters swarming about her like so many eager suitors. The marshals escorting her were not in obvious good cheer. Gubitchev, with his official escort, arrived shortly thereafter and the press dutifully, if unenthusiastically, made note of the Russian's appearance.

The courtroom was packed with reporters; also present were representatives from the Soviet delegation to the UN, various other diplomats and government officials, and a rather unusually large complement of the just-plain-curious. This would be the first arraignment on grand jury indictments for espionage in the Cold War, something worth seeing.

"All rise," intoned the bailiff as Judge Rifkind entered the room. Before him stood Judith Coplon and Valentin Gubitchev, nearly side by side, silent, without a glance at each other, without any sign of recognition. Rifkind called the case of *United States of America versus Judith Coplon*, and the defendant stood stock still, seemingly frozen in place. She might have been painted in the scene, almost as an afterthought, so small in the large, austere room, a tiny woman barely five feet tall.

Charges were read. Although a synopsis had been published in last night's and this morning's newspapers, somehow they sounded infinitely more ominous, infinitely more evil, spoken aloud in this austere and venerable setting. For a moment, there was absolute silence.

"Miss Coplon, how do you plea?"

"Not guilty," Judy answered, her voice so soft only those in the first rows could hear her. Rifkind nodded, consulted his calendar, and announced an April 1 trial date, scarcely more than two weeks away.

"In the matter of bail, Your Honor," Raymond Whearty began, "the government requests that the amount be raised to $50,000." If bail were not increased, Whearty insisted, this dangerous spy would escape to who knows where. The battle between the prosecution and defense waged as before.

"Your Honor, there is absolutely no reason to increase bail!" Adams objected angrily. "My client has the closest possible ties here, to her aging and desperately ill parents, to the rest of her family. Her father is a beloved philanthropist, a legend in his own and in our time, who needs to see and hold his only daughter. She will go directly to him; she has absolutely no intention of fleeing. This is a regrettably mean-spirited, unreasonable request, totally without merit."

Whearty, now furious himself, began to speak, but the judge silenced him immediately.

"I'm sure," he said gently to the accused, "that you won't get any silly notions about running away."

"No, Sir," Judy replied in the same low voice.

"Bail is continued at $20,000," Rifkind said, and Bert Coplon began breathing once again.

Ten minutes later, Bert handed over his four checks, grabbed his sister's arm, and left the courtroom. Judith could expect to be free of the FBI, courtrooms, and judges until April Fool's Day, the day set for her trial.

Valentin Gubitchev's arraignment was, by his own later analysis, only the first act in a comedy. It began with the Soviet national admitting that he was skilled in the English language but insisting upon an interpreter.

"Are you represented by counsel?" the judge inquired.

No, he was not, reported the interpreter after a brief conversation in Russian. "Mr. Gubitchev would like to retain a lawyer but cannot afford one."

"Very well, the court will assign counsel. Will you explain this to him, please?"

Another brief conversation in Russian.

"Mr. Gubitchev does not require a lawyer," the bewildered interpreter now reported.

"May I speak?" the Russian inquired in English. "I consider myself a foreigner and a member of the diplomatic profession, and I consider that the accusations leveled at me are a provocation pursuing a certain aim. They are a plot against me and against my country. Therefore, I will refuse to answer the questions of the court."

Rifkind, irritated nearly to the limit by now, announced that he would not allow Valentin Gubitchev to be arraigned without representation. He would appoint counsel, regardless of the defendant's wishes in the matter. Gubitchev's arraignment was now scheduled for March 14 and his bail continued at one hundred thousand dollars.

Judy went home to her parents. The man who was arrested with her went back to jail.

That night, a man called the Coplon residence, saying he was a friend of Judy's. He identified himself as Val. Bert Coplon refused to call his sister to the telephone, saying she could not be disturbed. Whether she ever knew of the call is a question that raises abundant other questions.

Justice Department lawyers in charge of the Coplon case were beginning to squirm. The diplomatic immunity complication could mean a delay in trial. They were monitoring the dispute between the Soviet ambassador and the State Department with growing concern. Even the president was now involved. It was within the realm of possibility, no matter who was saying what officially, that the international argument could go on for weeks.

It was imperative that Judith Coplon be tried almost immediately. Political posturing worsened by the day, along with criticism of the Justice Department and the administration. Far from lessening, media interest in Judith was increasing. Something had to be done, and quickly. The solution finally determined was to convene a secret grand jury in Washington and rearrest Judith there on related espionage charges that would not include Gubitchev and his annoying immunity claim. Doing so would ensure that, before long, one way or another, Judith Coplon would be tried in New York or in Washington. That the charges, however framed, were essentially duplicative was of little concern. Political expediency demanded a quick and highly publicized trial.

In Washington, Secretary of State Dean Acheson announced, officially, that the United States did not recognize Gubitchev's claim of immunity. Ever cautious, he added that the matter would be considered further before a "final" decision was made. Officially.

In Moscow, the case, "a vicious U.S. plot against Russia," was making headlines. While Gubitchev was unjustly held in captivity, reported Tass, the official Russian news agency, FBI agents had grilled him extensively on the subject of Russian defenses. In their effort to obtain secret information for U.S. intelligence agencies, the FBI was trying to elicit information about military installations where Gubitchev had worked in Russia, about concentration camps, and about slave labor. Those questioning the innocent Soviet engineer also wanted to know whether he "deemed possible a change in the foreign policy of the USSR." In all, bemoaned Tass, the American authorities were indulging in "crude, arbitrary action."

In Brooklyn, a terminally ill old man may or may not have realized that his beloved daughter had come home. Fifty years later, Judith's husband would insist that Santa was already lost in his own private torment, unaware of anything outside of self, unable to think or to feel. If so, it was a blessing.

During the evening of March 12, Bertram Coplon made two calls, one to his wife, Shirley, and another to Rose Zwick, his mother's sister. He asked the two women to start a chain system of calling friends to let them know that the telephone number at the Ocean Parkway apartment had been changed. The new number was Ulster 3-6417. Bert was concerned about unwelcome calls. He was also deeply concerned about wiretapping.

March 13–15, 1949

Life in the Coplon household remained in a constant state of emotional turmoil over these next three days. Judith's cousin, Bertram Kaye, spoke with Bertram Adams, saying that Judy was not ready to discuss the "facts of this case" with Adams or anyone else. According to Kaye, Judy refused even to speak with her family about the case and became "very emotional" every time the charges against her were mentioned. Adams expressed the feeling that public sentiment was, at this time, strongly in Judy's favor, which in some circles was the truth.

For Judy, whose public persona caused the press and public to see her as cool and confident, or smiling and cheerful, the truth was that she was struggling to maintain any semblance of control. On March 14, she told her sister-in-law that the situation in which she found herself was "becoming intolerable." She could not read the newspaper, listen to the radio, or watch television. Celebrity was killing her; she found herself everywhere she looked. The constant confrontation had reached a point where, she told Shirley, she was ready to shoot herself.

Discussion continued between Judy and her brother about legal representation. On March 14, J. A. Seidman suggested both George Wolfe, who had "represented Costello and others," and Sol Gill, who "knew judges." There were other suggestions as well, all of which were considered not only in terms of appropriateness, of course, but also in terms of cost.

Rebecca heard but did not join in the conversations. Daily, she lived in terror, initially just for her daughter, but later she began to worry about others in the family. She called her sister, Rose, on the night of the fifteenth, cautioning her against coming to the apartment frequently. Rebecca was afraid that something might happen to her because of her connection to the Coplons. How different from the days when the name *Coplon* brought to mind far more pleasant thoughts.

March 16–17, 1949

On March 16, a secret memorandum was sent from Attorney General Tom Clark to President Truman, a communication that would be kept secret until its declassification April 2, 1991. The subject of the memorandum was the deportation of Valentin Gubitchev.

Clark noted that the charges against Judith Coplon and Gubitchev carried possible penalties of thirty-five years imprisonment for Coplon and fifteen for the Russian. Arguing against the State Department's recommendation that Gubitchev be deported to Russia rather than stand trial, he offered Truman a number of reasons why the Soviet engineer should be detained in the United States "at least until after the trial of the New York case."

Among these was the fact that Gubitchev's absence would afford "vast opportunities to Coplon in her defense"; Coplon could complain that deportation prevented her access to his testimony. Further, sending Gubitchev back to Russia would imply that the United States never had a case against him and never intended prosecution. Another compelling reason, according to Clark, was that prosecution of the young woman alone, without Gubitchev's involvement, would be known to the jury and could appear as persecution of Judith.

Finally, wrote Clark, "Another alternative exists, i.e., to prosecute Gubitchev and then permit his deportation to Russia." Further, "it might be possible to inform the Russian Government that Gubitchev will have to remain in this country for the trial but that the consideration of his ultimate deportation after trial would remain open." In closing, the Attorney General asked President Truman to authorize him to "proceed with the trial of Gubitchev without delay."

Truman complied, and a secret deal was struck. It was vital that the government convict Judith Coplon.

For four days after her release from jail, Judy continued to live in painful, quiet seclusion in Brooklyn with Bert, Samuel, and Rebecca—quiet except for endless talk about finding, and paying for, a lawyer who could properly handle a major criminal case. Bertram Adams called to say that a press service had offered five thousand dollars for an exclusive interview with Judy. Adams thought it would not be "unwise" to accept—to have Judy make her case, as it were, with the public. Besides, the five thousand, accompanied by a commission for Adams, was worth consideration. Bert flatly rejected the offer.

Today, on the fifth day, what was left of her world suddenly collapsed at Judy's feet when, without warning, she learned that a secret grand jury in Washington had indicted her on new charges stemming from the March 4 arrest. She would be arrested again. There would be two spy trials, one in New York and one in Washington. Thomas Donegan, special assistant to the attorney general, offered her a choice. She could be arrested at her parents' home in New York or she could surrender to his people in Washington. "Which do you prefer?" he asked.

The niceties of such a question evaded Judy. She had already been arrested, indicted, and twice arraigned. The thought of being arrested and taken into custody at home terrified her. Judith, Bert, and attorney Sam Neuburger, a friend of the family, discussed the best strategy for dealing with the new indictment and arrest. They agreed that Judy would surrender in Washington, probably the following Monday. Bert was deeply concerned about additional bail. How could the family possibly manage it?

In the midst of the confusion and despair resulting from this seemingly incredible turn of legal events, a new lawyer entered the picture. He was Archibald Palmer, who called Shirley Coplon to say that he had just recently realized Judy was a member of the family of Samuel Coplon, an old friend of his. He would be pleased, he told Judy's sister-in-law, to offer his legal services. Archie believed in the cause, he would do anything to help. Money was not an issue; he would serve without pay. The charges against Judy, the attorney said, "constituted one of the greatest frame-ups he had ever known." With enormous gratitude, the family accepted Palmer's offer, and by the following day, Archie had the situation, the case, and the cause firmly in hand. The family's trust was immediate. It stemmed from Palmer's earlier relationship with Samuel and his convincing pledge to save Judy, coupled with the attorney's insistence that money was not a problem. A new defense team—Adams, Palmer, and attorney Max Rosenstein—was short lived. Before long, it was a one-man show. Archie's. Most likely his teammates welcomed this. Dealing with Archie's strong personality over an extended period could be taxing, and getting an appropriate fee for doing so could be iffy.

Judy found herself wondering how the government could arrest her once again for essentially the same alleged criminal act. Wasn't this some sort of double jeopardy? Could the government really do this to her? It could, and once again, the following day, Judith Coplon made headlines around the world.

The media, alerted about the new indictment and coming arrest, enjoyed yet another banquet of sensational press fodder, not only in the United States, but also abroad. Especially in England, where the appetite for news of Judy went unabated. The British *News Chronicle*'s coverage of the "Judith Story" noted that things had gotten a bit out of hand in the colonies, that "the air, in short, is heavy with news and rumours of spying—on and by the United States." A lead story from the *London Dispatch* carried a banner headline reading U.S. SPY SCANDAL FLARES UP, with sidebar stories totally filling page one of the prestigious newspaper and spilling over to several inside pages. The British adored the intrigue. After all, it was in England that the spy-counterspy business, universally in vogue since biblical times, was first institutionalized.

Official Soviet news, of course, dealt only peripherally with Judith Coplon, focusing on Valentin Gubitchev's "illegal" arrest and incarceration. What was happening to Judith was of little interest to them.

American newspapers, whose representatives scrambled after this new lead, were now portraying Judy either as sexy and sultry, the way female spies should be if they were worth their rubles, or as a young innocent failing dismally in this regard. There was no denying that Judy's gender was foremost in many minds. Here was a story referring to the alleged spy as "whistle bait," and another referring to her as "a cutie," all ridiculously silly. A column by syndicated writer Robert Ruark reported that although Judy had a "moody mouth, reasonably good legs, and raven hair," she fell short of the ideal woman spy.

"I would say," Ruark wrote, "that Miss Coplon is more optically believable than either the dumpy Elizabeth Bentley or Axis Sally. But Holy Cow, the names these dames choose! Mildred (that's Axis Sally), Liz and Judy! They sound about as sinister as Louisa May Alcott."

Female spies should have exotic Russian names, Ruark complained, like Olga. Further, they have the whole business of spying wrong if they get caught for "pinching and passing state secrets." A really worthwhile woman spy is supposed to lure a "brilliant young officer" or a "doddering old cabinet minister" into her bed and make him so crazy with love that he gives away keys to the secret store. Forget Judy, who is "barely out of her bobby-sox." Bring on instead a sexy traitor who is "lean and tigerish, a temptress like Ava Gardner."

Washington correspondent James Donovan described Judy as "chatty and vivacious," with "dark laughing eyes, long dark hair and white even teeth which flashed often as she smiled." More than forty years later, the authors found a copy of Donovan's article in Judith's FBI file. It bore an unidentified handwritten note indicating that Donovan, far from being a completely objective journalist, had been dating Judy. Donovan, suggests the FBI note, merited watching.

Other stories were far more frightening than annoying and reflected the mood of the country. Some called for "extermination" of spies, starting right now with Axis Sally, not yet sentenced, and, of course, this latest female turncoat, Judith Coplon, who should be considered a prize candidate for the ultimate penalty. "The security of our country is at stake. Spies and traitors should be eliminated," insisted the *El Paso Times*.

Press attention also focused on the beloved Santa Claus of the Adirondacks,

and on his devotion to and pride in his daughter. The full story of Samuel
Coplon, for so many years retold during the holiday season, was retrieved from
newspaper morgues and appeared in papers from coast to coast. Samuel, to the
family's great distress, was once again in the news.

Archie

Attorney-at-law Archibald Palmer, sixty-five, born and raised in Manhattan's
garment district, had never taken a criminal case in his life. He was a civil
attorney, strictly small-time, whose practice consisted almost entirely of
bankruptcy and small claims cases. Standing a mere five feet three inches tall,
Archie was pear shaped, with an amiable, heavy-joweled face. Routinely he
spent his days studying the financial dilemma of one or another of his less
fortunate clients and sucking on fruit-flavored Life Savers or candy mints.
The most notable legal work performed by Archie thus far had been representing a minority group of security holders in the financial reorganization
of the Philadelphia and Reading Coal and Iron Company in 1943.

Archibald Palmer, Esquire, had two trademarks: One was the ever-present
roll of candy or mints, and the other was an enormous, wide-brimmed floppy
black hat worn everywhere. About the hat, Archie would say, "Can't wear a
derby. The head's too round. So I always wear this kind of hat. Got a house
full of them." At times he expressed concern about the need to remove his
hat in "the building," meaning the courthouse. "I might forget," he worried,
"and there'd be trouble!"

For reasons never understood by anyone outside the family, Archie was
selected to represent Judith Coplon, defendant in the most controversial life-
and-death espionage trial anyone could remember. Granted, Archie was a
friend of the family, as was Adams, but friendship, said certain of those close
to the case, had its limitations. Although knowledge about Archie was far
from widespread, he was notorious among opposing lawyers for his eccentric
behavior and outrageous performances before judge and jury. But there were
colleagues in the legal field who never failed to praise Archie for his understanding of the law and for his "old school" individualistic and combative
demeanor.

Referring to his contentious courtroom antics, Archie would explain them away by recalling his boyhood training as a bantamweight fighter.

"I have to be punching all the time, even if I get licked."

Former FBI agent Hollis Bowers, half a century after the Coplon case was over, spoke about Archie's dealings as a bankruptcy lawyer. In New York, Bowers had worked on the FBI's accounting squad dealing with bankruptcy fraud. He knew Palmer in his role as an attorney representing individuals and businesses declaring bankruptcy. There were unanswered questions about legitimacy of claims, Bowers says, about merchandise that mysteriously disappeared from clients' stores and warehouses. Bowers believes that Palmer represented certain clients operating on the fringe of legality. "In every case, he abused the living hell out of everyone, including the judge," the former agent says. Bowers remembers that Archie "was a wild man, especially in the Coplon case," where he nearly drove "the poor old judge" out of his mind.

In his private life, Archie was happy, content, and self-confident, a good husband to his second wife, Rita, and loving father to sons, daughters, and stepchildren.

Despite appearances and the wonderment, even amusement, with which he would be greeted as Judith's attorney, Archie Palmer was no fool in terms of knowing the law. He was graduated at the head of his class at New York University and won a prize for his "learnedness" in the process. For reasons of his own, and by careful design, he had chosen to practice law in an unpretentious, and often financially unrewarding, corner of the world of jurisprudence.

Notified later in the afternoon of Archie's new role as Judith's defender, the prosecution team at Foley Square, headed by the highly respected John Kelley Jr., was in a collective state of total bewilderment. Not one among them had even heard of the small-time civil lawyer. They had expected someone like the costly Leonard Boudin or Samuel Neuburger, someone known as a defender of left causes.

It was immediately predicted that beating Archie would be like taking candy from a baby, and that Archie would have difficulty even finding his way to the men's room. The prognostication would prove only partly correct. It was true, much to the delight of the government team, that Archie got lost trying to find the men's room on his first visit to Foley Square. As for the candy snatching, no one ever touched Archie's Life Savers without an invitation to do so.

It was not predicted, at the time, that little Archie Palmer would soon be on his way to becoming a legend, a household name particularly repugnant to J. Edgar Hoover, President Harry Truman, Attorney General Tom Clark, and, of course, the prosecution team, including the impressive Mr. Kelley.

Archie, no longer a bantamweight, intended to be punching all the time and had no intention of getting licked.

March 18, 1949

Of the choice of evils that lay before her, Judy, with help, had selected surrender in Washington. On Monday, with Archie at her side, she would go to the capital, where she would be arrested—again. She was at home in Brooklyn this Friday, exactly two weeks from the night of her capture on a lower Manhattan street corner. Only two weeks. It seemed an eternity.

The indictment returned by the Washington grand jury was more serious than its New York counterpart. In the first of the two new counts, Judy was charged with "obtaining information respecting the national defense with the intent and reason to believe" that the information was to be used "to the injury of the United States and to the advantage of a foreign nation." The second charged violation of the statute forbidding copying, mutilation, or removal of government documents—specifically, material containing intelligence reports relating to espionage and counterespionage activities of the United States.

Announcement of the second count gave the public its first clue about the contents of Judith Coplon's purse the night she was captured. She was specifically charged with taking "certain extracts and summaries of reports of the FBI known as data slips, containing intelligence reports relating to espionage and counter-espionage activities in the United States." There was much more, of course, but the world would have to wait until May 30 before all of the secrets of Judy's purse were made public.

Had Valentin Gubitchev and the Russians been better sports about his arrest, or if the U.S. government had been willing to wait out the diplomatic wrangling that threatened to postpone the first trial of a Cold War spy, there would have been no need for the new indictments, another arrest, and two trials. But such was not the case. And regardless of any deal made concerning the Russian's post-trial deportation, the immunity issue had to run its conflicted public course.

There was enormous excitement across the country. Surely this unexpected turn of events meant that "little Judy Coplon, the ideal girl next door," was in fact a dangerous spy. Bigger, blacker headlines told the story; Congress worked frantically to draft even more anti-espionage legislation, and around the nation anonymous calls were made to the FBI with increasing frequency by people suspecting that one neighbor or another was a spy.

Terrified by the escalation of the case against her, Judith dreaded the coming Monday. Caught in a legal technicality that made possible two different, although related, sets of charges stemming from the same alleged criminal act, she could well spend much of the rest of her life in prison. To her it was madness and made no sense at all. A great many observers, some who thought her guilty and others who considered her innocent, agreed. Nevertheless, Judy Coplon would appear once again before a judge and would listen to a reading of indictments against her. She would once again reply with a plea of not guilty. The issue of her bond would be raised. That she was already free on bail was of no consequence; these were new charges. There would be a new bond required. If it was set any higher, she might be returned to the detention center.

Events of this night suggest that Judy's anxiety about what lay ahead had become overwhelming. There is no question that, as the hours wore on, she became increasingly desperate. The woman whom Kelley would later call "a tough little baby" lost control.

The agents were housed in a fourth-floor walk-up loft in mid-Manhattan, some ten blocks from Grand Central Station. There was no identification of any sort to distinguish the building from any other. Six men seated in the loft were about to share one of the most unusual experiences in their careers. Tom Mitchell was one of the six.

In the loft, a buzz in his headphones alerted one of the agents that the woman was making a call. Quickly he engaged the device that would identify the number called, then dropped the needle onto the blank recording disc in front of him.

"She's just called the night number at Justice in Washington! She's asking for Kelley!"

"Kelley!" The others crowded around the listener.

"She sounds pretty upset."

"Let me hear," the supervisor insisted.

A moment later, a call was placed from the same telephone to the home of Raymond Whearty. After three rings, the woman's voice could be heard pleading into the telephone.

No one answered.

"She's broken," the supervisor speculated excitedly. "We've got to help her. She wants to confess! Why else would she be calling the enemy camp in the middle of the night except to confess?"

Agents in New York immediately called colleagues in Washington. "Find Kelley. Find Whearty!" A frantic search around the capital city, monitored moment by moment in the Manhattan loft, failed to find either of the two Justice Department officials. Because the wiretap was a closely guarded secret, agents in both cities were limited in their options. And in fact, most of those in Washington had no idea why they were asked to locate Kelley and Whearty. Among those who knew, no one could very well call Judith with, "Say, we're eavesdropping and know you're trying to reach a couple of people at Justice. Just hang in there, and we'll locate them before the night's over." And of course, not one of them knew for certain what she so desperately wanted to say.

The Justice Department, with its crack intelligence capabilities, could not find two of its own, who simply happened to be out late at Washington functions. Agents in the loft nearly wept with frustration.

Judy's last frantic call to Whearty was faithfully recorded to the sound of unanswered ringing.

There were two other calls made that night, a night Bertram presumably spent at home with his own family. Sounding distraught, Judy told her brother that she was "going to take some pills." Alarmed, Bertram reacted violently. A conversation bordering on hysteria calmed only when Judy convinced him that she meant she was going to take some vitamin pills; she had no intention of harming herself.

Later in the evening, a terrible telephone argument ensued between the two. Judy accused Bert of having had too much to drink, and, in a fury, he referred to her as an espionage agent. Two weeks of relentless, terrifying events, plus the anticipation of Monday, had taken a tragic toll. The emotional collapse of a precious relationship did not last, but it cost dearly in the currency of shared pain.

March 21–22, 1949

March 21 was a landmark day in the case, a return to Washington's Constitution Avenue, where the most serious Coplon arraignment would take place. Appearing calm and confident, Archie Palmer and Judith left New York under the watchful lens of the press, Archie on a ticket Bert had purchased with the last forty dollars available to him at the time. Money worries had grown into hideous monsters plaguing Bert's every waking hour. He had managed to raise another seven thousand dollars from a Bob Cato and three thousand from "the boys on Ludlow Street," all good friends of his. His fervent hope was that the judge would not ask for more than an additional ten-thousand-dollar bond.

Archie was glad to greet reporters in both New York and Washington, enthusiastically encouraging their interest in his client. Puppeteer Archie pulled the strings, and Judy smiled and waved gaily from the door of the plane, laughing down at the photographers gathered on the tarmac. Archie especially wanted media attention today, when he planned to reveal an important clue to his client'defense: her book.

The manuscript Judith claimed to be writing could be a critical element in her defense against the charge of taking government secrets with the intention of passing them to the Soviets. Before going to Washington, Judy had told Archie her reasons for writing her book and had talked about its concept and contents. Whether he believed her, whether he thought a manuscript existed, or ever had, he behaved as if firmly convinced that she was telling the truth.

What she had to say was compelling. The jury would later hear the same story during her direct examination:

"I was going to call my book 'Government Girl.' It's autobiographical in a sense, but a novel. I started writing when I came back from a trip to Europe last summer; I guess I first started making notes in August. So far it's a series of sketches. Life of a government girl in Washington during a pretty disturbing time, but also some glimpses of Europe."

The "disturbing time" occurred more after the war than during the hostilities.

"I began writing about how wartime Washington felt, at least to me. There was a feeling of idealism about the war effort, the need to get things done, a feeling of 'we've got to win this war.' A wonderful spirit of cooperation, of everyone pulling together."

Judy wrote about that spirit in "reflections and flashbacks." And then she began writing about a period of disillusionment when the war was over, when the war effort ended in 1945 and people began a gradual movement from government to industry. These were good people, good citizens, yet their government had doubts about them. "During the war they were heroes of a sort; afterwards, everyone was suspect." Loyalty oaths and witch hunts, were, in her telling, a fact of everyday postwar life.

Did this affect Judith? "It changed my life, both personally and professionally. We used to sit around and talk, just generally, about our work and the fact that we loved it. Oh, not discuss anything classified, of course. But after the war, surprisingly enough, you couldn't even do that much in Washington. With all the hysteria about subversives, you never knew who among your friends might go back and misquote something you'd said, and the next thing you'd know, you'd be the subject of an investigation. The fun went out of being with people. You honestly didn't know whom you could trust.

"I suppose the most awful part of it was when it happened in families. For example, a boy of thirteen reported that he had heard his father say something sympathetic about the Russians. Not only was he praised by our people, but he was also encouraged to suggest that his friends spy on their parents as well."

Judy's job changed as well as her personal life. "I was assigned the task of deciding which organizations in the country to blacklist on the basis of someone's arbitrary definition of disloyalty. To decide which were subversive. I felt like a traitor."

Victim or traitor, the Government Girl came to the federal court for the District of Columbia, a mammoth stone building a full block square, where Pennsylvania and Constitutuion Avenues intersect. It is an intimidating edifice for those entering its portals as the accused. For Judith Coplon it was a very familiar place, one she visited in the course of her daily work in this capital neighborhood. Her office, in fact, was at Ninth and Pennsylvania.

When Judy left Washington on the one o'clock train to New York on March 4, seventeen days earlier, she fully expected to return to Washington the following day. She was a free woman. Then, between March 4 and March 21, she became notorious, was indicted for espionage activity in New York and Washington, arrested and twice arraigned in New York, and held a federal prisoner for a week. Her freedom at the moment was technical and based on a twenty-thousand-dollar bond. In a few minutes, even that might end. She would be a prisoner again.

Judith waited in the front row of spectator seats watching Judge Richmond B. Keech charge a murder-trial jury. When her name was called, she walked to the bench and stood with apparent calm while new charges against her were read.

"How do you plea?" Judge Keech inquired gently.

"Not guilty," she responded in a clear, carrying voice.

Judy stood with hands clasped behind her back as a vociferous, but brief, battle over bail raged between Archie and Raymond Whearty. Archie used the same arguments that Bertram Adams had used in New York, principally that Judy would go nowhere, could go nowhere, but home to her ailing parents. Whearty angrily countered with a description of Judy's elusive behavior the night of her arrest.

"Bail is set at $10,000," Keech decided. "Trial date, April 25th."

Judy closed her eyes momentarily as she was led, a prisoner once again, from the courtroom. She was taken to an office where she was fingerprinted and photographed. Archie, meanwhile, was going through the process of posting bail. A seven-thousand-dollar cashier's check and three thousand in cash. From Bert.

The third and most controversial of the arraignments was concluded.

There were questions about the need—and the legality—of bringing seemingly duplicative charges in Washington. The legal questions were disposed of easily: No law was violated, due process was not denied, rights were not violated. Insiders, of course, well understood the need to try Judy quickly, and alone.

Before leaving the courthouse, Archie took Judy to the pressroom, where he would do most of the talking. About the book.

"My client," the affable attorney began, "is a budding novelist. She was simply collecting material for her book when FBI agents arrested her for espionage. This little girl is not a spy, she's a writer. Actually, this whole case is much ado about nothing!"

Reporters grinned. "Her novel is partially political, partially government, and partially love," Archie continued. "She's a serious writer. She's not selling her soul for a mess of pottage—she's trying to write something that's going to stand out." A mess of pottage? Pencils paused midsentence.

One of the journalists, who had managed to move close to Judy, whispered to her, "Have you told Mr. Palmer about this book?"

"We've had discussions," Judy smiled.

"You see," Archie explained, "in Washington, it's customary for people in public office to write books, and authors have to get information so they have the proper historical background."

"Do you mean that at the time Miss Coplon is accused of having committed espionage she was collecting material for her book?" asked Andrew Tully of the *Washington Daily News*.

"Certainly," Archie replied.

When asked if the material found in her pocketbook was for Judy's book, Archie answered smugly, "I can't answer that question."

Judy sat quietly, at times obviously amused by Archie's performance. Now and again she would break into a smile, an entertained member of the audience rather than a part of the cast. Her attorney was clearly pleased by the number of questions about Judith's book, and he was well prepared with answers.

"But what about the Russian?" someone asked.

"Ah, the Russian!" Archie responded. "You meet all kinds of people from all countries at teas and cocktail parties. Meeting a foreigner doesn't mean much. It's like a foreigner kissing your hand—just a kiss."

Miriam Ottenberg of the *Evening Star* observed that Judith "never forgot" to refer any leading questions to her lawyer. One of the few women reporters present, Ottenberg duly noted that Judith kept her poise throughout the questioning and described her dress for the occasion, assuming, and no doubt rightly so, that women readers were interested. Did the new "Mata Hari" wear the country's latest fashion rage, the midcalf "New Look"? No, Ottenberg wrote, Judy's gray tweed skirt was somewhat shorter than the current fashion. With it, she wore a black beret tilted over an eye, a black cardigan sweater buttoned up the back, and a thin gold chain around her neck. Bright lipstick, Ottenberg added, "relieved her paleness." Judith's black beret worn over sleek dark hair became a fashion trademark suggesting both glamour and intrigue. Half a century later, Monica Lewinsky's black beret would do the same.

Asked if she had been able to return to her McLean Gardens apartment to collect personal effects and clothing, Judy responded that she had not had the time to do so. Time away from New York had become a serious problem. Not only were both parents ill, but now Bert Coplon was not feeling well.

"Look," she said, pulling off one of her black pumps, "just look at that. Thirty thousand dollars bond and a hole in my shoe!"

Archie called a halt to the proceedings, but not before he shared with his thoroughly baffled audience a few final, disconnected thoughts about Theodore Dreiser's *An American Tragedy;* William Shakespeare; *I Remember Mama;* and *The Busy, Busy People.* In that order.

In a masterpiece display of misdirected finger pointing, Archie scolded Judy the day following the press conference for making statements "too ridiculous and uncalled for" to reporters. Fine, Judy promised angrily, she would never, ever speak to reporters again. It would prove to be a promise impossible to keep.

That evening, Bertram Coplon told a friend that he was supporting five doctors, all needed to care for his stricken father and ailing mother, along with his own family's health needs. Five doctors, he said, and three lawyers, or would be, given the probability of having to retain a lawyer to represent Judy in Washington. He estimated that cost at twenty-five hundred dollars. Further, Bert said, he had withdrawn his savings from the Kings Highway Savings Bank because it had become the "general opinion" that his father-in-law was backing him financially, providing funds for Judith's defense. It was necessary that Bert do what he could to protect Shirley's father's reputation and his position at the bank. He would later tell Archie that he had no desire to become indebted to Seidman, that the relationship had not been good for some time.

Ever tactful, Archie told Bert tonight that people were beginning to refer to Judy's brother as a Communist. At the moment, both Bert and his sister must have believed that things could not possibly get worse. But they could. Infinitely worse, eight days later.

March 29–30, 1949

Filled with tingling excitement, the children listened each Christmas for the familiar sound of Santa's jingle bells ringing through the snowy mountains. Listened, and squealed with delight when, at last, they heard the joyous sound heralding Santa's long-awaited coming. No one knew how many thousands of children, and adults, had heard the ringing of Samuel's bells.

Shortly after midnight, in the early morning of Tuesday, March 29, the bells were silenced for all time. Even so, that same Tuesday, their resonance rang sweetly in the hearts, if not the ears, of all of those whose lives had been touched by the Santa Claus of the Adirondacks.

GIRL SPY SUSPECT'S BROKEN DAD DIES, SANTA DIES OF BROKEN HEART, and similar headlines screamed across America's newspapers. There was no doubt, at least on the part of the public and the media, that the frail, gentle man had died of grief. God had visited him with poor health and excruciating pain, which he had been able to bear; the world—most said *his daughter*—had delivered upon him an emotional burden he simply could not survive.

Today, Judith's husband insists that Samuel's death was not associated with her alleged espionage. "He was unaware," Albert Socolov says. "Completely." Yet one must wonder if his insistence is based on a continuing need to protect his wife, because, at the time, Rebecca's words revealed quite a different view.

"We tried to keep the news from my husband, and so he died two weeks later . . . she was my husband's darling." If he had been as "completely unaware" as Socolov contends, there would have been no need to shield him from the news of Judith's plight. And at the time, Archie Palmer told the press that Judith's arrest had "hit the father hard."

At eleven-thirty on the morning of March 30, Rebecca Coplon arrived with her son at Gutterman's Memorial Chapel on Church Avenue in Brooklyn. Judith arrived separately. Voyeurs watched a new Judy enter the church. Gone was the exciting, glamorous alleged spy; in her place was a fragile, grief-sticken daughter, her pain surely exacerbated by the devastating morning headlines. Judith wept openly and bitterly throughout two funeral services—Masonic and Orthodox Jewish—conducted for her father. In addition to the immediate family, other relatives and about 150 friends were present. The services were for Samuel, but attention was focused on his weeping daughter.

Outside, those who had gathered to catch a glimpse of the Coplons moved aside as the family left the chapel to accompany Samuel on his last ride, a trip to Riverside Cemetery in Rochelle Park, New Jersey. Under indictment for espionage, it was necessary for Judith to obtain court permission to attend the interment.

No bells sounded, no children cried out with joy, as they drove away.

April 1

As the day neared for the New York trial, two themes reflecting the public's interest dominated news coverage of the Coplon story. One was based on the anticipated arrest of additional members of Judy's "spy ring," along with the capture of other rings circling through government. Fear of communism, the Bomb, the Red Menace, was everywhere, exacerbated beyond measure by Judith's arrest. In truth, the Soviets *were* spying, the UN *was* alive with Soviet intelligence officers in the guises of various benign roles, and the Russians *were* working on the Bomb. But the fantasy, a group affair, was greater by far than the reality. With a failed national confidence at its heart, the prevailing American condition would have been an ideal laboratory for the study of latter-day psychohistorians. And it was not yet the era of McCarthyism, still a year away.

The second theme was punishment, that which was appropriate for espionage, for betrayal of one's country in such exceedingly dangerous times. It had been discussed all along, but the temperature of the debate rose sharply, along with demands for the government to move quickly in serving up Judith Coplon's just desserts. On March 25 John Kelley had put Mildred Gillars (Axis Sally) in prison for ten to thirty years. This month, April, was Judy's turn. Editorials called for Judith's immediate imprisonment. Others called for her execution. As soon as legally possible.

Also of great interest was the heated issue of Gubitchev's status, still not resolved. In the prosecution's hands were several unhelpful documents. One was a brief submitted to Judge Simon Rifkind in federal court in New York City holding that the Russian was not eligible for diplomatic immunity—if, that is, the State Department so decided. Prepared by Fowler Hamilton, an attorney acting as a friend of the court, the document acknowledged that there were "cogent arguments on both sides of the issue."

From the State Department had come various memoranda indicating that Valentin Gubitchev, once and for all, without question, was not entitled to diplomatic immunity, unless, of course, someone decided otherwise. Pronouncements always fell short of finality, with a door left open for the ultimate "official" decision. In truth, no one seemed prepared to make the ultimate, official decision.

In Washington, two versions of how the FBI "got onto" Judy suddenly surfaced. One was that revelations from a confidential informant led to investigation of Judy. The other, coming from Capitol Hill, held that she was discovered through a routine loyalty check no different from those made on all government workers. The two possibilities were not necessarily mutually exclusive. A routine check could involve a confidential informant; still, something did not ring true. What was the government hiding, people wondered, and why?

The man who knew was not talking to the press. FBI Special Agent Robert Lamphere, who had orchestrated the case from the beginning, would keep a low profile until his explosive appearance on the witness stand. For now, he remained in the shadows, quietly observing, while his remarkable counterintelligence drama continued to entrance an international audience. As for the answer to the question about a confidential informant, he would keep that secret for four decades.

Judith's New York trial had been scheduled to begin April 14 to allow her time to grieve for her father, with the Washington trial set for April 25. The prosecution team was not concerned about the Washington trial. Five days, they thought, from opening arguments to a jury decision. But the New York trial, with the continuing debate over diplomatic immunity, would be more complicated and could run in to a snag.

Fortunately for the prosecution, on April Fool's Day, 1949, Kelley received notice that Archie Palmer wanted his client tried first in Washington, on April 25 as scheduled, which would give her most of the month to "mourn properly." Palmer suggested May 2 for the New York trial. If the prosecution would find the new, revised schedule acceptable, he would petition Judge Rifkind to approve the change.

Kelley found the change eminently acceptable. Prosecutors immediately began to plan for the Washington trial, a five-day wonder that would have them all back up in New York by April 30, where they would tackle the Big Trial.

What they failed to anticipate were the plans of someone else. The little fellow with the slouch hat and the candy mints.

PART TWO

On the **Avenue,** with **Side Trips** to **Hollywood** and the **Balkans**

Opening Gambits

• I •

THE TRIAL OF ACCUSED COLD WAR spy Judith Coplon began in the district court of the United States in Washington, D.C., on April 25, as scheduled. From the outset, it was a two-ring circus, the first ring filled with the kind of entertainment provided by clowns, buffoons, dancing bears; the second, with the spine-tingling thrills of trapeze artists, knife throwers, and high-wire acts of enormous skill. From the opening moments, among the crowds of eager spectators jamming the corridors and hoping for seats, there was a perceptible feeling that this was going to be a great show.

Had there been a colorful billboard over the door of the historic courthouse, it would have given Archie Palmer well-deserved top billing. He danced cheerfully into the ring the minute proceedings began and the first veniremen were brought in to be examined. One moment Archie was skipping merrily between his seat at the defense table and the jury box; the next, he was offering prospective jurors mints. And the next, he would be asking a question that left his audience, including the prosecution, astounded; or, except for the prosecution, a query that left everyone amused and entertained.

"Tell me, have you ever had any association with the House Committee on Un-American Activities, or the thousands of investigating committees that spring like mushrooms out of the soil of Washington to display their investigative powers?"

At one point, while explaining that "Judy never gave a single thing to any foreign power or nation," Archie pulled Judith to her feet, dragged her chair in front of the jury box, pushed her back into the chair, and announced: "This is Judith Coplon. She will take the witness stand and tell you that she was a United States government employee for a number of years; that her forebears—"

"Objection," shouted John Kelley and Raymond Whearty in unison. "What do her forebears have to do with this?" Kelley thundered. "Besides, he is making a speech which should be reserved for his opening statement!"

"Oh, well," Archie interjected blithely, "I thought I'd put a little light and heat in the case, but since it's a hot day, I'll drop the heat."

"Sustained," said Judge Albert L. Reeves belatedly, already wondering what he had gotten himself into. He was all but retired, settled happily in Kansas City, when he was persuaded to come to Washington to assist with an overloaded docket in district court. He was elderly, crotchety, tired, and totally inexperienced with cases involving high crime. His discomfort was painfully obvious.

The first item of business this morning was a petition by the defense to quash the indictment charging Judy with taking documents from government files for the purpose of aiding Russia. Archie argued that the defendant's rights were violated because the grand jury returning the indictment had included nine government workers. Not fair, Archie claimed. Having taken the loyalty oath, these grand jurors could not possibly have rendered an impartial judgment.

"Congress settled this question in 1935, Mr. Palmer, when it made government workers eligible for jury duty," Reeves said in denying the petition.

With feigned incredulity, Archie then inquired of each prospective trial juror, "You mean you have been in the government for years and you could sit here without prejudice in this case? Isn't it true you would be afraid or embarrassed to find the defendant innocent?"

As each person denied bias, Archie moaned and shook his head, causing either Kelley or Whearty to demand that the judge admonish Archie for his behavior. In response to the judge's scoldings, Archie several times apologized for his lack of familiarity with the rules of the game. After all, he explained, he was unfamiliar with Washington and the legal niceties of the district court. He was a poor stranger, "come from New York, the land of Sodom and Gomorrah." From time to time, Archie would bow from the waist, as fully as his waist would allow, and apologize to the potential juror and the court.

During the nearly daylong wrangle over jury selection, Archie would eventually challenge for cause seven of the twenty-eight panelists who were government workers. Each challenge, however, was reviewed with Judy, whose dark head remained bent over her notepad, except when she watched Archie traipsing about the room.

"Your Honor," Kelley finally addressed the bench, "the government is willing to stipulate, out of an abundance of caution, that all government employees on the panel may be excused, providing it is understood no precedent is being set. Perhaps then we can move along."

Archie threw his arms in the air and whirled toward Kelley. "He hands me alms, for the love of Allah!" he shouted. "The defense will not enter into such a stipulation. I can't agree to the government's offer because I'd be waiving the rights of the defendant."

"What?" Kelley exploded.

"I don't understand, Mr. Palmer . . ." Judge Reeves began.

But Kelley understood. This whole business could be a basis for appeal.

Archie's questions of the first venire were soon going far afield. Were they prejudiced against a divorced person or against an unhappily married person seeking a divorce? What about an American who contemplated marrying a citizen of another country? If such a union occurred, how would they feel about a foreign spouse living in this country, or an American living abroad?

"Is all of this pertinent?" Reeves finally asked.

"It will be," Archie said smugly. "We do not deny there was a social relationship. Judith Coplon will take the witness stand and tell all about it." He fluffed his feathers. "She was with this man many times," he announced. The jury took notice. Was this whole business simply about romance?

Kelley and Whearty were on their feet with a ringing objection.

"To my chambers," Judge Reeves hissed.

After conferring with the prosecution and defense in his chambers, Judge Reeves took over examination of the remaining members of the prospective panel. This did not preclude Archie's asking Reeves, in a stage whisper, to make certain inquiries, requests Reeves most often ignored.

As the court's business for the day was gaveled to a close, no jurors had been seated. Their selection would continue in earnest tomorrow, Judge Reeves promised. Archie gathered up his papers, Life Savers, oversized hat, and his client. He was muttering to the press about "that Russian" as he steered Judy to the elevator. "Smile," he kept telling her, and she did. But she answered none of the shouted questions, not those from the reporters or from the simply curious.

Struggling through the crowd, Judy climbed into a taxi and returned to the Willard Hotel at the corner of Pennsylvania and 14th Street, where gawking onlookers watched her leave the cab and enter the hotel. Dinner, as would become routine, was a simple, quiet, and inexpensive affair. When her mother arrived, tomorrow, they would share the room and have dinner served there, avoiding prying eyes. This would be their pattern throughout the course of the trial, a pattern that kept them almost always to themselves, remote, savoring the quiet and escape from the press and the public. Now and again there would be a visitor, an old friend, or an evening walk along the avenue. But once outside their room, the eyes were watching, and often lenses as well.

Bertram Coplon would remain in New York, struggling with the toy business and spending as much time as possible with his family. On occasion he would drive to Washington, and on rare occasions his mother and sister would go to New York for a weekend. The compelling, directing, imposing issue was money, Bert's crushing burden.

• 2 •

ROMANCE! JUDITH IN LOVE, JUDITH WAS TO WED RUSSIAN, and LAWYER REVEALS LOVE ANGLE were the following morning's headlines. The painful process of jury selection and various procedural motions received not nearly as much attention as the prospect that love may have been the reason Judith Coplon and Valentin Gubitchev had been meeting secretly. There was speculation that, in an admittedly anti-Red climate of opinion, Judy might be simply a young woman in love who was framed for political expediency. Not everyone felt that way, however.

"We are no end sorry if romance has been nipped in the bud, but there are times when considerations of national security must intrude upon international necking; and particularly when there is cause to suspect that the dowry consists of top secrets pilfered from government files," wrote the editor of the *Nashville Banner*.

Regardless of the *Banner*'s unromantic position on the matter, the press loved this unexpected turn of events. Were Judith and Valentin *really* planning to be married? How long had the romance been going on? Did this mean that the only betrayal involved in this case was Gubitchev's marital perfidy? What Archie did not know at the time, and would not know until the very end, was that the love angle would become a dangerous triangle.

As she alighted from her taxi this second day of the trial, Judith once again offered only smiles and not answers to the waiting crowd. Despite the attention she had received thus far, she seemed surprised by the number of newsreel cameras, reflectors on tripods, and broadcasting teams outside the courthouse. For a moment she hesitated, and then Archie, a merry leprechaun in broad brim, took her arm and they made their way inside.

Moving with determination, Judge Reeves completed selection of the jury. Chosen were eight males, six white and two black; and four females, all black. Two of the female jury members were housewives, one was a charwoman at the Municipal Center, and the last was a telephone operator in the U.S. Bureau of Printing and Engraving. The average age of the women was nearly forty-eight, twenty years older than Judy.

Of the males, two also worked at the Bureau of Printing and Engraving; others were employed as a telephone repairman, a meat cutter, a civilian clerk for the army, a sheet-metal worker, and a housepainter. Only one juror was at a professional or managerial level; ironically, like Judy's father, he was a toy manufacturer. The average age of the men was thirty-seven.

The highlight of the day's judicial exercise was Archie's motion asking for return of the contents of Judy's purse, the so-called government secrets and private items she carried to New York on the night of March 4. Archie insisted that because Judith was arrested and searched without a warrant, these items must be returned and therefore could not be used in evidence. Judith was "seized upon violently," claimed the defense, her purse "grabbed" from her and its papers and other private articles illegally taken from her.

"Oh, come now," Kelley objected. "Nobody attacked the defendant as he describes."

"Ah, my good friend, the famous prosecutor who caged Axis Sally, objects to the truth."

"Your Honor, will you please ask defense counsel to quit referring to me as his friend?" Kelley paused. "And of course the government does not object to the truth."

"I was just trying to be pleasant," Archie offered. "You don't have to be nasty about my calling you friend. I think I will object to your behavior."

"Enough!" bellowed Judge Reeves.

The motion, one of critical import, would be addressed tomorrow, Judge Reeves announced, when the FBI would be called upon to defend the legality of the arrest. There was no question that if the court found the arrest without warrant unjustified, it was all over. Without the documents, there was no case against Judy.

The whole untidy business about the warrant had made the government apprehensive from the beginning. It was one of two weak links in the legal chain that bound Judith Coplon at the moment, links the prosecution feared could break at any time. The other, of course, was that Judith had failed to cooperate with the planned transfer of the documents in question; she had nearly spoiled it all by ending up with government secrets still in her purse when Bob Granville nabbed her.

Now, as the second day of the trial closed, the FBI and the prosecution team were suffering a contagious nervous condition brought on by Archie's motion. Tomorrow they would have to justify an arrest without a warrant. And a search to boot. Their attention focused once again on the requirements for such an arrest—suspicion that a crime had been committed, which was not much of a problem; and insufficient time to secure a warrant, with a concomitant concern about escape of the suspects, which was indeed problematic. To add to their discomfort, no one knew what to expect from Judge Reeves, the elderly novice on the bench.

Veiled and garbed in mourning attire, Rebecca Coplon arrived in Washington on the afternoon train from New York. To passersby, she was a vision of sadness, her large, luminous eyes ringed in charcoal, her face a startling chalk white against the midnight black of her head-to-toe costume. Reed thin, and weak from a chronic heart condition, she nevertheless moved boldly to the door of the train, then stepped down onto the platform and into the welcoming arms of the press.

In New York, the Russian embassy finally posted the necessary hundred thousand dollars and Valentin Gubitchev was released after fifty-three days behind bars. He was ordered to remain in the city and to stay away from train stations, airports, and docks—unless the Justice Department summoned him to appear in Washington, D.C., in the case of *United States of America versus Judith Coplon*. This was seen as likely, given John Kelley's announcement earlier in the day that he would produce Gubitchev in court at the appropriate time. The announcement seemed to titillate the entire country, except for Kelley, who had made it because he thought he must and who had no intention of calling the Russian; and for Archie Palmer, who felt that Gubitchev was the last person in the world he wanted to run into at the corner of Constitution and Pennsylvania Avenues. And except for Gubitchev, who, given the choice, would have preferred to return to jail.

• 3 •

Judy arrived alone on the morning of April 27. At her instruction, Rebecca would arrive later, after most of the crowd, including the media and its paraphernalia, had dispersed. Judy greeted her fans warmly, but declined to make a statement. Joined by Archie, and escorted by a helpful marshal, she walked through the melee and into the courtroom, where she placed her handbag and a small black case on the defense table before taking her seat.

When Rebecca Coplon entered the courtroom shortly before the appearance of Judge Reeves, tears stung the eyes even of those who were convinced that Judith Coplon was a spy. Judy jumped from her chair and ran to her mother, caught her in her arms, and held her in a loving embrace. For a moment, there was absolute silence, the quiet of people visually eavesdropping on a heartrending scene and then turning away. John Kelley cleared his throat and shuffled papers on his desk.

The jury would not hear arguments about the arrest. Judge Reeves dismissed the panel until eleven o'clock the next day, Thursday, to allow sufficient time to resolve what had become a sticky problem. There was no way now that the trial would end on Friday.

John Kelley began his justification of the arrest by stating that the papers found on the defendant's person involved national security and were stolen from Justice Department files for transmission to Moscow. They were absolutely essential to the government's case, Kelley insisted.

Palmer rose to his feet. "The government admits that if we are successful in suppressing the evidence they snatched from this girl's pocketbook without a warrant, they won't have any case," Archie told the judge.

Special Agents of the FBI Robert Granville and T. Scott Miller took the stand to defend the March 4 arrest. Miller was first, describing in step-by-step detail how the FBI had followed Judith Coplon on three different occasions, how she had met Gubitchev on all three, and how they had behaved suspiciously.

"Did you ever see this girl give a single thing to the Russian?" Archie asked Miller.

"No."

"Did you," Archie continued, "ever overhear anything about Gubitchev fearing that private detectives were following him? Detectives sent by his wife?"

"What?"

"Private detectives, Mr. Miller. Hired by Mrs. Gubitchev."

"No, I did not."

Miller testified that at one point during his February 18 surveillance he "drifted up behind Miss Coplon on an Eighth Avenue subway and got a look inside her bag, where I saw a folded piece of onion skin paper with typewriting on it." This was hardly incriminating.

Corroboration for Miller's testimony detailing Judith's behavior was provided by Granville, the competent, respected supervisor from Foley Square who had arrested Judith. Yes, surveillance of the defendant had taken place exactly as described; and no, to Granville's knowledge, there had been no sightings of any transfer of materials from the defendant to Valentin Gubitchev.

Now came the matter of information Judy carried to New York, information she did not transfer to the Russian engineer.

"Aside from personal articles, there were more than thirty sheets of paper known as data slips containing extracts from reports of the FBI relating to internal security matters and to suspected espionage agents in the United States. Such property was the property of the government." Granville paused. "The defendant's purse also contained other memoranda which may briefly be described as a statement of the defendant's efforts to obtain access to a top secret report of the FBI, a brief statement of her post-graduate educational background, and three statements [character sketches] concerning three potential recruits for espionage service." Not mentioned was a certain document in Judy's own handwriting. It would later prove to be of enormous significance.

Granville read into the record Judy's statement about her efforts to obtain access to a top-secret report of the FBI.

> I have not been able (and don't think I will) to get the top secret FBI report which I described to Michael on Soviet and Communist Intelligence Activities in the U.S. When the moment was favorable, I asked Foley where the report was (he'd previously remarked that he'd had such a report); he said that some departmental official had it and he didn't expect to get it back. Foley remarked there was nothing "new" in it. When I saw the report, for a minute, I breezed through it rapidly, remember very little. It was about 115 pages in length; summarized first Soviet "intelligence" activities, including Martens, Lore, Poyntz, Altschuler, Silvermaster, et al. It had heading on Soviet UN delegation but that was all I remember. The rest of the report I think was on Polish, Yugo, etc. activities and possibly some info on the CP, USA.

Pin-drop silence. And then, an excited murmur rippled through the courtroom. To both the initiated and uninitiated, this seemed unquestionably the business of espionage. In addition, the initiated recognized the names of individuals in the statement. Spies. Recruiters of spies.

Spectators, who could see only the back of Judy's head at the moment, were no doubt wishing they could see her face. They would have been sorely disappointed, for her expression changed very little during Granville's reading. As for Archie, he frowned and continued to chew vigorously.

Throughout the day, Archie argued that Granville's testimony was hearsay, that Judith should not have been arrested without a warrant and that, therefore, the papers she carried were private and must be suppressed. He left with the judge specific questions with regard to his motion, questions the judge promised to consider before court tomorrow morning.

"Who is Michael?" reporters called out to Judy. "How can you explain that memo?" "Why were you after a secret report like that?"

They were crammed into the courthouse pressroom, Judy and Archie perched on a table up front. Reaching into his briefcase, Archie retrieved a Bible, thumbed to a particular passage, and handed it to Judy.

"Miss Coplon," a reporter asked, "did you type that memo?"

She gave him one of her most brilliant smiles. "I did. It was part of the politically slanted romantic novel I'm doing. It has intrigue, it is straight out of Washington. But it's fiction."

"Who's Michael?"

"An allegorical character, Michael the Archangel. Here, listen." Judy read from the Bible in her lap.

"From Revelations Twelve. 'And there appeared another wonder in Heaven; and behold a great red dragon, having seven heads and ten horns and seven crowns upon his head. . . . And there was war in Heaven; Michael and his angels fought against the dragon; and the dragon fought against the angels.'"

The Red Dragon, Judy explained, was also an allegorical figure, this one representing Russia and her satellite countries.

There was nothing allegorical about people like Silvermaster and Poyntz and all, the reporters pointed out. These were real people. At least subversives, and perhaps spies.

"Of course they're real," Judy explained. "And all of them are people who figured in investigations by HUAC. There is no problem here." The fact was, Judy continued, she was using reality to help her devise a fictional plot. She was writing notes to herself, acting things out to herself. It was a part of plot development and a system that worked for her. She smiled reassuringly.

To many of the journalists, most of whom had a book in their minds if not in their typewriters, Judy's explanation seemed plausible enough. To others, it begged too much of one's reason. Whatever, they wrote their stories about this new turn of events, and the document in question became the "Michael Memorandum."

In closing the press conference, Archie told the journalists who continued to shout questions, "Look, this little girl worked her heart out on her government job. She worked long hours of overtime, her bosses will tell you that. They knew she took work home all the time. Ask 'em about it. If they deny it, they're not being honest with you. As a matter of fact," he announced, "my worthy opponent, Mr. Whearty, had himself written a sterling evaluation of Judy's work just last year, partly because of her extra efforts."

On the following day, Archie approached the bench the moment Judge Reeves's gavel sounded. His argument that the arrest was illegal and the contents of Judith's purse wrongfully taken turned to a new issue in support of his motion. There had been no ruling thus far as to whether the contents were evidentiary or private.

"In this particular matter before Your Honor on the motion to suppress, nobody has a right to publish the private paper . . . [until] those papers are properly in evidence."

Publication of the Michael Memorandum, now the subject of glaring newspaper headlines, was improper and injurious to his client, a wrong the court must correct, Archie insisted. Conclusions about guilt and innocence were being drawn in the media. The judge did not agree.

The defense motion failed, with Judge Reeves ruling that Judy's arrest, her search, and the seizure of the contents of her purse were in accordance with the law. She would stand trial. If the judge thought the matter would end there, he would be monumentally disappointed. Further, had the government, including J. Edgar Hoover, known what was to follow, it would have welcomed a different decision from the court every bit as much as the defense.

• 4 •

April 28, 1949, the day for opening arguments, and four days into what had been expected to be a five-day trial.

In the stillness of the courtroom, Raymond Whearty rose slowly and deliberately to deliver his opening to the jury. The courtroom was packed with an audience eager to hear his every word and those of Archie Palmer, which would follow. Whearty turned and for several seconds focused a chilling stare at the defendant, who appeared unmoved, and then addressed the jury, his icy countenance replaced by an indulgent smile. He began by explaining precisely how the government would open its case. First, he would read the charges against the defendant; second, he would describe the evidence that the government intended to introduce in order to prove its case; and third, he would provide an "over-all picture" as a framework for the jigsaw puzzle of evidence to come before them. Piece by piece, he told jurors, they would put together all of the bits of evidence required for conviction.

The assistant prosecutor introduced a reading of the two-count indictment with, "These are the actual words." They were ominous words, charging that Judy "did copy, take, make and obtain documents, writings, and notes containing intelligence reports . . . with the intention of giving them to a foreign government." That she "did willfully and unlawfully conceal and remove certain records."

Judy sat silent and unmoving, pencil poised above a yellow legal pad, throughout the reading of the charges against her. She was smartly dressed in a gray wool suit with a white blouse. Clear-eyed and composed, her full attention was fixed on Whearty, her former employer and ex-friend.

"As for a description of the evidence," Whearty told a thoroughly attentive jury, "I will recite the order of events of the case." This order he saw as beginning with Judy's employment in the Justice Department in 1943 as a staff member of the Anti-Trust Division located in New York. Since 1945, he said, Judith Coplon had been employed in Washington as a political analyst in the Foreign Agents Registration Section. In painstaking detail, Whearty described the work of the section and the defendant's job. A part of her job, he explained, was reading a variety of sources of information about foreign agent activity, including FBI reports.

Whearty, articulate and capable of quick, fiery speech, was speaking slowly and deliberately, condescendingly, giving the impression that he was concerned about the level of understanding of the charwomen, meat cutters, and telephone linemen who must be convinced of the defendant's guilt. There was repetition; there were long pauses.

For those who had expected a little fire and brimstone, a little excitement, Raymond Whearty was already becoming a disappointment. He droned. There was no drama. Jury members began to fidget. Whearty noticed a certain lack of attention and quickly picked up the tempo, his manner suggesting the advent of excitement just around the corner.

There came a time, he said, around the middle of January, when Judith's behavior had come to the attention of her supervisors and she was "taken off" internal security matters, her job limited to foreign agents' registration. She would no longer be using the secret files. The FBI now "picked her up," began to "observe her." Yes, indeed, the plot was thickening.

Archie Palmer leaned his head to the side and whispered softly to his client. She smiled, and he unwrapped a new role of Life Savers, offering her one. She shook her head and he stood the roll on end on the corner of the table.

On January 14, as was her custom, Whearty was saying, Judith took the train to New York to visit her parents. Along for the occasion, unknown to Judy, were several agents in the process of "picking her up." With the jury now very interested and spectators hanging on every word, Whearty segued into a lengthy description and history of the New York subway system and lost much of his audience along the way. He went back in time to "some glacial period" in describing the geological formation of the land, how early tunnels were built, where layers of rock existed. He carefully told his listeners about the development of the underground transportation system and how the streets were laid out and how, in general, Manhattan had moved its populace since the earliest days. Warming to his subject, Whearty told of gentle grades and lovely parks. Jurors cast quick glances at each other; spectators appeared puzzled.

After meandering through time and topography, Whearty got his subway system and his opening address back on track. He returned to the night of January 14 and Judith's visit to New York City.

"She got to Pennsylvania Station and she stayed around the station for a little while, oh, I guess, close to three quarters of an hour, in the ladies room, and then in a little book shop and then in a drug store getting a bite to eat, and then finally on the Seventh Avenue subway, which, you will recall, runs up to this St. Nicholas Avenue hill." A thought struck the speaker and he quickly held up a hand. "Wait, I should say this. I missed two details in the subway description that I should tell you about."

From the jury box came an audible groan. If the judge heard the sound he did not acknowledge it.

After additional details on which streets intersected where, Whearty returned to Judith on the night in question. He related every move she made, every shop she entered, every step she took. On Broadway and 193rd Street, she met Valentin Gubitchev and the two of them went into a small café. Gubitchev dined while Judy dropped coins in the nickelodeon. As they left the restaurant, there was some sort of argument and Judy shook a rolled-up newspaper at her companion.

Now, surely, something would happen! One of the evidentiary puzzle pieces would be forthcoming. But none appeared. Judy went to her parents' home in Brooklyn, and the Russian returned to his apartment.

"The Defendant Coplon next came to New York on the 18th of February," Whearty told his disappointed listeners. "The train was late; it was thirty-five minutes late." Judy broke a strap on her shoe and stopped to have it fixed. Obviously hurried and anxious, she boarded the Eighth Avenue subway, accompanied by several FBI agents, one of whom stood immediately over her right shoulder.

"As she opened her purse and he looked in, he could not see much of what was in there, but sticking up in one compartment, in one side of the purse, there were some papers, there was some typewriting on those papers. The typewriting was folded and it could not be told what was written there or even the nature of the paper . . . it appeared to be onion skin."

Was this a puzzle piece? Was there something here they were not getting? The jurors were now openly looking at each other, studying other faces for signs of enlightenment. They looked over at the defendant, who was now smiling broadly. It all seemed very peculiar.

In her rush to meet her Russian, Whearty said, Judith got lost in Tryon Park. Ironically, she even asked one of her followers for directions. Eventually, Judith and Gubitchev met, in the usual circuitous way, but only briefly. There was still nothing very exciting about it all, no sightings of Judy passing secret materials, no little bits of information to fit the puzzle. Two meetings so far, in which nothing much seemed to happen.

Whearty next took the jury back to Washington, where Judy expressed anger over having her access to secret reports curtailed. A woman lawyer would testify, Whearty said, that Judy contrived to see these materials after she was told she should not. He looked down at his notes, cleared his throat, and resumed his narrative. There came a time, after Judy's access to secret documents had been restricted, that her boss, William Foley, handed her a secret memorandum supposedly sent by J. Edgar Hoover to Assistant Attorney General Peyton Ford. The document was "spy bait." Coplon read the memorandum, made notes about its content, placed the paper on a desk, and shortly thereafter left for New York on the one o'clock train, earlier than was her habit on a typical Friday afternoon.

The date was March 4.

Back again to the step-by-step surveillance and the story of Judy's arrest. Another listing of the items in her purse, items she had not passed to Valentin Gubitchev.

"My friend, Mr. Kelley, says day-ta and I say dah-ta." Whearty grinned. "These dahta slips were used for ready reference to specific FBI reports." In Judy's office, Whearty said, were probably half a million such slips. She had thirty-two of them with her. When Whearty moved to the Michael Memorandum and began to quote from it, Archie leaped to his feet.

"Until anything you read from becomes part of the evidence, you have no right to tell the jury; you cannot, in advance of the Court's ruling as to whether anything is material or proper, say what is in the papers!"

The argument with the judge was short lived. Furious, Archie returned to his chair. "All I can say is, exception!" he shouted.

When the assistant prosecutor finally had finished, questions had been raised about the items in Judith's purse, but the information she had carried to New York would not necessarily make her a spy in the eyes of many in the courtroom. If she were a writer using plot and counterplot reality as grist for her mill, she might have carried any of this material. And there could be other explanations. Work at home, whatever.

Also, Whearty made a strategic error in his presentation. If he wanted to drop a dah-ta bombshell, he should have done so before spending more than two hours boring his captive listeners by constructing subways through ancient geological formations, riding various trains and buses, and walking

Manhattan's streets. To make matters worse, infinitely worse, along the way he promised the jury they would hear it all again. Several FBI agents would recount, step by step, Judy's movements in the city. Not only would they tell every single detail, and have their stories repeated and thus corroborated by colleagues, they would also have maps and charts to boot. The jury could hardly wait.

His remarks concluded, Whearty returned to his seat. It was fifteen minutes past noon.

• 5 •

Defense attorney Archibald Palmer exploded upon the after-lunch courtroom scene like a delighted child whose turn had come to bat. He fairly danced to a spot directly in front of the jury and raised both arms to the ceiling.

"May it please the Court, and ladies and gentlemen of this jury, the curtain is up." His cheerful look vanished and his brow furrowed. "This is a serious play. This girl's life is about to be brought before you through the medium of witnesses under oath." He whirled, went to the defense table, pulled Judy to her feet, and marched her to stand before the jury.

"Now, in this case, my client comes before you clothed with innocence. His Honor will tell you the law is that until she is proven guilty beyond a reasonable doubt, this girl stands here innocent." Judy remained motionless. "And this is the first time she stands before anyone for the purpose of defending herself and indicating the fact that this case was built up through government notions, perhaps distorted in a timely manner, because of being in government service." Eyes on the just-pronounced Innocent, minds attempting to follow Archie's reasoning, the jurors also were motionless.

"We want," Archie shouted, "to prove before you that the mountain labored and brought forth a mouse." The men and women in the jury box struggled with this one. The mountain was supposed to be the government, wasn't it? And the mouse an insignificant case? Or was the girl the mouse? There was some squirming about in seats, but not from boredom.

"In order to understand this case, you ought to understand the indictment," Archie continued, as he gestured for Judy to return to her seat. "There are two things in this indictment which I want to read to you and have you understand that you are the sole judges of the fact and His Honor is the sole judge of the law. You are kings of the facts.

"In the first count it says, 'that with intent and reason to believe that the information was to be used to the injury of the United States and advantage to a foreign nation.' And in the second, it says, 'did willfully and unlawfully conceal and remove certain of such records.'

"Now," announced Archie, and quite convincingly so, "if there was no intent to do any of the two things, then, so far as this case is concerned, it must fall." There were nods of understanding among the jurors. Intent was the key to guilt or innocence. "And it is based upon the law and based upon evidence, under oath, of those you believe that we feel that this mountain labored and brought forth a mouse." Drat. The mountain and mouse again!

Archie continued by poking fun at the prosecution's foray into subterranean Manhattan and then, in great seriousness, observed that topography and history played no part in his client's guilt or innocence. "We say to you what plays a part in this case is this girl and her intentions, this girl and her background, this man whom she met and the things they did, and the distortion they make of the things she did."

Before painting an innocent picture of Judy's meetings with Gubitchev, Archie promised to "unscramble this jigsaw puzzle, to see whether or not I can take away the attempt, unconsciously, on the part of Mr. Whearty, to becloud you."

And the UN had to be explained, because Gubitchev talked about the UN to the "little girl" who fell in love with him.

"It is supposed to be just what the word says, united for the love and affection and peace of the world. That is the theory for the whole business. Whether it is going to be carried through with such a peace in the world is beyond my understanding. My sons in the war did not find it. But, people are always seeking the light. So, we have the United Nations."

Archie returned to the defense table and picked up three packages of Life Savers. Slowly he returned to stand in front of the jury, where he opened all three packages and placed them on the rail, then offered to share. One woman in the front row reached out, but caught the eye of the judge and hastily retrieved her hand.

"No?" Archie smiled. "Very well, we will continue." He popped half a dozen of the candies into his mouth and began to speak around them. "Mr. Gubitchev was an engineer in connection with the building of the various propositions attached to the building of that marvelous institution, which our John D. Rockefeller gave so much money to, and other governments are aiding with the balance."

Having explained away the United Nations, Archie embarked upon Valentin Gubitchev, a "personable person," charming, who spoke to Judy as a man does to a maid, who became a friend and, eventually, a romantic idol. A gentleman, who, although he felt great affection for Judy, had never touched her, had never kissed her. In telling of the couple's meetings in New York, Archie revealed that Judy and her Russian friend had met at times other than those described by the prosecution. They had met on Christmas Day and on other occasions when they had not acted suspiciously. The prosecution, Archie noted, had failed to mention these earlier meetings.

"When she wanted to take him home to do what you would have done, bring him to meet her father and mother on New Year's Day and he excused himself, they met on January 14. Then, for the first time, in that restaurant, he told her he was a married man but that he was not on good terms with his wife, that he wanted to become a part of this great country. He admired it; that is what he told her." This, explained Archie, was the cause of the argument and newspaper wielding. It was after Judy learned about the wife that she realized why they were being followed. Later, Gubitchev would give her other explanations, Archie declared.

Why did the government go after Judy simply because she was seeing a Russian? "Is a Russian a leper? A short time ago, it was a leper or a Nazi or a German or a Japanese! The President of the United States shakes hands with the ambassador of Russia. We are supposed to have amity and good will. Never mind what goes behind statecraft and iron curtains. Never mind about the airlift that is about to be lifted." He rose to his toes and waved wildly. "Love knows no bounds," he hollered.

Kelley started to rise, then sat back down.

"Your Honor," Archie asked, "will you ask the prosecutor to stop bobbing up and down in his chair? It's very distracting." Kelley's face reddened.

"Just continue," the judge ordered.

Archie whirled and twirled, bowed and gestured. He popped more Life Savers. As a rule, when mentioning the prosecution, either Whearty or Kelley, he spoke of them in glowing, complimentary terms, his "good friends for whom I have great respect." But not always. As for the two good friends, they might as well have dropped down a rabbit hole.

Judy watched Archie's every move, rarely making notes during his opening remarks. The jurors and spectators watched as well, fascinated by his behavior, thoroughly entertained by his convoluted discourse.

"Then on January 14, the FBI missed their grand opportunity," Archie was saying. "There is a man they are suspicious of, a Russian! According to Mr. Whearty, the commander-in-chief of this exploratory search, and who attempts to prove backwards things he could not prove forward—why didn't the FBI at that particular moment, if what Mr. Whearty says are the facts, why didn't they seize both of them if that paper passed? If Mr. Whearty, who was not there, is not mistaken, why didn't they seize the two of them and search them and frisk them and find this piece of paper, which a woman can carry in her pocketbook, like tissues, Kotex, things of that type. They missed their grand opportunity," Archie yelled. Kelley and Whearty exchanged yet another desperate look.

The cat-and-mouse game on March 4, Archie said, was based on Gubitchev's offering various explanations about who was following them, and on his telling Judy to "go away." But Judy cared for him and wanted more information. Did he love her or not? In short, they were having a spat; one moment he said to meet him on a street corner and the next, fearing followers, told her to disappear. She continued the adventure because she was trying to decide "which is right, her head or her heart."

"What's the matter with common sense?" Archie roared. "Must the juror lose his common sense because he becomes a juror? Is there inscribed over that door, 'He who enters here leaves his common sense outside'? If she has papers to give away, and they were on the bus, couldn't she have passed the papers to him, and couldn't he have dropped off on 41st Street or 42nd Street and disappeared with the papers and she carry on?"

Handkerchief in hand, Archie pulled back, mopped his brow, then sneaked up on the spellbound jury. "It is because those things did not occur! It is because of what they tried to do by putting a cart before the horse!"

"And the planted memorandum? This hush-hush data represents an outrageous attempt at entrapment!"

As for the final period when the FBI lost the elusive pair, Archie scorned, "And now comes this great eclipse, this marvelous piece of FBI ideology. They tell you the pocketbook is in her possession all this time, and suddenly the chief of the supervisors says to flush this bird. Why now?"

Archie's language and logic wound around the courtroom like a dozen writhing snakes. Still, the prosecution seemed only hugely annoyed; irritated, but not seriously concerned. That would change with Archie's next words.

"Now, the law speaks about search warrants and the law speaks about warrants for arrest. If you have a warrant for a person's arrest, you have got to have an affidavit upon which it is based. That is the law of the land. And if you want to search people, under our Constitution . . ."

Whearty was on his feet in an instant. "May I interrupt? I would like to object to this kind of argument."

The court agreed. Archie was making an argument, not a statement.

Archie shrugged. "It will be conceded in this case that they had no search warrant and they had no arrest warrant." A statement. Unfortunately for the prosecution, there was no argument.

Archie complained bitterly about Judy's having been indicted in both New York and Washington, insisting that two of the counts in New York were essentially the same as those in Washington. He was right, of course. Judy was indicted in Washington, Archie speculated to the jury, because "the more years you have got to serve if convicted, the more willing you might be to bend the knee and bow the head and say things against other people." Partly right.

"How well do you know your own strength?" Archie asked the jurors. "Job in the Bible did not know his strength. God aided him. Abraham in the desert did not know his strength when he was asked by the angel to kill his son. You see, they thought they could break her down. This girl is a girl of moral fiber, of decency, of forebears that are honest, and just middle class people like you and I."

Going to stand by the defendant, Archie now spoke softly. "I give you Judith Coplon. You are to do with her what the evidence requires you to do, but please, all of you, I ask just one thing. Stay with open mind. Do not be satisfied because the government presents a case that a person must be guilty.

Do not be satisfied with the idea, as His Honor will tell you, when a person is indicted they must be guilty. Hold yourselves in readiness to hear the truth.

"Finally, I ask you, then, to give me back Judith Coplon, to restore her to what health or happiness she deserves, and give her back to her mother."

Archie was finished. Despite his unorthodox opening, with its convoluted thought and syntax, he had raised valid questions about entrapment, arrest and search without a warrant, and the fact that there was no evidence anywhere that Judy had passed secrets to a foreigner. The diminutive attorney turned and bowed, to the jurors, the judge, the prosecution, finally to his client, and then returned, smiling, to his seat.

The government's crack prosecutors, Kelley and Whearty, sat frozen in disbelief. And Archie Palmer had not even begun to perform. He was still on his best and most circumspect behavior, which would last only for the next day or so. Then he'd *really* be in his element.

The Case for the Prosecution

When Reeves ruled against us, that the Defense would be allowed to have the FBI files, I thought it was all over. I asked Kelley and Whearty, and they said Tom Clark would not stop the trial. I couldn't believe what I was hearing.

ROBERT LAMPHERE, interview, August 21, 1997

If the Government has something to hide, then the Government should not be here.

JUDGE ALBERT REEVES, June 7, 1949

• I •

William Foley waddled. He was pear shaped, although not as much so as Archie Palmer, with a cherubic face, narrow eyes, and a wide mouth. His trousers were a bit too short, and he swung his arms vigorously as he propelled himself to the jury box. Foley was the first witness for the prosecution. The trial, at last, was truly under way. The witness raised his hand, swore to tell the truth, and identified himself as Judith Coplon's supervisor. With enthusiasm, he described his job, Judy's job, and the work of the department, much of which the jury had heard in Whearty's opening statement. And then, in response to Kelley's questions, the witness told of relieving Judy of her "internal security" duties in January after he learned that she was "running around with a Russian." In a meeting with Judy, Foley had simply explained that he was reorganizing duties. He said nothing at the time to indicate a lack of trust.

"How did she react to this change?" Kelley inquired.

"She didn't like it. She was disgruntled. She felt as if she were being slighted."

Foley explained that he had been firm in insisting that Judy limit her work to the registration of foreign agents, that she not deal with any material having to do with espionage or counterespionage activities.

"Did she do so in spite of your instructions?" Kelley asked.

"Yes. Repeatedly." In fact, Foley testified, Judy had asked more than once to review a secret report he had let her glance through on one occasion.

"Did you do give it back to her?"

"I did not. I made excuses."

Thoughts immediately went to the Michael Memorandum. Surely this would be the report on which the typewritten memorandum was based.

After several additional questions and responses concerning Judy's attempts to see classified documents, it was Archie's turn.

"Did you tell my good friend, Mr. Whearty, that you feel sorry for this girl here accused?"

"I might have."

"Do you feel sorry for her now?"

"I pity her."

Archie postured and pirouetted. Judy giggled. "Suppose she's a victim?" Archie inquired, hand clutching his throat.

"I pity any victim," Foley responded uncomfortably.

The defense attorney moved quickly to the issue of reassignment of Judith's duties.

"Now, about taking her off internal security, you spoke of Judith's 'running around with a Russian.' How did you get this news?"

"From Peter Campbell Brown, who was acting for Peyton Ford, Assistant to the Attorney General."

Palmer walked over to the jury rail, carefully chose a roll of candy mints, slowly pulled several from the pack, looked at them in his hand, then popped them into his mouth. "Tell me," he asked, looking back over his shoulder. "Do you hate every Communist?"

"No."

"Do you believe Communists are the enemy of the United States?"

"Potentially so."

A shrug was Archie's unspoken implication. Mr. Foley's prejudice could mean that Judy didn't have to be spying to have her duties reassigned, only dating a Russian.

"Is every Russian a potential enemy of the United States?"

"Possibly," Foley answered. Archie snorted.

"He should stop that," Kelley complained.

"Stop that," Judge Reeves said.

"Isn't it true that, as a part of her job, Judith Coplon recommended prosecution of the Amtorg Trading Corporation for failing to register as a foreign agent? That for some time she had been trying to get you to take such action as a result of their failure to comply with the law?"

"I don't recall," Foley responded. Judy gasped.

"What?" Archie yelled. "What?"

Kelley was on his feet.

"Sit down and behave yourself," Archie hollered at Kelley. The judge, head darting back and forth, admonished Archie to behave *himself*. And quit, he ordered, making mountains out of molehills.

"I am so sorry," Archie responded politely. "Only God can make mountains and make molehills." Now, Archie asked, had Mr. Foley shown Judy the planted memorandum about Amtorg on the morning of March 4? Yes, Mr. Foley responded, he had. The prosecution interrupted with an offer to introduce the memorandum into evidence. Archie looked delighted.

"This tool of entrapment?" he asked.

Whearty quickly withdrew the offer. He would deal with introduction of the evidence later. Archie returned to the witness.

"Did you know it was fake? A tool of entrapment?"

"I did not know it was false."

"You didn't?" Archie shouted. "Did you describe it to this girl as 'hot and interesting?' as 'top secret?' Did you?"

"Yes, I suppose I did."

"And you insist you thought it was legitimate?"

"Yes."

Archie's eyes widened in disbelief. He shook his head and muttered to himself. Kelley complained about his opponent's treatment of the witness, the judge warned against making side remarks and mutterings, and Archie noted that Kelley's words were "contemptible."

"Stop," Judge Reeves yelled to no one in particular. Several spectators laughed, and the gavel sounded. Reeves was getting cross.

Foley's credibility, however, had suffered a serious wounding. On the one hand, as Archie had pointed out, Foley had demanded that Judy not see sensitive materials, some of which were not even classified, yet three months later offered her a look at a "hot and interesting" top-secret report. A setup, Archie implied, and his audience inferred precisely that.

Ruth Rossen, an attorney in Judy's office, followed Foley to the stand and testified that Judy had repeatedly asked to see internal security reports. Mrs. Rossen, claiming not to have known that Judy's access to these materials had been curtailed, had given Judy "some fifty or sixty reports." Long after she had taken over this aspect of Judy's job, Rossen testified, she had innocently responded promptly to Judy's requests for sensitive materials.

Archie spent considerable time in cross-examination, no small part of which was devoted to ridiculing Foley's management and organizational skills. To many, the end result was that Foley looked either like a very poor administrator or like a party to an effort to entrap Judy. All in all, Archie enjoyed himself immensely, took up much of the prosecution's time, and considered the day well spent.

It was Friday afternoon—five days, one working week into the trial of Judith Coplon—and Kelley and his staff were beginning to fear that the situation might be seriously out of control. Dozens of witnesses had yet to be heard. Foley and Rossen should have been on and off the stand in a matter of minutes, but Archie's cross-examination had taken hours. What could be done about Archie Palmer?

Judge Reeves adjourned proceedings until Monday morning at ten o'clock. Whearty and Kelley gathered up their papers and glumly made their way out of the courthouse. The side door. They could not tolerate witnessing another Coplon press conference. Neither did they want to respond to questions from reporters waiting to talk to the prosecution.

Outside, on the steps, Judy laughed and talked with journalists and waved to curious spectators, many of whom had been unable to get inside the courtroom and had waited all day to see Judy. It looked more like Hollywood and Vine than Constitution and Pennsylvania.

An observer at the time noted to a friend, "Who do you think ought to direct the movie, George Cukor?" His friend laughed. "I dunno, maybe Billy Wilder, with Gene Tierney starring."

● 2 ●

The preliminary rounds were over and for Archie Palmer the fun was about to begin. Twenty—not two or three, or even four or five, but twenty—FBI agents were scheduled to testify about following Judith Coplon's every step on her clandestine trips to New York. To testify that they had seen— absolutely nothing.

On the morning of May 2, Judy was devastated by reports of a *Newsweek* article just published that called her "Miss Giggles" and accused her of taking her predicament "lightly." Newspapers had the unflattering story, and reporters wanted Judith's reaction when she arrived at the courthouse.

"I don't think this is a laughing matter," she told them angrily. "My mother is here and she has a bad heart. My father died last month. Do you think I'd want to cry in front of her? I'm trying to keep up her spirits as well as my own." Further, she said, "I'm too well aware of the seriousness of what's going on here to laugh about it."

Archie held up his hand. "This little girl is like the Spartan boy who kept up his courage even though a fox was gnawing at his vitals. She has been smiling in court to reassure her mother, who sits just behind her. Those are not smiles of derision; they are smiles of courage." With a protective arm about Judy's shoulders, Archie added, "Her father died recently as a result of this case, and her mother is ill. I ask you," he said to the reporters, "what is she going to do, kill her mother, too?"

Judy rose as Judge Reeves entered the courtroom. She wore a dark blue dress with pleated skirt, gold belt, and plunging neckline. Her costume was in stark contrast to that of her mother, who still appeared clad from head to toe in somber black. Immediately after everyone was seated, Judy went to work. She became, from that moment on, Archie Palmer's full-time assistant, taking copious notes, sorting and arranging papers, locating documents for him. Judith Coplon at last had gone to work, seriously, on her defense.

First to testify was Special Agent Richard Hradsky, who described how he followed Judy on January 14—step by step along the streets, in and out of cafés and shops, on and off trains. John Kelley went forward, introduced a six-foot map of the Washington Heights section of New York, and handed Hradsky a long pointer. Jurors leaned forward, taking in the new visual aid.

Not only had Special Agent Hradsky followed Miss Coplon, he testified, he had also followed Gubitchev. In fact, he offered, the next morning he was on surveillance at 680 Park Avenue, home of the Soviet delegation to the UN, when Gubitchev emerged. He followed the Russian engineer to 64 West 108th Street, "which turned out to be his home," the agent explained.

The cat that leaped from Hradsky's bag would never go back inside. The FBI was watching the Soviet delegation to the UN! To most of the people in the courtroom, Hradsky's careless admission meant little; to some, it was a disaster. The FBI, which had routinely maintained such surveillance operations, had also consistently publicly denied doing so. The press would not let this embarrassing bit of information go unnoticed.

Special Agent Richard Brennan followed Hradsky to the stand and told essentially the same story of tailing an elusive Judith Coplon on Friday night, January 14.

"Would you describe the nature of Miss Coplon's walk?" Kelley asked.

Blustering, Archie rose to object. "What does that mean, pigeon-toed or what?" Spectators guffawed, and Reeves's gavel sounded sharply.

The entire surveillance scenario was repeated by Agent John Malley. In cross-examination, Archie had a few new questions.

"Did you see this man kiss this girl?"

"No."

"Touch her?"

"No, sir."

"Did you see tears flowing from her eyes after she and the man left the restaurant?"

"No."

"Well, then," Archie demanded, getting to the point. "Did you at any time see this girl give anything to this man?"

"No."

Roger W. Robinson, who had been in the room when Judy was interrogated after her arrest, who had suggested she fall asleep in a chair at three o'clock in the morning, was next on the stand. At this fourth telling of the surveillance story, the jury was becoming restless. They perked up, however, when Archie Palmer began his cross-examination.

"At Foley Square, after Judy's arrest, didn't you say that she was white trash?" Palmer asked. "Didn't you say the very chair she was sitting in had been sat in by dope fiends and white slavers?"

Startled, Robinson responded loudly. "At no time was she called any names by anyone."

"No?" Archie said sweetly. Years later, according to the man Judith would marry, she remembered those names, vividly.

"She refused to tell us her name or answer any other questions," Robinson continued. "But we absolutely did not call her any names."

"Isn't it true, Mr. Robinson, that the FBI was seeking funding, seeking appropriations when this army of agents went after this little girl?"

"Objection!" Kelley challenged. "This was not an army!"

"I agree," conceded Archie. "The number was less than a battalion." There was, in fact, some disagreement among the witnesses as to exactly how many agents had shadowed the suspect on January 14. One said eighteen, another said twenty-four.

In sustaining the objection, the judge noted that Archie's question about FBI funding was inappropriate. There seemed to be a lot going on that was inappropriate. He glared at the defense attorney.

Undaunted, Archie leaned across the witness box, his eyes locked onto Robinson's. "Now, sir, isn't it true you never saw Judith Coplon give or hand over or in any way transmit anything to Mr. Gubitchev?"

"It's true. I never did." With obvious disgust, Robinson brushed Life Saver grindings from his left shoulder.

Archie's cross-examination continued, sometimes going far afield. He was, the judge apparently thought, taking too much time and having too much to say. Judge Reeves suggested that counsel might want to be more concise.

"I am not a man of few words, Your Honor, and I apologize." Archie's merry face beamed at the judge. "I want to pay tribute to your own precision and economy in the use of words." He sighed. "I wish I was more like that."

Judge Reeves nodded. "It's unfortunate," he said quietly.

After a full day on the stand, the four FBI agents had testified that the alleged co-conspirators used antisurveillance tactics throughout their January 14 meeting, that they had spent forty-five minutes in the De Luxe restaurant on Dyckman Street, that they had some kind of spat on leaving the restaurant, when Judy "gesticulated" or hit at Gubitchev with a rolled newspaper. They also, to a man, testified that they had not seen any transfer of any papers from the woman to the man. In short, they testified to suspicious behavior, but no criminal wrongdoing. The day had not gone smoothly. Archie had interrupted frequently and had taken an inordinate amount of the prosecution's time. To make matters worse, the defense attorney insisted upon having more time tomorrow to cross-examine.

Across the street, six blocks down, J. Edgar Hoover was getting a firsthand report on the trial. When he learned about Hradsky's slip-up, he was furious. Adding to his anger was a copy of a *New York Daily Mirror* editorial commenting on the Coplon case.

"What is overlooked is the real issue, that our government seems to be an undisciplined administration in which job-holders on any level, from the office cat to the assistant to an assistant, can walk off with the files," read the editorial set in large type.

An undisciplined administration. Mr. Truman would not like to hear that. But it wasn't just the *Mirror;* more and more complaints were being aired about a sloppy administration, one that let a spy operate in the Justice Department. Things better get moving at the courthouse, and mighty damned fast.

They did.

• 3 •

Titles of the three proposed "chapters" that prosecutors said would make up their case were January 14, February 18, and March 4, named after three trips Judith took to New York to meet Valentin Gubitchev. It was planned that each would take no more than one day. Yesterday it was expected that Chapter One would be presented and completed, and that today, the pages would turn in orderly fashion to Chapter Two. Unfortunately for the prosecution, a new author became involved.

Archie Palmer rewrote Chapter One almost from the opening page, and then penned several new chapters, with additional date titles. He began by insisting that the agents who had testified the previous day be recalled for further cross-examination.

On the stand was Richard Brennan.

"The prosecution is purposely keeping out of the record this girl's movements of honesty and decency," Archie charged. "There were other times when the FBI army followed Judith Coplon in New York and she did not meet a foreign friend, right?" Archie knew the prosecution had no intention of ever mentioning Judy's "innocent" trips to New York, or, for that matter, her circumspect behavior in Washington. None of this fit the picture of a spy perpetrating evil.

"Objection! Defense is exceeding the scope of direct examination," Kelley protested confidently.

"Very well," Palmer retorted, "I'll now call him as my own witness and ask him anything I want to!"

"You can't do that!" Kelley shouted. "The prosecution is presenting its case!"

"Objection overruled," Reeves announced, amazing everyone but Archie Palmer.

Kelley sank into his chair. Would Archie be allowed to recall any or all of the government's witnesses and ask them anything he wanted, regardless of the content of direct examination?

"Now, Agent Brennan," Archie continued smoothly, "on what other dates did you follow the defendant?"

"January 19, 20, 21 and 22 and February 19," Brennan responded testily.

"Tell us what happened on February 19, when this girl was supposedly in New York doing the devil's business."

"I first saw Miss Coplon come out of an elevator in the Hotel Picadilly with an unidentified man, not Gubitchev."

"And what did they do, Mr. Brennan? Where did they go?"

"She and her male friend went to the Century Theater to see 'Kiss Me Kate.' Before the show, she visited some friends in Fresh Meadow, Long Island."

Archie's next questions were typical of the off-the-wall, totally irrelevant queries to which the prosecution objected the entire day. Objections frequently and amazingly overruled.

"Is it possible for a woman to enter the ladies' toilet in Pennsylvania Station in New York on one level and leave at a different level?"

"Yes, it is."

"Mr. Brennan, what did you eat during a four-hour conference in New York between your fellow FBI agents and government lawyers preparing the Coplon case?"

"What color are Miss Coplon's eyes and what is the condition of her teeth?" Even Judge Reeves was skeptical about the dental question, but Archie explained that it was critical that Brennan reply. "I am trying to determine if she was gritting her teeth."

Kelley moaned and put his head in his hands. Whearty reached over to give him a comforting pat on the shoulder, but the chief prosecutor pulled away and glared at his colleague.

To Agent Hradsky, Archie addressed a question about background for service in the FBI. "What qualifications do you have for an FBI agent after spending six years in the wholesale grocery business in Missouri after graduating from law school?"

At one point, after having been reprimanded by Reeves, Archie smiled up at the judge and said, "I beg your pardon. I don't want to tread on Your Honor's proverbial corns." Hastily, he added, "I know Your Honor does not have real corns."

Archie again recalled Brennan and asked, "On January 14, did you see Gubitchev paw, neck, hug or kiss this thin little girl less than five feet in height?"

"I did not," Brennan responded, looking wildly at Kelley. There was a feeling among the prosecution's witnesses that they were in the hands of a madman. They waited for Kelley's rescue.

"Your Honor," Kelley began.

"What's the matter?" Archie rushed over to him. "I'm not in heat!"

Not in heat? Whearty stood up, then sat down. Kelley, like a man in a trance, again sank into his chair. Archie returned to the witness box after passing slowly along the jury rail, where he scooped up two rolls of mints. In front of the box he took his time about peeling down the wrapper on one of them. He smiled over at the jurors, said, "help yourselves, anytime," and then offered Brennan a mint. The agent shook his head vigorously.

"Now, Mr. Brennan, did you know that our Mr. Kelley here, my good friend the prosecutor, prosecuted the traitor Axis Sally?"

With great exasperation, Kelley pulled his lanky frame from his chair. "Objection. Your Honor must ask Mr. Palmer to quit referring to Axis Sally. And he is not my friend!"

"Oh, what's the use," Archie shrugged. "I'm trying to make him famous and he won't let me."

Now Agent Robinson was back on the stand for more "cross-examination."

"Will you describe for us the pilgrims' progress of five armed agents following this little girl from Pennsylvania Station to Washington Heights?"

It was here that Kelley exploded. "Your Honor, please admonish the defense attorney to cease his buffoonery!" he yelled. "This so-called cross-examination has gone on for hours. I ask the court to prevent this unreasonable interference with the flow of the government's case!"

Before Reeves could respond, Archie rushed across the room to shake his finger under Kelley's reddened nose. "If you think that's buffoonery, you'd better read Bunyan's *Pilgrims Progress*."

Missing in the entire scenario, from the opening gavel to this moment, was the involvement of Judith Coplon. She continued to take notes and sort papers, but not an eye focused on her, not a moment's attention was paid to her. She was not the star of the show, but simply one of the spectators.

FBI agent Thomas McAndrews was called to the stand late in the afternoon to testify about the content of Chapter Two, February 18. He was quickly withdrawn, however, to allow Archie another crack at cross-examining Agent Hradsky about shadowing Judy on January 14. Back to Chapter One.

In the end, the judge finally admonished Archie about his disruptive tactics and cautioned him about staying on the matter at hand. But on this day the entire case for the prosecution had been reduced to confrontation and confusion. Archie had examined witnesses for almost the entire day. There was not a single point on the government's side of the scoreboard. The defense, however unorthodox its tactics, had scored heavily. Judith Coplon was pictured as behaving in a most unspylike manner for most of the time she was under surveillance by the FBI, as being a very normal young woman unfairly persecuted by a legion of FBI agents. Which was precisely what the "buffoon" wanted to accomplish, along with keeping the prosecution totally off balance. His unwitting assistant in the process was Judge Reeves.

At the end of the day, reporters, who besieged Archie Palmer with questions, asked only one of Judith Coplon. Who was the man with whom she had gone to the theater? "The mystery man," she laughed.

• 4 •

It was the morning of May 4, and a fired-up Senator Karl Mundt, the man who discovered spy ring tentacles, sat with the Senate Judiciary Committee urging enactment of his Communist-control measure. It was exactly two months since Judith Coplon's arrest, and Mundt and other lawmakers were still, daily, using her for inspiration in writing and proposing legislation.

"I admit," Mundt said for the record, "that my bill will drive Communists further underground. I suppose a lady like Miss Coplon would be more careful about meeting her contacts in the shadow of elevated tracks. She would make [her meetings] much further underground." Yes, he said, his bill would be certain to inhibit "romantic, giddy-eyed novitiates like Judith Coplon."

Senator Homer Ferguson reached for his microphone. "Do you think, Senator, that women who cooperate with Communists are always under the influence of love?"

"No, I don't, Senator, but you can't always drive love from a woman's heart."

Meanwhile, in federal district court, Archie Palmer was continuing to snatch the prosecution's witnesses and make them his own. Now, however, he was on a new tack, one of enormous import. "Isn't it true," he asked one FBI agent after another, "that you tapped this girl's telephone to listen in on her most private conversations, learning things like when and where she was going, who she was meeting?"

"I have no knowledge of wiretapping Miss Coplon's telephone," each witness would testify.

"Her brother's telephone? Did the FBI wiretap Mr. Bert Coplon's telephone?"

The answer, in each case, was "I have no knowledge of wiretapping Mr. Bert Coplon's telephone."

"Her parents' telephone?"

And so it went. Over and over again, in different ways, Archie tried to wrest from the witnesses an admission that the Bureau had tapped telephones in the course of investigating Judy's activities. Finally, prosecutor Kelley complained.

"I object to counsel's persistence in this matter!"

"If they didn't tap her telephone, they could say so and that would be the end of it."

"They said so," Kelley snapped.

"They did not," Archie insisted. "They said they have no knowledge of wiretapping."

The FBI agents who denied having knowledge of any wiretapping became more and more squeamish each time they gave this answer. Ends might justify means, but perjury was perjury.

Judith Coplon wrote furiously on her notepad throughout the morning session, looking up now and again to stare intently at the witnesses. She saw that Archie, from time to time, would attempt to improve his behavior. In the main, he was unsuccessful. He complained about the location of his chair, the prosecutor's chair, and the fact that his friend, Mr. Kelley, didn't want Archie standing near the prosecution's table. It all seemed mighty inhospitable to the stranger from Sodom and Gomorrah. On occasion, he would pout, skip across the room to stand where he knew he would block Kelley's view, or mutter aloud when Kelley or Whearty was speaking. And all the while, he chewed vigorously on his candy mints.

During the noon recess, a reporter asked Archie, "Have you heard what Senator Mundt had to say this morning?" He had not, and so he was told.

"Romantic, giddy-eyed novitiate?" Archie steamed. "Meet Communist friends underground? He's saying she's guilty!" Archie fumed and snorted and stomped, a lumbering bull in a black felt hat. This was unfair, patently prejudicial.

"Will this have any effect on your case?" inquired one of the reporters.

Of course it would. No legislator had the right to comment on the guilt or innocence of a defendant while her trial is in progress. Once he regained his composure, which many thought he'd lost for effect, Archie hinted that he might demand a mistrial on the basis of the senator's remarks, an indiscretion certain to come to the attention of the jurors.

In the afternoon, G-man Thomas McAndrews and stenographer Sappho Manos were taking turns on the stand to describe tailing Judith on the night of February 18. They recounted the story of Judy's reaching Manhattan later than planned, breaking the strap of her shoe, and getting lost looking for Broadway.

"I told her I didn't know the way to Broadway," McAndrews testified.

"And her response?"

"Oh, God!"

Miss Manos corroborated the story, the implication being that Judith was on urgent, secretive business when she lost her way.

Archie's cross-examination of Manos quickly hit pay dirt.

"How did you happen to be on duty that night of March 4, there at Foley Square?"

Kelley grimaced. He wasn't ready for March 4, which was his publicly announced Chapter Three. And there was the rather significant matter of March 4 timing, which he had not discussed with Miss Manos.

"Objection," Kelley called. "This is beyond the scope of cross-examination."

"The prosecutor forgets," Archie said kindly, "that I can call Miss Manos as my own witness." Then, turning to Kelley, he snapped, "Sit down, Sir!"

"Overruled," the judge announced belatedly. "You may continue, Mr. Palmer."

"Now, Miss Manos, about March 4 . . ."

"On March 4, shortly before 5:30 in the afternoon, Mr. Granville asked if I would work late that night to act as a matron in the case of Miss Coplon. He said she was being brought in."

Considerable whispering began at the prosecution's table.

Archie, the buffoon, had done it again. Through Miss Manos's testimony,

Archie established that the FBI knew all along that an arrest was probable, which meant that there had been ample time to secure an arrest warrant. Failure to secure a warrant, time permitting, made the arrest illegal, unless the suspects were ready to flee. The government, despite having set out a tasty bit of spy bait, had argued throughout that there was no intention to arrest Judith Coplon the night of March 4. It insisted that the decision to do so was made on the spur of the moment, only because agents believed a crime had been, or was about to be, committed.

Archie knew what he had accomplished, but continued without missing a beat.

"Did you see her stripped that night?"

"I helped strip her. I acted as one of the matrons. The other was Genevieve Charos, a registered nurse."

"So she became naked and stood there before you, naked?"

"That was so."

When Archie finally finished with the witness, Kelley called the young woman back for redirect. By now, it was apparent to her that she had made a dreadful mistake. She was not certain, however, just what that might be.

"Now, Miss Manos," he asked the flustered witness, "did Mr. Granville say on the afternoon of March 4 that Miss Coplon 'would' be brought in or 'might' be brought in?"

"Might!" Miss Manos gulped.

"Oh, Your Honor, I object!" Archie protested. "Mr. Kelley is guilty of rehabilitating the witness! She has changed her testimony to suit his whim!"

Archie recalled Manos. He yelled. Kelley demanded that Palmer quit yelling at the witness. "I'm trying to keep my voice up," Palmer replied, pointing to four boxes of cough drops sitting on the jury rail. "My first-aid," he told the judge.

"You wouldn't need it if you didn't talk so loud," the judge responded.

Turning back to the witness, Archie asked again for clarification of the "might" or "would" issue. The woman looked desperately at Kelley.

"Look at me, Madam, not Mr. Kelley. You must quit looking to him for succor."

"Oh, my God," Kelley said aloud. "It's not exactly pleasant to look at you."

"I'm a bad dose of castor oil," Archie shouted at him.

The gavel sounded. Judge Reeves, his patience as thin as his hair, explained in threatening detail the array of penalties at his disposal to punish ill-behaved attorneys. He took no sides. His look and his words slashed at the squabbling pair before him.

All of this was new for John Kelley, the cool, skillful, heretofore composed prosecutor. A man of great dignity, accustomed to deferential treatment, he had never before suffered such humiliation. It was not the only scolding he received. Later, when he returned to his office, he would hear dreadful warnings about wiretapping and arrest warrants. From the Very Top.

As for Archie, Judge Reeves's warnings had little effect. After yet another admonishment, he went back to the jury rail for a fix from his collection of medicinal treats, then ordered the next witness, Agent Miller, to step down from the stand and pretend to be Gubitchev. Miller had just testified that on the night of February 18, he had seen Judith place her hand on the opening of her purse and then reach the same hand toward Gubitchev. The Russian, Miller testified, extended his hand as though to receive something.

"Consider yourself as Gubitchev—you act as Pygmalian, please, while we . . ." Archie directed Miller, staging his drama. The judge complained, Kelley objected wildly, but Archie persisted. He now told Miller to "impersonate Judy," and tucked her leather purse under the agent's arm. Looking distressed and casting sidelong glances at the prosecution team, Miller/Judy walked in front of the jury box, mimicking the defendant. Next, Archie had Miller act as Gubitchev and called Judy up to play herself in the scene. The courtroom was spellbound.

Other agents followed Miller to the stand to testify as to the events of February 18, Chapter Two. The bottom line was that no one had actually seen anything pass between Judy and Gubitchev, although it appeared to surveillance agents that the couple's arm and hand movements indicated that something might have been transferred from Judith to the UN engineer. Might have been.

• 5 •

Palpable excitement, an eager anticipation, was growing as the trial, slowly, laboriously, sometimes entertainingly, moved toward the subject of the night of the arrest, March 4. It reached that point on May 10.

The prosecution's long-overdue Chapter Three opened with testimony from a young female FBI stenographer, Catherine Condon, and FBI agent Brewer Wilson, who testified how they had trailed Judith from Pennsylvania Station to the Eighth Avenue subway. In detail, they retraced the March 4 steps so familiar to the jury.

At the noon recess, a fiery argument flared between Judy and her lawyer as photographers rushed to take her picture outside the courtroom. Archie was all for the publicity, as always, but Judy objected furiously.

"You told me to smile for the photographers and you see where it got me," she yelled. ". . . People think I'm taking this trial as a joke, or as something wonderful and glamorous."

Palmer grabbed her arm. "Don't be a little fool," he snarled. "People had great admiration for you when they saw you smiling in the face of all this trouble." He concluded by suggesting that Judy remember the great heroes of history. "Think of Andrew Jackson," he advised.

"I don't want to be Andrew Jackson," Judy responded petulantly.

Besides, it was unbearable the way the trial was affecting her mother; terrible, the way strangers would stop Mrs. Coplon on the street and ask personal, hurtful questions. "This whole thing is killing my mother," she said. "I tell you, I'm afraid she's going to break."

"I'll have your mother laughing, too, before this is over," Palmer replied.

Frail, gaunt, still clad in mourning clothes, Mrs. Coplon had been asked to rise that morning so that Agent Wilson could identify her as having been seen during his New York surveillance. In tears, a reluctant Mrs. Coplon got to her feet.

Archie later pushed Wilson on the matter of how the FBI had decided to investigate Judith Coplon. He tried to establish that Mrs. Gubitchev, in a fit of jealousy, had tipped off the FBI that her husband was seeing Judy for the purpose of conspiring to commit espionage. Each time Archie popped the question, Kelley objected and Archie rephrased his query. What he finally was able to get on the record was Wilson's statement that he had no knowledge of how the FBI learned Judy was meeting Gubitchev. Very likely, this was true.

By May 12, Wilson was in his fourth day of testimony, now going over and over again the details of the March 4 pursuit of Judy and Gubitchev. In the process, he described Gubitchev as being approximately five feet four inches in height. Archie objected, demanding that the government produce a record showing Gubitchev's height.

"There's no need of that," Kelley sneered. "Mr. Gubitchev is available on subpoena if counsel wants to call him."

"That's an outrageous thing to say in front of a jury. I don't need him." Archie stomped over to Kelley, furious. "Why don't they call him? You know Mr. Gubitchev. I don't and I don't want to know him."

"Does the court direct us to produce a secret FBI document on Gubitchev's measurements for this man?" Kelley asked Reeves, pointing to Archie.

Incensed, Archie screamed, "This man! Your Honor, that's an outrageous insult. In all my years of law experience I have never heard a lawyer referred to in such terms in a court."

Reeves agreed, and instructed Kelley to refer to Archie as Mr. Palmer. "Gentlemen, let's not play the role of children here."

"God forbid that I be a child again," Archie sulked. "It took me too long to get where I am."

Undaunted as usual, Archie continued his disruptive tactics with Wilson. At one point he staged another of his off-Broadway performances, with Wilson playing the Russian role and Judy, as before, playing herself. The scene was their meeting the night of the arrest.

When the show was over, Palmer placed Judy in a seat directly behind the prosecution team. Kelley immediately asked that she be moved. Archie shouted that there was no reason to move Judy; he was planning to use her again.

"I have reason for not wanting the defendant near while I confer with counsel and take notes," Kelley snapped.

In tears, Judy returned to her seat at the defense table as the judge yelled, "I can no longer put up with this childish trial of a lawsuit." The red-faced Reeves continued, to Archie, "Her own interest forbids what you're doing here!"

Startled, Archie whirled at the judge. "I should ask for a mistrial on that! Your Honor shouldn't have said that!"

"I had a right to," Reeves began, but Archie would not allow him to continue. Screaming now, the lawyer shook his finger at the judge. "Anything Your Honor says influences my case. The jury looks upon Your Honor as a god."

With an enormous sigh, the judge responded, "No, they don't pay any attention to what I say."

The following day, May 13, now well into the third week of the trial, Archie Palmer suggested that Gubitchev was a counterspy used to trap his client. Wilson denied the allegation.

Before the day ended, Palmer again raised the wiretap issue. He asked for FBI records to clear up the issue once and for all, a request not immediately acted upon by Judge Reeves. Kelley was quick to call Archie's efforts to obtain the records "a fishing expedition," insisting that FBI agents already had testified that they knew nothing of any wiretapping in the case. If this was indeed a fishing foray, Archie certainly was using the right bait, although it would take months before he set the hook.

For twelve remarkable minutes on that day, Archie made a speech to the court. He said that Judith Coplon "has been crucified before the world" and "didn't get the chance a dog gets." He talked about Judy's family, about her trial in the newspapers, and about her reputation.

"Shakespeare said when you steal my name you steal trash. Shakespeare was wrong," he told his astonished listeners. "Judith Coplon's whole family's reputation has been assassinated." Further, "Her father has died, her brother has lost most of his business, her mother is ill and"—he paused dramatically, pointing to a pale, terrified Rebecca Coplon—"there she is!

"Since when," Archie continued, "you don't take home government documents to work at night on them?" Judy only took documents home to catch up on legitimate, routine work. What was wrong with that?

Judge Reeves, in enormous wonder at Archie's latest exhibition, observed that the speech was an "amazing procedure." And, of course, it was. Lawyers were not allowed to make speeches and present arguments during examination of witnesses, and especially not during the opposition's case—at least not in other courtrooms.

As the day, and the third week, closed, poor Reeves tried to encourage the jury by acknowledging that there had been some rather peculiar goings-on, but that they should not be impressed by, or concerned about, the distractions.

"You and I have a job to do," he told them. "Let's try to do it well."

• 6 •

G-men who had been silent shadows following Judy's footsteps on March 4 continued to detail to the court what happened that cold, historic night in Manhattan. On May 17, Judy celebrated her twenty-eighth birthday in the courtroom listening as one after another of the parade of FBI agents testified about her devious behavior.

During recess, reporters asked her if she were planning a birthday celebration. "No," she answered. "I'd feel better if I knew what plans I could make for my next birthday!"

This same day, Judge Reeves ruled that love was not and could not be an issue in Judy's case. Agent John Daly was on the stand when Archie asked about the likelihood that two people in love would choose "a quiet eddy" rather than a busy street for a walk so that they could "talk to each other about sweet nothings." Before Daly could answer, Reeves rose from the bench and shook his finger at Archie, telling him to get on with the issues of the case.

This *was* an issue, Archie insisted, "whether this man was in love with the girl or . . ."

"I'm telling you, that's not the issue and you can't make it the issue," the judge yelled. But Archie would continue to do just that. So would Kelley, in the end. The question of romance, not espionage, or the obverse, would be a dominant issue in the trial, Judge Reeves or no.

Later, on a different topic with a different witness, Archie again implied that Gubitchev was a Russian counterspy employed by the U.S. government to trap Judy. In attempting to set up a relationship between the government and the Russian UN delegation, he asked Agent Robert Wirth, "Does the United States have agents in embassies, ambassadorships, consulates and UN delegations of other nations here, including Russia?"

"Yes," Wirth replied.

It was a bombshell, critical information that would cause enormous embarrassment for the government. The FBI had just admitted the presence of U.S. agents in places they were not supposed to be. If ever there was a loose cannon threatening Washington, it was Archibald Palmer. Newspapers the next day ran stories with headlines proclaiming, U.S. HAS SPIES IN FOREIGN MISSIONS. Quite a number of people, both inside and outside the government, were outraged by such a breach of international ethics. The U.S. diplomatic community was especially distressed, considering the earlier admission by Agent Hradsky that the FBI had been watching the Russian UN delegation.

As the fourth week of Judith's trial was coming to a close, Archie's tactic of deliberately trying to confuse witnesses on the stand led to a verbal battle between him and the judge, who warned the attorney, "I'm not going to put up with any more of your nonsense!"

Archie took exception to the word *nonsense*, and the fight was on. It ended with Judge Reeves fining Archie one hundred dollars for contempt of court and Archie yelling that the judge must tell the jury, ". . . it should not be held against my client that she might have picked the wrong lawyer."

On May 20, the prosecution's contention that Judith and Gubitchev were behaving like spies in New York was strengthened by the testimony of yet another parade of agents. By now, the jury, bored silly, knew the script by heart.

The scene brightened considerably when Archie began his spirited cross-examination, quickly focusing once again on the wiretapping issue, the so-called fishing expedition. No one had any knowledge of wiretapping; no one ordered taps on anyone. Really? Archie rolled his eyes and sighed deeply. Archie's persistence about the matter was causing people to wonder, including the folks in the jury box.

On May 25, exactly one month into the trial, Robert Granville, the agent who had arrested Judith, recounted his story of the pursuit and apprehension of Coplon and Gubitchev. This is the point the prosecution had intended to reach in a matter of two or three days, at most. The government, if not the defense, was ready to be done with the trial, but Archie, still in the center ring, was still master of the show.

"Now, you said on the night of March 4 you turned to Mr. Scheidt . . . and said you wanted to put the two people under arrest; is that what you said?" Archie asked Granville.

"No."

"What did you say?"

"I said I was *going* to place them under arrest," the agent said firmly.

Granville had made the decision and the arrest. It was he who had deployed the surveillance team and had given instructions. Archie wanted to know if Granville was "assured . . . that by putting twenty-one people on this job . . . and all these cars, that you would be successful in finding any legal evidence upon which to arrest Gubitchev or Coplon on the night of March 4th?" Had Granville known what Judy was carrying? An objection by Kelley kept Granville from having to answer. The question was one of critical import. A question he did answer concerned wiretapping. He had not ordered taps on any Coplon telephones.

There was a bit of silliness this day as well. Palmer grilled Agent Edward McCarthy about Granville's description of Gubitchev, given to the agents. Any description of the chin, as to weak or strong? Of full lips, voluptuous, or thin lips? Of a nose that was stub, or "acquiline"? What about the Russian's ears? Were they flat against his head, or did they protrude?

As the fifth week began, on May 30, the government had shown only suspicious behavior on the part of Judith Coplon. It had been unable to prove that any information had passed from her to Valentin Gubitchev. On the other hand, Palmer had made a reasonable, if not yet recognized, challenge as to the legality of the arrest and search, had forced a response from each prosecution witness that he had seen no wrongdoing on Judy's part, and had raised questions about wiretapping and entrapment that were not easily dismissed.

All of this, and not a shred of significant evidence against the defendant had been entered. But the time had come to link Judy to the evidence found in her possession the night of the arrest, and to wrap up the case against her.

• 7 •

On May 30, the prosecution turned to the subject of Judith Coplon's purse; some would later call it "Pandora's Purse." Attention immediately focused on twenty-two of the thirty-four FBI data slips it held the night of March 4, 1949. The slips were summaries of, or excerpts from, secret FBI reports on U.S. counterespionage. One, which made page one everywhere, concerned Dr. Ruth Gruber, aide to Harold Ickes at the time he was secretary of the interior. Information on the slip read that Gruber "was reported to have been a contact of F. A. Garanin of the Soviet embassy."

Gruber immediately denied the allegation and an outraged Ickes, reached by telephone at his Maryland farm, attacked the FBI for its sloppiness in having raw, unverified data in its files. "If that's a test of the accuracy of the FBI, they better disband," he said. "If she's a Red, I'm a Hottentot!" Besides, Ickes pointed out, the department of interior didn't deal with secrets.

The background descriptions of three Washington residents said to be potential Soviet espionage recruits also created a sizable public stir. Two of the subjects of the sketches were Lorraine Elkin Sinderbrand and her husband, Alvin. Both Sinderbrands had attended the Coplon trial on several occasions. The third subject was a man named Albert Boynton Stevenson.

Lorraine Sinderbrand was described as a high school classmate of Judith's with "progressive political leanings." Judy had written of the young woman, "She remembers me as a Communist." Lorraine's husband was described as "more politically mature than his wife, and financially comfortable." As for Stevenson, a civilian employee of the Signal Corps and a pro-Communist, Judy wrote that he was a bit of a "wishy-washy idealist and politically naive."

Sinderbrand, reached at the Brooklyn home of his father-in-law, told the Associated Press that he had been warned about the biographical sketches but was assured by the Department of Justice that they would not become a matter of public knowledge. The couple was considered to be "innocently involved." It was a complete shock to learn that the sketches existed, he said, but an even bigger shock to have them made public. Distressed, Sinderbrand insisted that "our connection with Miss Coplon has been purely a social one. My wife attended high school with her." So, people wondered, is Miss Coplon in the spy business or not?

In court, attention turned from the biographical sketches to the decoy document that Foley had routed to Judith's desk immediately prior to her final clandestine meeting with Gubitchev. In Judith's handwriting, her summary of the memorandum, found in her possession March 4, said, in part:

> Bureau using 2 highly placed Amtorg officials as informants. One is Needleman with whom Bureau maintains "a rather indirect contact through an intermediary." . . . Bureau has recently learned thru an informant that Amtorg has been in contact with the Geophysical Research Corp re geophones. The fact that these are used for the purpose of making blast

measurements at Alamogordo and other testing points is highly restricted but Amtorg apparently must have some knowledge of their use.

Now the full report was made public. The fact is that poor Needleman never was an FBI informant, but saying so made the information irresistible bait, and Judy apparently swallowed it. For his part, attorney Isadore Needleman said within a few days that he would bring criminal libel charges against Attorney General Clark and FBI director Hoover because of the false information about him planted for Judy to harvest. "A person's lifelong reputation can be ruined beyond repair if such practices by powerful U.S. Government agencies are allowed to go on," Needleman complained.

In addition to the false Amtorg tale, there were real, substantive data in the report that would prove embarrassing and troublesome to the government. FBI agent Robert Lamphere, who had written the information Judy was intended to steal, was on the stand. Lamphere was instructed to explain to the court the extent of his poetic license as opposed to valid secret data in the enticing espionage bait. The agent admitted the Needleman business was false, but said that information relating to the shipment of atomic-energy instruments to Russia by Amtorg, the Russian trading company, was authentic.

This immediately set off a public firestorm of charges and countercharges, of fault finding and excuse making. The United States, at a time when protecting anything and everything to do with atomic energy was top priority, had allowed these shipments to take place. Some of the material shipped required licensing, but in fact had no such license. Orders from various manufacturers were reviewed in court and duly reported in the media. Included in the essential atomic-energy industry equipment that went to Russia were Geiger-Müller counters, ionization chambers, electroscopes—all used in detecting ionizing radiation, the emanations given off by fissionable materials. Also shipped were proportional counters, scaling units, and count-rate meters, used to register the frequency of emanations. Here were indications, recognizable even by laypeople reading their morning newspapers, that the Russians were fast at work experimenting with atomic energy, perhaps on their way to snatching the key to doomsday. And government laxity was allowing U.S. manufacturers to profit in the process. People were outraged.

The government explained on the day its exhibits were entered as evidence that most of the information in Judith's purse had been placed in two envelopes, sealed, and hidden inside a Belle Sharmeer hosiery package. The handwritten message that so distressed Needleman was enclosed in a plain white sheet of paper, folded into a two-inch by one-inch package, and marked with an arrow apparently showing how to open the tiny rectangle.

In all, the impact was devastating. At last there seemed to be a real case against Judy. No amount of discussion about writing a novel, or working overtime at home, or using the materials to refresh her memory about her work experience (as she would later claim) could change the impression this evidence made on the public who had so faithfully followed Judy's trial from its beginning. One could only speculate about the jury's reaction.

On June 1, the day following release of the twenty-two data slips, the biographical sketches, and the Amtorg memorandum, prosecutor John Kelley told the court that twelve additional data slips found in Judith Coplon's purse the night of March 4 would not be introduced as evidence for fear that doing so "would jeopardize the security of the United States." As had so many controversial elements of the trial, the existence of the twelve slips was uncovered in a bit of fancy-footed cross-examination by Archie Palmer. Agent Scott Miller, who had searched Judy's purse when she was arrested, was on the stand. Archie, his curiosity piqued, began questioning Miller about the missing data slips.

Kelley leaped to his feet, insisting, "The security of the United States is involved!" He asked to approach the bench.

"There's no such thing as security when you go into a courtroom, Your Honor. I do not care to approach the bench," Archie protested. "I want the jury to hear everything said in this trial."

Without ruling on suppression of the contested documents, Judge Reeves did allow a listing of all items in Judy's purse, including the contested data slips. Kelley was forced to agree that a simple listing would not threaten the United States of America. The missing twelve slips contained information furnished to the FBI by informants whose identities and reports the government desperately wanted to keep secret.

The historic list, which seemed at first to be innocuous, would later create a monumental stir in Hollywood and halfway around the world. It also would lead to J. Edgar Hoover's greatest embarrassment, and some indications that he might resign. It read:

> Gen. Nicolae Radescu and Austria, French military authorities (closed); "T-one," an informant of known reliability, Washington; Harold Beerman, Newark; Stuart Legg, New York; Eli Potash, Los Angeles; Lidia Pavil de Pavigle (Tacconi), New York; Michael Walden, T-2 advised Los Angeles; Boris A. Evanoff Goregoff, Los Angeles; Samuel Gordon, New York; Eugenio Chavez, El Paso; Irina (closed) Efemovna Aleksander, New York, Washington; Novaya Arya (Russian language newspaper printed in California).

Archie immediately began pushing for release of the withheld documents. He badgered Miller, demanding to know if he had personally selected the twelve to be omitted. Miller said he had not. Kelley was on his feet objecting to the line of questioning, and the judge promptly sustained his objection. Archie, however, was not about to be silenced.

"These papers are needed by this girl to show her innocence," he shouted, insisting Judy had needed, and had carried, the secret information for use in connection with a civil service examination she intended to take in order to qualify as an intelligence specialist. He shuddered and wailed and demanded relief. He must have the missing papers. In fact, he now demanded the full background reports on which all thirty-four data slips were based. Kelley was aghast. Judge Reeves, at his judicial wit's end, slapped another hundred-dollar fine on Archie—his second in two weeks—calling Archie guilty of "obvious contemptuous conduct."

As for the disputed papers, they were given to the judge to study before he ruled on whether the government would be required to produce the full FBI reports. From all thirty-four data slips. J. Edgar Hoover and company were beside themselves.

The following day, nervous federal attorneys were speculating that the government might have to drop its espionage case against Judith Coplon if Reeves ruled that the secret files must be opened to the public. Clearly distressed, Kelley told reporters that if the government "must expose its files in their entirety to prosecute one criminal—or let the criminal go free, it is a very sad choice to make."

Further, he added, "In this modern world of espionage and counter-espionage, the government will find it extremely difficult to prosecute a criminal if it must expose secrets. Where would this demand for government secrets stop? Is the defendant to be allowed to go into every file in the Federal Bureau of Investigation?"

The six-week trial could well be over. If the judge ruled against the prosecution, top Justice Department officials, certainly Attorney General Tom Clark, and perhaps even President Truman, would have to decide whether the case would continue. Archie was riding high, insisting that the U.S. government was using "national security" as a pretext to withhold evidence necessary for Judy's defense. Kelley made every effort to assure the court that there was nothing in the full FBI reports that would tend to "enlarge, diminish or explain the guilt or innocence of the defendant," which made no difference to the court. The issue was more basic—a defendant's right of access to an entire body of evidence, versus the government's right to withhold a portion of that evidence for any reason.

A *Wall Street Journal* editorial, published during Judge Reeves's consideration of the matter, presented a thoughtful assessment of the problem, cautioning against considering the disputed documents of no importance, even if they would prove to be of little use to the defendant.

Suppose, the editorial questioned, some future spy shows discernment and steals only papers labeled "Top Secret." Does this mean the spy cannot be prosecuted? And if he is, how does the government prove his guilt? The choice seems to be either exposing national secrets or asking the jury to convict on the sole basis of an FBI agent's testimony. "Either we risk letting a treasonable man go free of punishment, or we abrogate our whole system of trial by jury and substitute therefore a system under which a man is found guilty by declaration of a government official."

A final observation made in the provocative piece notes that while it may be necessary to "travel this secrecy road," the nation will have to dump, along the way, traditions and rights to which Americans are accustomed. "The Coplon trial offers but a small hint of what we shall have to leave by the wayside."

When Judge Reeves's decision was finally delivered June 7 to an electrically charged courtroom, he responded to Kelley with confidence and conviction. "If it turns out that the government, which is the litigant in this case, has come into court exposing itself, then it will have to take the peril." Further, "I am not charged with the responsibility of protecting the security of the government." Those responsible for the security of the government's secrets were the same as those responsible for the lawsuit; in essence, the government had made the bed it now found itself lying in. No courtroom decision ever had greater impact on the FBI.

In ordering release of the disputed documents, the judge said that he had examined them and found that "they do not suggest danger to our national security . . . they could only produce irritations and maybe endanger individual lives." *Only* endanger individual lives? An insider quotes Tom Clark as saying privately at the time that "Reeves never should have been allowed to hear this case!"

FBI Special Agent Robert Lamphere said half a century later that he still found it difficult to believe that the government chose to go forward with the case once Reeves had ruled that the contested documents could be made public. Lamphere knew immediately what the outcome would be. It was not, as they say, a pretty picture; instead, it was a multitextured, brazenly colored collage, one fabricated by both truth and fiction.

"I assumed, we all assumed, the trial was over," Lamphere said recently. Earlier, he had written that "the [background] information thereby divulged was devoured by the press . . . much of it was hearsay and things that should never have seen the light of day. Hoover was livid, and blamed Tom Clark for the debacle, though not publicly."

Newsman Don Whitehead, in his 1956 book *The FBI Story*, quotes from Hoover's letter to his executive assistants and district offices explaining release of the secret documents. (Because the Bureau's Coplon files have been kept secret, one assumes that Whitehead was given the letter by Hoover, who wrote the forward to his book.) Hoover's letter insisted that blame for release of the documents should be placed at the door of the Department of Justice and not that of the Bureau. He expressed having no objection to release of documents that could be introduced "without compromising sources of information, other investigations, or embarrassing innocent persons." Reports that would "reveal the identities of confidential informants or embarrass innocent persons" were another matter entirely, and he strongly objected to their release. Finally, the Bureau's furious director explained, he had had no knowledge that the reports would be introduced until "after they had been presented in court." And it was the Department of Justice, not the Bureau, responsible for selecting which reports would be introduced into evidence.

In truth, it was Judith Coplon's choice of data slips, and Archie Palmer's maneuvering, that resulted in the "selection" of secret files released to the public.

Reeves's ruling would make judicial history. "No trial in memory has reached down into the lives of so many persons, little and great, as that which began seven weeks ago in the tiny District courtroom," the *Washington Post* wrote. In the process of touching so many lives, the newspaper observed after the first day's revelations, a record would be set for trials in an American courtroom. The *Post* estimated there would be recorded between "a quarter and a half million words for the first day alone, most of the words from the documents, some of them the length of short novels."

As the readings continued, the prosecution contended that one life that might be endangered was that of Confidential Informant SF 1463. Lamphere was again on the witness stand, with Palmer demanding to know what the letters *SF* on one of the data slips represented. Lamphere refused to answer, and Kelley was once again on his feet.

"The mere location of the informant might be a serious threat to his life," the prosecutor insisted. Lamphere was furious. But Palmer, ignoring Kelley, went back to the witness, raging, demanding an answer. Lamphere set his jaw and refused to respond. Unlike so many earlier witnesses, he would not be intimidated. Judge Reeves rose slightly in his chair, leaned over the bench, and instructed Lamphere to answer. "I will take full responsibility," he said.

"The SF stands for San Francisco," Lamphere snapped after a moment's hesitation. "I had no choice," he reflected many years later.

Palmer asked another question, and Lamphere replied in a voice too loud for the lawyer who had shouted and screamed throughout the day. "Don't raise your voice to me!" he yelled at Lamphere.

"I *am* raising my voice to you," Lamphere raged back.

"Behave yourself!" Archie demanded.

Their faces were inches apart as the FBI agent yelled, "Don't badger me!" Their fury was real. This was no performance for the audience, and the jury, along with others present, feared the battle would escalate from a verbal to a physical altercation. Everyone, except the defense attorney and the witness, looked to the bench.

Judge Reeves, as usual slow to act, finally called a halt. It would take several minutes before the storm subsided, before the court could get back to the business at hand.

On June 8, the FBI's secrets continued to be exposed, tumbling one over another for the next few days, indiscriminately revealing names and histories and sins—either real or alleged. Secret FBI reports, until now carefully locked away from unauthorized eyes, protected with all of the vigilance afforded the government—reports of fiction and fact that ruined reputations and actually caused loss of life—became matters of public knowledge.

Washington Post journalist Bill Brinkley wrote of June 8:

> The Judith Coplon trial has had enough stormy and dramatic moments for a dozen trials. But nothing has approached the crescendo, almost the breaking point, it reached yesterday. It was a court day packed with naked emotions on the faces and in the voices of attorneys—prosecution and defense—of the witness, and of the slight girl who is the defendant.

Slight girl. Judith, now twenty-eight and possibly the most famous woman to be called a spy since Mata Hari, was still a delicate child in the eyes of many. Even an innocent child.

In an incredible turn of events, during the *prosecution's* case the defense began to introduce the full reports from which the twelve contested data slips had been excerpted. Archie chose the twelve, of course, because the government had fought so diligently to prevent introduction of their excerpts or synopses.

Palmer began with the data slip that named Stuart Legg, a filmmaker. The slip had consisted of two lines: "Stuart Legg—possible Russian espionage agent; Frink, NY 1/14/49; Re: Frederic March." It was the last line that was of interest. The defense attorney received and began reading the entire FBI file on prominent actor Frederic March and his wife, actress Florence Eldridge—aloud, in the open courtroom.

A highly exercised prosecutor Kelley asked, first, that the full report be read only to the jury and the parties to the trial, and second, that names be deleted from the report. But Judge Reeves overruled, saying, "When a matter is admitted in evidence, the newspapers and the public have a right to know." And thus began one of the most incredible scenarios in courtroom history.

What made the beginning of this grand exposé so especially intriguing, so doubly enticing, was that the first chapter involved not only March, but also others among Hollywood's most famous movie actors. Two years earlier, in the highly publicized case of the "Hollywood Ten" who refused to cooperate with HUAC, the suspected subversives who went to jail were writers and directors. In the late 1940s, the moviegoing public loved to read about film stars and pored over slick fan magazines for regular inside information on the cinematic world and its glamorous inhabitants. What came out at the Coplon trial was far better than what could be found in any magazine. It was real— perhaps true, partly true, or not true at all—but *real*. It came from the FBI, not from the creative juices of one press agent or another.

Archie began to read the entire March document. It opened with FBI agent Robert Frink's report that Confidential Informant ND 407 "advised subject was CP member 1947." Page after page cited every organization supported in any way by March and Eldridge, what meetings and conventions they attended, where and when March spoke, with whom the Marches associated. A list of his "Communist Front organizations" was offered. Among the subversive acts of both Marches was signing a petition to abolish HUAC. Another: March contributed five thousand dollars to the World Today, Inc., a documentary film production company headed by Stuart Legg and another party, both of whom were subjects under investigation as possible Russian espionage agents.

There was no indication as to which, if any, of the allegations against the Marches had been verified or discounted through investigatory measures. Busy Informant 407 (who did not provide all of the information on the Marches—others contributed as well, T-5, T-6, and ND 382 among them) reported to the FBI that he was satisfied March was a member of the Communist Party, along with, among others, actors Edward G. Robinson and Paul Robeson. Also included as members were writers Dorothy Parker, Donald Ogden Stuart, Ruth McKinney, Alfred Maltz, Alvah Bessie, Dalton Trumbo, Millen Brand, and Michael Blankfort.

An item concerning a 1939 article in a German-language literary magazine implicated not only the Marches but also actors Sylvia Sidney, Paul Muni, and Melvin Douglas. Among the dozens of names appearing elsewhere in the report were those of actors Helen Hayes and Danny Kaye, and writer John Hersey. Writers, intellectuals, musicians, actors—it was quite a collection of talent the Communist Party apparently had snagged for itself, or at least whose favorable attention it and other leftist causes had received. The country was enthralled.

Not all of those named were accused of being Communists, but their inclusion in the report amounted to much the same thing for many observers. The public had no way of discerning fact from fiction, of knowing that "facts" in raw reports could be merely gossip, innuendo, rumor, or silly allegations reported to the Bureau. But as is so often the case in such matters, once derogatory information appears in print, it registers in the psyche as truth.

Reaction was swift. In Hollywood, Dorothy Parker said she was "appalled" by the accusation and claimed not even to "understand what a Communist front organization is." She was also quoted as saying that she regretted knowing not a single Russian, but wished she did. "Maybe it would help understanding if we all knew some Russians."

Screenwriter Blankfort said he most certainly was not a Communist; that the only organizations he had belonged to in his entire life were a Princeton club and the Marine Corps Officers' Association, neither of which he felt to be especially dangerous. Writer Brand also denied the allegation, and Boston University president Daniel Marsh called the charge "grotesque," claiming to despise communism.

Although the *Washington News* reported that Robeson had been reached in Hollywood and denied being a Communist, the *Journal American* filed a different story. It reported that Robeson was unavailable for comment, but had made his feelings "clear" at a concert in Moscow the night before, where he reportedly said, "You know how I feel to be back again on Soviet soil."

At Bryn Mawr, Pennsylvania, March called the charge against him "the most absurd thing I've ever heard of." Asked if he had ever attended a Communist meeting, he answered, "Good God, no!"

Edward G. Robinson was vehement. He had never been a Party member. Such accusations and innuendos, he said, "come from sick and diseased minds . . . it is time for this madness and character assassination to stop." But it had just begun.

Helen Hayes was not at home when the press tried to reach her, but her husband, playwright Charles MacArthur, was. "You might as well interview Helen as the American flag . . . I'm appalled," he exploded.

"We knew that political censorship of the screen was the objective of certain Congressmen like Mr. Rankin and Mr. Thomas. . . . However, until today, we did not know that the Department of Justice was engaged in any such unconstitutional activity . . . this report . . . is probably a case of misplaced zeal of some individual investigator," said screenwriters Maltz, Bessie, and Trumbo, speaking through an attorney.

The three writers were among those earlier cited as "unfriendly" by HUAC. Maltz issued an additional statement saying that the contents of Judy's purse were much like those of the minds of Representative J. Parnell Thomas, since "there is an unpleasant smell of herring about both."

Brand said he was not a member of the Party and never had been. Wondering why his name was included, he said, "I sure am in distinguished company."

Almost immediately after the Hollywood names were revealed in Washington, and as a direct result of the Coplon trial, the California Un-American Activities Committee announced that New York and California were the nation's "principal centers of Communist activity." It added its own list of names of people who might be disloyal: bandleader Artie Shaw, director John Huston, and actors Katharine Hepburn, Lena Horne, Orson Welles, Frank Sinatra, Danny Kaye, Gene Kelly, Charlie Chaplin, Gregory Peck, John Garfield, Robert Dekker, Larry Adler, and Vincent Price. Also named, prominently, were the already maligned Frederic March and his wife, Florence Eldridge.

With the opening of the FBI secret files to the public, the Coplon case acquired a historic significance above and beyond Judith Coplon's guilt or innocence. In fact, it seemed for a time that the basic issue—whether Judy was a spy—was lost in the flood of government surveillance data made public for the first time.

From the Legg report, attention turned to the "T-1" document, a comprehensive report about a suspected spy, which revealed the obvious presence of a U.S. mole inside the Russian embassy in Washington. The mole, T-1, had reported confidential details about an embassy employment applicant, details he could have learned only by being on the scene, a dangerous revelation for the unfortunate T-1.

A side effect of release of this particular document was the exposure of its author, Special Agent Robert K. McQueen, the FBI's case agent in charge of surveilling the Soviet embassy. McQueen says today that he was shocked to find himself featured on page one of the *Washington Post* the day after his report was made public. There was a much more significant link to the Coplon case for McQueen; at the time, he knew a secret about her that nearly all of his colleagues would not know for decades to come. And it had nothing to do with the Russian embassy.

T-1's investigation of an embassy job applicant led to one of the woman's friends, the Russian-born wife of an American citizen. Because of her association with Vasili Zubilin, then a top-level Soviet espionage officer in this country, she was suspected of being a spy, something the world now knew. Others entered the reports in much the same way, one person suspected of being a Communist agent or sympathizer associated with another by various numbered informants who provided one or more pieces to complete a scarlet jigsaw puzzle.

Without televised drama, without *All My Children* and *General Hospital*, the American public looked to the incredible FBI revelations as the most compelling, spellbinding, and exciting entertainment of the day. And it went on for day after captivating day.

Some of the detailed information on suspected subversives was ridiculous, such as tennis dates and trips to Baltimore to buy Polish sausage. But there were some juicy and some tragic revelations as well.

One concerned Morton E. Kent of Chevy Chase, Maryland, a Harvard graduate and New York lawyer. On the Saturday before Kent's name and activities were to be read into the Coplon trial record, his wife drove him to a boat-house on Washington's Potomac River, where he rented a canoe. Kent paddled to the Three Sisters rock formation in the river, climbed on the rock, and sunned himself for a time. There, with a cheap kitchen knife, Kent slashed his throat. The coroner's office said "hesitation marks" in his throat suggested that the young lawyer's hand had faltered before he made the fatal stroke.

There was obvious reason for Kent's suicide. He was soon to be revealed at the trial as having been a contact of the Soviet secret police. Information in the Kent report indicated that in an effort to reach the police, Kent had approached Emilie Condon, whose husband, Dr. Edward U. Condon, was director of the National Bureau of Standards. This provocative little tidbit immediately created a monumental uproar in the highest circles of government. Condon was outraged and demanded an apology directly from J. Edgar Hoover. Attorney General Clark promised to ask President Truman to force Hoover to apologize to Mrs. Condon for the unverified item in the FBI file. Nothing doing, Hoover said predictably. Condon continued to demand an apology, and rumors were rife that Hoover was going to resign over the entire Judith Coplon affair.

In the reports, read aloud page after page, was the 64,000-word life history of a suspected Soviet agent living near Washington at the time, a woman accused in the secret FBI report of having caused the execution of her first husband in Russia. Who needed Chekov? Irina Aleksander, a Russian-born author, was prominent in both Washington and New York in 1949. She was described as being "very friendly" with Soviet officials in New York—in fact, she recently had been in touch with Pavel Mikhailov, "reliably identified by the Bureau's informant as being in charge of Red Army espionage."

Irina's file included details of apparently wild all-night parties in Arlington given by friends whose guests included briefcase-carrying army and navy officers from the Pentagon. Neighbors had told the FBI that on different occasions people were seen "moving around the house in a nude state." What did all this mean? Could sex-for-secrets orgies be taking place in the Pentagon's backyard?

There was more to interest the prurient. In September of 1948, a former secretary to Republican Senator Ball of Maryland filed a breach of promise suit against Harvey W. Wiley Jr., father of her baby. Wiley, son of the doctor largely responsible for the Pure Food and Drug Act, was nationally known as the country's "best-fed baby." The suit was dismissed, but the information was read to the court because, it seems, the woman had become pregnant following a Soviet Embassy party. As this history was read to the court, it became obvious that the names of Washingtonians who enjoyed Embassy parties, with or without sex, might be found in secret FBI files.

(For years, Marcia Mitchell's public broadcasting office on 16th Street in Washington was next to the Soviet embassy, and on occasion she attended receptions there. She wonders now if her visits might have been recorded in FBI files, or if anyone noted her irresistible attraction to Russian caviar.)

Balkan intrigue entered the picture, complete with plot and subplots, in a story centered around Romanian munitions manufacturer Nicolae Malaxa and Gen. Nicolae Radescu, former Romanian Prime Minister. Both were living in New York at the time of the Coplon trial.

In 1933, according to the Radescu file, Malaxa bribed Romanian King Carol's private secretary and was able to secure the appointment of his own men to high state offices. During 1937, said the report, Malaxa began collaborating with the Nazis in Germany, including Albert Goering, brother of Herman. Malaxa reportedly gave Goering an interest in all of his companies, including the Resitza iron and steel works. Now a millionaire, Malaxa helped finance the Fascist Iron Guard.

When the Russians took over Romania, Malaxa shifted sides and collected millions as reparation for his damaged factories. At the time his file was read in the Coplon court, Nicolae Malaxa supposedly had every official in the Romanian Legation in Washington on his payroll. Allegations that Malaxa was financing a resistance movement in Romania were vehemently denied by the Central Intelligence Agency, said by some to be helping the Romanian entrepreneur.

A story of special interest concerned David K. Niles, a White House assistant to the President whom Hoover suspected of being a spy. Apparently, Niles had intervened to secure passports to visit Mexico for one Philip Levy, thought to be a Communist agent, and his wife. It seems that Niles had previously been in love with Mrs. Levy.

Among the most titillating and fascinating files was one with the tragic tale of beautiful Russian singer Tatiana Lestchenko, revealed in letters to a Mrs. Dorothy Bloch of New York City. Mrs. Bloch met Tatiana in Greenwich Village through a New York attorney, Benjamin Pepper, who had fallen in love with Tatiana on a visit to Russia, married her, and brought her home to New York. On a return visit to Russia, Tatiana became pregnant by Russian sculptor Dmitri Tsapaline. After the birth of their daughter, Tatiana and Dmitri went off to Majorca to live, and Pepper, justifiably annoyed over the whole affair, got a divorce. But this was not the end of poor Tatiana.

After Tatiana and Dmitri returned to Russia, where he was made an honored artist of the Republic, the Russian songbird fell in love with an American writer, Louis Fischer, and bore him a son, Vanya. Dmitri's response was much the same as Pepper's had been, and Tatiana and children were packed off to live in miserable, deprived conditions with her parents.

For a while, Tatiana continued to sing. "I sang for Lillian Hellman last year," she wrote, "my songs, to me, are a source of joy, sorrow, love . . . I live through them." She described her circumstances to a sympathetic Mrs. Bloch, who responded with gifts of clothing, makeup, and food, which she sent through World Tourist, the company operated by confessed spy Elizabeth Bentley and her Russian controller, Jacob Golos.

Transfixed, the courtroom sat deathly silent as episode after episode of the Tatiana romance-tragedy unfolded in minute detail, hanging onto each and every word. Tatiana wrote lovingly about Vanya and about her feelings for each of the men who had been a part of her life. Finally, the report that Tatiana was dying of tuberculosis left many in tears as they heard the singer's words read aloud. "They say you in the States have a marvelous medicine for tbc [tuberculosis]. Is it true? Could you send me that? Oh, if!!!"

There were other stories, stories of "little" people, poor people, like the unemployed barber accused by someone or other of being a spy at the White Sands Proving Grounds. Revealing the most intimate, and often most damning, suggestions about so many public and private lives was totally for naught. It was all proof of nothing.

The whole fiasco did provide Richard M. Nixon with the delicious opportunity to charge Attorney General Clark with using bad judgment in allowing introduction of the files. The Congressman proposed immediate hearings to explore ways of protecting the FBI's files from future legal safecrackers.

Archie Palmer had started reading the reports aloud, but even his iron throat eventually gave way. The judge took pity, and others were assigned the task of reading word after word, page after page, report after report, day after day. Unfortunately for J. Edgar Hoover, the "others" included red-faced, outraged FBI agents. The ultimate irony perhaps came when Scott Miller was ordered by the court to take a turn at reading the reports the Bureau had so valiantly fought to protect. In his worst nightmare, Hoover could not have imagined such embarrassment.

When it became apparent that there was nothing to be gained by continuing its case, which for so much of the time had been in the hands of the defense attorney, the government, in enormous disarray, rested. But not even this could occur without argument.

"Your Honor, the government rests," said a weary John Kelley.

"Objection," shouted Palmer.

"That," observed the astonished Kelley, "is one thing I've never heard a defense object to."

Incredibly, the judge allowed Archie to read notes taken at the time of Judith's and Gubitchev's arrest and once again to cross-examine Judith's former supervisor, William E. Foley—still as a part of the prosecution's embattled case. If it did nothing else, this last bit of examination reminded jury members of the reason for which they had been impaneled. A few hours more, and the government's case was over. More than twenty different bureau witnesses had been called, many of them several times.

It was the first day of the eighth week of the trial. The government had been expected to complete its case halfway through the first week. In the deluge of irrelevancy, Judith, all but forgotten, sat quietly for much of the time, a nonentity, twisting her hair around her fingers, lost in the proceedings. By now, her circus trial was a brilliantly colored spectacle with film stars, tragic Russian heroines, Balkan intrigue, a suicide, suspected Pentagon orgies, and White House indiscretions.

And it had come a long, long way from Broadway and 193rd Street.

The Case for the Defense

• I •

On the stand . . . Miss Coplon was dressed in a neat black suit, a white blouse muffled at her throat. Her dark, soft-looking hair, one of her most attractive features, was held in place on the top by two barrettes, her curls tumbling sideward to frame her rather small face. Her face . . . a paleness dominated through the slight coloring . . . projected out over the filled courtroom outside of which hundreds more waited for a glimpse of her. Her eyes, dark eyes, behind which lie the answers to so many questions people all over the world are asking these days, and mainly one question:

Was she or was she not a spy against her country?

Washington Post, June 18, 1949

It was true that people the world over were anxiously awaiting Judith's appearance on the stand. The Coplon audience was now in the millions. In the United States, newspapers had been filled daily with the color and excitement of the judicial proceedings and often included full pages of trial transcript; now they were filled with speculation about what was to come next. The phenomenal Coplon trial coverage was unequaled in America's journalistic history.

There was no question that the Coplon trial had thus far exhibited all the elements necessary to gather and hold a wide audience. But all of it was merely the warm-up, the parade before the main event, the setting of the stage. The time had come for the defense to enter the ring, for Judith's performance before the jury.

June 16, 1949

The line of potential spectators forming outside the courthouse before dawn was longer than usual on this morning. The defense would launch its case, and no one wanted to miss a word. Perhaps the star would perform. The possibility of seeing Judith Coplon in person, live on stage, answering questions, was irresistible. Some of those who could not get inside the courtroom waited around, hoping at least to see her enter or leave the building; others left, resigning themselves to settling for news photographs and stories of her appearance. Inside and outside the building, the air was charged with anticipation.

The moment came at 3:05 in the afternoon, in a scene so touching that some spectators wept openly.

Archie Palmer had opened with three witnesses—both Condons, Dr. Edward and Emilie, and Harold Ickes, Dr. Ruth Gruber's boss. Condon was asked about the atom bomb, Mrs. Condon was asked if she was or had been a Communist, and Ickes was asked if the Interior Department had relations with the FBI. A flurry of sustained objections by Kelley quickly established the irrelevancy of the witnesses' testimony, and, in an unexpected move, Archie abandoned plans to call other potential witnesses (including Frederic March and J. Edgar Hoover), announcing at 2:57 that he was ready to put the defendant on the stand. The judge called a brief recess, and he and the jury left the courtroom. Everyone else remained seated.

Moments later, the courtroom stilled as Judith rose slowly at the defense table, pushed back her chair, turned, and walked three steps to kneel before her ashen-faced, trembling mother. Mrs. Coplon, still clad in black, sat ghostlike, hands twisting beneath the handkerchief in her lap. From across the room, Archie called to the ailing Rebecca, "Please try to smile." Distraught, Mrs. Coplon burst into tears, and Judith, still kneeling before her, grabbed her hands and held them tightly. Palmer turned away from the sad scene and walked over to stand at the jury rail.

"Clear a pathway, clear a pathway," a marshal called in the corridor, moving the crowd aside as the seventy-five-year-old judge, followed by the jury, entered the courtroom. Judge and jury were seated, the doors closed, and Palmer's voice boomed, "Judith, take the stand."

Judith responded "I do" softly, in swearing that she would tell the truth. In the witness chair she crossed her legs, seemed relaxed, swung her foot with a black shoe dangling. Archie urged her to feel "as comfortable as you can under strange circumstances."

The attorney began his direct examination by reading the first count brought by the grand jury, charging her with copying and taking government documents "with intent and reason to believe that the information was to be used to the injury of the United States and to the advantage of a foreign nation."

"Is that true or false?" Palmer asked.

"False."

As to the second count, charging her with removing FBI data slips containing intelligence reports relating to espionage and counterespionage activities in the United States, Palmer again asked, "Is that true or false?"

"False," she said again.

"Judith Coplon, are you now or were you ever a Communist?"

"I was never and I am not now," she replied.

"Were you ever involved in subversive activities against these United States?"

"Never."

Archie paused, walked toward the jury box, then turned. "I ask you, Judith Coplon, before this jury before which you are being tried, are you guilty of any offense against these United States?"

"I am not!"

Noting that the first indictment specified unlawful behavior beginning December 10, Archie asked when she and Gubitchev had first met. She responded that the meeting had taken place during Labor Day weekend.

"I met him at the Museum of Modern Art in New York City," Judy told the court. "I went to the museum on Saturday of Labor Day weekend, and I was looking around at the pictures, surrealistic and cubistic pictures . . . There was a small group in front of this picture. A man, as if addressing the group, said, 'What do you make of that?' I happened to be standing right next to him and I said, 'Not much.' He turned out to be Mr. Gubitchev."

"From that particular conversation, you began to talk to each other . . . to walk around that building for a while with him looking at pictures?"

"Yes, we did, and discussing various pictures, as well as other things."

From this first meeting, Archie turned to the subject of Judy's family. When he asked about her father, Rebecca Coplon's sobs could be heard throughout the courtroom.

"Your father was in the Spanish-American War, wasn't he?" Yes, she said, he was. "Is he dead now?" Yes, he is dead. And wasn't it true, Archie wanted the jury to hear, that Samuel Coplon had died since the case started, after the second indictment, in Washington? Yes, yes, it was true. He had been ill about five years, Judy said.

"Your mother is here in court?"

"She is."

Judy, "daughter of a patriotic family," was asked if her brother had served in World War II.

"That is correct," she replied.

Palmer then led the witness through a brief overview of her employment history, including her most recent role with the Justice Department. Judith explained that a political analyst was "someone who does research work and collects information about, has knowledge of, various political trends . . . which would include organizations, individuals, connections . . ." Judith first worked with France and Belgium, she said. But by the time Raymond Whearty, now one of her prosecutors, joined her department, her responsibilities included Russia, Poland, Yugoslavia, Italy, Latin America, "the Baltic field, and perhaps at that time I also had in my assignment sheet Communist and Left Wing matters. "

Archie briefly asked Judith about a "Cook's Tour" she had taken to Europe, a trip that did not include Russia, then turned to the documents found in her purse the night of her arrest. It was important to Archie's defense that their presence be explainable by reasons other than spying.

"During the time that you were working here in Washington, did you have occasion, from time to time, night after night . . . to bring home work from the department and carry on your typing and your work in your own apartment?" Archie asked.

"Yes, I did."

"When you took the work home, what did you do with it after you brought it home?"

"Bring it back."

Archie now focused on Judy's personal contacts with Gubitchev, picking up again at the first meeting. Gubitchev had told her he was a construction engineer at the United Nations, a member of the UN Secretariat. Judith, in turn, had told the Russian she worked in Washington, with the Department of Justice. The friendship developed quickly. Asked if they had been in touch since the time of the arrest, Judith said they had not, directly or indirectly.

Palmer led Judith to her alleged discovery that Gubitchev was a married man on the night of January 14, Chapter One of the prosecution's case. Archie had arrived at a key point in his defense argument: Judy in love.

"Now, during this period of time, during these . . . occasions on which you met him . . . did Mr. Gubitchev ever tell you or had you any reason to believe he was a married man?"

"Never."

"When, for the first time, did you discover the fact that he was married?"

"The night of January 14th."

"Before that time had he, in word or any other manner, informed you of the fact that he was in love with you?"

"He had."

"By that time . . . had you returned his affection?"

Judy hesitated in a courtroom absolutely silent, with the audience leaning forward to catch her answer.

"I thought I was in love with him, yes."

Back to the restaurant, back to Chapter One. "As you left this restaurant, explain to this jury just what occurred—and in that connection the scenes that have been depicted by the separate FBI men who watched you and followed you—tell us what occurred in connection with his conversation with you on January 14 about being a married man."

"It was either just before we were leaving the restaurant, or when we had left the restaurant . . . I was so astounded and so furious, and I felt imposed upon and everything . . . I guess I let loose and I started to cry; and I had a newspaper and I was brandishing it, I guess, and he tried to calm me, tried to put his arm around me, and I pushed him off with the newspaper. By this time he was getting excited, too. He was saying that I was completely unreasonable. He said I was provincial, like American women, that I was not trying to listen to him . . ."

"Judy, agents have testified—and the reports are in evidence now—that on Sherman Avenue you beat him with your fist. At times, Judy, do you lose your temper?"

"Yes. You know."

"You have lost your temper from time to time among your fellow workmen here in Washington, have you not?"

"I guess so."

"When you feel hurt and distressed, you show it visibly, do you not, and you do cry and you do hit?"

". . . I guess I was not completely sure of what I was doing."

The argument in front of the restaurant was now explained, at least to Archie's satisfaction. The row had had nothing to do with spying and everything to do with a suitor who had lied about being married and the anger of the woman to whom he lied.

The defendant described other dates with Gubitchev between the time of their initial meeting and Christmas, when, she claimed, she gave him a gift of a tie and a box of cookies.

"We met at Rockefeller Center," she said, her audience following every word, clearly enjoying the romance theme, "right near the skating rink. It was rather a cold day. We went into a place on 6th Avenue for coffee. I saw him for a short time on Christmas Day, because he had been operated on during the month of December and he did not feel well. Again on Christmas Day, I asked him whether he could come over the next day and meet my family."

"In connection with this Christmas Day," Archie said, "the government has made claim before this court and jury that you had papers which you"— and here he paused—"*intended* to give to this man, Mr. Valentin Gubitchev. Did you," he demanded, "ever *intend* at any time in your life to give any papers of any kind, not only affecting the United States, but any paper of any kind or character?"

"Never," Judy replied with conviction.

On most occasions the couple simply walked, talked, and dined; on one, they went rowing in Central Park. Who did the rowing? "He did," she admitted, smiling. "I'm not good at it." Afterward, they dined at Longchamps.

"And that charm grew on you, and now we have you rowing in Central Park and we have you eating in Longchamps . . . when is the next time you met him?"

They had met on a Saturday night in October, Judy answered, when they had dinner at Charles Restaurant. Only once, on the night of the Central

Park date, did Gubitchev take her home. Because her father normally was asleep by eleven o'clock in the evening, Judy's escort rode with her in the elevator but did not go into the apartment. Archie asked and Judy answered questions about Gubitchev's telephone calls to her.

There was another meeting of greater interest, when the couple met at Columbia University's South Hall, then went up to the Cloisters. The Cloisters, Judy explained for the jury, was part of the Museum of Modern Art, a collection of remains of medieval churches brought from all parts of the world. A beautiful setting, Archie suggested, and an appropriate place for people to meet; a place, he said, that was in the vicinity "of 192nd or 193rd Street." In the vicinity of Broadway and 193rd. He hoped the jury would get the point.

"Anyway," Archie said, "during all of those years you had not met the man whom you had fallen in love with, or the man who had fallen in love with you, successfully. I mean by that, giving lawyers a chance to get them a divorce after they got married." Never mind, the jury understood.

"That is right."

Archie asked if Judy had found Gubitchev to be a charming person when she first met him, and what was "impressing to your female heart and mind" about him.

"I thought he was attractive. Also, he had an enormous knowledge of literature, art and music, like I had never experienced in any other person . . . he was sensitive, intelligent. He was a gentleman, respectful. I found his personality attractive and I thought he was charming."

In all, Judy was on the stand for fifty-five minutes. She had done well, but when it was over she mopped her brow with a handkerchief, a gesture caught by press photographers. Leaving the courtroom, she made her way through a pushing, autograph-seeking crowd, not responding to the greetings and questions called out to her. With her mother, Judith Coplon returned to a quiet, but surely troubled, night at the Willard Hotel. Cross-examination was ahead; if not tomorrow, then soon.

The official transcript of Judy's appearance for the defense, which numbers more than a thousand pages, shows remarkably few objections or interruptions from the prosecution during Judy's first day on the stand. All of that would change, and soon.

• 2 •

Friday, June 17

Appearing calm and confident, Judy took the stand at 10:05 in the morning, when her attorney asked for extensive details about the policies and procedures of the Foreign Agents Registration Section of the U.S. Department of Justice. Who was required to register and why, and what happened if those required to do so did not comply with the law? In particular, he focused on the Amtorg Trading Corporation, the Soviet business agency named in the handwritten summary found in Judith's handbag the night of her arrest. He wanted to show that the defendant had done nothing to protect Amtorg from the law and, in fact, had sought compliance from the Russian organization.

On several occasions, throughout Judith's ordeal, she insisted that she had tried to make a case against Amtorg, but had been unsuccessful in securing the support of her superiors. Her superiors included both Whearty and Foley.

Ironically, Thomas Mitchell—then an FBI special agent—had shared her professed goal and participated in a wee-hours inspection (aided by the building superintendent) of the premises of the Amtorg Trading Corporation, located on the fifth floor of a mid-Manhattan office building. The elevator was operated by the superintendent who, with the inspecting agents, set up a warning signal to be used should a Russian unexpectedly arrive on the scene. As a safeguard, Mitchell was assigned as a lookout. After delivering agents upstairs, the superintendent returned to the lobby, where he and Mitchell decided to do a trial run of the alert drill. It was taken for granted that the helpful building employee would advise agents of the test when he took his elevator back to the fifth floor. He did not, and pandemonium erupted when the signal sounded and agents, who had removed their shoes to avoid tracking newly polished floors, slipped and slid among the shoes scrambling to retrieve their own. Confusion was aggravated when Agent Robert Wirth, a star in the Coplon wiretapping escapade, flushed the toilet and dashed from the office rest room, only to have the toilet overflow on the lovely floor.

"Not our shining hour," Mitchell admits. He says nothing about what was learned during the early-morning misadventure.

Now, at the trial, attention turned directly to the FBI and Judy's relationship with the agents who worked there. Archie Palmer asked for the physical location of Judy's section and its proximity to the FBI, and about shared access to doors and files. The FBI and FARS were neighbors of a sort. Access was fluid, easy. It was clear that Judy had frequent contact with FBI agents who came and went in her department, that she was on comfortable terms with them, that she considered them colleagues.

"In other words," Archie said, "the FBI . . . came to the offices from time to time, were working in conjunction with your office, to do the footwork necessary to get the information to see whether the people had registered properly. Now, then, did you know that the Federal Bureau of Investigation, the FBI, the *glamorized* FBI . . ."

"I object," complained Kelley.

"I will take the glamour out of it," Archie offered with a smile. Not satisfied, Kelley complained to the court about the use of *glamorized* and demanded that his opponent once again be cautioned.

"Cautioned about what, Your Honor?" Archie asked innocently. "Everybody glamorizes."

A friendly picture, the FBI agents swapping stories with Judy, visiting in her office, having access to her files. Having access to her.

With the jury and spectators now wondering about the openness existing in the Department of Justice, Archie turned his attention to the critical issue of the top-secret report Judy mentioned in her now-famous Michael Memorandum, noting that she had been unable to obtain the classified document despite efforts to do so.

"Now, there came a time in connection with Mr. Foley, did there not, in the early part of this year, when Mr. Foley had contact with you concerning what is referred to in one of the exhibits here as a 'top secret report?' Do you remember that?" Archie asked, and Judy replied that she did.

"Now," he continued, "in connection with this top secret report, which is the one we had the argument about in court, and His Honor made the ruling which, of course, must suffice—will you kindly tell me, before that time, had Mr. Foley spoken to you about releasing you of certain of your duties?"

"No," Judy said, he had not, refuting Foley's earlier testimony.

"Did Mr. Foley come to you and talk to you about the top secret report?" Yes, Judy said, he did.

"At that time or at any time before you were arrested, did you know you were under surveillance? That you were being spied upon by the FBI?"

"I had no idea."

"Did you know that your phones were being tapped?"

"No," Judy answered, "except about three days before I was arrested, I suddenly noticed . . . in this room in Washington a sort of regular crackling in the wire."

"Did you understand what it was?"

"I didn't know what it was. I asked a friend of mine. He said it is probably not being tapped; they do it so quietly you don't hear anything."

Kelley objected to what Judith's friend said, but not insisting, as he had before, that there had been no wiretapping. Archie grinned smugly, pleased with a score. Slowly he walked to the jury rail and carefully considered the rolls of mints, chose one, then turned quickly. His witness was relaxed in the chair, shoe dangling again.

"Now, I call your attention to the fact that I began this discussion by asking you about this top secret report . . . Had you ever, up to the time when Mr. Foley came to you in January of this year, the investigation of your activities . . . having been started without your knowledge after Christmas, 1948—had you ever seen anything labeled 'top secret' before?"

"Never."

Archie gestured expansively, then whirled and said, "In comes your boss, Mr. Foley, with this top secret, something you never heard of before. Go ahead and tell us what occurred."

"He walked into the room. He said to me, 'We just got a top secret report on Russian espionage in the United States.' I said something to the effect of top secret . . . So far as I know, the highest rating I had seen was 'strictly confidential.'"

In response to a question from her attorney, the defendant gave a fairly lengthy explanation of the "confidential" classification as it was considered in her department. Often, material so labeled reached her office after it had been widely disseminated in the nation's newspapers, or after open hearings of HUAC, especially in the case of Elizabeth Bentley. Judy said she and her colleagues frequently considered the confidential label "laughable," since the general public already had seen the information.

"Continue," Archie instructed.

"He came in and said it was top secret. I asked him whether this was about the Atom Bomb or some more information given by Miss Bentley. He said he did not know, that he had not seen it, but he wanted me to look at it. He made a specific point of that. He wanted me to look at it. Later on, he came in and said, 'Maybe you shouldn't.'

". . . A few days later he came in and threw the report on my desk. He put it down grandiloquently. I said, 'Oh, is that top secret?' That was the first time I had ever seen it . . . it had a black cover. I think it was in silver letters. It said, 'Top Secret.' It stood out on the book. He said, 'There it is, glance through it' . . . It is my belief that was a decoy of some sort."

Judy's typewritten note, her Michael Memorandum referring to the report, would not be fully explained until the next day. Archie next turned to the subject of the attorney general's "blacklist" of subversive organizations and the standards used to determine which organizations were placed on the list. Thus began an exchange that proved to be yet another embarassment for the prosecution, at least for Raymond Whearty, who had been partially responsible for administering the controversial loyalty program.

Begun with President Truman's Executive Order 9835 in March 1947, the program marked the first broad-scale effort of the government to protect itself from subversives within its ranks. By now, two years later, national disharmony over the legal requirement to pledge fealty to the United States as a condition of employment had reached a crescendo. Along with the pledge, employees and recruits were required to list organizations to which they belonged, organizations that might or might not ultimately be classified as subversive. Numerous institutions, organizations, and individuals were now strongly objecting to what they considered to be a gross violation of civil and constitutional rights.

Who wrote the loyalty standards for organizations, Archie asked Judith, and what was her role in determining whether an organization was "subversive"? Judy testified that, as far as she knew, the writers were attorneys in the Department of Justice, and she was ordered to be among those deciding which organizations would be blacklisted. She added that the established "loyalty standards" were considered "revolting" by Justice Department employees.

"What did Mr. Whearty, who was the head of this department . . . tell you or anyone else . . . regarding his opinion concerning this loyalty program that you folks were working on in internal security?" Archie asked.

"When we got those . . . most of the lawyers, as well as the two political analysts, at the time, were pretty sick, because of the nature of the standards which we felt were capricious and un-American . . . Mr. Whearty came into the room; he had a long talk with us, and he said that he felt equally sick about this violation of civil liberties."

Archie offered the prosecution team a slight bow. "In other words, Mr. Whearty, whose name was on the mimeographed memorandum, when this doctrine of subversive disloyal organizations, of people connected with it, blackened if they ever belonged to it . . ."

"I object to this speech," Kelley said.

". . . Anyway," Archie continued, "Mr. Whearty, at that time, was big enough and brave enough to tell you people openly that he despised—words to that effect—this loyalty section himself?"

Judy looked directly at Whearty, who sat motionless. "Yes. He said he would like to become a member of the American Civil Liberties Union, when he looked over this material."

Archie turned to Whearty. "To fight? That is what Mr. Whearty, the prosecutor, said?"

"Yes, especially because he was nominally in charge of a part of it."

At the time, the ACLU was actively engaged in battle against Attorney General Tom Clark over provisions of the loyalty program. Justice Department senior staff members, and certainly Whearty, were expected to take a strong and vocal stand against the ACLU.

Whearty rose. "Could we have on the record where this conversation took place?" he asked evenly.

Judy's eyes never left the prosecutor's face. "Yes, this took place in my office in the presence of Mr. Norris."

Other questions followed, including whether individuals, and especially lawyers, could lose their jobs if they failed to sign the controversial oath. The topic was concluded with a tedious reading of all the entries on the attorney general's lists of various subversive organizations. While most of those named clearly were associated with foreign groups, others, innocent sounding, raised spectator brows. Some were schools—such as the Abraham Lincoln school in Illinois, the George Washington Carver school in New York. People wondered. Were Reds *everywhere?*

Archie moved quickly to Judith's arrest, focusing on the interrogation that took place the night of March 4 and the early-morning hours of March 5 on the sixth floor of FBI headquarters in Foley Square. She spoke of being strip-searched and the indignity of having her body orifices examined, of being advised that she could have but could not call an attorney, of her concern about notifying her parents of her whereabouts.

She told of endlessly repetitive questioning, about one instance in particular.

"I said, 'no comment, no comment.' At which point, Mr. Robinson, in such a loud voice that even Agent Wilson jumped, said, 'What do you mean by answering, no comment? Who do you think you are? You're just a piece of trash. I have had all kinds of trash in that chair.'

"He said, 'I have had racketeers, white slavers, all kinds of crooks and low form of life in that chair . . . Who gave you the idea that you could answer, no comment?' So I said, 'Mr. Miller.'"

The courtroom was completely silent. There was no wavering, no hesitation in the defendant's voice. She was direct, articulate, firm. And convincing.

"Did you at that time know," Archie asked, "that upstairs sat, in another room, your ex-boss, Mr. Whearty, the man who had given you a promotion?"

Judy looked at Whearty, then replied, "The first time I saw Mr. Whearty was when they brought me before a judge and he came over and he handed me a subpoena. He said, 'Here, Judy. Here is a subpoena.'"

"He said, 'Here, Judy?' After four o'clock in the morning?"

They had been coworkers, Whearty and Coplon, even friends. There was an attachment of sorts, Whearty had admitted. Now, even to those who were beginning to believe she truly was a spy, this seemed to have been a particularly cold and heartless moment.

Judith told the court that when she finally was taken to a room where she could lie down, she was afraid to fall asleep for fear of missing the opportunity to call an attorney. Besides, she said, the nurse with her kept up a "constant stream of talk. What was I doing with my life? I was so young, I could be so glamorous. I could be like Elizabeth Bentley, if only I told all."

A lot of chatter, but no one had told her there would be an arraignment;

she was told nothing about what would happen next. In fact, at one point Agent Miller told her, "You should know a lot about law; you worked for the Department of Justice." She disagreed, saying that she had been in the Economic Warfare Section and FARS, and was not familiar with judicial procedure.

"Well, you went to law school," was Miller's reply.

"For six nights," Judy had told him.

Archie left March 4 and asked if Gubitchev had called her after their spat the night of January 14. "Yes, he did. Before this whole outburst I told him that I was coming in on inaugural weekend, which was the next weekend. He called me twice at home in Brooklyn. The first time I was rather curt, and I told him I did not want to have anything more to do with it." A curious choice of words. She said "it," not "him."

"He told me to think a little bit about it," she continued. "He said it was all right, he did not have to see me that weekend, but would I think over what he was trying to tell me, that he wanted to see me to explain. I was curious and at that time I felt that I was still very much attracted to him."

"Very fond of him?" Archie wanted to know.

"Yes."

Turning to the night of February 18, when Judy broke her shoe strap and got lost, Archie asked about the subway trip uptown during which Agent Miller was looking over her shoulder.

"He told the jury about your opening this pocketbook and he saw a piece of onion paper which was folded in so that he could not understand it. You carry in your pocketbook, as ladies do, letters and things of that kind?"

"Yes," Judy answered. "When I heard Mr. Miller testify about that, I was trying to think what it would be." Perhaps, she went on to say, it might have been something in connection with the Barnard Occupation Bureau regarding getting a new job in New York.

As for the timing of Judy's arrest, March 4, Archie speculated there might have been a reason for the FBI's action other than the obvious. The Department of Justice had been criticized roundly for not being aggressive enough in pursuing subversives.

"Did you know at that particular time that your particular case, or the alleged crime, as stated by Mr. Whearty, immediately deflected negative attention from the Department of Justice who now had caught the great spies, you and Mr. Gubitchev?"

"I object," Kelley said.

"Sustained," said the judge.

"Did you know it? I'm asking you," persisted Archie.

"Sustained," repeated the judge.

The fact is, the timing had been fortuitous for the Department of Justice. Initially, abundant favorable attention resulted from the clever capture of suspected Red spies. With the advent of the sideshow trial, however, the department's image quickly spiraled downward.

Archie turned his attention to the circuitous route taken by Judith and Gubitchev the night of the arrest.

"Did you know at the time you were under surveillance . . . that he was under surveillance?"

"No; but he thought someone was following him."

"What did Gubitchev tell you before you got on that train with regard to anyone following you?"

"He told me two things, one on February 18th, and then the beginning of March 4th. When I met him on Broadway he told me that he thought his wife had hired a detective, or more than one detective, to follow him . . . Then, when I argued with him about this ridiculous idea of not sitting together in the bus and not sitting together in the train, you know, going across town, he said to me at that point, 'Well, I am not sure, it may be the NKVD . . . the Russian Secret Police.'"

"When he told you it might be the secret Russian police in this country following him, what did you say to him?"

"I said, 'This is too much.' It was the most petrifying idea, because, first of all, this idea of being followed by his wife's detectives, I did not know what reason she would have, except to use me in some divorce suit . . . That was bad enough. This idea of secret police . . . I said, 'This is the most horrible thing in the world. What are they going to do, kill us?'"

This was Judith's explanation of the elusive behavior that had so occupied the attention of the prosecution. Because no one had seen anything pass from one of the alleged spies to the other, much needed to be made of the covert way in which they met.

With an orchestrated stroll from witness box to jury box and back again, Archie returned to Judy's note about the "hot and interesting" report about Amtorg, the "tool of entrapment."

"Would you tell us here in the courtroom all that happened on March 4th, 1949, between you and Mr. Foley in connection with the handing to you of this Exhibit 13, which we now have found out was a decoy letter."

"As I said, it was early, about nine o'clock, and Mr. Foley walked in, and he gave me this letter and two others . . . He handed me the three and said, 'This is hot and interesting,' or words to that effect. I said, 'What do you mean, all three?' He said, 'No. The top one.' He said, 'Look at it,' and he pointed to 'Needleman.' He said, 'I want you to make a note of this and give it to Lenvin' [her office mate]. He told me to make a note of the highlights . . . in connection with possible prosecution under the Act.

"Then Mr. Foley came back and said, 'Did you make a note of it?' and I said, 'Yes.' He said, 'Let me see it,' and I handed it to him and he read over the note."

Archie was playing the entrapment card. "After he told you to make a note, you then prepared Exhibit No. 117, and then he read the note . . . What did he say then?"

"He said, 'I would like for you to work on this over the weekend.' I said, 'You know I am going to New York' . . . He said, 'I want you to take this note to New York with you and think about the matter.'"

"What did he tell you to do with the note?"

"I asked, 'What do you want me to do with it, put it in like this?' He said, 'Oh, no; put a wrapping around it, or something' . . . I took another piece of paper and I put a wrapping around it, and put it in my pocketbook."

"In Mr. Foley's presence?" Yes, Judy replied, and Archie said, "So, before you left for New York that day, he had told you to prepare this memorandum, had read the memorandum, told you to put it in your pocketbook; you put it in your pocketbook, and he knew you were leaving at 1 o'clock."

"He did."

"So, when you got to New York and you found out later on that day there were twenty-six or more FBI people ready to receive you with great honors— Mr. Foley had known that before—that this particular piece of paper, referring to the fake decoy letter, was in your pocketbook at his request?"

"Yes."

Throughout the day's testimony, the country's undisputed soap opera star had remained calm and controlled, playing her role with confidence. When she stepped down from the stand, her attitude changed and she hurried to her mother's side. The older woman, still clad in black, leaned forward to hold her daughter. Not a soul in the courtroom moved.

Mother and daughter left together, heading for two days away from the courtroom, two days of breath catching. As usual, crowds of spectators pushed and shoved toward them and bundles of fan mail were handed to Judy; and, as usual, the media loved every chaotic moment, even though the star and her mother would not respond to their questions.

The weekend would be especially quiet, a time to rehearse mentally, to talk with Bert on the telephone, to hide from the curious. To have one quiet walk, alone.

Monday, June 20, 1949: Direct Examination

Would they never get enough of her? "Hey, Judy!" "Will you sign this?" "Give us a smile!" With Archie at her side, and carrying an armload of note-books, Judy smiled broadly, offered greetings, and disappeared inside, declining to stop and sign the autograph books waved at her. Later, her mother slipped silently into the building alone and found the seat reserved for her directly behind Judy.

There was an unmistakable air of anticipation this morning as Judy rose to testify. Archie immediately raised questions about William Foley's testimony for the prosecution, particularly his saying that suspicion of Judith had led to his removing her from internal security matters and access to classified data. Foley testified that Judy had disregarded his orders and, essentially, tricked her successor into letting her see sensitive documents. This was an important point; spies did sneaky things like that. Did Judy?

Not so, the witness now testified. Mrs. Rossen frequently had come to Judy for help in handling reports, showing them to her in the process. A very practical reason for this, Judy explained, was that Foley had failed to give the poor woman sufficient instruction to allow her to do her job properly. Time and time again, Judy said, Mrs. Rossen had come to her, classified documents in hand, to ask how specific tasks should be handled—even after their supervisor allegedly "had taken Judy off internal security" and prohibited her access to sensitive documents. Further, Judy's testimony revealed that restricted materials were kept in unlocked cabinets and drawers throughout the FARS offices. When the FBI searched her office and found sensitive materials in Judy's desk, it was nothing out of the ordinary.

A murmuring went through the courtroom. With the specter of Reds lurking in the halls of government, this sort of carelessness was an open invitation for espionage activity.

It was clear that there were legitimate questions surrounding Foley's management. Judy, confident, seemingly competent, now appeared more reliable, to some, than did William Foley.

Archie, for his part, appeared to be enjoying himself immensely. The day, which would soon take on the characteristics of a course in literary criticism and would see Judy explaining away the troublesome data slips, was well under way. It was destined to end with the bombshell du jour.

"On January 14, 1949," Archie asked, "and anytime besides that, before that, even before the government dreamt of having you surveilled, either in Washington, or in New York, did you ever pass a single thing of any kind, involving the United States Government, or any internal security to this man Gubitchev?"

"Never!"

"Did he ever ask you for anything at all?"

"Never!"

Archie paused, letting Judy's strident denial hang there, glowing; and then, in one of his characteristic quick switches, he turned to the night of the arrest and the personal belongings taken from Judith. Included in those belongings was a novel, Alfred Hayes's *All Thy Conquests*, which, to everyone's amazement, the attorney began to read aloud. "Rome has many conquerors . . ."

"Just a moment," Kelley said. "Let's go right to the ending, so we can see how it comes out."

"There is one thing about you," Archie responded. "I am sure literature never gets its chance to spread its glories upon you."

"Let's get along," said the judge amiably, and everyone save for Archie undoubtedly was wondering the same thing. Get along to where?

Why, to other literary matters, of course. Discussed were Trilby and Svengali, and Somerset Maughan's *The Summing Up*. Archie brought up Milton—"the blind poet," he yelled, "the man who wrote *Paradise Lost*. The man who dictated that work to his daughter when he was blind . . ."

"We all know that," Judge Reeves observed.

Archie was not through with the subject. "Shelley? You know Shelley was the famous English poet who wrote about love in every shape, manner, and form." The point of most of the discussion, if it had any, was that Judy and Gubitchev shared a passion for literature. It played a significant role in their romance.

Grinning, Kelley said, "Let's go on to the end of the book. You're not going to leave us dangling." But Archie was through with Hayes and Rome.

Left dangling, the court watched Archie skip over to Judy and ask how she felt when Gubitchev told her the night of March 4 that their pursuers might be deadly NKVD officers.

"I was struck numb with fear and terror. It was just a devastating thought."

Enter Svengali and Trilby again.

"The way Svengali took charge of Trilby," Archie said.

An unusually relaxed Kelley tipped back his chair. "He was her lover," he offered. Was this a literary tea, some wondered, or a trial for espionage?

Now, Archie wanted to know, in planning to use the papers found in her possession March 4 as material for her novel, did she follow Maugham's advice on how to become an author? He pulled out a copy of the autobiography and, noting that Judy had been accused of the "foulest of crimes," the attorney quoted:

"Breathes there a man with soul so dead, Who never to himself has said, This is my own native land." He thought a moment, then speculated quietly, "I guess that applies to women as well as men."

A different kind of literature entered the picture, when Archie asked Judy what kind of reading was required for her work. She cited a number of Communist and Soviet publications, noting that she could read but neither speak nor understand spoken Russian. Did exposure to material of this nature cause her to want to betray her country? It did not, she insisted.

Now, to the data slips. Judy explained that these were her own notes, indexes to full reports, as it were.

"My method of work was to take these FBI reports and to make slips on any information which might be of interest to me . . . What I would do would often be to make notes so that I could use them as a basis of a memorandum which I would write." Either she wrote the data slips or instructed a secretary to do so from "mark-ups" on the original reports. The process was part of her research and analytical work.

"Will you kindly tell me, my dear Judy, why did you take the notes to New York?"

"On this specific occasion, I took them in connection with the civil service examination." It was, Judy said, an "unassembled exam," meaning that candidates submitted their papers individually and not in a classroom. (Records show that in February, less than a month before her arrest, Judy had made at least two calls to inquire about the examination and to ask that the necessary forms be mailed to her.) Archie asked why Judy wanted to take the examination, and she responded that it was for the purpose of furthering her career. This brought a question that confounded everyone within earshot.

"While you were here in Washington and getting this salary, thanks to Mr. Whearty's aid and assistance, of $102.25 every two weeks, on which you had to pay taxes, will you kindly tell me whether during this period of time you had any idea that you could better your condition by obtaining the acquaintance of people like Gubitchev or attempting, if you please, to sell these United States by divulging information of the kind and character that comes in the possession of this particular FARS, wherein there are no locked doors and there are no locked cabinets; was that your intention, in any way, shape, manner or form?"

The silence was profound. And then a dazed Kelley rose and objected, saying, "That has a tail on it as long as a kite. I don't know what he's talking about!"

Neither did anyone else, and the "question" was dropped. Judy went through a lengthy explanation of the civil service exam she had planned to take, which required her to write about three specific aspects of her work. Those she selected were the loyalty program, the Communist Party USA, and informational activities of Eastern European representatives working in this country. Data slips, which only served as indexes, would remind her of the cases about which she wanted to write. She would not, however, use real names in her exam.

Aha, thought some. Was this really stealing secrets? It didn't sound like a serious matter at this point, at least to some observers. To others, insiders, it sounded extremely serious. It was a matter of names, names that would be of interest to the Soviets.

Archie began a relentless effort to establish Gubitchev as an operative working for the United States (or for Russia, for that matter), who had been put in place to trap the innocent young political analyst "to see if they could catch you in connection with anything to do with our government."

Judy professed no knowledge about such a possibility, but did mention, more than once, that Gubitchev had left her ten minutes prior to the arrest to make a telephone call. This, in retrospect, seemed mighty suspicious to her.

"Now, Judy, in connection with treason, or matters involving things of that type, those are usually done, according to the standards, for either love or money. Now, on March 4th were you in love with this man, the inexplicable Mr.—I beg your pardon—were you in love with him?"

"I don't know." A different answer, causing speculation. Did it come from a growing suspicion about the Russian's motives, or perhaps from something nearer to the hidden truth? Archie pushed on. Did she give papers, give anything, to Gubitchev because of love for him? Of course not.

"Will you kindly tell me if Mr. Gubitchev, at any time, anywhere, ever gave you one cent of any kind, to sell our country?" Never.

Archie's next questions came in a huge roar. Did her master's degree studies at American University, her learning to read Russian, her work-related reading of Communist literature, lead her to performing, or wanting to perform, treasonable acts?

"No!"

"You still love to be an American?"

Yes, yes, of course.

Enter Anna Karenina.

"Did you read *Anna Karenina*?"

No, no, interrupted the judge, we'll not go into that one!

Very well. Did Judy know anything about the makings of an atomic bomb? She did not.

Every day of the trial had its explosions. Today's was not atomic, but still caused a blast heard from one end of the country to the other.

Archie was asking Judy if there was "other decoy bait" that might have been set out for her, enticing bits not yet discussed, that might have been planted to entrap her. Possibly, Judy said. "Mr. Whearty told me that the FBI had prepared a list of all individuals in this country whom they recommended for custodial detention in the event of war with Russia."

Gasps could be heard throughout the courtroom.

"In concentration camps?" Archie was horrified.

"He said in custodial detention. He said Mr. Campbell [assistant attorney general in charge of the Criminal Division] has taken that list and had . . . it delivered to Mr. Foley." The list, Judy had been told, was not even in an envelope. It was "bare," the obvious implication being that the list was easily accessible.

"It was a story he was telling me," Judy continued. "In the light of all the testimony, and in the light of this talk about top secrets, I think it might have been some sort of bait he was giving me." But then again, it might have been the truth.

Murmuring in the courtroom revealed discomfort about the latter possibility. It had not been all that long since Japanese Americans, and others whose loyalty to the United States was in doubt, had been placed in concentration camps. But it was long enough that people spoke openly about friends or acquaintances, loyal Americans, who had been unjustly sent to wartime detention camps. For many, this whole business of secret lists and mass incarceration was frightening. It was especially so because this audience had so recently been exposed to the FBI's raw files, where rumor and nonsense alone could lead to one's name being placed on a list.

Author Tom Mitchell acknowledges that yes, certain lists of this nature did exist. Before the days of computers, there were lists in FBI pockets, names of Russians, just in case. And when Puerto Rican nationalists mounted an armed attack on Congress in the early 1950s, within hours a list of suspected Puerto Rican militants living in the United States surfaced. The morning following the brutal attack, at precisely five o'clock, they were picked up. Every one of them. Stationed in New York, Mitchell participated in planning the operation, which he says was "a preventive measure."

As the day was ending Archie made a repetitive, but futile effort to explain Judy's arrest as a result of entrapment, a government plot based on its embarrassing failure to put Alger Hiss behind bars and on HUAC's continued criticism of the Justice Department. Judy was an innocent lamb sacrificed on the altar of bureaucratic incompetence. Shouted down by the opposition and scolded soundly by the judge, he changed gears and charged again. Back he went to the single issue most disturbing to the prosecution, the messy business of wiretapping. Time ran out, but Archie promised to take up the contentious issue the next day, and both Kelley and Whearty experienced simultaneous heartburn.

All in all, it was a day that found Judy none the worse for her appearance on the stand, and perhaps better off for time spent. Tomorrow, however, the crash could come. She would face Kelley, fresh from convicting Axis Sally, a prosecutor who did not lose. At times embarrassed, even humiliated in this circus of a trial, he was ready for blood. He could taste it, and it would be rich.

Newspapers around the world carried the story of Judy's day on the stand, beautiful Judy, "sensuous" Judy, Judy the spy, Judy the innocent victim of a troubled time. Outside the courtroom, the crowds were even larger than before. Her fan mail rivaled that of Bette Davis, and she was receiving at least as many marriage proposals as the actress.

Tuesday, June 21:
Direct Examination Continued, Followed by Cross-Examination

This was The Day. In a sense, the denouement. It dawned unremarkably, like any other late June day in Washington, warm, sticky, heavy. On Pennsylvania Avenue, traffic slowed as it neared the federal courthouse, then came to an abrupt stop where pedestrians, oblivious of honking horns and shouted curses, ignored crosswalks and crowded across the street. Prosecutors Kelley and Whearty arrived early, wanting to avoid the melee, but it seemed as if no hour would have been early enough to miss the madness.

Kelley seemed confident, Whearty distracted as they mounted the wide steps, heavy briefcases in hand. Part of their prosecution team, young attorney Harold Shapiro, would not be in the courtroom today, although he would play a starring role. Better to keep him out of sight throughout the trial, Kelley had decided. As for Shapiro, most likely he was in total agreement, and the stage was thus set for a historic courtroom drama without one of its principals.

The day began with an old issue as promised—wiretapping. Once again, agents testified that they had no knowledge of any such thing.

"In connection with your telephone at your home, after you got home, did you discover . . . that after your arrest that your phone was tapped?" Archie asked.

"I object to this 'discover!'" Kelley complained.

Moving right along, Archie asked, "After you got back from prison [Judy spent a week in detention awaiting bond—she never went to "prison"] . . . and you were followed in the fashion you described, and in so far as you are concerned, and the phones were tapped, will you kindly tell me . . ."

"Just a moment," Kelley said. "I object to this. There's no such evidence."

Palmer turned to Kelley, smug, certain. "You *deny* they were tapped?" The proverbial deer in the headlights, Kelley stood transfixed, waiting for the judge, who toyed with his pencil.

Belatedly and finally, Reeves sustained Kelley's objection, but Palmer ignored him and demanded of Kelley, "Do you know anything about it?"

"Talk to the judge, not to me," Kelley snapped.

With a sigh of disgust Archie walked back to the jury box and took his time selecting a roll of mints. Affably, Archie smiled at the jurists, offered the array of mints with a gesture of his hand, then turned back to his witness, chewing vigorously.

"What was it that induced you to write a book?" he asked.

She sat relaxed, leg swinging, hands folded in her lap. "Well, what was it? I guess it was a creative urge. I had been thinking of it for a while, thinking that I would like to do some writing, because my writing . . . was of the most routine type on my job. And I went to Europe . . ."

"What did you write?"

Judy described for the jury, as she earlier had for Archie, her novel-in-progress, describing it as a series of sketches, as "more or less" biographical, the story of a "government girl in Washington." She spoke of postwar suspicions of friends and family. When she talked about wives going through their husbands' pockets and reporting what they'd found to the FBI, about children reporting on their parents, and how this kind of behavior was not only condoned but also encouraged by the government, her listeners were aghast. No wonder, for hadn't they recently listened, day after mesmerizing day, to FBI reports of the most intimate details of personal lives, details that were as much rumor and gossip as anything else?

Judy wrote, she told the jury, about "this whole espionage hysteria, the witch hunts, the loyalty program." Also, she said, she included personal glimpses from her European tour, "being in the war-torn countries, Italy and France, these devastated regions such as in Genoa and parts of Florence, this beautiful cultural city, which had just been bombarded after the Germans had declared it an open city."

None of this discussion bored the jury or anyone in the courtroom, even though they had heard bits and pieces of it before. They were spellbound. The witness was an articulate, fascinating storyteller, and they hung on her every word.

"Too bad she didn't have that book on the market today," an observer noted. "She'd have a best-seller." His companion said, "*If* there ever was such a book!"

The prosecution, in an objection, raised this very question. Where was this alleged novel? Destroyed, Judy said.

"I didn't want it to get into the hands of the FBI. By that time, the newspapers had made such a ridiculous spectacle of me—I had been blasted, my name and reputation—I didn't want to be held up to any more scorn."

"What did you do with it?"

"I tore it up and threw it down the incinerator in the apartment house."

It was established that Judy had attempted to arrange meetings to discuss publication of her book with Simon & Schuster. This, Archie contended, proved there was a book, or at least that there had been one.

With the audience entranced about her book, or at least her talk about it, the time had come for Archie to solder the link between some of the material found in Judy's purse and her novel. He began by entering the full text of the character sketches of Lorraine and Alvin Sinderbrand and Albert Stevenson, and it was not difficult to make the case that the sketches, political in nature, could serve very well as models for characters in her novel. Having placed the three subjects of the sketches into the context of the missing novel, Archie turned to something far more damaging, the Michael Memorandum, which he read aloud.

Archie asked, "Tell me about Michael." He referred to her words, "I have not been able (and don't think I will) to get the top secret FBI report which I described to Michael on Soviet and Communist Intelligence Activities in the US."

"This was a note from the book I was writing." Michael happened to be one of the characters in the book, Judy continued, as well as the "holy scribe" who was doing the writing. "I put in the part about Foley, when he came over to me first and said we had a top secret FBI report, and said, 'I want you to see it.' Then he came back later and said, 'Maybe you should not see it.'"

She smiled. "I put that in and changed it, fictionalized it, because it was a very amusing incident."

Amusing, Archie acknowledged, but what about the people named? "Martens, Lore, Poyntz, Altschuler, Silvermaster, et al." Was there anything amusing about these people?

"Poyntz is dead, supposed to have been killed in New York by the NKVD about 1938. Martens was the unofficial Soviet delegate to the United States, deported in the '20's." Lore, she said, was at one time a leader of the Communist Party in the United States and later was thought to have been involved in Russian intelligence activities. Lydia Altschuler was "involved some way with Spain, with the Spanish War." Silvermaster's activities had been revealed in detail by Elizabeth Bentley.

The news, at least as far as these people and their activities were concerned, was indeed "nothing new." In fact, the public had read much of the same information in their newspapers. This was what Judy had found amusing. It was hardly top-secret stuff, and the point surely was not lost on the jury.

As Judy's direct examination drew to a close, her attorney led her back to the subject of the specific data slips found in her possession on March 4. Why these? Yesterday, she said she had chosen the slips as reminders of reports she wanted to use in writing about the loyalty program and "hysteria and witch-hunting." Archie wanted the jury to hear more about this.

"I call it that, hysteria and witch-hunting," Judy said.

She was not alone, Archie noted. "The President called it that?"

"Including the President."

The data slips she carried referred to reports she particularly wanted to have in mind when she wrote about the loyalty issue. In addition to pocket-searching wives and tattletale children, to "everyone reporting on everyone else," the FBI had other means of collecting data on suspected subversives, Judy told the court.

"They would get it from phone conversations, also trash cover. They would go through waste paper baskets, tap telephones . . ." The vision of their government sorting through garbage and listening in on private telephone conversations, perhaps of ordinary, innocent people, was disturbing to many of the spectators. There was a good deal of elbow poking and whispering in the room, and if some felt more secure knowing the government was snooping in the alley, others were clearly outraged. This sort of thing could happen to any of them! Hadn't it happened to Frederic March and Mary Pickford?

"The data slips I chose were selected because I was interested in that kind of material. That was my job."

Archie concluded his examination with the contention that Judy had, by now, explained away all of the government's evidence—the handwritten note about Amtorg and geophones, the Michael Memorandum, the character sketches, her own biographical note (written for her novel), and, now, the data slips. He was satisfied with her answers, or at least claimed to be. There was really nothing left to dispute. No one had testified to seeing Judy pass a single document to anyone. He crossed over to the witness box and nodded to Judy.

"You started with the glamour of the job and ended with the dirt and degradation of a trial." He waited, but there was no response. The attorney stood quietly for a moment and let the tension rise. Then he turned slowly and gave a magnanimous bow to the lanky prosecutor waiting his turn.

"Your witness, Mr. Kelley."

The courtroom was absolutely silent. Not a soul moved, except for Rebecca Coplon, who could be seen moving forward in her seat, her face taut and pale, her eyes glistening with tears.

Tuesday, June 21: Cross-Examination

The immediate connection was apparent throughout the courtroom; it sizzled, strung like an electric wire from the prosecutor's eyes to those of his witness, a line drawn between two highly intelligent, clever antagonists. Like two prizefighters, they were certain to dance and feign and test each other before striking. Archie sensed it, and quickly asked a marshal to "bring this girl a glass of water."

"We can wait until after the recess if she's tired," Kelley offered, his voice surprisingly gentle, and Judith smiled at him. "I'm not tired." Words carefully delivered, courteous. They were playing with each other.

Remaining seated, Kelley, in the same gentle, almost sympathetic tone, began questioning Judy about her romance with the Russian. As the exchange went on, and the expected harshness had not materialized, Judy seemed to relax, but only slightly. Kelley asked about her various meetings with Gubitchev, what they did, where they went, how they felt about each other. He was easy, kind. If Judy seemed more relaxed, Archie became increasingly wired, ready to spring at any opening.

"In the course of these nine meetings with Gubitchev, Miss Coplon, I believe you testified that you experienced three overwhelming emotions, love, fury, and terror; is that right?"

"One moment," Archie said.

"What?" asked Reeves.

"Love, fury, and terror," Kelley repeated. "Those are her terms."

"She said nothing of the sort," Archie snorted.

"She can take care of herself!" Reeves insisted. "You let her answer."

Kelley's point was that Judith had testified to loving Gubitchev, to being furious when she discovered he was a married man, and to feeling terror at the thought of being followed by the NKVD. Love, fury, and terror, but for now, he said, the issue was love.

"Let's deal with this emotional experience. Let's see if we can determine, as the song title has it, 'What is this thing called love?'"

"I did not hear that," Archie complained.

"He wants to know what is this thing called love," Judge Reeves solemnly explained, and the courtroom burst into laughter. Too funny, the spectators thought, coming from the crotchety, aging judge. Banging his gavel and yelling at the audience, an embarrassed Reeves threatened to clear the court-room. One more outburst and that, he promised, would be that. Even so, it took several minutes to restore order.

The next voice was Archie's. "I heard something about title."

"There's been so much confusion that I cannot understand what is going on," fussed the judge, and the spectators struggled to keep silent.

Archie continued to fight about the love question. "In the first place, you cannot diagnose love. It is an emotion. You cannot use a thermometer or geophone for it." At another point, he interrupted with the fact that there is "quite a difference between love and love, crescendos and minuendos."

Kelley threw up his hands in surrender. He would drop the question. The prosecutor asked about Judy's initial impressions of Gubitchev, and what he had told her about himself. He was from Moscow, she told the court, but had lived elsewhere in Russia, particularly the Urals. As a boy in Leningrad he had hung around ships. In a surprise statement, Judy said Gubitchev had told her he was "anti-Soviet," that he had hoped to become an American citizen. Wasn't a revelation like that "unhealthy," Kelley wanted to know? Judith said it was not. She thought the opposite.

"You considered marriage to him, didn't you?"

"I did. It hadn't got that far, though."

Judy called him Val, she said, and he called her Judy, sometimes "Dear." Kelley nodded, lazily got to his feet, walked over to Judy, and suddenly the gentleness was gone. "Did you ever before allow yourself to be picked up by a strange man and give him your phone number?"

Yelping, Archie cried out, "It's a dirty, contemptible . . ."

"Stop!" ordered the judge.

"You know what I mean by picked up, don't you?" Kelley's cool voice asked. "Did you ever pick up before with a total stranger?"

Furious, but under control, Judy snapped, "Yes, I have."

Frequently? Kelley asked, and Judy gave him a curt "No!"

In rapid fire, prosecutor and witness exchanged questions and answers about why, if Judy had been contemplating marriage, she had not inquired about Gubitchev's family, income, even his marital status. It didn't sound much like a real romance, suggested Kelley. He went back to the night of

January 14, the night when Judy said she learned that her Russian paramour was married, that he had been two-timing her.

"Up until that moment did he appear to be completely candid, honest, and forthright with you?" Judy said, yes, she believed he had been honest about "his profession of love." Was he being true to her alone? A debate ensued over what "being true" constituted, and Archie observed that this sort of commitment was different for men than for women. Kelley continued: When she entered the restaurant that night, had Judy any idea of the shock she was about to experience, the shock of finding out he was married, that there was another woman in the picture? She had not, not the slightest hint.

Kelley enjoyed the process of setting his trap, asking needless questions about exactly when Gubitchev made his startling revelation, whether it was before or after he paid the check, other questions to get the witness off guard. And why, he wanted to know, was she so furious about his being married when they'd had only a few dates? Because, she explained, they had loved each other.

"He had done you no harm?"

"No."

There were other stage-setting questions, including several related to her testimony the previous Thursday about the depth of her love for Gubitchev. At one point the audience sat absolutely silent in an electrified courtroom.

"I had never been in love as deeply with anyone as I thought I was with Gubitchev," Judy told Kelley.

"And up to that moment, when he told you he was married, you had complete faith in his sincerity, did you?"

"Of course."

"He said he wanted to marry you?"

"He did."

"He had not even kissed you?"

"No, not up to that time he had not."

Kelley's questions, although often sarcastic in tone, had been spoken in a normal, sometimes even quiet voice. He was suave, smooth, biting. She was fielding his questions skillfully, articulately. Neither had scored a definitive win. Suddenly, John Kelley leaned forward and thundered at the young woman before him.

"Isn't it the truth, Miss Coplon, that you and Gubitchev never were in love whatsoever in the slightest degree?"

She paled at the prosecutor's fury. "As far as I know, I was very deeply in love with him. As far as I know, from what he said to me, I thought he was very deeply in love with me."

"Is it not the truth that just one week prior to that date, prior to January 14th, which would be the night of January 7th, you spent the night in room 412, in the Southern Hotel in Baltimore, Maryland, while registered with a man under the name of Mr. and Mrs. H. P. Shapiro, from 122 Burnside Avenue, East Hartford, Connecticut?"

It took a moment for her to react, the shock was so complete. And then Judy screamed hysterically, "That's a damn lie! Why are you doing this in front of my mother?"

Archie shouted his objection, demanding attention from the bench.

"You deny it?" roared Kelley.

"I deny it!" Judy screeched.

Kelley sunk the hook. "Is it not true that on the following night, the 8th of January . . ."

"I will tell . . ."

"The 8th of January," the prosecutor yelled at the witness, "you spent the night in room 1523 of the Bellevue-Stratford Hotel in Philadelphia, Pennsylvania, while registered with the same man, under the name of Mr. and Mrs. H. P. Shapiro?"

"I object," Archie raged, "I object upon the ground, in the first place, it is irrelevant and incompetent and has nothing to do with this particular case . . ." He stopped for a breath, and in that split second of entranced silence, a shrill scream came from Rebecca, who jumped to her feet, pointing wildly at Kelley.

"I knew he was going to do this; I expected this from him!"

Now Reeves was yelling and pointing. "Remove her from the courtroom," he ordered, and two marshals rushed at the bereaved woman in black.

Archie was apoplectic, stomping, shouting at the judge. "You're going to ask the *mother* to leave the room?"

Another tormented wail from Mrs. Coplon. And then, "No, no, I want to hear it all." The marshals hesitated, and Rebecca collapsed into her chair. She could stay, Reeves said, "As long as she behaves herself."

It was complete and utter chaos, a mass of hysteria and pain. Members of the pencil press scribbled furiously in their notebooks. Kelley charged ahead, thundering over the sounds of Rebecca's crying and Archie's screaming to be heard by the judge.

"Answer my question," he demanded of a badly shaken witness, "did you not spend the night with Mr. Shapiro on those occasions?"

Judy's voice now became surprisingly controlled. "I do not know how he registered. I spent the night with him, during which time I did not sleep or make any attempt to sleep."

"In Baltimore on the 7th?"

"Baltimore on the 7th."

"In Philadelphia on the 8th?"

"It was the week-end."

"Did you not spend New Year's Eve of this year with Mr. Shapiro, in fornication, in an apartment of a friend of his in this city?"

"I did not."

"Have you not spent nights during the month of February in Shapiro's apartment—in fact, to be specific, the 17th of February, the night before you went up to meet Gubitchev—bringing your bag there with you, when you entered, taking it with you the next morning when you left the apartment to go to the Department of Justice and leaving for New York?"

"I think I did that night."

"And have you not spent other nights in his apartment during the month of February?"

"I have."

"Now," said Kelley, fully in command, "let's go back to the second time you met him . . ."

"What?" Archie stormed. "The question was fornication. I submit the lady has a right to answer the question." The court agreed.

Judy addressed the judge, who told her not to do so, but she continued despite his order. "Is this related to the issues of the case? Has he a right to besmirch me in the presence of my mother?"

"You can answer the question about this fornication," Kelley said, but before she could reply, the prosecutor turned and charged at Archie, who had left his seat and was on the move. "Sit down!" Kelley hollered. But Archie would not, and the fireworks continued until the judge finally intervened and Judy had an opportunity to respond.

"I did not spend the night with him in fornication."

Oh? Kelley wondered. What were they doing, discussing literature?

Kelley showed the witness hotel registration cards naming Mr. and Mrs. Shapiro, and produced a bill for breakfast in bed. Judy claimed she did not sleep with Shapiro, although they shared a room, and breakfast, she said, certainly was not served in bed.

As the prosecutor began his next question, Archie interrupted, asking that Kelley be made to stand still; he was blocking Archie's line of sight. Grinning, Kelley moved. "Does Counsel object to me standing here?"

"You stand over there! I want to see!"

More sniping, with Reeves finally insisting that Archie sit down. He did so; his compliance exaggerated by a great flailing of arms, whirling, muttering, gasping, looking pleadingly at the mesmerized members of the jury.

"Did you tell Gubitchev that night, the night of January 14, that you had spent the Sunday previous in a room with Mr. Shapiro, registered as his wife?"

"I did not."

Kelley entered into evidence two hotel bills along with the breakfast check. He then passed these items to the jury.

"I object!" This evidence was immaterial, Archie insisted. And besides, "I will say on the record that *fornication has nothing to do with espionage!*" In so saying, he wrote the next day's lead for newspapers around the world.

"It has something to do with love," Kelley countered. The implication was clear. If Judy had been in love with Gubitchev, the reason she gave for meeting with him, she would not have been fooling around in bed with Shapiro. With the revelation of her affair, Judith's defense had shattered, its shards a brilliant fusillade across the courtroom.

"You might have something to do with love before you get through," Archie threatened.

After another heated dispute over who was to stand where, Kelley returned to the issue of love, tying every loose end, tying the witness to her claims of love and devotion. From time to time he demanded that Judy look at her jury, but she kept her eyes riveted on him. At the moment, the fact that the prosecution had provided no evidence that Judy had given away, or sold, government secrets, or that she had ever *intended* to do so, mattered not at all. The only evidence that mattered was that of the gutter, of behavior not associated with "nice girls," especially in a postwar society where young women gave their jobs back to returning heroes and stayed home to make babies. The picture of Judy as the "typical girl next door" was tossed to the winds by the public, and, of course, by the jury.

When the ordeal was over, the defendant, in a dark V-neck dress with a patterned silk scarf at her throat, mopped her brow with a large white hand-kerchief, a gesture caught, as before, by one of the multitude of photographers fighting to get close to the young woman. The cutline under the photo, which appeared in the *Washington Post* and elsewhere, read, "She admitted she spent the nights with a man in Baltimore and Philadelphia hotels." It was Big News that day, and not just in the United States.

The Coplon women went home to the Willard, two small figures skirting onlookers and hurrying to seclusion. Rebecca, head bowed, was downcast in both body and spirit. In contrast, Judy's head was held high, perhaps filled with enticing thoughts of a few minutes alone with Harold Shapiro and a blunt instrument.

Wednesday, June 22: Cross-Examination, Continued

Prosecutor John Kelley strode into the courtroom clad as the victor. He looked at no one, went to his table and, with a thud, slammed down his brief-case and several file folders. Make no mistake, his manner declared, I am ready for the day, I am in control, and I am the winner in this game. Judith Coplon entered with an amazing calm, moving gracefully, a slight smile on her face. She would not play the role of Guilt, of fallen woman and spy. Bustling and muttering, hat in hand, Archie arrived on the scene, the last of the major players in the drama. Whearty had been there before the others, sitting quietly at the prosecution table, at the moment a minor figure.

To make certain that the most prominent twelve members of his audience understood the finer points of yesterday's tempestuous proceedings, Kelley began his examination this morning with a review of Judy's failure to ask of Gubitchev the kinds of questions a young woman considering marriage would ask of her lover. Her lover, Kelley implied, was not Valentin Gubitchev. The prosecutor then moved quickly to the classified nature of the documents with which Judith worked and those in her possession when she was arrested. In her direct examination, she had testified that at times she found the "confidential" label "laughable." Kelley took issue with Judy's statement.

"You would distinguish between these reports; one, you would say was laughable, and the other not?"

"At the time I said laughable, I said a lot of this information marked 'confidential' was known in public records, had been blasted across the pages of newspapers. It was available in the files of the old Dies Committee or the Un-American Activities Committee, was available in columns of people like Drew Pearson or Walter Winchell. It was common knowledge among individuals interested in it . . . I said that was a laughing matter, in the sense that this is marked 'confidential' and then you read it in the newspapers . . ."

"And do you follow your own opinion, as far as disseminating information, or do you submit to the FBI decision?"

Of course she always respected the Bureau's confidential stamp, whether or not she agreed with it. "I never disseminated any information outside of the Department of Justice where that stamp was . . . I would not walk along the street and say, 'Gee, just guess what I read in the FBI report.'" But Kelley was not satisfied. If the witness disagreed with the FBI's classification criteria, it followed that she had little respect for the FBI.

"You had contempt for the FBI, did you?"

"I have been arrested by the FBI."

"You thought the FBI agents were witch hunters?"

"I made a statement yesterday in which I discussed the FBI and witch hunters and the loyalty program. Yes, I think the nature of much of the material in these reports is disgraceful, and I always thought it."

The data slips were confidential, Kelley noted. The materials, all of them, found in Judy's possession on March 4 were of a secret nature. But Judy, he said, didn't seem to think so. Hadn't she, in fact, said as much to a New York reporter?

"At any time, did you make a statement to one Mary Harrington, 'They were not important documents nor could they have hurt anyone'?"

"I did not."

"May she make an explanation?" Archie asked.

Despite the thermal nature of their earlier confrontations, nothing approached the heat of the new battle that now erupted, as Palmer complained that Judy wasn't allowed sufficient leeway for explanations of her actions. At one point, a bellowing Archie exploded across the room and shook his fist in Kelley's face; Kelley, in return, swung back, ready to strike. Bailiff and marshals were at the ready when Judge Reeves, nerves to the breaking point, gaveled for a cease-fire. The case had to proceed, or else, he demanded. Or else what, was never explained.

"Let her say what she said," Reeves ordered.

"Can I tell you?" Judy asked.

"Yes," Archie said. "His Honor said, yes. You don't have to look at Mr. Kelley."

Kelley was furious. "I must say, if this man doesn't stop parading between me and the jury, I assume I will have to go to the other side . . . May the record show he is within three feet of me, constantly bobbing up and down, sometimes within twelve inches, and reads the time off my watch."

"Mr. Whearty is within twelve inches of you."

"Let's stop this," insisted the judge. Then, turning to Judy, "Do you have an explanation to make?"

"Yes, I would like to explain."

Archie closed in on Kelley. "Behave yourself," he hollered, and by now everyone had forgotten the question before the court. Today's show was marvelously entertaining, and the audience, straining to watch every move, but having no trouble hearing it all, chuckled and poked and whispered. Eyes of the jury left the players only infrequently, when they studied the faces of their jury box colleagues.

The question repeated, Judy began to answer when Kelley interrupted her, launching Archie into orbit once again. The furor ended only when the judge, red faced and pounding his gavel, threatened to put Archie into prison. Archie calmed, but continued to object to everything Kelley said and did, with the prosecutor plodding on, brushing Archie aside like an annoying insect. He turned now to the night of Judy's arrest and her having said she was "struck numb" with terror at the thought of being pursued by the NKVD. But that wasn't the worst of it, she now testified.

"There is only one impression in my mind which was a greater terror . . . and that was when Mr. Granville, and with what seemed to me one hundred agents, seized me."

"They told you they were FBI?"

"FBI."

"Why didn't you throw your arms around their necks and say, 'Thank God; I thought the NKVD was after me?' Didn't you feel some measure of relief when you found you were in the hands of the FBI and not the Russian secret police?"

"I did not. Not from the treatment I got. You asked why didn't I throw my arms around them? It would have been difficult, because they had their arms about me. If you want to know what I felt, I felt some measure of a frame-up; that is what I felt."

"You were innocent?"

"I was innocent."

"You had been working with FBI agents for years?" Yes, Judy said, they came into and out of her office daily. Kelley asked if she had a horror of them before March 4.

"No, but I have developed a terrible horror of them since then. I think this whole thing is horrible; this whole case is horrible, not only what developed that night, not only that brutal treatment. I think other things are horrible. I knew nothing about arraignments, and I told that to Mr. Miller and the other FBI agents. I knew nothing about what was going on. I begged to have my family notified. I begged to have a lawyer. I was told I didn't have to answer any questions; yet, they pounded me with questions."

Kelley wanted to know why Judith didn't complain about her treatment to Judge Rifkind when she was arraigned. Uncertain as to what would be appropriate "in terms of remarks to the judge," she kept quiet, she said. Well, then, the prosecutor continued, why, when her old friend and former boss, Whearty, appeared, didn't she run to him for help? "Why didn't you say, 'Mr. Whearty, this is all a big mistake'?"

"Why? Because, Mr. Whearty came over and said, 'Here, Judy; here is a subpoena.'"

Kelley paused, then, glaring at the witness, he rumbled, "You didn't do anything wrong?"

Judy looked her interrogator straight in the eye and spelled it out for him. "No, I didn't do anything wrong, and I have never done anything wrong. You don't know the dumb terror something like this can bring you when you're being questioned hours and hours by the FBI, when they say 'sleep in your chair,' and don't let you notify your family, when they call you the vilest names. You suddenly don't go up to Mr. Whearty, whom you have known for years, who hands you a subpoena, and say, 'Look, Mr. Whearty; what is this about?'"

Kelley wanted to end with the love story. More to the point, with Judith's love life, with the "fornication" issue. But his witness had had enough. Suddenly she sat forward sharply in her chair:

"I want to explain!" she cried out. "You branded me as a spy and now you are trying to brand me as a harlot! Why don't you tell the jury Shapiro is in the Department of Justice and an attorney under Mr. Whearty?" Kelley turned away, and she screamed, "I want to look you straight in the eye, Mr. Kelley!" It was a scene that would be replayed in every news broadcast and on the pages of the country's newspapers. It also played well in Europe, especially in England.

Judith Coplon was indeed branded as a harlot. It was only left to brand her, to the jury's satisfaction, as a spy.

Thursday, June 23: Cross-Examination, Continued

More marriage proposals, more bundles of mail, more demands for autographs. Disclosures about Judy's romance and new calls for her execution did nothing to stem the ardor of those who were starstruck. No longer the girl next door, now the seductive vamp, the exotic spy Robert Ruark had called for, so different from dowdy Elizabeth Bentley and Axis Sally. The picture was out of focus, however, for it was she who had possibly been lured into the enemy's bed, not the other way around. Regardless of who had lured whom, the nation finally had a woman spy who was *really* interesting, sensuously, provocatively interesting.

Crowds surged toward Judy this morning, and Archie cheerfully pushed them out of the way. The press was not so easily dispatched. How about some comments, Archie? What about the mysterious Shapiro? Nothing mysterious about the rat, was Archie's position. Handsome Harold—whose middle name, Archie hooted, was Platonic—was a living, breathing, tool of entrapment, a member of the *prosecution's legal team!* How obvious could the government get? There would be new motions, Archie promised, motions to dismiss. When asked on what grounds, he did not elaborate, although entrapment seemed an obvious choice.

Among those who only wanted to be done with Judy were J. Edgar Hoover and Harry S. Truman. For them, the Coplon embarrassment factor increased exponentially every day. Hoover never did apologize to Mrs. Condon, and her husband, still miffed over the whole affair, had enough influence to keep pestering Truman. Truman pestered Hoover. Hoover was a silent mass of anger; an apology was out of the question. Tom Clark pestered them both. Hoover continued to brood over the humiliation brought to his sacrosanct Bureau; Truman brooded over the mileage Richard Nixon and company had gotten out of the devastating mess. This trial, this supposed five-day railroad to prison, was now sidetracked in its ninth week of entertaining the nation. Get it done, Kelley, was the drill ordered from two different Pennsylvania Avenue addresses.

Judy, dressed in a green plaid dress with black accessories, went first to embrace her mother, and then to the witness box. She looked cool and refreshed, not easy in a courtroom already too warm from the late June weather. Mrs. Coplon began to sob quietly into a white handkerchief even before Kelley launched his penetrating examination of the data slip issue.

Judy placed the slips in a stocking package just as a means of carrying them, she said. She needed them for the civil service examination, she said. She didn't put them in her suitcase because she didn't have a suitcase that night, she said. He pounded; she replied in short, snappy answers. They weren't good enough, he said. He asked her "orally to write out" a portion of the exam showing how she planned to use the slips. Archie yelled and pitched, but to no avail, and his client did an admirable job of writing on the wind.

Now to the decoy letter and Judy's note dealing with its contents, with Amtorg and the faux double-crosser Needleman. It was found in a tiny packet, also tucked into the stocking package. How could this possibly be explained? It was a tiny package, wasn't it?

"It was a small package," she agreed.

"And you put an arrow on it in pen and ink?"

"I did. I would like to explain that arrow."

"Do you have to explain *everything?*" Kelley asked, feigning exasperation.

Archie demanded that she be allowed, once again, to offer an explanation to the court, and Kelley, with a great sigh, gestured that she could do so.

"I would like to explain, because I believe someone said the arrow would show how to open the package. I marked it with an arrow just to identify it to me, so I would not confuse it with a wad of gum or something else that I might have wrapped."

"Confuse you with a wad of gum?" Kelley was astounded.

"Yes, in a piece of paper."

"You put wads of gum in your purse?"

"I might."

"Do you?"

"I might." The prosecutor was disbelieving.

"An arrow points to something, doesn't it?"

"Not necessarily. I made an arrow . . . I would like to know what that would point to."

Today, the arrow pointed to Judy. Moving quickly, Kelley turned to Judy's typewritten Michael Memorandum and the three character sketches. Kelley was getting it done.

"Now, that [Exhibit 115, the memorandum] was one of the documents that you wrapped with the data slips, isn't it?"

"That's right."

Kelley gave Judy the material she had placed in two envelopes and then in the stocking package. "Put that together like you did in your apartment that evening."

Judy had difficulty getting everything into the envelopes. "This is the same trouble I had that night. I did not have an envelope that it could fit into," she said, which was why she placed the material in a stocking folder. She had included the Belle Sharmeer insert to make the package more secure.

"Do you deny that you put that in for the purpose of having it appear to be a pair of stockings?"

"I deny that most emphatically."

It was a stretch, even for Judy's staunchest supporters, whose numbers were dropping dramatically. By now, Archie's client was damaged goods. In fact, the entire day, in which Kelley had unrelentingly revisited the evidence in Judy's purse, had been disastrous in terms of the defendant's credibility. Judy had remained calm, but if ever there was a storm to follow the calm, tomorrow, when Kelley would finally give her up, would be the day. She would be the storm in a courtroom scene like no other.

Friday, June 24: Cross-Examination, Continued

Rebecca Coplon accompanied her daughter to the courthouse Friday morning, but did not enter the building with her. She waited a few minutes in the taxi, until the cameramen were satisfied and Judy had disappeared inside. Every moment since Kelley had begun his cross-examination had been a poisoned needle in Rebecca's heart. Lonely and alone, frightened, widowed less than three months ago, she was nearly paralyzed by fear for her daughter. Added now was the shock, the public humiliation, of Judy's sexual exploits and lies. She did not fool herself, this frail woman with an ailing heart and tortured soul. The worst was yet to come. Certain members of the press, understanding that Rebecca still believed her daughter innocent of espionage, wondered how she had survived this far, and whether she would simply give up and go home to Samuel.

Kelley's manner this morning showed no sign of change in demeanor. He was bigger than life, meaner than life, and ready to go.

Spectators stood as the bailiff announced the opening of the session and Judge Reeves, appearing exhausted, settled himself at the bench, arranging his robe around him, removing and then replacing his spectacles. His manner was clear: Let's get on with it, because I am very, very tired of all of you.

Kelley began with questions about Judy's proposed novel, which both his body and verbal language suggested never existed, not even in the defendant's mind. Equally not in existence, he intended to show, was a single legitimate reason for Judy's having had the materials found in her purse at the time of her arrest. Dropping his voice, he asked Judy about the Michael Memorandum. Archie complained that he was unable to hear Kelley.

"I don't want to stand near the witness, but I want him to talk a little louder. Let him talk in his natural way. Let him not assume a new pose, fortissimo and pianissimo."

Fortissimo and pianissimo? The audience chuckled. Archie was in good form.

"You will have to sit or stand somewhere else if you can't hear him. His voice is loud enough for me to hear and loud enough for the jury," Reeves snapped.

"Did you have a living person in mind when you referred to someone as Michael?"

No, Judy did not. Well, then, the Michael in her mind was a matter of interest, observed Kelley. "Where, in your mind, did you conceive that you met and conversed with this fictional character, in the sense that you said, 'I told Michael.'"

"I didn't say, 'I told Michael.' I said, 'I described to Michael.'"

Kelley took issue with the autobiographical sketch found in Judy's purse, which was not a government secret but certainly, to the prosecutor, appeared to be information provided to her controller in the hope of advancing in the spy ranks. Not so, said Judy. Kelley wanted to know when she had written the sketch and she said it was on Thursday, the day before her arrest. Kelley did not wink at the jury, but he might as well have done so.

"And it was your method, you had to write a note to yourself and seal it in that stocking thing to take it up to your parents' home, to use two days later, to remind yourself when you entered the university?"

"No, I wrote a note to myself. That was my method of work. I sealed it, because I was taking this other material; so I put it all together in one little package like that." Kelley's skepticism was shared by many. His masterful questioning made the fateful Belle Sharmeer package seem more and more as if it had been destined for someone else's use, not Judy's. And yet, and yet.

The same evidence ground was revisited, Kelley paving it over and over again with his suggestions that the witness was lying about everything. In terms of facts, there was little that was new in this rerun of the evidence game, and yet everything was new today because Judy had lied, for a while so convincingly, about being in love. Nothing else seemed to matter.

Something new was the efficacious (for the government) appearance, albeit only in spirit, of Igor Gouzenko. Among the documents the young Soviet cipher clerk carried to the West was a list of questions to be explored with potential espionage recruits. The document became a part of a Royal Canadian Commission report.

After noting that every piece of evidence from Judy's purse had to do with communism or Communists, Kelley handed Judy a book and asked if she had read any of it. The book was the Canadian report.

"What is it?" he asked.

"It's *The Report of the Royal Commission to Investigate the Facts Relating to and Circumstances Surrounding the Communication, by Public Officials and Other Persons in Positions of Trust, of Secret and Confidential Information to Agents of a Foreign Power*. It was written on June 27, 1946."

"Now, I address your attention to pages 50 and 51 of this report; and would you read to yourself, please, this portion." He leaned forward, his face inches from Judy's, and pointed to a section of text, "including this sentence on page 50 . . . the book recites, does it not, that the Canadian officials secured a secret Russian document which outlined the information the Russian espionage system wanted in relation to possible Canadian recruits for further espionage, does it not?"

"I just read that part about social contact," Judy answered. "I didn't see anything about secret Russian documents."

"I direct your attention to this portion," Kelley said. "While this document refers only to two men, it is an excellent example of the system employed in cases of men they hoped to recruit by this means."

Archie was on his feet, booming an objection to introduction of the book and its contents. All of this had nothing whatsoever to do with the matter at hand, he insisted.

"Overruled, and sit down!" Reeves told him, and Archie marched back to the defense table and snatched up a roll of mints. Eyes left the witness box to watch, much to his delight. Kelley waited for attention to turn back to him.

"Now, Miss Coplon, please look . . ."

"May I comment on what you told me to read?" Judy asked. Kelley nodded, and she continued. "I think, from what I read, this gives a very good outline of what sort—what a person is, what a person is made of . . . I resent this implication. I wrote certain character sketches . . ."

"You understand, do you, that this is the information the Russians desire in connection with possible recruits for espionage?" She did not.

"Let's look at your documents," Kelley said. Line by line, he read Gouzenko's outline, and, line by line, Judy's "character sketches." They matched perfectly with the Russian model in form, content, and even terminology. Especially damaging were those portions referencing communism and the Party. It was either a case of remarkable coincidence, or compliance with Soviet instructions.

More questions and more answers, all turning what could have been, might have been, innocent observations into tools of espionage.

Unable to contain himself a moment longer, Archie pleaded again to the judge. "Your Honor, I ask . . . that the book . . . is no criteria of evidence that can be admitted in a court of law, that that is the way the Russians get their information, or want information. I object on the ground that the entire examination was improper and I ask therefore that all the questions and answers be stricken out as not being based upon anything in evidence."

"Overruled." The inevitable argument came, with the inevitable answer. Archie lost. What continued to amaze was that Archie, bouncing, bounding, an inflated balloon-man, never lost any of the combustible material that filled him. Knock him down and he sprang back to his feet. Neither the judge nor the prosecutor ever punctured the balloon skin. No enthusiasm, no determination escaped from him, disaster after disaster. Throughout the day he had pranced and preened and objected, his stereophonic, surround-sound voice resonating off the walls and ceiling.

Now, and for the last time, Kelley went over Judy's movements during the time she was under surveillance in New York. It was time to close, and Kelley set out to do so.

"Now, Miss Coplon, do I understand that it is your testimony before this jury that, as respects this prosecution, you are an innocent woman and that there is a conspiracy afoot to frame you. Is that your testimony?"

The witness, whose manner and voice had been controlled throughout the day, suddenly transformed. "My testimony is, and it always will be, I am innocent and I have been framed!" She was a screeching Wind Fury, reborn from mythology, come to life in a steamy federal courtroom.

Startled, Kelley stepped backward. Recovering, cool, eyes hooded, he asked, "And do you think that many persons have participated in this framing of you?"

Shaking with outrage, Judy yelled, "I don't know who has participated, but I feel a frame-up."

"Do you think the Attorney General of the United States has participated in framing you?"

"I do not know who has participated in this!" she shrieked. The judge, wide-eyed, sat stunned. Kelley pushed on.

"Do you think my associate, Mr. Whearty, has participated in framing you?"

"Yes," Judy cried. Oh, yes, yes, yes!

"Do you think I have participated in framing you?"

"I understand, from your testimony, that you came on the scene later, but I will say that you have participated in asking me some of the lowest questions that I have ever heard," she spat, shaking her finger at the prosecutor. He turned away in disgust, then, with his back to her, said, "You had some strange doings, Madam." And then, "Do you think William E. Foley participated?"

Judy demanded that the prosecutor turn and look at her, which he did, slowly. "I definitely think Mr. William E. Foley participated in this frame-up." Foley, the man she said lied about the Amtorg note, "which he told me to take to New York. He wanted to make sure I had something in my pocketbook! This whole arrest was conceived—

"Why did Mr. Miller open my pocketbook? Did he know it was going to be there? Why did he pull it out there? Why did he know it was going to be in that position, just where I told Mr. Foley?

"Why did Mr. Whearty take the Congressional train and go to New York?

"Why did Mr. Granville tell Miss Manos to stay around for the arrest? Why?"

Judy was shouting, wounded, driven by raw fury. Kelley was unmoved, a dog with a torn rag doll in its mouth. "You knew you had been surveilled on two earlier occasions?"

"I did *not!*"

"You knew they expected you to meet Gubitchev again?"

"I did *not!* They might have expected me to meet Gubitchev again. This whole case is so fishy it smells to high Heaven! For all I know, *Gubitchev* told them. He made a phone call around the 15th Street region and within ten minutes I was arrested. I would like to know who this Gubitchev is, too." Judy sank back in her chair, moaning.

Watching, Rebecca Coplon was near hysterics. The judge looked at her but said nothing. The place was a madhouse anyway. What difference could a hysterical mother make at this juncture?

"Do you think Mr. Nathan Lenvin participated in framing you?"

"I don't know what Mr. Nathan Lenvin's part was in this . . . he might have sat around and informed people I was making data slips . . . he is still an employee of the Department of Justice under Mr. Whearty." Judy's voice was filled with venom.

"You think, last but not least, that Mr. Shapiro and Mr. Gubitchev participated?"

The ultimate insult. "As far as Mr. Shapiro goes," she said, "I think that he participated very much in framing me. As far as Mr. Gubitchev goes, I still don't know. If you people were waiting and expecting something to be passed, why didn't I pass it to him before?" she demanded. "Why didn't I pass it on the bus? Why didn't I pass it when . . ."

"Because you knew the FBI were on your tail? Because you knew it was not safe?"

Furious, she yelled, "What do you mean, I knew it was not safe? I had no idea who in the heck was following me. For all I know, the NKVD was running around there. Mr. Gubitchev thought some such thing." Oh, she knew why that paper was planted on her person! "So when I was arrested, there would be something in my pocketbook."

Spectators were struck dumb. Many looked at the judge, expecting a recess, or at least an attempt to restore some semblance of order; he did nothing but sit and watch, however, as spellbound as the rest. He was the failed referee in a championship bout.

Kelley asked if any of those persons named, persons Judy believed had conspired to frame her, had anything to do with the fact that the materials placed in evidence had been in her possession the night of March 4. None had, she answered, but then hurried to clarify.

In the process, she made an extraordinary speech, screaming her accusations, defending herself in a way later said to have been unique in the annals of U.S. courtroom history. Witnesses under cross-examination were required to respond to questions and not to add clarifying information unless instructed to do so. No extra words. No unseemly behavior.

She was responsible for what was in her handbag, she said, "but I was *not* responsible for the document on the Amtorg Trading Corporation . . . And God knows how many decoys and all kinds of frame-ups you have put in this case! I was not responsible for that! Mr. Foley was responsible for that . . . From every single thing he says, as far as I am concerned, he has told a tissue of lies . . . about this internal security, the foreign agents. He said he took me off. Maybe he thinks now he should have taken me off, and he did not do it adequately, according to you people . . . He gave an impression that I had no authority to look at these reports. I certainly had authority to look at these reports . . .

"His whole statement on the top secret . . . That consists of what? Consists of material from newspaper files. A real top secret report, yes," she cried.

"All your decoy—this custodial detention, why did he tell me about that? Why did he tell me about all of these things? What kind of bait were you trying to use? What did you think he was doing? Weren't you happy? . . . If that isn't entrapment, I don't know what that is.

"If this whole thing isn't a frame-up—why did all the FBI agents say they didn't know I was going to be arrested? It is ridiculous on the face. *Of course* they knew I was going to be arrested. Mr. Whearty was going into New York. What for? Mr. Mendenhall was going into New York. What for? Mr. Granville told that woman that held me while they stripped me, he told her to stay there and act as a matron. How did they know? Through tapped phone wires, or because Gubitchev was some sort of plant or counter-espionage agent, used to trap me in some sort of way? I don't understand this whole case. All I know is I have been framed," she ended with a final wail, then leaned back in her chair, head shaking back and forth in disbelief.

Relentless, merciless, Kelley asked Judy once again if she alone was responsible for the materials found in her purse. The court upheld her earlier response; she already had answered the question.

Kelley turned to Palmer with a huge sigh. "I give you back your witness." The witness he gave back was not the one he had received from Palmer.

Back on direct examination, a clearly shaken Archie called Arthur Shimkin, who had been a high school friend of Judy's and who worked at Simon & Schuster. Shimkin said yes, Judy had called him to discuss some writing she was doing, although not specifically about a book. They spoke of meeting, but never got together.

Judy was indeed branded a spy and a harlot by now. Few had doubts that she would soon have a new label—"felon." What escaped the notice of most was that even now, at the end of nine weeks, there was not a single shred of direct evidence that she had ever passed secrets to her Russian friend or, in fact, that she had ever intended to do so. Except for hotel receipts, every bit of evidence was circumstantial.

And, of course, there were Judy's valid questions about a frame-up. (The authors are in vehement disagreement on this issue.) By whatever name, however, some of the people Kelley named had been building something from scratch, and it wasn't a flower box.

Fame had come to Judith Coplon with its attendant miseries, chief among them a total lack of privacy. Instead of becoming bored with Judith, the country grew more fascinated day by day, and the press, fully aware of this fact, was becoming increasingly intrusive. Joining reporters and photographers as they camped outside her hotel and followed her every move were ever more autograph seekers and, as always, the simply curious. The everyday act of getting into a taxi, normally much less challenging in Washington than in New York, became an exhausting struggle, both physically and emotionally. This horrible day, the end of the case for the defense, concluded with Judy nearly in hysterics, although she would later claim she had never "broken." Together, Judy and her weeping mother ran the gauntlet of shoving press and public, finally managing to climb into a taxi and head for the Willard Hotel. Another crowd was on the sidewalk when they arrived, and another bout of pushing and shoving ensued before they could reach the door. Hotel staff tried to help, but to little avail. Mother and daughter, desperately holding on to each other, hurried inside and into immediate seclusion. Judy would mark this as a red-letter day in her year of Hell.

End Games

Monday, June 27: Rebuttal

Another motion filed by Archie Palmer for dismissal of charges based on "entrapment and lack of evidence" was quickly denied by Judge Reeves. Rebuttal witnesses were called, and Judith's former supervisor William Foley, along with lawyer coworkers Nathan Lenvin and Harold Koffsky, took the stand for the prosecution.

Foley categorically denied that he had ever instructed Judy to make a note about the Amtorg decoy letter and take it with her to New York. Absolutely a lie, he said. In cross-examination, Archie took a different tack, charging at Foley, demanding, "You know Harold Shapiro, don't you?" Archie quickly garnered two admissions. One, that Foley and Shapiro were friends who had at one time roomed in the same boardinghouse, and, two, that they played cards together.

Koffsky, who identified himself as a friend of Judy's, denied her claim that she had at one time told him of Foley's speaking to her about a top-secret report. "Miss Coplon never mentioned a top-secret report to me," he said.

In her earlier testimony, Judy claimed that she had told Lenvin about her boyfriend at the UN, someone she was seeing during her trips to New York. Not so, Lenvin now said in his direct rebuttal. She had never breathed a word about any friend at the UN. In cross, Archie went after Lenvin with the same queries about Shapiro. Oh yes, Lenvin freely admitted, they were good friends, card-playing buddies. Archie asked Lenvin about Koffsky. Wasn't he also a part of the card-playing cabal, Palmer wanted to know? Yes, indeed, said Lenvin. Not only cards, but Koffsky also played squash with Shapiro. It all sounded very cozy to Archie.

"Objection," Kelley fumed, insisting that Archie had no right to pursue this line of questioning. Shapiro's name had not been mentioned in direct rebuttal, Kelley said, meaning Archie was out of line in raising the issue in cross-examination. Reeves sustained and instructed Archie to drop the subject. One can only wonder at this change of tactic on the judge's part. The man who was allowed to introduce new topics at will, to waste hours with questions about literature, the defendant's teeth, or an agent's previous work experience, was suddenly told to keep quiet. The elderly judge, seeing the light at the end of this miserable tunnel, was not about to let Archie regain control of the proceedings.

All three former coworkers denied Judy's statements and called her a liar. She sat calmly, demurely, listening, not reacting. She was dressed in red-checked gingham and looked particularly young and vulnerable.

Testimony in the trial of Judith Coplon ended without the jury hearing from the two men who played such prominent roles in the case, Valentin Gubitchev and Harold Shapiro. Either could have shed revealing light on the love-versus-espionage issue, which, one would surmise, is precisely why neither was called.

Testimony was finally over. Tomorrow, the jury would hear three closing statements, two from the prosecution and one from the defense. Judy Coplon's day of judgment was fast approaching.

Tuesday, June 28: Closing Arguments, Mr. Whearty

Of all the characters in the Coplon case, none was more enigmatic than Raymond Whearty. Few who observed his reserved demeanor in the courtroom, who noted how unfazed he appeared by Archie Palmer's persistent invective against him, were aware of the suffering and personal torment this case brought to the prosecutor. He seemed all business, sometimes—as in his opening statement—to the point of being tedious, even boring. Although on two occasions he had argued heatedly for increased bail, Whearty showed strong emotion only on very rare occasions during the course of the trial. Even during Judith's damning words about his hating the loyalty program, he remained calm, stolid, resolute. From time to time, if one caught him in an unguarded moment, it was possible to discern the conflict that raged within.

At the beginning, he was disbelieving. Not Judy. Not a young woman he was admittedly fond of, a friend, a trusted colleague. A protégée of sorts. No, Whearty had said, I cannot participate in this case. He declined involvement in her prosecution and asked to be excused from the case. But the government insisted that he be a part of the team to prosecute Judy, that he "do his duty" as the government myopically saw it. That duty was to put his personal feelings aside and go about the business of convicting Judith Coplon of espionage. A problem for Whearty had to do with the nature of the business.

From disbeliever to believer, from friend to foe, Whearty traveled the road in painful style. At some point, he apparently reached an accommodation of sorts with his conflicted feelings about Judy. Surely there was solace in the anger he felt, a personal anger, for betrayal not only of country, but also of Raymond Whearty. Yet there were those moments when he turned away from the scene in front of him, his solemn face revealing overwhelming sadness. It was different for the relentless Kelley, unhampered by remnants of personal feelings for the Coplon woman. Ironically, it was Whearty who took the brunt of Archie's accusations for instigating the case against Judy, for setting out to entrap her, for forming a conspiracy to destroy the "innocent little girl."

Whearty's closing comments would come first today, and he was well prepared. Indicating that the prosecution was ready, he rose slowly and approached the jury. The courtroom was silent, waiting. Archie Palmer and his client sat side by side, Archie toying with a pencil, Judy motionless, watching her former friend with undisguised bitterness.

"Ladies and gentlemen," Whearty began, "we've come a long way—ten weeks in a trial we thought would last ten days. Now we have come to that part of a case to which every lawyer looks forward—looks forward with anticipation and some apprehension." He paused. "This is a deadly serious case. This is the first case in which an employee of the Department of Justice has been charged with a crime of this sort."

Whearty spread his hands on the polished rail in front of him and cast his eyes from one juror to another. "It is deadly serious to the Government and to the defendant. It is not a laughing matter. It is not a farce," he said, glancing over his shoulder at Archie Palmer. Serious words, spoken so softly those in the back of the room were straining to hear. How different this manner, this ambience from that which had prevailed here the past ten weeks. This gentle gentleman, speaking softly, was an incongruity.

Each paper Judy had with her the night of March 4, Whearty told the jury, had been "taken." This, of course, was misleading, as neither her own biographical sketch nor the three character sketches of the Sinderbrands and

Stevenson were taken from anywhere but her own mind. The data slips were taken from the Justice building, and information was taken in the form of papers she created, the Michael Memorandum and the Amtorg note. But it was not true that all of the papers found in Judy's purse were "taken."

"So," he said, "the case narrows down to an operation of the mind—what was her purpose in taking them?"

It was not, Whearty explained in painstaking detail, for a single one of the various purposes the defense had claimed. It was not for the purpose of preparing herself for a civil service examination, or for use in a novel she was allegedly writing. It was not to comply with instructions from Foley to read a secret memorandum and summarize it in a handwritten note to be carried to New York for study. These purposes, Whearty said, were "silly," "ridiculous," "false and fictitious." They were the stuff of "hocus-pocus."

Still without raising his voice, without any of the dramatics the spectators had come to expect, Whearty cited his own conclusion regarding the intended purpose for each piece of evidence found in Judith's purse. That single purpose, beyond a shadow of doubt, was espionage. It was to deliver to the Soviets the information contained in every one of those papers. No other reason was credible.

Speaking gently, Whearty told the jurors, "This is a matter for your conscience. I have never yet asked a jury to find a defendant guilty. I have asked a jury only to do that which before their God and their conscience they can justify—and I ask this jury to do that."

Jurors were clearly moved by Whearty's closing. They had listened intently, had taken in every word. Raymond Whearty was believable. He had behaved like a gentleman, and a gentleman wouldn't lie. As for the defendant, she had alternated between looking at the enemy and staring off into space, twisting a strand of hair around her finger, distancing herself from the speaker and his audience.

Closing Arguments, Mr. Palmer

The center ring was dressed for Archie Palmer, the air charged with excitement, the spectators sitting forward in their seats, respectfully silent, waiting for the act to begin. And no one doubted that it would be an act, that what they were about to witness would be a performance of extraordinary greatness, filled with brilliant color and pageantry. Archie did not disappoint. It was his finest hour. More to the point, his finest ninety minutes.

The volatile defense attorney bounced up and down and tripped along the jury box, as always waving his arms, gesturing, pointing, pounding on the jury rail; at times, causing startled jurors to jerk back in their seats or even, on a few occasions, to duck from what they likely thought would be at least the defense attorney's arm, if not his entire body, vaulting over the rail and into the box. He sang, he shouted, he sobbed, and he shrieked. It was high color, and the audience, except for the prosecution, savored every moment of Archie Palmer's closing.

"Friends and neighbors," he began from his podium on the clerk's platform, "I read to you from St. Matthew." Opening his Bible, he recited, "Judge not that ye be not judged. For with what judgment ye judge, ye shall be judged; and with that measure ye mete, it shall be measured to you again." His voice had taken on the resonance and style of an evangelical preacher the final night of the annual tent meeting. He was speaking of God and man and sin and forgiveness. His audience was transfixed. "And why beholdest thou the mote that is in thy brother's eye, but considerest not the beam that is in thine own eye?"

Solemnly, Archie turned to the jury. "I came here to defend a poor girl whose family I've known for years." But, Archie wondered aloud, would the jury do the right thing by this poor girl, or would the fact that some of the jurors worked for the government make them incapable of rendering a fair decision? Governments could do wrong, he let them know. Tenderly, he closed his Bible and walked to the defense table, where he deposited the Holy Book with a fond pat on the cover.

Skipping a few centuries, Archie continued. "Abraham Lincoln said you couldn't fetter men's thoughts. George Washington Carver said you couldn't fetter men's thoughts. When you fetter men's souls you make them slaves. That's what they do in Germany and Russia. It's what the Wheartys and the Kelleys are trying to do here when they fight a little girl like this."

Voice booming now, Archie yelled, "The half-truths they want to bury this girl with and put another nail in her coffin of fate." Coffin of fate? And wasn't something missing in this statement? Some were confused, but no one seemed to mind.

Off the podium and up to the jury box, leaning forward into a juror's face, Archie screamed, "You! Juror Number Seven!" Poor Number Seven, eyes wide, twisted in his seat. "They used the words 'in fornication' and they used them in front of her mother! It means plain sleeping together." Turning toward the press table, eyes narrowed, finger waggling, he stormed, "The papers in this city lied and they're sitting there." Juror Number Seven nodded. It seemed the right thing to do.

Leaving the jury box for the moment, Archie leaped up on the witness chair and waved his arms in his trademark gesture. The audience tensed. An important point was certain to follow. "I am proud to present to you not the United States versus Judith Coplon, but Judith Coplon against the United States of America." He told the jury that although prosecutors had expected her to confess, Judith Coplon did not. Instead, she did the right thing, she fought back. "People have admired her courageous struggle against the python snakes in the hands of the two trainers, Kelley and Whearty." The prosecutors sat quietly, staring straight ahead, never reacting, never looking at each other or making comments, even as Archie spoke of the two as "whipping their pythons out!" Indeed, Judith was a "fresh and fragrant innocent" and the prosecutors "pythons seeking to strangle her soul and ruin her reputation."

Now out of the witness box and bounding onto the floor, Archie called the prosecutors "ravening wolves" and "bloodhounds." The attorney's voice was in a constant rebound against the dark wood-paneled walls, filling the courtroom, where only one other sound could be heard, and only during those rare seconds when Archie paused for breath. It was the background piece scored for the performance, the pitiful dirge of Rebecca's wailing.

There was a conspiracy behind Judith Coplon's arrest, Archie insisted. At the center of the evil web was Raymond Whearty, who used Judith to "feed the personal glory of this Nero," Whearty, the man who "would be Attorney General and, ultimately, President of the United States." Judith was an innocent pawn in Whearty's grand scheme. But Kelley also received an epithet from history. "Mr. Kelley is standing in front of you like the Hero of Thermopolae."

Wanting to make certain that the jury was still focusing on the key issue, Archie charged at them with, once again, "Judge not lest ye be judged."

"If this happened in Germany or Russia, we'd want to hang from the housetops the people who did it . . . the Whearty's who framed her, the agent provocateur." Gesturing toward the defendant, Archie said, "There's a girl who's been under his wing . . ." Judy had been his protégée, his friend, and he had become "so cold, so glacial . . . that by comparison an iceberg would be a desert."

In a quieter voice, as he looked around the room, "We're just the little people." On the other hand, he noted, there was the FBI. "In every door, in every window, is the eye of the FBI."

From the FBI, Archie turned to Christ, his voice rising to a fevered pitch. "By reason of His sufferings, when Christ suffered, the world got religion. By the sufferings of this girl, the lot of government employess will be improved. Even the FBI will be cleansed. Beware," he hollered at the top of his lungs. "Beware! Under the old law, women caught in adultery would be stoned in the public place until Christ wrote in the sand." He dropped to the floor and traced the words with his finger, "'Let ye who be without sin throw the first stone.'"

In the event Kelley and Whearty failed to get the message, Archie clamored to his feet, pointed an accusing finger at them, and said ominously, "Judge not lest ye be judged!

"I won't even go into the psychology that love has nothing to do with fornication. Fornication! That fancy word conceived in the brain of Mr. Kelley! You decent people," he screamed, "are you willing to send this girl to jail and her mother to Hell and damnation and not to Heaven?" Eyes turned to Mrs. Coplon, who shrank in horror.

Archie went to the jury box and now favored Juror Number Eleven with his bombastic attention. Why, he demanded did the government feel the need to disclose Judith's personal relationship with Harold Shapiro? "Why didn't Shapiro come here and say he was not in love with this girl? They didn't call him because they didn't want to defile the Department of Justice, but they smeared her with pitch and tar that can never be eradicated." Number Eleven, as had Number Seven, nodded in agreement.

Satisfied, Archie leaned against the jury rail and refreshed himself with a few mints. "If they had brought Shapiro here he would have had to testify she had never slept with him." By now, with the new supply of mints already grinding away, Archie had a rim of white at the corners of his mouth and on his lips. It gave him the disquieting appearance of frothing at the mouth.

Upping the volume, Archie spun around to confront the jury as a whole. "This lover was no young Lochinvar out of the West. This Shapiro, he was not a good fellow." Ah, Shapiro, a dangerous kiss-and-tell betrayer, gave information to the government, which led to those filthy lies about Judy told by the vile prosecutors, Archie explained. At no time had the defense admitted to a sexual relationship with Shapiro, only to having been in his presence overnight.

"Shapiro wanted this girl but didn't have the key," Archie said. Poor Judith, trusting, caring, had been sold down the river by the prosecution team, by Kelley and Whearty in the courtroom and by Harold Shapiro in the bedroom.

As for Gubitchev, "the man of her dreams," here was real love. "He was the man who filled the niche in her empty heart. She loved him and that can be shouted from the housetops, even though they try to drag love in the mire."

As he neared the end of his performance, Archie closed his eyes, becoming blind Justice, scales in hand. He quoted from Omar Khayyám: "The moving finger writes and having writ moves on." He reminded the audience once again that "you and I are the common people," that God, who takes care of the little sparrow, will take care of His own. He made a final attack on the enemy, speaking briefly of William Foley: "Foley, you saw him, that fat, oozing face of his, his leering face . . ."

Archie Palmer concluded his closing remarks with the Thirty-fifth Psalm. "Oppose, Lord, those who oppose me; war upon those who make war upon me. Take up the shield and buckler, rise up in my defense . . . Let those who seek my life be put to shame and disgrace. Let those who plot evil against me be turned back and confounded. . . ."

Judith's fate was placed in the hands of the jury. "I told you at the beginning I'm turning over to you the soul of this little girl. Go thou! Do as you would be done by." With a slight bow, Archie turned and walked back to his seat after having delivered, arguably, the strangest closing in America's judicial history.

Closing Arguments, Mr. Kelley

He stood nearly a foot taller than the whirling dervish who had preceded him. Now John Kelley placed himself a mere two feet from Palmer, looming over his opponent as he began his summation before a hushed audience. No one had moved during the recess between Archie's closing and Kelley's. No one wanted to risk losing a seat or missing a single word.

"Your Honor, Judge Reeves, my esteemed and cultured friend Mr. Palmer, my associates, ladies and gentlemen of the jury," he began, turning to face the twelve men and women who would decide the fate of Judith Coplon. Esteemed and cultured friend! Archie sizzled.

"My function," Kelley said, "is to rebut against my adversary. I find it difficult, not because of what he has said, but the way he has said it—flitting about like a woodpecker in a storm." His voice, now scornful, boomed, "All the venom that can be brought up from an evil man has appeared in this trial!" Palmer blanched, then reddened as the prosecutor turned and glared down at him. "He dug deep to find epithets sufficient to describe myself and my associates, to tell you we had betrayed our trust, had taken part in a conspiracy to frame this defendant." He looked down at Palmer as if he were something other than a human being, something more like a malodorous fungus growing out of the defense table.

"If you believe that, ladies and gentlemen," Kelley nodded to the jury, "in Heaven's name acquit her and go directly to a grand jury and indict us. This tale of hate and passion charging everyone from the Attorney General on down in a 'plot' to frame the defendant! Challenging the integrity of everyone who had anything to do with this case!" Moving to the jury box, he leaned toward the jurors, who sat transfixed by this imposing man of the law. "In his invective so freely hurled against Mr. Whearty and myself, Mr. Palmer reached the heights. He took liberties seldom taken with a fellow barrister."

If Archie was stunned by the bitterness of Kelley's words, the spectators were even more so. In an atmosphere of palpable hatred, they watched Kelley rail against the opposing attorney. Known for his cool and reserved demeanor, Kelley was clearly succumbing to a passion much like that he excoriated. Ten weeks of anger had festered, and the sore was raw.

"He described the hate he said he found in my face. He said we took liberties which, if they had been taken in Germany and Russia, we would have been hanged. I wonder what would have happened to Judith Coplon if she had been in Russia and had betrayed Russia! Mr. Archibald Palmer," Kelley sneered, "has done a splendid job of trying everybody but the defendant.

"They're all out of step but Judy," he yelled. "*Everyone* is a liar but Judy!

"Why wouldn't she look at you, the jury, when I asked her to? Why did she insist on looking at me? 'Look at your jury,' I kept repeating. But she would not. Why? Because"—he paused—"because somewhere in her face it would show that she wasn't telling the truth."

Referring to Judy's outburst the previous week, he said, ". . . from her came the greatest stream of invective I've ever heard from womankind."

Hate. It would now be attributed to the defendant. The Russians, he said, found in Judith Coplon a girl who hated the U.S. government. A very clever girl into the bargain, and oh, the Russians knew how clever she was!

"I would like to pay tribute to the skill, the cunning and the dead earnestness of Russian espionage agents in the United States . . . they know what they want. Don't think they picked Judith Coplon hastily. They took their time about it. . . ." The Russian agents penetrated Judith's "veneer of innocence" and were not fooled by her "pretty face." Ah, Kelley said, no truer words were ever spoken than Archie's: "Judith Coplon against the Government."

"They found precisely what they wanted. They found a girl instilled with hate against the United States and willing to sell out her country. A girl with courage of a kind, a girl who wouldn't be frightened in dark alleys." And now, at full volume, he shouted, "They found a clever spy!"

The clever one sat listening intently, but not reacting outwardly. Kelley did not look at her as he continued. "When she was released on bond, that clever, agile little mind like a Swiss watch went to work, aided by a counsel equally clever." Another look of disgust shot at Palmer, who glared back with equal repugnance. Where Whearty had gone item by item over every piece of evidence found in Judy's purse on March 4 and dismissed any and all innocent reasons for its presence, Kelley took a far different tack.

"She figured out her explanations for these things in her purse. 'The data slips?'" He piped in a falsetto imitation of Judith. "'What'll I do about those?

Got it! I'll say I was going to take a civil service exam. This'"—he reached for the Michael Memorandum—"'is going to take a little more trouble. I can't say that was a civil service exam. Got it! I'll write a book . . . but they've got my Corona now, the FBI . . . I'll say I destroyed the book. I've got everything now.'"

Posturing before the jury, Kelley was Judy again. "'And then my lawyer's talking entrapment. So I'll go after old whipping boy Foley again. I'll say he ordered me to take the notes on that decoy to New York.'"

In his entire career, stylish John Kelley had never before been so undignified, so nasty, so vicious. The expected panache was gone, replaced by histrionics. Kelley, who had decried Archie's antics throughout the trial, now stormed and shouted and mimicked the young woman he was prosecuting. And said unprofessional things about a fellow attorney. Kelley had lost it.

There was the matter of Judy's claim to meeting Gubitchev because she was in love with him, and of Kelley's having revealed Judy's overnight assignations with Harold Shapiro. The government, according to Kelley, would never have revealed Judy's sexual exploits without good cause.

"You may be sure," Kelley charged, "that the visits to the hotels, the visit New Year's Eve in a friend's apartment . . . also the visits to Shapiro's apartment on R Street, would not have been brought out by me if Judith Coplon had not said she loved Gubitchev.

"Since Mr. Palmer brought up Mr. Shapiro again, I also must go into it again," Kelley said. "The defendant slipped up when she said she never slept on the nights in Baltimore and Philadelphia hotels, and her attorney slipped up on another important point. He kept asking why we did not bring Mr. Shapiro to the stand. He implied Mr. Shapiro could not have answered on grounds he might incriminate himself under the Mann Act. But if his client told the truth, that they only talked on the nights in question, why would Mr. Shapiro incriminate himself?"

Wound tightly, Kelley pounded on. "When these facts were brought out, Miss Coplon screamed a denial. 'Oh, no, I was there,' she said, 'but there was no fornication. I never slept or lay down,' she said." If everything was on the up and up, Kelley wondered, why didn't Judy simply lie down and sleep in comfort?

Finally reaching the point of his argument, Kelley announced that the "sole importance" of the testimony about her relations with Shapiro "was to prove she was lying in her teeth when she told you she was head over heels in love with Gubitchev. If you find she has lied about Gubitchev, then all other reasons given for her meetings with him can be disregarded."

The link between espionage and fornication was thus solidified. Neither Kelley nor anyone else seemed to entertain, even for a moment, the possibility that Judy could have been in love with Gubitchev and in lust with Shapiro, that she might have been having relations with two men.

Moreover, the prosecutor was speaking disingenuously. Make no mistake: The government did not tail Judith Coplon to Baltimore and Philadelphia, did not monitor her stays in Shapiro's apartment, simply to pass the time of day. If they had not intended to use the information against her, Judy's romantic escapades would not have been so meticulously reported. Further, the government would not have pressured one of its own, Harold Shapiro, to reveal what happened behind closed doors with Judith unless it had good reason to do so. The government planned to play the sex card from the very beginning. But now, to the members of his audience assembled in the Foley Square courtroom, Kelley was successful in conveying the impression that, ever so reluctantly, he had been forced to embarrass the defendant with such sordid revelations.

Because Judy "told the monstrous lie," the prosecutor said, "it became my duty to bring these facts before you. I did not enjoy it. Defense counsel charges that we killed Miss Coplon's father, that we are imperiling her mother. Why didn't Judith Coplon think of her mother when she was standing in the lobby of a hotel in Baltimore waiting for Shapiro?" Kelley asked the jury. "Why didn't she think of her mother when she was in Shapiro's apartment?" And, finally, the worst of all:

"Why didn't she think of her mother when she sold out her country!" he thundered.

Kelley paced, then studied his hands.

"And now she would have you believe that she was cornered into this in some kind of conspiracy. She would have you believe Shapiro was part of a conspiracy starting with the Attorney General; and, fantasy of all fantasies of this seven-headed defense, is the suggestion that Gubitchev himself is a counter-agent working for the FBI!" A slow walk to the jury rail, and now, more composed, Kelley calmly addressed his final comments to the jury.

"The government has been pictured to you as a horrible ogre. It's your government. The government of the people of the United States. I represent the people of the United States. On their behalf, I ask you to find this woman guilty."

Of the three closings, Raymond Whearty's was the most substantive, the most reasonable, the most compelling. With great aplomb and sound professionalism, he had discussed the evidence and argued the case. Ultimately he made sense. Both Palmer and Kelley were so vitriolic, so angry and emotional, that neither effectively addressed the evidence, the issues, or the arguments. For Palmer, it was a case of modus operandi; for Kelley, it was an astounding aberration. In any event, if the closing was far from the textbook ideal, it was unquestionably fabulous entertainment.

Wednesday, June 29: The Case Goes to the Jury

The historic and tumultuous Coplon case went to the jury at twelve minutes after eleven o'clock this day, following Judge Albert Reeves's solemn charge to the jury. His instructions were detailed and precise, consuming some twenty typewritten pages of the trial's official transcript.

Throughout, Judith Coplon sat unmoving and unmoved, clad in a simple skirt and blouse. Her mother, as usual a study in black, wept softly from the moment Reeves's gavel sounded until the jurors left the courtroom.

In his charge, Reeves repeatedly differentiated between the "law" of the case and the "facts" of the case. "With the law of this case the jury has nothing to do," he told them. "On the other hand, with the facts of the case I have nothing to do." To aid, but not to control their judgment, he would review the evidence and express opinions "upon the evidence" as he remembered it. His memories and opinions might differ from theirs, in which case they were to rely not on his observations, but their own. However, everything that he might say to them regarding the *law* was binding upon them.

He commented on the "apparent friction in this prolonged trial and probably many irritations," asking them to forget that sort of unpleasantness.

Before getting to the law and the facts of the case, Reeves spoke about the preamble to the Constitution, congressional establishment of an intelligence service "known as the Federal Bureau of Investigation," and the duties of that agency. He talked about national security.

Reeves reviewed the entire case, its facts, and its evidence, from the grand jury indictment to the testimony and arguments presented. He reviewed the documents found in Judith's possession the night of March 4, and the conflicting reasons for their presence as presented by the prosecution and the defense. Intent was a significant issue, as was entrapment. If the government caused her to be accused, this would indicate entrapment, and the jury should return a verdict of not guilty.

"In considering the question whether the defendant had a purpose to deliver documents, data slips, and papers in her possession to the person named, Valentin A. Gubitchev, a Russian national, you will take into consideration all the circumstances attending her meeting with him on January 14th, February 18th, and March 4th, 1949, the places where they met, and their actions at such meetings," he instructed.

Jurors could find the accused not guilty or guilty of one or both counts of the indictment.

Observers were shocked by the dramatic change in Judy following the jury's exit. As usual, she hurried to her distressed mother, and, holding her tightly, led her to the elevator. Most unusual was Judy's obvious terror, her grief, her weeping openly and desperately. Gone was the stalwart young woman of the past several weeks. The elevator arrived, Rebecca Coplon entered alone, the doors closed, and Judy stood for several moments staring straight ahead, like a lost child left behind. Never before had she publicly exhibited such pain. But when Judy turned, there was a second amazing change. She was the "old Judy" once again, smiling, almost lighthearted. It was not the first, and would not be the last, occasion when people would wonder, "What makes her tick?"

A reporter asked if she would return to her old job if she were acquitted and she answered that she could not comment on the future. "I just can't let myself think of anything until this is over." She went back to the courtroom, where she refreshed her makeup and combed her hair. A U.S. marshal brought her two fat envelopes: "More crackpot letters," he told her.

One week after her March 4, 1949 arrest in New York, Judith returns to court for a second arraignment on charges that could mean life in prison, or death. Corbis Photo

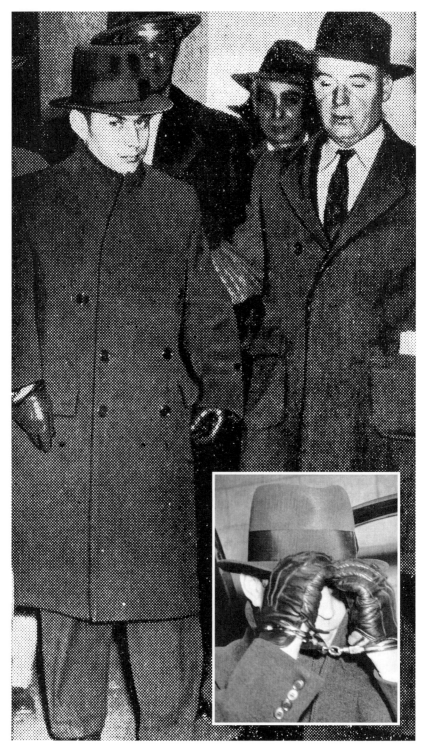

Arrested the night before, Valentin Gubitchev leaves the Federal Courthouse in Foley Square following his arraignment on espionage charges. Photo courtesy of the *San Francisco Examiner*
Inset: Gubitchev shields his face with manacled hands as he heads to court for his second arraignment. AP Photo

Gubitchev's passport used to enter the U.S. in 1946 — an intelligence officer in the guise of a Soviet engineer with responsibilities at the UN. National Archives and Records Administration, Northeast Division

July 1, 1949. Judith in her Washington D.C. hotel room reading news accounts of the jury's decision. Reporters followed her into her room and listened while she and Archibald Palmer, her lawyer, broke the news of her conviction to her mother. Corbis Photo

Judith and Palmer on July 1, 1949, surrounded by reporters at La Guardia Field following their return from the disastrous Washington trial. Corbis Photo

Palmer calls the Washington trial "a farce," and for two hours rages about his determination to appeal "everything." July 1, 1949. Corbis Photo

Judith prepares to make a recording of her voice for comparison with the hotly disputed recordings made by the government. With her are Palmer, and, at right, audio expert Robert Solvy. January 5, 1950. Corbis Photo

More popular than a film star and the media's darling for more than a year, Judith attracted crowds and autograph hunters wherever she went, including Foley Square. January 26, 1950. Corbis Photo

Judith with her ailing mother Rebecca in Palmer's office as the New York trial gets underway. January 28, 1950. Corbis Photo

Judith and her brother, Bertram, in court on the day she fired Palmer. Corbis Photo

Judith and her lawyer, Albert Socolov, marry on May 28, 1950. She has been released on bond but faces twenty-five years in prison. AP Photo

Judith and a jubilant husband/lawyer Socolov, after her New York spy conviction is set aside. December 5, 1950. Corbis Photo

Reissue(T212.1)

From: NEW YORK

To: MOSCOW

No: 27

8 January 1945

To VIKTOR[i].

SERGEJ's[ii] conversation with SIMA[iii] took place on [B% 4 January]. SIMA gives the impression of being a serious person who is politically well developed and there is no doubt of her sincere desire to help us. She had no doubts about whom she is working for and said that the nature of the materials in which we are interested pointed to the fact that it was our country which was in question. She was very satisfied that she was dealing with us and said that she deeply appreciated the confidence shown in her and understood the importance of our work.

SIMA's transfer to a new job was made at the insistence of her [D% superiors]

[64 groups unrecoverable]

generalizing materials from all departments [OTDELY]. SIMA will probably start work on 15 February.

On the basis of this preliminary information there is reason to assume that in her new job SIMA will be able to carry out very important work for us in throwing light on the activities of the KhATA[iv]. The fruitfulness of her work will to a considerable extent depend upon our ability to organize correct and constant direction. It should be remembered that SIMA from an operational point of view is quite undeveloped and she will need time to learn conspiracy and to correctly gain an understanding of the questions which interest us.

A final decision on the question of direction and liaison can be taken [B% only] after she has moved to CARTHAGE [KARFAGEN][v] when it will be ascertained [B% specifically] what her new job consists of.

No. 22   MAJ[vi]
    8 January
_____

Comments:
    [i]   VIKTOR: Lt. Gen. P. M. FITIN.
    [ii] SERGEJ: Vladimir Sergeevich PRAVDIN.
    [iii] SIMA: Judith COPLON.
    [iv] KhATA: The Federal Bureau of Investigation.
    [v]   KARFAGEN: WASHINGTON, D. C.
    [vi] MAJ: Stepan APRESYaN.

29 January 1974

Pravdin's meeting with SIMA, reported in this message to Moscow, reveals much about SIMA's commitment to helping the Soviets. Venona decrypt

Reissue (T212.2)

From: NEW YORK

To: MOSCOW

No: 992

26 June 1945

To VIKTOR[i].
    Your No.4195[a].
    After SIMA's[ii] transfer to CARTHAGE[iii], she was instructed to refrain from [C% removing] documents until she was quite sure that she was trusted. As you were advised earlier, on the advice of her superiors S. is studying the Russian language with the aim of [1 group unrecovered] a post in the department [OTDEL] of the CLUB[iv] which is investigating the actions of the USSR and the Communists. S. was given the task of studying the CLUB, its methods of work, the way in which documents are kept. On this matter S. [D% compiled]

[121 groups unrecoverable]

Notes:
    [a] Not available.

Comments:
    [i] VIKTOR: Lt. Gen. P.M. FITIN.

    [ii] SIMA: Judith COPLON.

    [iii] CARTHAGE: Washington, D.C.

    [iv] CLUB: Presumably the Department of Justice, or possibly a specific Division of the Department of Justice.

① Bureau using a highly
Amtorg offi...
D...

② a violation + any questions
which should be asked of N.
Ask if N. is registered as
foreign agent.
___Bureau has recently___
learned thru an informant
that Amtorg has been in
contact with the Geophysical
Research Corp re geophones.
The fact that these " are used
for the purpose of making
blast measurements at
Alamogordo + other testing
points is highly restricted
but Amtorg apparently must
have some knowledge of their
use.
II Bureau Memo, 3/3/49.

Judith's handwritten notes, made the night before her arrest, were based on Lamphere's decoy memorandum, "irresistable spy bait," set out by Peyton Ford. Mention of geophones was key to the government's charge of espionage. Washington National Records Center

Office Memorandum · UNITED STATES GOVERNMENT

TO : Mr. Peyton Ford
The Assistant to the Attorney General

DATE: March 3, 1949

FROM : Director, FBI

STRICTLY CONFIDENTIAL

SUBJECT: AMTORG TRADING CORPORATION
INTERNAL SECURITY - R

As supplementary to my memorandum to you dated January 27, 1949, regarding the Amtorg Trading Corporation, I want to call your attention to a recent development in this investigation which may be of potential significance in any prosecutive steps contemplated.

In the referenced memorandum, I mentioned that we are presently using on a confidential basis, as informants, two highly placed officials of the Amtorg Trading Corporation. One of these is Isidore Gibby Needleman, the Amtorg legal representative with whom we have been maintaining a rather indirect contact through an intermediary. We have not been entirely satisfied with this arrangement or the extent of the information being supplied by Needleman and for that reason, in order to check on his sincerity, we desire to obtain from him more complete information on a variety of matters including his knowledge of the activities of the Amtorg Trading Corporation which would be in possible violation of the Foreign Agents Registration Act.

We would, therefore, appreciate your making available to us a memorandum outlining your views on what would constitute a violation on the part of this Corporation and any questions you think should be asked of this individual. We would also like to know if Needleman is registered as an agent of a foreign principal.

I have previously furnished you information concerning the efforts of the Amtorg Trading Corporation to obtain equipment relative to atomic research developments. In this connection, this Bureau has recently learned through an informant that the Amtorg Trading Corporation has been in contact with the Geophysical Research Corporation concerning geophones to measure blast pressures which this company manufactured in small quantities for the original bomb test at Alamogordo. The fact that these geophones are used for the purpose of making blast measurements at Alamogordo and other testing points, is highly restricted but apparently the Amtorg Trading Corporation must have some knowledge of the use of these instruments.

The above represents another example of the security risk present in the activities of this Corporation. We are continuing our investigation of this Corporation in an effort to determine whether Amtorg is sending out of the United States information and equipment relative to our atomic research.

William Foley's insistence that he believed in the authenticity of this memorandum, subject of Judith's notes and the suspicious "missing conversation," influenced the course of both Coplon trials. National Archives and Records Administration, Northeast Division

BELLE-SHARMEER

leg-size stockings for leg-wise women

Belle-... ...always are full fashioned, not only in the leg and ankle but
in th... ...ns why Belle-Sharmeer stockings are full
Th... ...shioned machines:
fas... ...ly the finest stockings
It... We believe that

Irina (Iraida) Efimovna Aleksander, was
Bozhidar Kossimir Aleksander, was

This report predicated on info received from I-1 that subjects (especially
Irina), were extremely friendly with officials of Russian Consulate, NYC.
On 9/29/45, Irina conferred with Mikhailov, at Consulate, stating that she
wanted him to know that she was always ready to help him as much as she
could and in whatever way he might require. (Bureau emphasis).

(24) 3/4/47...

#Murphy, NYC, 5/29/46, Re: IEA etc., Int. Sec.-R, Refer 5 IS
****
Bernard Koten, Research Director of American Russian Institute, is
friend and contact of William Hermann Eckart Johnson and his wife Annette F.,
Johnson, who are employed at present on the Secret Russian Desk of the
War Dpt, Washington, DC and who are suspected of giving out info to the
NKVD.

#Murphy, 9/5/46
****
Additional data received re subject Irina further indicating she may
be Russian espionage agent. One anonymous letter indicates she acted as

SUBJECT NO.	NAME OF ...		
DOC. NO.	DOC. DATE	PAGES - LINES	

Stuart Legg—possible Russian espionage agent.

SUBJECT NO.			
DOC. NO.	DOC. DATE	PAGES - LINES	

In March 1946, subject had in her address book the name of Ruth ...
has been reported to have been ... a contact of F.A. Garanin of the ...
Embassy, Wash. Gruber was secretary to Harold Ickes, ... Secy of Interior.

#O'Brien, NY, 11/12/38, Re: Ursula Wasserman, Int. Sec.-R

...harmeer *Stockings*
in all leg sizes
to fit all sizes of *legs*

YOUR FOOT-SIZE HAS A NUMBER — YOUR LEG-SIZE HAS A NAME

Data slips, hidden in a stocking wrapper sealed with cellophane tape, led to the historic
release of secret FBI files during the Washington trial. National Records Center

Tolson ✓

Ladd ✓

November 7, 1949

Memorandum for Mr. D. M. Ladd
From: H. B. Fletcher
Subject: Tiger

HBF

The above named informant has been furnishing information concerning the activities of Coplon since her conviction. <u>In view of the ~~immediacy~~ *IMMINENCY* of her trial, it is recommended that this informant be discontinued ~~immediately~~ *IMMEDIATELY* and that all administrative records in the New York office covering the operations of this informant be destroyed.</u> Pertinent data furnished by the informant has already been furnished in letter form, and having in mind security, now and in the future, it is believed desirable that the indicated records be destroyed.

O.K.
H.

HBF:tlc

(In print:) THIS MEMORANDUM IS FOR ADMINISTRATIVE PURPOSES. TO BE DESTROYED AFTER ACTION IS TAKEN AND NOT SENT TO THE FILES.

7269870

The infamous "Tiger" memorandum confirming previously denied bureau wiretapping and deliberate destruction of evidence. Meant to be destroyed, its shocking revelation dealt a serious blow to the prosecution's case. "O.K. H." indicates Hoover's approval. Tattered and taped, the memorandum survives in the New York archives.

Special Agent Thomas Mitchell, working Soviet counterintelligence during the Coplon years, on surveillance at the docked *Queen Elizabeth*.

The old Judy looked up and laughed. "I got one from a 59-year-old disabled veteran the other day. He wanted to marry me," she told the marshal. "I've gotten several letters asking me if I were interested in marriage."

Half an hour after leaving, the jury requested copies of the original FBI reports from which the data slips were taken, a massive amount of material that could not be delivered until two-thirty in the afternoon. Jurors were dismissed until the files could be retrieved. Judy left the courtroom as well, going for lunch at Harvey's on Connecticut Avenue, where journalists dutifully watched and later reported that she had clams on the half shell, chicken fricassee, spinach, boiled potatoes, and iced tea, a rather hearty lunch for a woman waiting to learn her fate. Ironically, most likely J. Edgar Hoover lunched there that same day, unnoticed in the quiet corner where he regularly dined with Clyde Tolson. A man driven by such habits, it was only much later, after Harvey's had the temerity to move from Connecticut Avenue, that Hoover switched his daily allegiance from Harvey's to the Mayflower Hotel. On Connecticut Avenue.

With more than two million words of testimony, and a multitude of documents to consider, jurors had their work cut out for them. Eleven hours after the case had been given to them, very late into the night, they asked for further instructions. Judge and attorneys returned to the courtroom to hear jury foreman Andrew Norford ask for a definition of *intent*. Reeves explained that jurors must find that Judy "purposely" took secrets with the intent to injure her country and to aid another country.

At 11:40 P.M., the jury was locked up for the night. The accused, who had appeared in good spirits throughout the evening of waiting, smiled and posed for news photographers. Judy took the opportunity to complain once again about being framed then, after a cheerful farewell to the reporters, took a taxi to her hotel, the mask firmly in place.

SEX DREW THE CROWD TO JUDY COPLON TRIAL was the headline for Frank Conniff's column of this day in the *New York Journal American*. "Sex, that funny thing, has once again proved its box-office value here at the Judith Coplon trial, where would-be spectators queued up as early as six A.M.," he wrote. The long lines were comprised mainly of females, he said, but there were males queuing up as well. Students studied textbooks as they stood in line. The reporter quoted "an elderly school-teacher type" as saying, "Every woman in Washington would be down here if she got the chance. Who would want to miss it?"

Conniff, who could see Judy "striding sexily down the aisle during a recess, a magnet for admiring glances from the governmental girls thronging the courtroom," called her animated and vibrant. "It was worth a six-hour wait to get a fleeting look at Judy," according to Conniff.

In its final edition of the day, the *Washington Daily News* ran a bulletin with the headline, U.S. DOESN'T PLAN TO PROSECUTE SHAPIRO. It reported that the government would not prosecute Harold Shapiro for violating the Mann Act by spending nights in Baltimore and Philadelphia hotel rooms with Judith Coplon. The Mann Act, which provides for penalties for taking someone across a state line for immoral purposes, requires a complainant. The reason the government would not prosecute, determined Alexander Campbell, head of the Department of Justice's Criminal Division, was "There's no complaining witness. We can't bring a charge without a complaining witness."

Further, the bulletin noted, Judith Coplon had denied that she and Shapiro had sexual relations during the occasions when they left Washington for Maryland and Pennsylvania. Dare one note the dissembling here? Department of Justice lawyers never would have prosecuted one of their own, a valued kiss-and-tell insider whose revelations saved a difficult case for them, sex or no sex. Not Kelley, not any of the DOJ legal team, believed Coplon and Shapiro spent those nights in platonic pleasure.

June 30: The Verdict

Judith Coplon arose early, after only four hours of fitful sleep, and was having breakfast when photographers arrived at seven-thirty. Not quite her usual pert self, she willingly posed for several photos at the table, then left for the courthouse and more picture taking. The media loved every moment this rainy summer morning, talking with Judith, watching, waiting, watching her waiting.

Judy's mood lightened as the hours wore on and rumors of a hung jury circulated throughout the building. A hung jury for Judy would be, she figured, tantamount to acquittal. Few thought the government, with the New York case ahead, would want to retry the Washington case, difficult as it had been.

"What do you think the jury will do?" a reporter asked shortly before noon, some twenty-four hours after jurors had left the courtroom.

"Archie told me not to think about the jury," the defendant responded. He grinned. "Can you truly say you're not thinking of that jury?"

Archie took Judy's arm. "Let's go to Harvey's for lunch," he suggested.

With a grimace, Judy said, "Oh, God, not again!"

"Don't like Harvey's?" the reporter asked.

"It's one of those restaurants men like."

Whether they liked Harvey's or not, it was where the press once again went to lunch, where, once again, they could watch and report on what Judy ate and what she drank (smoked turkey, a salad, and coffee) and record her every movement and mood. She was cheerful, they thought, almost happy, certainly far more relaxed than might have been expected. As for Archie, he told jokes throughout lunch, and Judy could be heard laughing, "a full-throated laugh."

One of the journalists approached the table with, "Judith, how have you been able to stand it all this time?"

"Time," she said, "loses all meaning in something like this. The days just run into each other." Then, looking at her watch, she said to Archie, "It's nearly two o'clock. Don't you think we should be going back to court?"

They were not even alone in the cab, where Archie continued to entertain a reporter. "This will give you a laugh," he said. "Listen—once there was a bankruptcy case I had, and in my inimitable way, I sidled forth and I told the judge, 'even a Persian kitten can look at a queen . . .'"

"Oh, my God, you can't stop him," Judy laughed.

Still laughing at Archie, Judy, with Archie following, went directly to the pressroom to continue waiting. At the door, a marshal rushed up to them with, "The jury's coming back."

"From lunch?" Archie inquired.

"No. They have a verdict."

Judy paled and Archie reached out to her, took her arm, and led her to the elevator. Neither said a word. With the announcement of the jury's return, the waiting crowd surged toward the courtroom doors, and marshals shouted, "Hold in line, hold in line!"

Judith Coplon and her attorney arrived together, he still holding her arm. They walked to the defense table, where she removed her black raincoat and settled back in her chair. She wore a black-and-green-checked dress and little makeup. Archie pulled out the chair beside her and sat down, reaching out to her. In turn, she stroked his face and smiled. He patted her hair, then put an arm around her shoulder. No one ever before had witnessed this sort of tenderness between the two.

John Kelley and Raymond Whearty arrived and took their seats, avoiding eye contact with Judith and Archie. The stage was set, with all the actors on their marks.

The gavel sounded, and Reeves cautioned spectators. "Now people, when the verdict is brought in, regardless of what it is, they'll be no demonstrations of any kind, no outbreaks."

The defendant sat motionless, her attorney stroking her hair, as the jury entered.

"Mr. Foreman, has the jury agreed upon its verdict?" the clerk asked Norford, a telephone company repairman.

"We have."

"What say you as to the Defendant, Judith Coplon, on Count 1 of the indictment?"

"Guilty."

"On count 2 of the indictment?"

"Guilty."

In a steady voice, Reeves said, "Members of the jury, your foreman says you find the defendant, Judith Coplon, guilty as indicated, and that is your verdict, so say you each and all?"

In unison, they replied "guilty."

All eyes went to Judy, who gave no satisfaction to those expecting a dramatic reaction. There was none, not a blink of the eye. She sat, chin in hand, motionless, her expression unchanged.

Archie rose, asking that the jurors be polled on each of the counts. He then raised questions about the judge's definition of *intent*, and about his client's bail and punishment. Reeves replied that this was not the time for dealing with such matters. He would discharge the jury, then hear what the attorney had to say.

Worried, Archie said, "I didn't know whether Your Honor was going to leave the bench."

Surprisingly, when the matter of Judy's remaining free on bond until sentencing was raised after the jury was discharged, Kelley responded, "The government has no objection."

Archie next asked that sentencing be deferred until completion of the New York case. Kelley opposed a delay of this length, saying, "The case in New York is a mere accusation. We are now dealing with a reality."

Ah, said Archie, he too was dealing with reality. He was not asking anything "excepting that the sword of Damocles, which, if Your Honor passes sentence now, will presently fall upon the girl. According to the ancient days they tell you if a drop of water falls on your head, one drop or two drops, you won't go crazy, but the continuous drop of water, as I recall one of the stories of Edgar Allen Poe, can drive you crazy." Surely poor Judge Reeves, after ten weeks of Archie Palmer, well understood the slow torture of an incessant annoyance.

Addressing the issue of bail, Palmer noted that Judy's bail was not furnished by any one friend but rather a great number of them who might now want their money back, making Judy unable to post bond. "The girl would have to go to prison, pending an appeal, unless bail would be continued in some fashion or another." The moment his client was sentenced, Archie said, she would lose her bail, be incarcerated in Washington, and unable to work on her defense in New York, where trial was scheduled in eleven days. Archie's plea became a lengthy and passionate speech. Let us get through New York, then we will return to Washington.

Kelley asked to make the government's position clear. "It is not the desire of the government that pending the trial of the case in New York, this defendant be confined. Her bond may continue. She shall be free to consult with counsel and to prepare in that case her defense." A compromise of sorts. Kelley wanted immediate sentencing, but bond continued to allow Judy to remain free until resolution of the New York case. "A jury has found this woman guilty. Let her be sentenced," he told the judge.

Before Reeves could respond, Archie said, "I will not rise on my hind legs and be pyrotechnical or attempt to be oratorical," whereupon he spoke of justice being what it is, and of the probability of trial errors that would have to be rectified. The debate continued, with the judge finally deciding not to decide. The question of timing would be taken up again in the morning.

Judith sat quietly throughout the discussion, distant, in a world of her own. Following Reeves's adjournment, Archie and his client gathered their belongings and prepared to leave the courtroom. Judy placed a Gideon Bible, the one Archie had used frequently during the trial, into her small valise. If Judy was silent, Archie was not. He was fuming and muttering about government workers illegally impaneled, about passion and prejudice, about appealing everything "from soup to nuts."

Leaving would not be easy today. Spectators pushed and shoved to catch a glimpse or to touch the convicted spy. Autograph seekers were vicious. Reporters demanded statements. "She has nothing to say," Archie told them, "she can't sing and she can't dance."

"No comment," Judy continued to say, until, "Really, it's silly isn't it? But I don't want to say anything." The media, with representatives not only from around the United States but also from abroad, were relentless.

"Look over here, Judy!" "Hey Judy, how about one for me!" "Hey Archie, put your arms around her." "Pat her on the cheek again, Archie!" When a cameraman yelled, "Come on, smile for me Judy, a great big smile," she answered, "Look, I'll pose for all of you, but please . . ."

"It's only a verdict," Archie told her as he put on his trademark hat. They would appeal. Judy would not go to jail. To the press he yelled, "She's got the guts, boys." Slapping her on the back, he repeated, "She's got the guts." He led her through the screaming throng and outside to where newsreel cameras waited on the lawn.

"Judith Coplon has told you people, yes, that she's innocent," Archie said to the cameras. "Today a jury found her guilty. No battle was ever won in the first round. We're taking this to the Circuit Court of Appeals," he promised. "Anyone who looks at her, talks to her, reads her face, knows she's innocent."

One of the newsreel cameramen was not satisfied. "Judy, say something," he pleaded. With Archie's permission, she made her first comment about the verdict. "The only thing I can say is that I'm innocent."

More pictures. Photograph after photograph was taken before Judith Coplon could escape the crowds and climb into a taxi with the help of her attorney. Flashguns caught her in the cab, Archie beside her, stroking her hair.

A solemn-faced Judy, with Archie at her elbow and the media at her heels, was followed into the hotel room she and her mother shared. Photographers pushed their way in, snapping photos of mother and daughter, listening to Judy and Archie break the tragic news to Rebecca, who had not been in the courtroom today. Fearing what the outcome would be, Judy had not wanted her mother to be present when the verdict was announced.

"Don't get hysterical, don't get hysterical," Archie cried, advice that had little effect on poor Rebecca. "How can I sleep tonight?" she wailed. Later, once her mother was quieted and resting, Judy and her lawyer went for a walk, stopping to peer into shop windows on F Street, where Judy saw a dress she liked. "I might buy that tomorrow, if I'm allowed to remain free on bail," she told Archie.

It is doubtful that any of the three slept this night.

One of Judy's jurors had not slept the night before. Mattie Taylor, a housewife, was the lone holdout for acquittal, standing firm for nearly twenty hours. Judy's fate was in her hands. "I couldn't sleep," Mrs. Taylor said the day the verdict was announced. "I was so upset. I am a Christian, and I wanted to do what was right." She held out until noon, when she finally agreed with her fellow jurors. It was she who had asked for further instructions about *intent*. The added instructions, she said, helped her change her opinion, something she insisted she had done on her own. "I wasn't going to let anybody tell me what to do," she explained.

Most jurors were convinced of Judy's guilt from the beginning of deliberations, but at least two, Mrs. Taylor and one other woman, initially were for acquittal. Juror John Pugh said that there was no discussion of guilt or innocence the first day. "We tried just to examine everything without making any decision." Several observers believed toy manufacturer Gould might feel a connection, might be sympathetic toward Judy. But Gould had no doubts from the very beginning. "I believed her guilty." Other jurors called Gould "the most learned one on the jury, the one who could talk best." For jurors, the key issue was the matter of intent. They believed Judy was not telling the truth when she declared that she had no intention of passing the information in her handbag to Valentin Gubitchev.

Said juror Henry Burrell, an employee of the Bureau of Printing and Engraving, "I think the verdict spoke for itself."

Friday, July 1: Sentencing and Return to New York

The new dress would have to wait. Instead of shopping this afternoon, Judy spent hours in a detention cell, waiting for her brother to post additional bail.

Bombastic Archie had arrived in court prepared to do battle, but he was outgunned from the outset by a hostile, vindictive John Kelley. Kelley, who had so readily agreed to Judy's remaining free until sentencing, and who implied he would have no objection to continuing the existing bond so that she could return to New York and prepare for her trial there, stunned both Archie and his client when he announced his new position.

"Since the proceedings of yesterday," the veteran prosecutor said, "I have been instructed, following sentence, to request that the defendant be held on $100,000 bond."

Archie let out a yell; Judith paled. "Your Honor said yesterday upon the record the girl could continue on her present bail," a wild-eyed Archie complained to the judge. "So that we can understand each other, Your Honor, yesterday it was said by Mr. Kelley in this Court, and it is upon the record, that the girl will not be hampered in connection with her defense . . ." Archie had been worried all along, he told the court, that Kelley might change his mind, might go back on what he had said in open court. Clearly, he implied, Kelley's behavior the day before had been nothing more than an act to please the public.

Kelley was adamant: one hundred thousand dollars, and nothing less. Over and over again, Archie insisted that maintaining the existing level of bond was difficult enough; to find additional money would be nearly impossible. And certainly impossible in the amount Kelley demanded. In essence, the agitated Archie said, the higher bond would mean his client would be jailed in Washington until time to appear for her New York trial. Not fair, he pleaded, implying that Kelley had deliberately misled the defense.

"We find out suddenly, a message came from somewhere, maybe from Mars, to the effect they want bail of $100,000. That is done for one purpose, to prevent the girl from trying her case in New York, to give her no chance, despite the hump upon her back today of a guilty verdict—a guilty verdict, with all due deference to the court, which is not justified by any evidence whatsoever."

Reeves called a halt to Archie's ranting. "If you have disposed of your preliminaries," he told him, "it is time for me to impose sentence." Before doing so, however, Kelley, Palmer, and Coplon would be allowed to speak. Kelley smugly declined.

Archie immediately called upon the judge to set aside the jury's verdict, citing several reasons for his motion, including a multitude of judicial errors made throughout the course of the trial. He went on at such length that the judge finally insisted Archie make his motion and be done with it. "Will you finish your motion without argument?" he snapped.

Saying that the case was tried, "in passion and in prejudice," and based on the reasons he had presented to the court, Archie asked the judge "to set aside the verdict of guilty and grant this girl a new trial." Immediately and predictably, Judge Reeves responded, "The motion is denied."

It was Judy's turn to speak. With deliberate calm, she approached the bench.

"Your Honor, I understand now that I could plead for mercy," she began. "That, I will not do, because pleading for mercy would mean an admission of guilt, and I have said from the very beginning, and I say it now, and I said it under oath from that stand," she nodded toward the witness chair, "that I am innocent. I am innocent before all the Wheartys and all the Kelleys and all the government, whatever they want to do against me. They may gloat in the glory of their hollow and Pyrrhic victory."

The convicted raised the issue of bond. "They have done everything to prevent me from meeting with my lawyer. They know I am a person of limited means. I can never make $100,000 bond." They wanted to break her, she told the court, but "they will never break me." She also insisted that media accounts of her becoming hysterical on the stand at the end of Kelley's cross-examination were grossly exaggerated.

"Mr. Kelley asked me who was in this conspiracy which I believed to be underfoot to frame me, and I told him, and I told him with the deepest indignation which I knew, but the newspapers said that I was hysterical.

"I wasn't hysterical then. I am not hysterical now, when I say I do not think I got a fair trial."

Was she through, Reeves wanted to know?

"That is all. I can keep on, saying the same things. I've said it all before, but this is something new, this $100,000."

Judge Reeves was irritated. He regretted that, in view of statements made this morning suggesting a lack of fairness, he found it necessary to review the evidence of the case. He began by meticulously detailing Judy's movements during her three meetings with Gubitchev. He reviewed every piece of the government's evidence, which he found compelling. Voice rising, he spoke of Judy's "glaring indiscretions in her association with a Russian national when her pocketbook bulged with government secrets." It did not seem to bother the judge that no one had seen Judy pass information to the Russian, or that there was no evidence that she had ever done so. Miss Coplon should have known better than to fool around with the enemy when she carried information that could prove helpful to a foreign country.

Reeves defended the legality of the arrest without warrant, which Archie had so strongly questioned. And he was most annoyed about the defending attorney's having kept Judy on the stand for three days when, the judge believed, Archie knew all along that his client was lying. Further, there was the matter of Archie's having taken over the prosecution's case and wasting weeks of the court's time.

"I question whether the courtesy and comity of this court ought not to be withdrawn from him, so he never again is permitted to appear in a case, either civil or criminal, in this jurisdiction," Reeves speculated in his scathing denunciation of Judith's counsel.

Most revealing were Reeves's heated personal observations about Judy. "She is twenty-eight years old, of a brilliant mind, graduated cum laude. She understands the conventionalities of America. Here she was running around, not only with a foreign agent . . . but, in addition to that he was *a married man* and she knew it! Here, where our conventions forbid that sort of thing! According to her own testimony, she *repeatedly* met him," a horrified Reeves complained.

The elderly judge continued his speech, to the total amazement of his audience. There was the tragic case of Benedict Arnold, a good man gone wrong. Reeves talked about the jury, the jury system, and the Coplon verdict, which was unquestionably correct. He spoke about Congress and what it had in mind regarding punishment of criminals. And, he said, despite suggestions to the contrary, he had been fair.

"I even went so far, at the instance [sic] of her attorney, and opened the files of the government, and even imperiled the government's best interests in doing it, in the interests of her fair trial."

More than one FBI agent present was groaning inwardly, wondering for the thousandth time why President Truman, a personal friend of Reeves, would have wanted this man on the bench for this particular trial.

Finally, the judge asked Judith Coplon to rise for sentencing.

On the first count, he announced, time to be served would be forty months to ten years; on the second count, one to three years, with sentences to run concurrently. Mildred Gillars had earned ten to thirty years, a tougher sentence. In Judith's case, knowledge that there would be a second trial may well have inclined the judge to pass down what those demanding blood considered inadequate punishment. Reeves suggested that the attorney general confine Judith to the women's reformatory at Alderson, West Virginia, the prison to which John Kelley had so recently sent Axis Sally. Bond would be set at twenty thousand dollars, and she would be free pending appeal.

Following sentencing, the issue of Reeves's fines against Archie was raised, a final bit of courtroom housekeeping to be taken care of before the trial was finally, and officially, over. Archie petulantly observed that he had expected them to be forgiven; after all, he was only trying to do his best for his client. Ha! exclaimed Kelley. Archie should be punished, the prosecutor insisted. His courtroom tactics were so reprehensible that he not only had paid fines in the past, but also had served five days in jail on contempt charges. This was clearly news to the judge and to the entranced media.

So what? Archie wanted to know. He'd rather sit in jail for speaking out on behalf of his client than spend time in a house with Kelley. Reeves had had enough. He granted a stay of execution with regard to the fines.

With a sound of a gavel, the torturous ten-week ordeal was over. Spectators and reporters surged forward, reaching out to Judith as she was led away by one of the marshals. They called out to her, but she did not respond.

Bertram Coplon was finally able to raise an additional ten thousand dollars for his sister's bond. The Weinstein Bonding Company agreed to provide funds, but only after Judith's appeal of the Washington verdict was filed. Archie filed by midday, and Judith was once again free, or as free as one could be under the circumstances.

Judith, Rebecca, and Archie went to the Willard to finish packing, but not without the ever-present media. Late in the day, Bert and Rebecca began the long drive back to New York, and Archie and Judy boarded a flight at Washington's National Airport. When the pair arrived at La Guardia at six-thirty that evening, Judy, exhausted and pale, declined to comment on her conviction.

"This is the first opportunity I've had to get any rest since I was arrested," she told reporters. "I don't know where I'm going to spend the weekend—probably with friends—so please don't try to contact me."

Archie did not decline to talk to the press. Judy waited patiently for more than an hour while her attorney spoke about the trial and his plans for an appeal on "dozens of grounds."

For Archie and Judy, it was one down, one to go. And in the next go-round, the public would learn a great deal more about lying under oath, a favorite complaint of John Kelley. The liars, however, would include a number of people not under indictment, individuals working for the U.S. government.

PART THREE

In **Foley Square**

The Soap Opera Continues

Every newspaper in the country, every writer with a forum to do so, had something to say to the public about the latest episodes in the captivating Coplon drama. The day following Judith's return to New York, the day after her sentencing, was a delicious feast of spicy copy. Shoot her, said some. Most were happy to have her locked away. Very few suggested that the trial had not been fair—that there might be more to the story than had been revealed in Washington. While Judy sought a restorative peace and quiet, an escape from the madness for the first few days after the verdict, others sought the attention of the media spotlight. Chief among them was John Kelley.

Judy was a much better actress than Axis Sally, the government's star prosecutor told the press in a titillating interview. Sally, Mildred Gillars, may have been a professional on stage, but Judith performed far better in the witness box.

Sally's performance was dull and "predictable," but not Judy's. "With Sally, we knew she was going to give us this act or that act." Judy, on the other hand, "a tough little baby, with a mind like a Swiss watch," was full of surprises. As far as appearances, Judy was an attractive, sensuous woman, while Sally was not.

The prosecutor was pleased to offer a comparison of the two cases, that of the Nazi propagandist and that of the government political analyst. Sex was involved in both, with Axis Sally claiming to have had a platonic relationship with a married man, a German named Max Koischwitz. Max, like Valentin, was "sensitive, intellectual, intelligent and soul-searching." A major difference was Sally's admission of having been led along the rosy garden path by the sensitive, etc., Max, and Judith's insistence she had never even entered the garden.

Both women were poised during their time in the witness box, "but both had their moments," Kelley said. Judy, who claimed to have loved Gubitchev, "cracked" when confronted with evidence that she and Harold Shapiro had spent several nights together, but Sally "hardly batted an eye" when questioned about the same kind of two-timing adventure. Sally's moment came when GIs testified about her cruel visits to prison camps where she manufactured her propaganda.

Of the two, Kelley found Judith "a more clever woman, intellectually. She really had it," he added.

Pressed by the media about why Judy could betray her country, an act she denied, Kelley said he simply didn't know. "Isn't it enough for you to know that these people do these things?" he responded. That Kelley would grant such an interview at this time seems highly inappropriate. He was to be Judy's prosecutor in New York, and one would expect a measure of propriety in the hiatus between the two trials. Instead, he made inflammatory remarks, offered judgments, made sport of her. In the end, he said, the convicted woman showed a "veneer of courage," but that he found her "peculiar."

Archie Palmer had a few well-chosen words to share with the press. He would appeal on more than twenty points. Loss of the case had been entirely his fault; he should have done a far better job. "It's the old story of a bad lawyer and a poor client," he said. "There's no other way out. Poor people have no choice but bad lawyers. She can't afford any better than me—or worse."

The *Washington Times Herald* introduced an extensive Coplon photo spread with a decorative, and uncharacteristically poetic, statement in bold italics and set off by a double box:

> This is the face that launched a thousand slips . . . FBI data, that is. One girl, slender, five feet tall, against the United States. Small and smooth and a way with clothes. And so smart! Even as a little baby, her mother said. At 2:30 P.M. yesterday, grown-up Judy Coplon heard the jury's answer. Guilty!

A copy of the photo essay is in the FBI files at the Hoover Building. Cutlines read: "Palmer Does the Talking," with Judy looking on; "The Whole Case is so Fishy," Judy holding her nose; "Now You Brand Me as a Harlot," Judy, chin in her hands; "No more smiles," a solemn-faced Judy the day of the verdict; "I Am Not a Drinker," Judy sipping a cup of coffee; "I Was Going Crazy," Judy looking pensive; "They Met in New York," Judy telling of her first encounter with Gubitchev; and finally, "He Told Me He Loved Me," Judy looking especially pretty and vulnerable, wiping a tear from her eye.

If the country had not remained mesmerized by the sullied image of the typical girl next door who went astray, the media would not have devoted such an enormous amount of space to reflecting on the case and its outcome. It was clear that the public still could not get enough of Judith Coplon.

Two days after Judy's arrival in Brooklyn, stories circulated that the government had "taken up" her passport and had placed security personnel at airports and other "international transport outlets" to keep her from fleeing the country. She was pictured as a dangerous, desperate woman. There followed an immediate backpedaling, with a State Department information officer insisting that passports of persons convicted of crimes are *always* taken up, and international transportation lines are routinely notified of the action as a matter of course. The flurry of police activity at East Coast airports and shipping terminals that followed Judy's release in Washington was, however, far from routine.

On the day newspapers reported the government's precautions to keep her from escaping, Judith did indeed board a boat. It was a ferry, and she took it to view the Statute of Liberty.

The *New York Daily News* ran a gloating editorial headlined HOW'S THEM

HERRINGS, HARRY? Reminding the public that President Harry S. Truman had called probes of Communist activities in the United States "red herrings," the paper wanted to know Mr. Truman's latest name for these activities. Although the "herrings" label had received the most notoriety, Truman had also called the various probes "headline hunts" and "symptoms of mass hysteria." The paper now had a question for the embarrassed leader of the free world. "How's that red-herring crop doing now, Mr. President?" Miss Coplon, who had screamed on one occasion that her trial was "so fishy it smelled to high Heaven," had done away with the president's herrings.

In an erudite column on the same subject for the same newspaper that same day, I. F. Stone raised legitimate questions about the arrest, the lack of evidence that Judith had given secrets to the Russians, and inconclusive speculation about intent. He cited the failure of the government to show how the memos in Judy's purse had anything to do with "national defense" as defined in the Espionage Act under which she was charged and tried.

"The decoy letter was a fraud," Stone wrote. "The memos had nothing to do with defense. The data slips dealt with FBI information on agents in this country from the Soviet Union and its satellites." About the slips, Stone determined, "The judge would have seemed to foreclose the question when he ruled weeks ago that not only the data slips but even the full FBI reports from which they were taken could be made public without danger to national defense or security."

The columnist took issue with the failure of the government to identify the confidential informant in a case "so tenuous and circumstantial," citing a memorandum of law in which the government itself held that confidentiality is not a privilege when identification of the informant is essential to the defense.

Stone paid tribute to "the dogged energy and irrepressible fighting spirit of Miss Coplon's lawyer, Archibald Palmer, who put devotion ahead of decorum and achieved much that no 'gentlemanly' lawyer could have accomplished." Too bad, Stone said, that Judy, "for all her courageous 10-week fight, was unable to provide a more convincing explanation of the material in her purse."

Left-wing press had a field day. A "peeping-Tom" government submitted evidence tending to cast doubt on Judith's "conventionality as a woman, and from the jury's verdict, it evidently worked," declared Ted Thackery, writing in the *Compass*. And Judge Reeves certainly should have taken care to ascertain that the jury was "fully aware it was not charged with finding Miss Coplon innocent or guilty of unconventional conduct." The charge, Thackery reminded, "involved espionage."

"Fornication is not espionage," Archie Palmer had shouted in court following the Shapiro revelations. In truth, the soap opera's first-season finale suggested otherwise.

A week after the initial media deluge about the case, its stars, its implications about spies in government and what should be done with them, Judith emerged from self-imposed shadows to speak publicly about a work of fiction, "The Government Girl," and its relevance to a work of fact, the government's evidence against her.

"Reporters take notes, writers takes notes. They don't just carry material in their heads. Read Somerset Maugham's account of how he puts down ideas, notes about people, and how they grow into stories," she said. "Writers collect odd bits of information that will be useful in this or that story. I took notes for my novel." She read aloud excerpts from Maugham's *The Summing Up* and talked about the use of the "character sketch" technique in story development, the use of real people to breathe life and substance into people created of words on paper.

She would be the heroine. "I wanted to tell the story of how I came to Washington, how it felt that first day when the weather was warm and spring-like and how the trees looked down by the river. I wanted to put into it the hope and the excitement that Washington means to a new Government Girl." Her eyes were misted, her voice soft, gently convincing. "And I made notes about people I knew and figured to put into the book, but I made a mistake in putting down their real names in my notes."

Judy continued, "And then, as I got the feel of the place, and came to realize what those buildings were, I wanted to picture Washington as a great big mausoleum with all the fretting workers, policed, probed, frightened, running in and out like . . . like cockroaches." It was to be a story of disillusionment, one she could write better now than before.

With regard to other evidence, her story about Foley's having given her "secret" information and asking her to take it with her to New York remained firm. As for the geophone business, it had been discussed and written about publicly for years. Even abroad. "Look at this magazine published in India," she said. "It contains a complete description of how geophones work, and tells where you can buy them in the United States, but the court wouldn't allow it into evidence." Bureau of Standards chief Condon would later testify that the information had been public "for more than 20 years."

Even timid Rebecca now had something to say. She spoke of her terror over the past four months since her beloved daughter's arrest and her unfailing belief that Judy had been wrongfully charged and convicted.

"I'll stand by Judy until the day I die," she declared. "I will never lose faith in my Judy's innocence." She talked of life before the arrest, of Judy's growing up, of a happy, safe family filled with love. And she admitted her own shyness.

"I've always been timid," she despaired, "and when people stare at me, I feel I can't take it much longer. I get panicky in the subways, not because of what people might say to me but what they might say about Judy. And there was the woman in Washington who asked me how many years in jail I thought my daughter would get! How can a person be that cruel?" she wanted to know. "How can a woman ask such a question of a mother?" How, indeed. How did people shout cruel questions to baby Lindbergh's mother? Half a century later, how did people approach a distraught Bill McVeigh and want to know how soon he thought his son would be executed for killing 168 men, women, and children?

"Every day since Judy was arrested the mail has brought me scores of letters, some of them wonderful notes of encouragement from people I've never met, but many of them penny postcards openly vile, obscene," Rebecca said. "Generally, the first filthy word shows what kind of lewd message is there and I rip the cards into a million pieces."

If there was nothing new to report to the public on a given day, the press rehashed the excitement of the past four months, speculating and speculating again about what had happened and what might happen in the days and weeks ahead. Usually, however, there was fresh fodder on which to feast—the diplomatic immunity issue, new views on punishment, a series of delays of the New York trial date (for a variety of reasons), Judy's work on her appeals, opinions on the issue of double jeopardy. Questions were raised and would continue to be raised about the fairness of a second trial, questions, for some, never clearly answered. There was also another unanswered question many found troublesome—who *really* told on Judy? Who was the real "confidential informant"? Into the mix, and always related to the Coplon case, were developments in the Hiss-Chambers affair, the mercurial events surrounding the trial of the Communist leaders, and more. All of this kept Judith Coplon, and sometimes her costar, Gubitchev, before the audience throughout the summer.

The American public responded to the media barrage with a flurry of letters written to the editors of various newspapers, congratulating a reported position, or objecting to it. And they wrote objecting to or supporting the letters of other readers. The FBI duly noted all of these and kept copies of them in their files, where they still remain.

On July 11, Judith Coplon, clad in a chic green dress, entered room 318 of the Federal Courthouse Building in New York's Foley Square. She took a seat, waiting for federal judge William Bondy to arrive for the purpose of setting a new date for her espionage trial with Valentin Gubitchev. With a start, she realized she had selected a seat directly behind the nattily dressed Russian. Quickly she rose and crossed to the far side of the room. He glanced at her with bored disinterest; she ignored him completely. The press loved it, one reporter writing that Judith's reaction to Gubitchev "out-chilled the air-conditioning system." One headline read, HER VALENTIN IN MARCH JUST A JERK TO JUDY IN JULY. Ever-verbal Archie got into a brief exchange with Bondy, whose demeanor was far different from that of Reeves. "Listen to the court and keep your mouth closed," Bondy ordered an astonished Palmer. The date was now set for October 17, the original April date long since left by the wayside on Constitution Avenue.

In getting set for the next soap opera season, scripts would be rewritten by both sides. What worked for the twelve-member audience in Washington would be retained, what failed to convince tossed out, and new scenarios explored. But the basic story line would remain the same; it could not be otherwise, because the charges, if not truly duplicative, were as connected as two welded links in an iron chain. As for the cast, it would be made up mainly of the same characters reading many of the same lines. New principal players would be added—Valentin Gubitchev and his brilliant lawyer, and, much later, some surprising understudies for Palmer.

Behind the Scenes

The Coplon family moved painfully through the summer, an increasingly frail Rebecca, a pencil-thin, nervous Judy, and a dangerously angry Bertram, whose obsession with his sister's plight grew day by day. Judy stayed with her mother and her aunt at the Ocean Parkway apartment, and Bertram went home to his wife and family. Reports of his telephone calls revealed his anger with the government and his continued warnings of the likelihood of FBI wiretapping; this, despite the Bureau's repeated denials, under oath, that phones were tapped.

For Judy, accustomed to a challenging job and the stimulation of work on her master's degree, days were endless. Every day had "a hundred hours," every day was the monotonous same. She tried to get a job, but as a convicted felon, was turned down for even the most menial tasks. Not only did she need something to pass the time, but she also desperately needed money for her appeal.

"One man did want to give me a job to publicize something he wanted to sell, but I didn't want to be connected with anything like that," she said. "The others were tactful, but I guess they just didn't want me around."

If any FBI agents were shadowing her, she thought, they would be finding her life "pretty dull." She had quit looking behind her, suspecting that her activities were of so little interest that the FBI had turned its attention to more interesting pursuits. It should be noted that her brother had the more realistic view.

In an interview late in July, Judy said that a "lot of ordinary people" followed her when she walked to the grocery store, wanting to get a look at "that girl spy." They pointed at her on the few occasions when she went out to dinner with a friend. "I'm getting used to all the attention now," Judy told a reporter. "I really don't mind anymore." Still, she said, she would keep her "nose in a book" when riding the subway to avoid looking at the strangers who stared at her.

Walter Winchell's column carried a report of a supposed altercation between Judith and a journalist. Not true, she insisted, calling the item "a piece of sheer fabricated nonsense. It said I had smashed a newspaperman's camera in a nightclub. That simply did not happen." The story, however, did not go away.

During the summer months, discussion of her punishment became more and more prevalent. While she tried to remain quietly behind the scenes during this period, it must have been exceedingly difficult to keep from crying out when strangers debated whether she should be executed, put behind bars for the rest of her life, or, possibly, forgiven for sins she insisted were not hers. Although there had been considerable interest paid to the issue prior to her trial and conviction, it now received a great deal more attention.

"While I do not know personally whether Miss Coplon is a spy or just a sex-happy little girl, she was duly convicted of espionage. She might have pulled more time for shoplifting," wrote Robert Ruark in the *Chicago Daily News*. This was the "kind of rap" they hand out for misdemeanors, Ruark, who rarely missed a chance to castigate Judy, complained to his readers. He was not alone. Others complained as well. Here was Judith Coplon, convicted spy Judith Coplon, running around loose! Was anyone safe?

Judy's daily early-summer routine almost never varied. It was reported that she rose about eight-thirty in the morning, had breakfast, shopped for groceries for her mother, returned home. She listened to classical music for hours at a time. Now and again she would venture out on her bicycle. On occasion she would sit on the steps and watch the neighborhood children at play. Friendly children, unfazed by the spy next door.

"Children are wonderful people," she said at the time. "There are a lot of children in our apartment house. Sometimes I tell them stories for an hour or so in the morning."

Neighbors were kind and supportive, wishing her good luck and raising money to help with her appeal. They did so because of Rebecca, who was much loved by all of them. Some expressed concern about Judith, who appeared frail and emotionally exhausted. Archie joked about Judy's loss of weight. "You're right in style these days, you little five footers," he told her. "I weigh 100 pounds," she protested, which no one believed.

Judy missed her Washington friends. Some had remained loyal, but many had not, her conviction understandably changing personal feelings toward her. She had her family for comfort, and she had Archie. On one occasion, she spent the weekend with the Palmers at their farm in Milford, Connecticut.

Whenever anyone asked, she would insist that she was confident there would be a reversal of her conviction. Whether she truly believed what she said is questionable.

Judy's outlook and activities changed dramatically once she began going each day to Archie's office, usually spending her time there working on her own case, typing, recording information about exhibits, and collating evidence. It was a welcome change for her, and she threw herself into her new role. By mid-August, she had read 4,000 of the trial's 8,504 pages of testimony. She also did some typing for Archie, who boasted about his new assistant's skill. "She's a good typewriter," he explained to grinning reporters. "Great help, this little girl. Don't know what I'd do without her in this case."

"He exaggerates my contribution," Judy countered. "My job is to boil down the record on basic points. My advantage is that I can remember things visually." Judy's onetime ambition to earn a law degree, which had to be abandoned due to the demands of her job, had given her a modicum of exposure to one area of criminal law. "My knowledge of the law is actually limited to assault and battery," she smiled. "Do you suppose I could use it in this case?"

In discussing Judith's appeal, Archie noted that "Judith found the government had built its case on two circumstances. She told her friends openly in Washington she was going around with a Russian in New York." As a result, Palmer held, the FBI investigated, found this was true, and arrested Judy simply on suspicious behavior.

"All FBI agents who watched me admit they never saw any papers passed," Judy added. "Therefore, the arrest was on suspicion." Was this legal? Further, there was no warrant. In her case, did the government have the right not only to arrest but also to seize papers without a warrant? To Judy, these seemed to be the most important issues in appealing her conviction.

Preparation for the October 17 New York trial and working on her appeal of the Washington conviction consumed essentially all of Judith's and Archie's time as this difficult summer progressed. The appeal, after several delays, was finally filed on November 3 for the October 1949 term of the U.S. Court of Appeals for the District of Columbia, with the 119-page document reviewing the entire case and citing numerous alleged errors in the trial court's decision. At the same time motions and petitions had to be drafted in preparation for pretrial hearings. Then, on October 5, the trial was once again postponed, this time because of a shortage of federal judges. The new date was now set for November 9; however, Archie Palmer advised the court that he might ask for another delay, pending the yet-undecided outcome of Judy's Washington appeal. The trial judge was not selected; in the interim, motions would go to New York federal judge William Bondy.

A visitor to Archie's office observed that the loquacious attorney "seemed to pep Judy up." It was clear that Archie cared deeply for Judy, and often told people he loved her as a daughter. Their relationship had the unique emotional complexity of father and daughter, attorney and client, friends sharing a mission, and, ultimately, combatants.

Normally, it was Archie who would explode and Judy who would soothe. Their roles reversed when speculation began late in the summer concerning whether Judy would testify against Gubitchev in exchange for a reduced sentence—a maximum of one year in prison.

"These stories are vicious because they are directed at the idea of my being guilty," she stormed. "I've told my story. I don't have any other stories." She was innocent. There would be no bargain.

To those who wondered if Judy still had feelings toward the Russian, she would say, "I don't know Mr. Gubitchev anymore. To me his is just the name of someone in New York who is a co-defendant in my trial."

On October 19, Judge Bondy denied Judith's motion to quash the charges against her, a petition based on "evidence that was insufficient and incompetent." She would have to stand trial once again. Bondy did not rule on Judy's request for return of documents found in her possession the night of March 4, a filing based on "illegality of the arrest." He did rule on Palmer's request for permission to examine the minutes of the grand jury proceedings that had led to the indictments against Judy and Valentin Gubitchev. The request was denied.

Archie and Judy went back to work, reviewing, rewriting, preparing pretrial motions. At the end of the day, Judy would return to her mother's apartment, have dinner, and talk with the two older women with whom she shared the residence. Bert was faithful about coming to visit and to encourage. It was an exhausting, draining time for the family. Often missing from the picture was Bert's wife, rumored to dislike his sister. Whether or not this was true, she was rarely seen visiting the three women on Ocean Parkway.

The issue of double jeopardy was brought before Bondy the week prior to the scheduled opening of trial, along with a petition for dismissal based on the illegality of arresting Judy without a warrant. Bondy ruled that both were matters to be decided by the trial judge. After dealing with Judith's petitions, Bondy listened while Gubitchev, in Russian, insisted at length that he could not be tried because he enjoyed diplomatic immunity. Couldn't he speak in English? Bondy wanted to know. Yes, he could, Raymond Whearty told the judge, producing copies of statements made in English by the Russian defendant. At the end of an argument during which Bondy was clearly annoyed, the judge warned that Gubitchev "had better prepare himself [for trial] or he will pay the penalty." Gubitchev then sought a delay so that he could find an attorney, explaining that he hadn't taken this espionage business seriously, having considered it merely a "provocation." Bondy was unmoved. You've had time enough, he told the Russian.

On November 10, after a full week of arguments, Judge Bondy set November 14 for the start of the second Coplon espionage trial, this one with the enigmatic Russian engineer as codefendant. On November 18, the second perjury trial of Alger Hiss was scheduled to open. Reruns perhaps, but spy shows were now the biggest hits off Broadway.

The national focus turned to Foley Square, to the government courthouse where Judy's trial would be held. It was the same building where eleven leaders of the Communist Party had been recently, and finally, sentenced. She would stand trial in a courtroom essentially unchanged in more than half a century. A courtroom well known to Tom Mitchell at the time, and one where Marcia Mitchell would stand many years later and see the defendant, but only in her mind's eye.

The Off-Broadway Rehearsals

The curtain went up on *U.S. Government versus Judith Coplon and Valentin Gubitchev* on November 14, 1949, launching pretrial hearings that would detonate in a two-month orgy of accusations, unexpected and seemingly incredible new revelations of wrongdoing, and public demands for congressional investigations. The New York case was not to be the anticlimactic finale in the Coplon drama so many had expected. It was during these pre-trial hearings that the entire Coplon saga would truly unfold, that what would happen to Judith over the next eighteen years would be determined, that axes would fall and futures would change.

Surprise and shock over the unexpected pretrial fiasco caused the media, once again, to jump on the showtime bandwagon. Although Judy remained in the public eye—and thus the lens of media—there was another target that seemed so monumentally, so wonderfully insidious that it garnered top billing for a time.

During the entire pretrial hearings, Judy moved more quietly and less publicly through her life, rarely appearing in court, going out in the evening to dine and dance with "boyfriends" in places off the beaten track and away from the cameras. The media's relentless pursuit of news from Foley Square, whether or not she was present, made the respite possible and served her well. Both Judith and Valentin Gubitchev successfully dropped out of the camera's focus for much of the proceedings in the federal courthouse, while their attorneys jousted daily with the opposition.

Gathering at Foley Square

Valentin Gubitchev arrived at the federal courthouse this cool November morning dressed, as always, in a well-tailored business suit and fedora, looking as if he were on his way to work in one of the nearby office build-ings. He was icily composed and totally self-contained. Still refusing to have a lawyer or to accept the legality of the charges against him, he took a seat, alone, at the front of the courtroom, and with great deliberation ignored those around him. He was particularly careful to ignore his codefendant, who returned the favor. Simply dressed and wearing very little makeup, pretty Judith Coplon seemed prepared for what was to come, while brilliant Judith Coplon *seemed* quietly confident. And yet, and yet. Scenes from the Washington trial surely must have been replaying in her mind. Disembodied faces of government witnesses floating in and out of a cerebral cinema, images ready to confront and accuse once again, joined by chilling visions of the despised Kelley and Whearty. Difficult moments, frightening moments, but Judy revealed nothing but calm composure, handling her entrance with assurance. It was expected of her. Every eye, except for the Russian's, was upon the young woman now branded both spy and harlot.

Archie Palmer, flustered and muttering, thumped his books and files and Bible on the table beside his client and tossed his hat on a nearby chair. An affectionate glance passed between the two, and Judy picked up a legal pad and pencil. The defense, at least half of it, was ready. The other half, comprised only of Gubitchev, sat staring stonily ahead, the table in front of him bare.

Federal judge Sylvester J. Ryan, who would have his judicial hands full from start to finish, was no Albert Reeves. He was sharp, confident, no-nonsense. It was clear from the outset that he intended to settle Archie Palmer's hash in short order. To begin with, Palmer would not chew candy while he questioned witnesses, or, in fact, at any time he was in Ryan's courtroom.

"But I've done this for twenty years!" Archie protested.

"You won't do it in *my* courtroom," Ryan snapped. Furthermore, Archie would not be a "buffoon." Any deviation from proper lawyerly behavior and Archie would not be fined or jailed. He would be out on the street. Archie would not be allowed to call the prosecution's witnesses as his own and would not be allowed to derail its case. Given these caveats, Archie Palmer, for the first time in his entire courtroom career, was slightly intimidated. But only slightly.

Immediately, Archie was on his feet introducing defense motions to dismiss. He added the issue of double jeopardy to his usual filings, claiming the arrest and seizure were illegal. The hearings were expected to last only a few days, and it was almost universally assumed that these efforts would be futile, with the trial itself most likely getting under way within a week's time.

First witness for the prosecution was Robert Granville, who began a lengthy testimony about the FBI's surveillance of the defendants. Immediately, Archie bolted headlong into his argument about the arrest and search, surely his best bet for dismissal. They had done this dance before, Granville and Palmer, but that no longer mattered. Winning the point now, each felt, was everything.

Did Granville not know, Archie questioned, that there were U.S. commissioners in this very building who could have issued a warrant? Yes, Granville said, he knew that. Did he "attempt to go to any particular commissioner or federal judge to ask for a warrant?" Archie asked the handsome, taciturn agent. "No" was the response. Technically, this was true.

What Granville did not tell the court was that the Bureau had gone to the top, asking Assistant Attorney General Peyton Ford for a warrant, only to have Ford insist there was "not sufficient evidence" for an arrest. Ford's denial was the result of Hoover's deliberately keeping Ford in the dark about the identity of the confidential informant; had it been otherwise, agents would have had their warrant in short order. But if Ford had known the truth, Hoover figured, he immediately would have shared the exciting news with President Truman, who immediately would have shared the information with certain trusted aides, men Hoover believed were spying for the Soviets. Suspected White House spies, close to a president who would never believe his aides could be traitors, could soon know one of the Cold War's most critical, most closely guarded secrets.

Keeping secrets from the White House was nothing new for the intelligence community; Roosevelt, too, was told only what the covert corps wanted him to know. J. Edgar Hoover often decided what the most powerful man in the world would or would not be told.

It seemed mighty peculiar to Archie that Granville would put seven cars and nearly two dozen agents, plus himself—a rarity for the supervisor—on the street March 4 when he was uncertain about an arrest, when he had not called out the troops and big guns on two earlier occasions. Why *this* night? Was it possible, Archie wondered, that agents *knew* Judy was carrying the infamous decoy memo? The implication went beyond the legality of the arrest. If agents knew Judy was carrying information about the "hot and interesting" memo in her purse, then perhaps Foley, not she, was the liar. Perhaps he really had seen her place notes in her handbag, and the agents knew for certain that she was carrying classified material on her person that particular night.

"When, for the first time, did you find out that a decoy message had been prepared to be given to this girl?"

"It was sometime after the arrest. I believe it was on March 5th."

"In other words . . . at the time when you made the arrest, you knew nothing from any source whatsoever that a decoy letter had been created by Mr. Lamphere and turned over to be read or given to this girl before she left Washington?"

"I did not know that, no." Granville replied. More than fifty years later, Granville would say that he "suspected" Judy was carrying secret information, "suspected" that the Bureau knew she had "something" on her person.

Archie pushed on, asking about the only other decoy letter planned for Judith, sent January 27 to her office via regular communication channels, Lamphere's first attempt to bait the trap. From all of the various trial and hearing testimonies, it is clear that no one knew whether she had taken this first tempting bit of faux secret information about Amtorg. Judith and Gubitchev were tailed on Feburary 18, during their first meeting following Lamphere's initial creative writing effort, but there was no full-scale arrest operation like that in March. It all made Archie very curious indeed. Granville said he had known nothing about an earlier decoy until this very minute.

Later, after Granville left the witness box, when Archie was questioning Scott Miller about the arrest, he observed that it seemed to him as if "it indicates that this entire arrest was prearranged—they could have got a warrant if they had anything for it—and they were trying to seize, first, whatever papers they might find on her as a pretext to make the arrest good."

Archie asked Miller: "Had you ever discussed these decoy messages or the proposed sending of them with Mr. Granville before March 4th?"

"Well," Miller answered, "the discussion limited itself to the fact that the Bureau had told us that they were contemplating doing it. We received no information as to what was contained in the messages except possibly that it might pertain to the Amtorg Trading Corporation." Miller also testified that Granville had discussed with him the possible arrest of "that girl that night." Yet only moments later, Miller said he didn't know that "this girl was going to meet this man that night and didn't know anything was going to happen between them."

In the event that this pattern of response seemed dissembling or contradictory in nature, Judge Ryan from time to time would wisely clarify: "He could not *know* the future."

"Had you received instructions from anybody before you made the arrest without a warrant . . . discussed it with anybody?" Archie asked. Granville said he had not. And then, "Well, we discussed the possibility of the arrest in the afternoon . . . with the agents assembled for the conference." Aha! was Archie's unspoken reaction.

Robert Granville told the authors that he alone made the decision to arrest without a warrant. Robert Lamphere says the Washington, D.C., group made the decision. Hollis Bowers says that J. Edgar Hoover made it.

The authors believe that those in charge in Washington and New York likely participated in the decision-making process, confirming the New York supervisor's authority to arrest, but interviews with Granville and review of his affidavits and testimonies suggest that his was the final call. It was his whistle, and he put it to his lips.

In conducting these first examinations, Palmer at one point directed Granville's attention to the topic most problematic for the Bureau. "While you were here in New York in charge of this matter, did your FBI agency in anywise tap the wires of either her home telephone or the telephone of her brother or anyone else connected with her?"

Kelley leaped to his feet. "Objection!"

"Overruled." Kelley registered raw shock. This was an unexpected and frightening response.

"I have no personal knowledge of that," Granville answered. (According to Tom Mitchell, "no personal knowledge" or "no direct knowledge" was standard protective language used in such circumstances.)

Palmer's eyes narrowed. He tensed, closing in, determined. What happened in Washington would not happen here. "I didn't ask you that. I asked you, did you get any information from anybody connected with the FBI that the wires connected with her home or anywhere else, or where she lived or worked, were being tapped."

Kelley, who successfully had objected to this line of questioning throughout the Washington trial and who was now dealing with a new judge, was once again on his feet. "I object to this question!"

Ryan overruled. In the crashing silence that followed, every eye was on the New York espionage supervisor.

"Yes," Granville answered firmly.

Judy Coplon sat stunned, pencil poised in the air.

Granville would not continue the company line. The ax had fallen, and stirrings in the courtroom made it clear that everyone within earshot, including members of the press, heard the thud.

"Who told you they were being tapped?" Archie calmly asked. Given his perverse nature, perhaps his failure to grandstand at this moment of triumph was a part of doing the unexpected, of not wanting to reveal absolute joy.

"Mr. Belmont."

As a lawyer, didn't Granville know it was against the law for federal agents to tap telephones, Archie inquired? Kelley, red faced and furious, began an exchange as to the relevancy of this line of questioning.

"It may be relevant," the judge responded evenly. "He may have acquired knowledge through these telephone interceptions which would be the basis for probable cause." Judge Ryan's words made it clear that queries about wiretapping would not be taboo in his courtroom.

Archie beamed throughout the ensuing Kelley-Ryan exchange, announcing his intention to stay out of the argument: "I retire and prefer to remain under Your Honor's banner."

"You won't remain under my banner," Ryan told him. "I hold no banner except the banner of justice."

"That's the banner I want to be under," Archie told him happily.

"That's the banner we are all under."

"I want it to remain unfurled," Archie said, and even the surly Gubitchev, who well understood English, smiled.

"Yes, we will have it unfurled and floating in the air. But you stand here on your own feet. I am not conducting any examination for you."

Archie bowed to the court and continued. "Did you know whether Mr. Gubitchev's telephones were tapped?" Ryan overruled another heated objection from Kelley.

"I have no personal knowledge of that, no."

"I am asking you, did you hear of it?"

"Yes, I had."

Everything had changed, not just the tenor of these hearings but also behavior in court for years to come. Observers were filled with "why" questions, and the matter of trust in government integrity became a national issue for some. For certain others, those most directly involved, there were no questions, only answers. Secret answers.

On November 16, Archie paraded eleven witnesses before the judge in his attempt to show the arrest was illegal. Included was Willam Foley, who gave his standard recital piece about the hot and interesting decoy memorandum. In asking for return of the decoy notes and all other items from Judy's purse, Archie, arms waving, told the court, "She is no more a Communist than I am, and I'm a Democrat." Furthermore, he insisted, the Bureau had ample time to secure an arrest warrant, a nicety certain others, like the "Nazis," never deemed necessary.

The following day, the seventeenth, Fred E. Strine, special assistant to the attorney general, told the court the arrest was based, in part, on fear that Judy and her Russian friend would seek refuge in the Soviet embassy if they were not arrested the night of March 4.

"This would be as safe as going to Europe," Strine declared.

Further, Strine, acting very mysteriously, suggested that the FBI had "knowledge far beyond the realm of suspicion" that the pair were into espionage and not romance, but offered no clue as to what that knowledge might be. After four days of arguments, the defense lost its fight for the return of the papers found in Judy's purse. Ryan held that the arrest was legal, and papers taken from Judy's purse would not be returned to her. Immediately, Archie sought to have the case dismissed on the grounds of double jeopardy. To many, the legality of the arrest remained problematic; so did this latest issue. Ultimately, it was decided that the charges against Judy were dissimilar. "It is evident that the indictments charge different statutory offenses, and that, therefore, the defendant Coplon will not be subjected to double jeopardy by standing trial on the present indictment."

The heart of the matter was the Washington indictment charge of crimes committed by one person, as opposed to the New York indictment charging conspiracy to commit criminal acts. It takes two to conspire, held the court. The reasoning was sound, many agreed, but at the same time they wondered about the need for two trials when all six charges could have been part of a single indictment. They certainly were inextricably related. If not directly questioning the government's motives, more than a few questioned its wisdom in separating out the charges and putting the defendants—and the nation—through two controversial, high-profile, and costly trials.

It took Judge Ryan only one more day to throw out all defense motions and declare that the trial would indeed take place. He delayed the start of the trial until November 22, giving Archie a chance to appeal his decision. With the battle to avoid the trial lost, Valentin Gubitchev changed his attitude about counsel and decided he had better have one. In furious Russian, he repeated his earlier contention that he had believed the charges against him to be merely a "provocation," and for this reason had not taken steps to hire an attorney of his choosing to defend him against "a fanciful tale of the Department of Justice and the FBI." Now, he said, he needed three weeks to find acceptable counsel. Fat chance, the judge said in essence. Gubitchev had been fooling around since last March and he had best appear next Tuesday, November 22, with an attorney. If he did so, the judge said, his request for a delay to prepare his defense would receive favorable attention.

By Monday the twenty-first, Archie's petition had failed and the Russian had found a lawyer through "mutual friends." He was the distinguished Abraham L. Pomerantz, who had served on the prosecution staff at the Nuremberg trial of Nazi industrialists in 1946. There could not be a greater contrast between two defending attorneys than that which was immediately obvious between the smooth Pomerantz and the exceedingly rough Palmer. If the tall, graceful Pomerantz was a stately pine, Archie was a gnarled redwood stump. In announcing his new role, Pomerantz said he would immediately ask Judge Ryan for a month's delay. On the twenty-second, Ryan was as good as his word, and the trial was postponed until December 27.

United States of America versus Judith Coplon and Valentin Gubitchev, the nation's second Cold War espionage trial, failed to open on that date; instead, contentious hearings would continue for a month after the scheduled opening. During the protracted hearings, more and more devastating revelations would surface about government activities that appeals later would call "illegal and deceptive." The drama played on in the stormy hearings and in an eager press as the Bureau entered the most humiliating period it would experience for another half century.

Judith Coplon continued to be an observer in absentia during this time, going for days and sometimes weeks without appearing in the courtroom, leaving these preliminary (but vital) matters in Archie's pudgy hands. Legally with, but personally far from Gubitchev, she avoided much of the courtroom furor.

The Bureau Boys and Their Electronic Recorders

Judge Sylvester Ryan announced that FBI agents would be quizzed about illegal tapping; days later, in response to a plea from Kelley, he changed his mind and declared they would not. Then, with yet another change of mind, he determined that he had better look into this matter, after all. For the second time in the Coplon case, the first being the opening of the raw files, a Pandora's box spilled secrets embarrassing the FBI and infuriating its director. Not only had the Bureau conducted tapping activities denied under oath in Washington, but agents had actually maintained their activities *during the trial and almost up to the day of the announced beginning of the New York trial.* Furthermore, and more incriminating, would be the revelation that discs and logs had been destroyed. The judge was not happy.

On December 13, Judge Ryan declared that evidence secured through wiretapping was "tainted." Further, the judge was quoted as saying that he was "determined to find out to what extent." Toward that end, he ordered the prosecution to prove that it could try its case without relying on "tainted," wiretap evidence, warning that he would suppress any evidence that "flows through" it. Headlines told the public that Judge Ryan might well throw out the case entirely. That same day, Kelley attempted to assure the judge that, as far as he knew, the indictment and the case he would present were not based on wiretap information. The press reported every word. The "tainted" story was now big news and the subject of conversations and speculation across the country. Who were the bad guys?

A nervous prosecution team on the following day, the fourteenth, asked for and was given forty-eight hours to confer among themselves about the wiretapping mess. That morning, they had failed to respond to the judge's order to arrive in court armed with the names of all agents who had eavesdropped on the defendants, along with a log of all the taps. The task was monumental and the order impossible. It was now patently clear that the judge meant business, and if the government did not move quickly to extricate itself from the tainted-evidence quagmire, the case would be lost, sunk in oozing muck. Not only lists and summaries must now be provided, but also proof that each and every bit of information learned through the taps had come from other, independent, sources.

On the fifteenth, a surprise affidavit was filed by Dr. Edward Condon, who alleged that his telephones had been tapped "constantly for the last three years." Poor Dr. Condon had waged more than one battle with the government. The House Committee on Un-American Activities had, the year before, called him "one of the weakest links in our atomic security." His response had been to demand a public hearing; at the time of his wiretap affidavit filing, however, he was still waiting for one, not satisfied by a recent clean bill of health given him by the Atomic Energy Commission. After receiving the affidavit, Ryan ordered Condon to appear before him on December 21.

Four days later, in the midst of the wiretapping debate, Ryan denied motions to dismiss the conspiracy count in the indictments against the two defendants. Two other motions would be argued this day, one from Pomerantz claiming the Russian was outside the court's jurisdiction, the other from both defense attorneys asking for dismissal because of the government's illegal wiretapping.

The court-ordered response affidavit of Howard Fletcher, the "boss" of the Coplon operation in Washington, was filed on the twentieth of December and gave the court details on the who and the where of the great listening-in operation. This was embarrassing information from a team that had earlier testified, under oath, to not having a clue about any wiretapping, anywhere.

(a) The telephone tap with respect to the COPLON, Washington, DC residence . . . was installed on January 7, 1949 and was continuously maintained thereafter until March 19, 1949, on which last date said tap was discontinued.

(b) The telephone tap with respect to the Department of Justice office occupied by the defendant COPLON . . . was installed on January 25, 1949, and was continuously maintained thereafter until March 12, on which last date said tap was discontinued.

(c) The telephone tap with respect to the COPLON New York City residence . . . was installed on February 1, 1949 and was continuously maintained thereafter until May 2, 1949, on which last date said tap was discontinued. That said tap

was re-installed on July 12, 1949 and was continuously
maintained thereafter until November 10, 1949, on which
last date said tap was discontinued.

(d) The telephone tap with respect to the GUBITCHEV residence . . . was installed on February 1 1949 and was continuously maintained thereafter until September 27, 1949,
on which last date said tap was discontinued.

In addition to the telephone taps, Fletcher's affidavit read, a microphone
installed in Judith's office on January 25 was maintained until March 12,
1949, eight days after Judith's arrest. Among the tap monitors named, one
who had testified falsely six months earlier was Richard Brennan. During his
questioning in Washington, Brennan had been asked by Palmer, "Do you
know whether or not there were any agents of the US Government, the FBI,
tapping the wires of her home?"

"I have no knowledge of such," Brennan had replied, answering over
Kelley's shouted objections to the line of questioning.

Now Brennan was one of the agents responding to Judge Ryan's order to
show cause, admitting in his affidavit that, yes, he had been "aware of the
nature, substance and content of intercepted telephone conversations in
which the defendant Judith Coplon purportedly participated." Later in the
pretrial hearings, Brennan also admitted having discussed all of this with
Scott Miller, Bureau liaison with Kelley and Whearty during the
Washington trial. He told the court, "Mr. Miller handed me some slips,
which had summaries, short summaries of material contained on discs. I
reviewed those slips and listened to the discs, prepared a memorandum for
Mr. Miller," confirming the communication link between Brennan, Miller,
Kelley, and Whearty.

Whearty, too, would later confirm reading the daily reports, and Miller
would confirm having made them. "I did make summaries of conversations
that I overheard prior to May 2nd, 1949," he said. He had begun to make
them "during the early part of February, probably the first or second."

Typical of the materials given the court to demonstrate the independent
source of information was William Foley's affidavit. Foley stated that,
regardless of electronic eavesdropping on Judith's conversations about her

trips to New York, she had personally told him when she planned to travel to New York. Thus, of course, the wiretapped information was extraneous.

Court Exhibit 46A, a February 28 New York wire from Special Agent in Charge Ed Scheidt to Hoover and Washington's SAC, reads:

> JUDITH COPLON . . . AT NINE THIRTY FIVE PM, FEB TWENTYSEVEN COPLON ADVISED HER MOTHER [by telephone] THAT SHE WOULD COME TO NY FRIDAY, MARCH FOURTH. MRS COPLON WANTED TO KNOW IF JUDY WOULD BE IN FOR DINNER. JUDY SAID THAT SHE WOULD NOT BUT WOULD TRY TO GET HOME AROUND NINE PM. MRS COPLON ASKED IF JUDY HAD SENT "THAT" IN THE MAIL TO HER. JUDY SAID SHE HAD NOT BUT WOULD WRITE HER MOTHER MONDAY NIGHT AND SHE WOULD GET IT BY WEDNESDAY. DUE TO TIME JUDY STATED SHE WOULD BE HOME, STRONG POSSIBILITY SHE MAY MEET GUBITCHEV AT SEVEN PM. WASH FLD SHOULD SURVEIL HER TO NY AS IN PAST. NY COVERAGE WILL BE SAME.

To counter this sort of bothersome evidence, it was necessary for the government to explain, as Foley's affidavit did, that Judith always told William Foley when she would be leaving the office early on a Friday. It might be noted that it is doubtful she told Foley of her plans to meet Gubitchev.

The prosecution responded to Judge Ryan's order through the flurry of affidavits, but the process and concomitant arguments would take weeks. What the court was not told, and what has not been revealed elsewhere, was the probable other "who." Who had orchestrated the dissonant theme of government witnesses lying under oath?

According to Robert Lamphere, it was none other than the senior prosecutor, John Kelley. Lamphere, especially, should know. He was a key player in the orchestra and helped write the score for the entire production. Lamphere insists that agents simply followed John Kelley's instructions when they testified.

"If you didn't actually see them place the tap," Lamphere says Kelley told his witnesses, "you know nothing about it." Agents who objected, concerned about perjuring themselves, were sternly warned to follow the prosecutor's playbook. Now, of course, it all came back to haunt, but it wasn't Kelley who had to deal with the ghosts, it was the agents who had testified falsely.

"The agents shouldn't be blamed," Lamphere insists. "Kelley told them to say 'I have no personal knowledge about any wiretapping.'" It makes sense that Kelley, who met daily from April 25 forward with Whearty, Miller, and every government witness, who saw Bureau reports—along with Whearty—and who raged so against this particular line of questioning, well knew what was going on.

John Kelley himself appeared on the stand during these chaotic, extended pretrial hearings. If the foregoing is true, the highly respected prosecutor lied as well, testifying that he knew nothing about the wiretapping operation until *after* the Washington trial was over. He declared now that, despite the heated exchanges about wiretapping that had taken place in Judge Reeves's Washington courtroom, he had not thought to explore the issue with his witnesses.

"Did you make an inquiry to find out whether or not there had been any wiretapping?" Archie asked.

"*Designedly* no," Kelley answered.

Well, Archie asked, what about inquiring in "the ordinary way"? Another denial.

"I never knew that until very recently when I discussed the matter with Mr. Fletcher in connection with the preparation of the affidavit filed in this case," Kelley replied smoothly.

At one point during Archie's Washington examination of Judith, he had asked her to say, "to the best of your belief," whether the phones in her office were tapped. An angry Kelley had objected, and Archie had turned on him with, "Do you deny the fact that they were tapped?"

"I have no knowledge at all about it, sir . . ." Kelley had replied.

Scott Miller had also been questioned in Washington, where Archie asked him, "Did you know that the phones of Mr. Gubitchev were tapped, and the phones of Miss Coplon were tapped? Do you know that?"

"Not from my own knowledge."

Again, at the beginning of these pretrial hearings, when Archie had asked Miller the same question, he had given the exact same answer.

On December 22, however, Miller talked about wiretapping Judith's telephone conversations, saying that until the time of her arrest they had only been about such mundane matters as "babies, schooldays, health, and business." After that time, the subject matter was quite different. Judge Ryan had a problem with Mr. Miller. As an attorney, an officer of the court, wasn't Miller bothered, sitting in the Washington courtroom knowing that agents were making "incorrect" statements? Was it not Miller's *duty* to take issue with them, Ryan demanded?

"No," Miller answered. He didn't see it that way. Even though he had read slips and summaries of the tapped conversations, he "had no personal knowledge" of the electronic operation.

Raymond Whearty, in his June 28 Washington closing, had scoffed at the idea of wiretapping. Why would anyone in the world ever accuse the government of such unseemly activity? "What made her think her line was tapped? What reason would she have to think, if it wasn't a consciousness of guilt, a consciousness of the activity in which she was engaged—why should a thing come across her mind, a thing of that nature?"

Judith's former boss, now one of her prosecutors, had access to, and admittedly read, the Bureau's surveillance records "set out in memoranda and reports."

Try as he would, Archie Palmer was unsuccessful in wresting an admission from government witnesses that they had discussed the covert tapping operation either with Kelley and Whearty, or within their hearing. Time after time he raised the question, only to have Kelley's inevitable objections sustained. Typical of his futile attempts is his examination of Leo Laughlin, in which the judge not only would not allow Laughlin to answer this particular question, but also would not let him say where discussions about tapping were held.

It was on December 20, when the batch of affidavits reached Ryan's desk, that the most disastrous of all wiretap misadventures came to light. In the mandated summaries of their listening experiences submitted by thirty agents who monitored Judith's mother's telephone, they reported having eavesdropped on at least fourteen conversations between Judy and her attorney. It is safe to say that, at this point, the government would have cut and run if it had been able to do so gracefully. All hopes for a brief pretrial phase and a slick, cut-to-the-finish trial were lost.

The judge granted Archie's request to question all thirty agents, plus another twenty who monitored Judith's office telephone and the hidden office microphone. Spy or no spy, members of the press and the general public figured, here was a serious wrong committed by the Bureau. Weren't people assured of the right to private communication with their lawyers? The government, Kelley at the helm, scurried madly to explain away this whole messy business, while the media had a glorious time. FBI TAPPED PHONE TALKS BETWEEN MISS COPLON, LAWYER, the *Washington Post* announced in bold type on the twentieth. On the following day, FBI AGENT ADMITS COPLON WIRE-TAPPING. And on the next, COPLON WIRETAPPING OUTLINED AT HEARING. The *Post*'s coverage was typical of what appeared in newspapers around the country. Publications from the left had a splendid time. The *Compass* railed against the bureau for tapping conversations between Judy and her attorney in an article headlined FBI MEN DESCRIBE COPLON WIRETAPS. The nation reacted strongly to the concept of violating private communication between the accused and counsel. Editorial writers pontificated on the entire wire-tapping issue, reflecting the public's outrage at what was seen as an egregious violation of basic rights.

Testifying on December 21, FBI agent James Lynch, a wiretap monitor, said the only specific call he remembered listening in on was between Judy and Archie. Lynch's colleague, Agent Daniel Gunn, admitted listening in on Judy's conversations into late August, when Judy and Archie were working on her appeal and preparing filings for the New York court. Reporters loved hearing this sort of testimony; it made such good copy and such compelling headlines. John Kelley and Raymond Whearty did not share the media's appreciation for the agents' testimony, or for the kind of government-bashing that had become a part of the daily news. Archie savored every article, considering each a transcript of his long-sought vindication.

At one point during the embarrassing revelations, Archie shouted, "I could go into a confessional box and I wouldn't be safe there!"—an explosion reported by an entertained press.

Dr. Condon also testified this day, ridiculing the government's contention that the decoy information Judy had in her purse was "secret." "It's been in the public domain for at least twenty years," he scoffed. Besides, the idea that this information had anything to do with making atomic bombs and national security was ludicrous. For the life of him, he couldn't imagine how instruments that measured explosive force could be used in bomb making.

In order to make their case for espionage, it was necessary for the government to allege an act that threatened national security. Robert Lamphere had chosen geophones. In the first week of the pretrial hearings, Lamphere testified that Howard Fletcher had made the national defense connection and had given orders accordingly. "I was instructed to place in the memorandum information relating to the national defense."

Early on in the November hearings, with Lamphere on the stand, Archie explored the national security issue with the witness, calling attention to an article about geophones "printed by the Hindus. I call your attention to page 85 thereof with regard to . . ."

Judge Ryan was disturbed. Was Archie pulling his judicial leg? "I am reluctant to think that you are trifling with the court," he warned.

"Why should I trifle with the court?" Archie pouted, then continued, "and I ask you to read this particular paragraph . . ."

Glancing at the frowning judge, Archie interrupted himself, offering to cite a precedent for the judge's consideration. With a deep sigh, Ryan surrendered. "No, no," he pleaded. "Go ahead." And Archie did just that, asking about scientific information getting out to the "entire civilized world." (In particular, did the civilized world know about geophones?)

Record Breaking at the Bureau

T. Scott Miller, whose name was quickly becoming a household word among those households following the Coplon drama, admitted on December 22 that he had taken it upon himself to approve destruction of certain wiretap records after reviewing transcripts and listening to discs. A week earlier, Whearty had told the court that some of the wiretap data had been destroyed. "In the regular course of established procedure, matters which no longer have any pertinency to the case are taken from the files and destroyed." It sounded like a simple, routine procedure.

Miller testified that he, alone, decided which of Judith Coplon's conversations would be destroyed and which would not. With some of this evidence no longer available, the agent was forced to rely on his memory about the content of Judith's conversations overheard throughout the whole tapping exercise. He stressed that he had not discussed any of his decisions with his supervisors. Alone, he "tore up and threw away" certain evidence obtained through the taps. Some of that included records of talks between Judith Coplon and her attorney.

Newspapers reported that Miller "blushed" at some of the conversations he overheard, because they were so "profane." He did not divulge in court just what he had found so embarrassing, but did say that the Coplon wire carried nasty words about the FBI, vilifying and pillorying the agents. To Miller, they sounded rather like an angry mob, warning each other about the Bureau, saying "watch what you say . . . the phones are being tapped."

Miller would not say whether the shocking profanity had anything to do with his decisions about what evidence would be destroyed.

Asked if it was possible that the agent had destroyed evidence that could have been valuable to Judith Coplon, possibly proving her innocence, he sat stonily silent while the prosecution shouted its objection. The question was repeated, in various guises, objected to, in various ways, and the objections repeatedly sustained. Ryan's rulings kept Miller from the embarrassment of having to answer such an exceedingly awkward question. In the end, it was clear that Miller had determined everything he deep-sixed "valueless."

Later, on December 28, Robert Wirth would testify that wiretap recordings are ordinarily destroyed by the FBI after being held for sixty days, unless instructions to the contrary are issued. This did not happen in the Coplon case, Wirth said. Remarkably, Wirth was allowed to respond to Pomerantz's questions, saying he did not consider that defense counsel might want to examine written wiretap reports. "When you were destroying these memoranda up to July 1st, did you give thought to the fact that they had been sought in April by Mr. Palmer?" the attorney queried.

"No, I did not."

Given Archie's persistent hammering at the issue throughout the Washington trial, Wirth's answer had the definite ring of untruth. Now, Pomerantz asked, didn't Wirth know that "the defendant has the right to call on the government to open up the material for examination?" No, Wirth told the court, he did not, adding that he, as an attorney, was aware of a Supreme Court decision on wiretap evidence, but not of "the details."

The exchange ended with Pomerantz asking Ryan to order the appearance of the person who actually destroyed the original recordings. "I think he should be produced as a witness to determine when, where, and under what circumstances they were destroyed."

Those circumstances were revealed in testimony not by one, but by two witnesses who came to court to explain how Judith Coplon's words—and those of other suspects—were forever silenced. Mrs. Sophie Saliba, head of the FBI's file room, testified that recordings were filed in her office, first in an active file and then, unless specifically noted for retention, in an inactive file. Usually, she said, she had possession of a record for from sixty to ninety days.

Saliba's colleague, John Ware, apparently a man of many talents, was a file clerk in the same office, a chauffeur, and a record eliminator. From time to time he would take recordings from the inactive file, drop them into hot water, take them out, and peel off the waxed surfaces. Next, he would cut the peelings into small pieces and transport them to Hackensack, New Jersey, for incineration.

Once a recording fell into Ware's hands, there was no going back, no possibility of retrieving its contents, no matter how valuable they might have been.

The Case of the Missing Conversation

As was true in the infamous missing eighteen minutes in the Nixon White House tapes, a missing segment in the Bureau's recordings of in-room conversations at Judy's office created yet another furious battle during rehearsals for the New York trial, this one of critical import. Although the microphone was in place and monitored in Judy's office from January 25 until March 12, there was no record, either in the log or on disc, of the critical exchange between her and Foley shortly after nine o'clock the morning of March 4. This is when she claimed her supervisor told her to take with her to New York information on the "hot and interesting" memo, ostensibly to work on it over the weekend; and when, she said, he saw her put her notes on the memo into her handbag. Foley contended she lied; he had said no such thing.

Foley also insisted that he did not know the original memo was false. It is safe to conjecture that not even his mother would have believed him, given the circumstances surrounding his receiving and passing along the memorandum.

Judith's former supervisor was disingenuous in his testimony about getting the decoy information into Judy's hands. In his November pretrial testimony, he said he had been given the decoy by Peyton Ford in an evening meeting on March 3, with instructions to "give it to your Foreign Agents people" the first thing the following morning. And who were the Foreign Agents people to whom Ford referred? "Mr. Lenvin and Miss Coplon." Well, Archie wanted to know, did Ford tell him to give it, specifically, to Miss Coplon? "I don't recall that he did, no," Foley said.

The decoy was accompanied by two unrelated letters. The decoy, however, had a note at the top saying, "Give this your immediate attention." There was no mistaking a sense of urgency.

Judith was alone in the office at the time, on the morning of the fourth, when Foley arrived with the memorandum and the letters. Archie asked Foley what he said to her about the papers handed to her.

"I said, 'These were given to me last night too late to deliver to you.'"

"Too late to give to *you?*"

"I don't recall what the language was," Foley said, quickly correcting himself. Actually, giving it thought, Foley recalled that what he had said was, "'too late to bring in here,' indicating that I got them after hours."

Raymond Whearty's stipulation during a November examination of Lamphere suggests that Foley was not quite truthful:

The government stipulated that "this memorandum was delivered to Mr. Peyton Ford on the evening of March 3rd by Howard B. Fletcher . . . that I [Whearty] was present at the time; within a very few moments of that delivery, Mr. Foley was summoned to Mr. Ford's office and appeared there. At that time in my presence Mr. Ford handed this memorandum, Exhibit 1, to Mr. Foley *with instructions to see to it that it was delivered to the defendant Coplon.*" [emphasis added]

Nothing in this unusual meeting made William Foley suspicious or caused him to wonder about the legitimacy of the message he was told to give to

Judith Coplon, whom he knew was suspected of espionage. There was no conversation such as Judy had claimed, no instructions to study the memo and take the information with her that day.

Nine months after the fact, on December 16, Agent Bedford, who had been listening to and recording the conversations in Judy's office, testified that there was nothing unique about this particular conversation being inaudible. After all, he said, he had complained from the beginning that the microphone was unreliable, and yet the Bureau had done nothing to correct the situation. Amazed, Archie asked if the agent had continued to record inaudible conversations from January 25, the date of installation, until March 12, when it was removed.

"This bad recording continued from week to week?" Archie asked.

"It continued as it always did," Bedford answered carefully.

"By and large," Archie continued, "would you say that the room conversations were virtually wholly indistinguishable on your discs?"

"That is correct."

Pomerantz entered the picture, calling Bedford's attention to the missing conversation.

"On that specific morning, at that specific time, you recall a male voice and a female voice coming over your earphones as a result of this monitoring. Now I ask you what, if anything, fastens this specific day and specific hour in your memory?"

"I just recall that I remember it."

Interposing, the judge asked, "Anything particular that occurred that brings it back to your memory?"

"Because on that particular date I know Miss Coplon was arrested in the evening in New York City, and I recall it at the time of her arrest that conversation had taken place between the persons in there, a woman and a male." Sadly, their voices were so muffled by the faulty microphone that he could hear nothing else.

There appears to be something fatally wrong with Bedford's explanation. The authors have a copy of his handwritten log of in-room conversations clearly heard and recorded both prior to and following the missing exchange between Foley and Coplon.

Mar. 4—10:55 A.M. Room Conversation. COPLON said to
SHAPIRO that I will call you Saturday. Spend some time
Sunday. COPLON said she would like to leave the office by
noon. Record #97, Cut #8.

The entry is signed "LWB," Bedford's initials

This same microphone was working well enough for Bedford to hear, at
9:10 A.M., Judith moving alone about the room and to make note of the fact.
Thus, it was performing at 9:10 A.M. and 10:55 A.M. on the morning of March
4, but not between 9:10 and 10:55, when the most critical conversation
debated in both trials took place. The microphone had also worked the day
before, as Bedford's log shows:

Mar. 3—9:23 A.M. Room Conversation. COPLON said to
FOLEY that she wanted to leave on the 1 P.M. train tomorrow.
She also said she wanted to get in New York early to pick up
something at downtown New York and she considered 42nd st.
as downtown New York. Not recorded.

Again, the entry is signed "LWB."

Judith, presumably alone until she left for the train that Friday, had no
further conversations in her office. The following Monday, the microphone
was still in place, however, and working well, as Bedford noted:

Mar. 7—10:08 A.M. Room Conversation. LENVIN said she
was a wonderful actress, she would sit down and read the Daily
Worker and laugh at its comments and editorials. Not
recorded.

And shortly thereafter, he noted:

11:50 A.M. Room Conversation. LENVIN said "Didn't she
have some data slips with her?" Miss TAYLOR said she had
typed some data slips from FBI reports for COPLON. Not
recorded.

There were also numerous calls clearly heard in the days prior to March 3.

In Foley's pretrial testimony, on December 10, he said he did not know there was a microphone in Judy's office. Archie quizzed Judy's former boss at length about where he was standing and how he spoke during the electronically missing conversation. Did Foley place himself in any particular position with the idea that his voice would not be recorded? Did he speak in such a manner that the microphone would not pick up his voice? No, he did not, because he had "no idea" that a microphone was present. Archie clearly had two possibilities in mind: one, Foley knew about Bedford and his recorder and was careful to stage the conversation so that it could not be clearly overheard; or, two, Foley did not know there was a microphone present and, therefore, the agents had tampered with the recording to protect an unsuspecting Foley.

"The Affair Shapiro" and Heading toward a New Year

It was Abraham Pomerantz who began calling Judith's ill-fated relationship with her Justice Department lawyer boyfriend "The Affair Shapiro." He did so when he joined Archie Palmer in objecting to evidence of the affair being used in the upcoming trial. On December 28, as the anniversary of Judy's admitted New Year's Eve tryst with Harold Shapiro neared, the combined defense argued that the FBI had learned of the illicit affair through illegal wiretapping. Therefore, the fact of the affair, and any implications with regard to Coplon's and Gubitchev's relationship stemming from it, should be suppressed. Ryan was inclined to agree about the source of information, but found electronic eavesdropping insufficient reason to dismiss the indictment. It was Pomerantz who heatedly argued that "The Affair Shapiro" never should have been brought into the case. Shortly after the holidays, Shapiro, for the first time, would take the stand in pretrial hearings and publicly discuss his romance with Judy and his involvement with the prosecution team. The nationwide audience eagerly awaited hearing from Judy's former lover, the alleged Lothario she accused in Washington of having been a part of an elaborate frame-up.

It was a troublesome day for the defense, with both Palmer and Pomerantz suffering scoldings by the judge. Although his previous warnings had been firm but gentle, Ryan's patience with Archie Palmer was near its end.

"I don't know whether your unorthodox tactics are the result of contemptuous buffoonery or personal eccentricity, but I want them stopped," Ryan declared, angered by Archie's constant interruptions. And there had been some lozenge chewing. No more, ordered the judge. As for Pomerantz, his clash with Ryan over whether or not the Bureau's wiretap summaries would or would not be a part of the record led to a testy exchange. Pomerantz wanted them out; the judge wanted them in, and the power was with the bench. After all, Ryan noted, Pomerantz had given his oral consent to inclusion last week. Not so, said the defense attorney.

"I move that if any remark of mine was interpreted as a concession to public divulgence—which I strenuously deny—I respectfully beg to retract any such stipulation." Respectfully or not, Ryan instructed Pomerantz to say no more on the matter. Contents of the summaries would be a part of the record.

There was only a brief holiday hiatus in the Foley Square proceedings. Pretrial hearings were taking far too much time and delaying the opening of the main event. But New York would have its Christmas, high-profile legal battles or no. The mega-city was dressed in its finest for the occasion, wearing its traditional accessories—twinkling Christmas lights, beribboned wreaths around the lightposts, silent reindeer staring from store windows. The air was filled with the music of carols and the squeals of children dragged along by mothers doing last-minute shopping. Storybook dolls and toy trucks and games lined the shelves of brightly decorated department stores, irresistible treasures these same children dreamed of finding under the tree on Christmas morning. With all of the beauty of the season, all of the joy, there was something tragically missing from the scene.

Santa, the real Santa, was dead.

This, the first-ever Christmas without their beloved husband and father, brought Judy, Rebecca, and Bertram unspeakable sadness. Throughout the East, a multitude of once-children now grown thought back to those Christmases when, through enchanted eyes, they had seen the real Santa in the mountains. The Coplons observed the holidays, this year of 1949, but not as any of them ever could have imagined a year earlier. And a year earlier, Judy had been deeply involved with Harold Shapiro, planning a festive New Year's Eve party.

Their relationship had been much more than the revealed overnight liaisons. They spoke every day and saw each other several times a week. Tap logs show that they discussed when, where, and with whom each would have lunch that day (if not together), whether they would join for dinner that night, whether, in fact, they would go home together. They discussed every-thing—books and music and feelings—and one would fret if the other suf-fered even a slight cold. This clearly was not a promiscuous sexual fling. It was something more richly textured. All of which must have made Judy's dis-illusionment profoundly bitter, believing as she did that Harold knew they were being trailed everywhere, and that, most likely, he had arranged for their conversations to be overheard by FBI agents. There is no indication that he had been in touch with her since her arrest. She must have wondered if he had ever loved her at all.

There was little break for Judy from work associated with the trial during the holiday season. There was abundant analytical and clerical work to be done, but no money to hire workers, so Judith spent long hours in Archie's office—a diversion that no doubt helped her through this difficult time.

On December 29, Archie moved for a new trial in Washington based on the wiretap disclosures. The motion would fail, as would Gubitchev's peti-tion for dismissal of the case against him based on his having a diplomatic passport. Pomerantz argued the point.

"To paraphrase Gertrude Stein, a diplomatic visa is a diplomatic visa is a diplomatic visa," the Russian's attorney said. Testifying for the government, Fred Strine disagreed with the literary analogy, arguing that "persons of dis-tinction" received diplomatic passports and visas "only as a matter of cour-tesy." Gubitchev's having one meant nothing.

What a surprise this news would be to diplomats worldwide, Pomerantz observed.

As the new year dawned, the Coplon case—now, of course, the Coplon-Gubitchev case—was once again making headlines, with a continued emphasis on the adventures and misadventures of the FBI. The show, and hence the reviews, had new and intriguing stars: the secret wiretappers. A *Washington Post* editorial reflected the sentiments of many, following release of a statement by

Attorney General J. Howard McGrath curtly saying that the FBI "has been tapping the private telephones of American citizens" by his authorization, and, furthermore, he would continue to do so. The *Post* observed:

> Congress wisely classified wire tapping among the forbidden police methods because the danger inherent in it to innocent persons outweighs the benefits it may yield to law enforcement. All wire tapping . . . is dragnet in character. It involves invading the privacy of innocent conversations, the disclosure of confidential relations. The mere knowledge that the police may resort to wire tapping puts a restraint upon the communication of ideas by wire that is intolerable to a free people. There is now a real need, we think, for a thoroughgoing congressional investigation of wire tapping by the FBI and a firm restatement of congressional policy unequivocally forbidding what Justice Holmes aptly called "such dirty business."

Congress had been asked, specifically, the year before to authorize wiretapping in certain circumstances, including "against those persons not citizens of the United States and those few citizens who are traitors to their country, who today are engaged in espionage or sabotage against their country." It had not done so. The law, despite what the attorney general declared, prohibited wiretapping. Period.

On January 1, a major left-wing newspaper, the *Compass*, reported that Judith Coplon would ask the Supreme Court to order the attorney general to "confess error" in the Washington trial and to join in her appellate motion to have the judgment against her set aside. Judy's petition said that, "in flagrant violation" of the Supreme Court's warnings in this regard, "and the clear language of the Federal Communications Act . . . the agents of the FBI, in full knowledge of the rulings of this court, constantly engaged in tapping of the petitioner's wires before the indictments . . . and even during and after the trial."

On the second, Archibald Palmer went to North Dakota senator William Langer to ask for a Senate Judiciary Committee investigation of the FBI's methods. At the same time, Robert Daru, board chairman of the New York

County Criminal Courts Bar Association, announced hearings on the wiretapping issue and said the association would present legislation on the subject to the next session of the New York state legislature. In short order, the American Civil Liberties Union and the Americans for Democratic Action hopped on the bandwagon heading into this new and compelling investigative territory—the FBI and its electronic information gathering.

Days later, a prominent headline at the top of page one of the January 5 *New York World-Telegram* read, INSIDE THE FBI: HOW IT TAPS. A subhead read, SYSTEM STARTED 10 YEARS AGO BY ROOSEVELT.

That same day, the *Washington Daily News* offered its readers inside information on how the Bureau reached decisions to tap wires, explaining that "original instructions and authorization to approve wire-tapping went to the US Attorney General in a confidential memorandum from President Roosevelt in May 1940." Never mind about Roosevelt and his memorandum, critics observed. This was a matter of law, and the law held that wiretapping was illegal. Later, in the appeals process, dozens of pages of argument would debate Roosevelt versus Congress, two sides of a very sticky issue.

The *Daily News* story defended the FBI's use of wiretaps, citing solved kidnapping cases and the apprehension of a group of Nazi saboteurs who landed on Long Island in 1941. There was good reason, the article held, for using listening devices. Again, two sides. The country read and thought about these questions. Thought about situations such as telling the parents of a precious child saved because of wiretaps that those taps were illegal and never should have been in place. Thought about saboteurs and terrorists whose evil plots were foiled because of someone listening in on their plans. Still, the law was the law, and if a law enforcement agency could operate beyond the law, how could it enforce compliance on the part of others? Across the land, this issue, debated so publicly, led citizens to contemplate not only civil law but also moral and ethical law, natural and universal law. What, and who, was "right" or "wrong"? This case had become not only a source of national entertainment, but also one of thoughtful contemplation.

On the day this story was released, Judge Ryan ordered Foley to appear immediately if not sooner to tell the court about the missing conversation. In the murky middle of wrangling over the legality of tapping, Ryan ordered, once again, that Archie give up his lozenges and drink water instead.

"It's an order of the court to stop stuffing your mouth with candy," announced the judge, noting that he had been tolerant long enough.

Archie pleaded for return of his chewing privileges, but the judge was adamant. If he were forced to replace his candies with drinking water, the distraught attorney warned, he "might deplete the city's short water supply."

"I hope the more you drink, the less you'll talk," Ryan said.

The prestigious *New York Times*, in relating the exchange, made note of the fact that Archibald Palmer, counsel to Judith Coplon, drank eight glasses of water during courtroom proceedings on January 5, 1950.

For the next four days, stormy arguments surrounded the issue of the sound recordings made in Judith's office and the handwritten logs made at the scene by the various monitors. Archie questioned two sound experts, and discs were played for the court. It was true that they were, for the most part, inaudible except for a few understandable (and unimportant) words here and there. The attorney observed, with ill-concealed suspicion, how curious it was that while the Bureau had kept these particular recordings for ten months, "nobody ever found out they were unintelligible" until the secret monitoring had come to light. Archie wanted to find out, he explained, if they had been rendered unintelligible by a deliberate act.

From witness Robert Solby, an audio expert, Archie learned that the discs appeared to have been "excellently cut." Solby also said the system in place at the time should have produced distinct recordings. Archie's nose quivered. Could someone have tampered with the discs in question? Could the conversations have been ruined after the records were made?

Oh yes, the expert testified. By any number of methods.

The second witness, Jack Meyerson of Musicraft Records, said the acetate discs would retain their transcriptions for a long period of time unless they were "mishandled or stored in extreme heat." Once again, the behavior of the Bureau was called into question—if not in specific words, then certainly by implication. Was there, in fact, a sinister reason behind the torn-up written records and the missing and unintelligible conversations on disc? The pernicious plot thickened day by day.

Pomerantz and Palmer, clearly excited, announced that they would bring sound engineers to court to make "scientific and microscopic" examination of the discs. As the day ended, Judy learned she would be able to review written logs and listen, as much as possible, to all of the discs available to her.

It was on January 9, exactly one year and two days from the time a telephone tap had been installed in Judy's Washington apartment, that Archie complained to the court about the discs the FBI had produced for the court. They were dubs made from the originals. The Bureau itself had determined which of the original conversations would be dubbed for the court, eliminating, it was explained, information it considered to be of no value, as well as that relating to other cases. It was difficult to understand this sort of fox-and-henhouse activity; it was also difficult to believe that a single disc would have on it recordings from more than one source.

A sudden illness kept John Kelley from appearing in court that morning. Whearty, acting as understudy, explained to the court that Mr. Kelley had collapsed on the train. The prosecutor, shuttling back and forth between his home in Washington and Foley Square, apparently was suffering from exhaustion. One might conjecture that fear of losing the most important case in his career, along with increasing pressure from the court and a pack of baying media jackals might well have played a role in the hardworking prosecutor's condition.

The Killer Tiger Memo

Fifty-one years after it came to light in the New York pretrial hearings, the authors held in their hands the original, yellow, and cellophane-taped draft of the FBI memorandum that rocked the courtroom on January 12, when Judge Ryan confronted the prosecution with its existence. The message, from Assistant Director Howard Fletcher, was directed to Mr. D. M. Ladd, one of Hoover's key assistants.

Its subject was Tiger. It read:

> The above named informant [Tiger] has been furnishing information concerning the activities of Coplon since her conviction. In view of the imminency [sic] of her trial, it is recommended that this informant be discontinued immedi-

ately and that <u>all administrative records in the New York office</u>
<u>covering the operations of this informant be destroyed.</u>
Pertinent data furnished by the informant has already been
furnished in letter form, and having in mind security, now and
in the future, it is believed desirable that the indicated records
be destroyed.

(emphasis as it appears in the original)

THIS MEMORANDUM IS FOR ADMINISTRATIVE
PURPOSES. TO BE DESTROYED AFTER ACTION IS
TAKEN AND NOT SENT TO THE FILES.

A handwritten note angles across the lower right of the page: "Tuchy
advised 12:10 P.M. 11-8-49 . . . disct 1:30 P.M. 11-10-49." Someone, it
appears, noted compliance with the disconnect order. Significantly, "O-K.
H.," Hoover's traditional indication of approval, was handwritten below the
text of the message. Corrections in pencil apparently guided preparation of
the final draft.

Tiger was the Bureau's Coplon wiretap operation. Tiger was now out of
the jungle and into the open.

The memo was given to the defense by Judge Ryan during Archie Palmer's
examination of Special Agent Arthur Avignone. Likely, Ryan had asked for the
memo after Fletcher's secretary, Teresa Cuddy, in earlier testimony had mentioned the existence of a written statement concerning destruction of records.
At the time, apparently, the defense had not realized the significance of
Cuddy's revelation. Avignone had admitted expediting destruction of eight to
twelve recordings of Coplon conversations, all of which had been on hand in
the New York office as of November 10. The secret document appeared to
put the lie to Bureau testimony and, for many, to belief in the country's most
revered law enforcement agency. Destruction of the discs was far from the
"routine" matter Whearty had described for the court. Avignone testified
with rare honesty and directness that he had been specifically instructed by Al
Belmont to ensure destruction of the wiretap recordings.

Pomerantz, stunned, said he had "never heard a more forthright and honest declaration from a witness." Judge Ryan nodded in agreement. "I make the same observation," he said, then turned the surprise memorandum over to the defense. It was read aloud.

The courtroom was in a collective state of shock. Even Archie Palmer was speechless, at least for a moment or two. A short recess found attorneys huddled, with the defense clearly far happier in this wildly flustered hiatus than was the prosecution team. With a sound of the gavel, the proceedings resumed, with Avignone still on the stand.

The agent testified that he was responsible for making written summaries of the Ocean Parkway telephone from July 12 until November 10, when the order to shut down and destroy the records was issued. He admitted to thinking at the time that Belmont's order seemed "a bit unusual."

Arthur Avignone had become, for some, the ultimate hero; for others, he had earned the stripes of a traitor.

The defense based high hopes for dismissal on the released memorandum, holding that destruction of critical evidence gained through illegal wiretapping amounted to obstruction of justice on the part of the government. Two issues were present—the manner in which the evidence was obtained and the manner in which it was destroyed. Ultimately, on January 18, Judge Ryan would settle the question.

"It is immaterial whether this investigation was touched off by an interception or knowledge was gained by a person who acted as an informer." Wiretapping was thus blessed. About destruction of the records, he said, "I am satisfied from the testimony . . . that destruction of these records was not for the purpose of obstruction of justice." Another blessing.

During final arguments on the issue, Al Belmont testified that he knew some of the intercepted and recorded conversations were between Archie and Judy, and, for "ethical reasons" sought Fletcher's approval to destroy them to protect client-attorney privileges. Archie did not appear to be pleased with Belmont's justification. Neither did Pomerantz, who brought to the court's attention the fact that Fletcher's signature on the controversial memo was in conflict with his earlier testimony that he "had no knowledge" of destruction of the records. On the stand, under Pomerantz's questioning, Fletcher now told the court that he "must have been in error" when he denied knowing anything about the matter.

While other matters took center stage the day following release of the memo, its existence and the possible implications coming from it were in everyone's mind. However, the court's attention, of necessity, was directed elsewhere. At the moment, it was directed to the witness stand, where Archie Palmer was once again examining pudgy William Foley. Archie immediately caused a stir when he inquired about a possible social relationship Foley might have had with his subordinate, Judith Coplon.

"Isn't it a fact," Archie asked, "that you and Miss Coplon went out socially—to see 'Hamlet'—and you brought her refreshments, and weren't you jealous when you found out she was going out with Gubitchev?"

"Not at all!" exploded Foley. Later, he told reporters who found this bit of gossip particularly interesting that he hadn't really dated Judy, but that they had attended the same Justice Department parties, that they were "together at parties." On occasion, he had taken her home. There was no relationship.

Foley was beginning to test Archie's limited patience. Judy's former supervisor continued to insist that he didn't know the decoy message was a decoy and gave it to the suspected spy in complete innocence, and that he never told her to take information from the decoy home over the weekend. He did, however, tell the FBI about Judy's every move during the time she was under surveillance. In Archie's mind, all of this did not compute, and his bombastic temper, never far from the surface, flared. Nerves frazzled, Archie raged against Foley, and, more particularly, against Kelley and Whearty, whom he clearly considered to be, at best, a pair of lying miscreants.

He had gone too far. "I don't believe in fining lawyers or sending them to jail," Judge Ryan steamed, reminding Archie of his threat to toss him from the courtroom and the case. "I would be very much grieved if your conduct in this case should be the cause of terminating your long career in this court!"

Chastisement aside, Archie boldly inquired of witness Dudley Payne whether Judith Coplon and Harold Shapiro "had their clothes on" when they entered and left a Washington apartment house the night of January 6, 1949. Were they, possibly, naked? Startled by the question, Payne paused a moment and then answered that the subjects were properly clothed and, in fact, had been out of his sight for only five minutes. It was the following night, and the one after, when Judy and Harold had their now very public nights in Baltimore and Philadelphia. An attentive Judge Ryan told lawyers for both sides that, if called, Shapiro's testimony "might be admissible on a limited scale" with regard to his affair with Judy.

"I want to hear from Shapiro's own lips" about The Affair Shapiro, Archie told the court. He wanted to know if Shapiro had been a pawn of the FBI. Of special import was whether the Bureau had learned of the Baltimore and Philadelphia assignations from overheard conversations.

"You mean you want to find out if he is what is, in common parlance, a stool pigeon?" asked Judge Ryan.

"He being a Yale man, I wouldn't use that expression about him," Archie replied in his most gentlemanly fashion.

Agent Payne assured the court that it was physical surveillance alone that led agents to follow the couple to the Washington apartment house (where they went in and out with their clothes on) and then to Baltimore. Judy's tap had been installed at 4 P.M. on January 6. Physical surveillance began an hour later, not long before the first call was intercepted, at 6:57 P.M.

The Mystery Man from Yale

Valentin Gubitchev was never the mystery man in this case; perhaps, under other circumstances, the enigmatic foreigner might well have carried this distinction. Even though he did not appear in the Washington proceedings in person but rather as a symbol of enemy intrigue, even though his surreptitious behavior left people wondering if he had been lover or spy, and, finally, even though he was now a defendant in a high-stakes espionage trial, he was not the mystery man.

Harold Shapiro was.

Why hadn't Harold been called to testify in Washington? Had he revealed intimate details of his romance with Judith to the FBI? Had Harold *led* the FBI to Judith? Was he a part of the conspiracy she claimed was behind her arrest? Had he made love to her per instructions from the FBI? Why hadn't Shapiro been caught by the press hurrying to visit Judith when she was first arrested, and why hadn't he publicly expressed support or concern? In fact, why weren't there photographs of Harold in their newspapers?

The public, filled with questions about and for Harold, eagerly anticipated his courtroom appearance, hoping for answers. They couldn't wait to
unveil the mystery surrounding the young man, now thirty-four, who had
played one of the most significant roles in the Washington case while assid-
uously keeping out of sight. In spite of himself, Harold had become famous,
like it or not. At first, it seemed, he did not; later, he was reported to be
enjoying his celebrity status at cocktail parties around the capital, always with
an attractive woman on his arm.

Like so many other aspects of the case, Harold's finally entering the courtroom took place not in either trial, but in the historic pretrial hearings now
under way.

He did not look the part of a romantic mystery man. Dark-haired Harold
wore Coke-bottle eyeglasses that, from time to time, he nervously shoved up
the bridge of his nose. He hardly seemed the sort of man the brilliant and
vivacious Judy would have chosen. But he was clearly intelligent, and apparently as interested in the arts and music as she was. At this time of her life,
Judy would later complain, she was feeling "dissected," that the public had
taken her apart, physically and morally, examining every piece of her substance and her spirit. Now the public wanted to dissect Harold as well, this
time with a scalpel of patently prurient curiosity.

The microphone in Judy's office was still in place on March 7, the Monday
after her arrest in New York. Lyn Bedford's log details a conversation
between two of her colleagues that morning and gives a clue to Shapiro's
feelings following Judith's arrest:

> 9:55 A.M. LENVIN to MICROUTSICOS at Ext 175 in Justice
> Dept. They discussed the arrest of COPLON. Both stated that
> they were shocked, surprised, and thought it unconceivable
> [sic]. LENVIN said Harold Shapiro was out to our house and
> he is completely dissolved. LENVIN said it was a wonderful act
> on her part and you would have to crawl inside her to figure out
> her mind . . . Record #98 Cut #6 and Record #99 Cut 1.

Signed "LWB," the log entry went on to detail reactions of various friends
and associates to Judith's arrest. Later, in the afternoon, Shapiro called Lenvin.

2:30 P.M. SHAPIRO to LENVIN. Shapiro said he was going to call Foley and wanted to know his extension. Record #100 Cut #4. LWB

As both an attorney working for the Department of Justice and the boyfriend of a woman arrested for espionage, Harold was uncertain about what he should, or should not, do. First, he had gone to see Raymond Whearty, telling him that Judy was a very close friend. Very close. With Harold on the stand at last, Archie asked:

"When you told him about your friendship for the girl, and you came there and asked him what it was all about, what did Mr. Whearty say to you?"

"That in his opinion she was guilty of these things that she was charged with."

Had Judith's boyfriend gone to Whearty "to exculpate" himself? "I wasn't involved," Harold told the attorney. "I had nothing to exculpate myself about."

Judge Ryan asked for further information on what Shapiro had told Whearty. "I don't remember," the witness answered. "I remember that the main purpose of my going in there was to ask if it could possibly be a mistake, or what it was about."

"Did he ever tell you at the time," Ryan asked, "or at any time, that your conversations with the defendant Coplon in her room had been monitored through a microphone?" No, Harold answered, Whearty did not.

"Is Your Honor through?" Archie asked; then, at the judge's nod, he turned to the witness. "Based upon what Mr. Whearty did tell you, or what the agents did tell you, did there come a glimmering to you, or any idea that what they were talking about could only have been obtained through the use of a microphone recording of the conversations on the disc or through interceptions of her telephone? Did that suspicion arise in your mind from what they said, or from the leading nature of the questions that they asked you?"

"From nothing that Mr. Whearty told me." Harold explained that when he learned the FBI knew all about his relationship with Judy, he simply assumed that she had told them about him, that all information had come to agents from her.

Well, then, Archie asked, what about anything he might have heard from the agents with whom he had spoken after Judy's arrest? Did anything said to Shapiro ". . . give you the idea at all that some of the leads they were given came by reason of intercepts of telephone calls or through microphonic conversations intercepted?" No, no, no, the witness knew nothing.

Pressured, Shapiro finally conceded that yes, at the time, he had thought "it might have been so." The judge, undoubtedly annoyed at Archie's failure to move quickly to the heart of the matter, resumed his questioning.

"In your acquaintance with Miss Coplon, did you act under the instructions of any law enforcement agent . . . or cultivate her acquaintance or arrange to meet her at any time under instructions of any law enforcement agent?"

Members of the press leaned forward to hear the young attorney answer softly, "I did not." The courtroom was completely silent, waiting for the next questions. One chair at the defense table was empty. It was Judith's.

"You did at times pay social visits and she paid social visits, and you went out together. On those occasions were you acting under instructions of any Federal law enforcement agent . . . [and] when carrying on telephone conversations with her, at any time was there any agent or any person from a law enforcement agency present telling you what to say or suggesting what should be said?"

"No, sir."

"Or did you make any of those calls at the suggestion or at the request or direction of any law enforcement agent or agency?"

Again, "No, sir."

Archie angrily approached the bench. "I am taking an exception to all this. I was looking at him, but I am taking an exception to all of Your Honor's questions upon the ground that they are leading in character and improper as to form."

Astounded at this sudden role reversal, Ryan demanded, "And *improper to form?*" Absolutely flabbergasted, yet with grace and dignity, the judge returned a most uncomfortable witness to the audacious Archie.

Smoothly, Archie asked Shapiro if he was still a friend of Judith's.

"I don't hate her," he said.

Harold denied that Judy had ever spoken to him about Valentin Gubitchev, claiming he had heard nothing about the supposed love of her life until after her arrest. According to the witness now testifying, her statements to the contrary were lies.

By way of background, Shapiro acknowledged knowing Whearty and having once lived in the same house with William Foley. There was no discussion of their being his card-playing friends.

Foley Has the Last Word

As the highly publicized pretrial hearings drew to a contentious close, Abraham Pomerantz demanded a grand jury investigation of what he called "mammoth" crimes admitted by FBI agents. Further, Pomerantz wanted Judge Ryan to appoint a special prosecutor to conduct an inquiry. Pomerantz's plea would fail.

On January 20, Judge Ryan handed down the last of his rulings. Judith Coplon and Valentin Gubitchev would be tried; their contention that the indictment should be dismissed because it was born of poisoned fruit was invalid. In thirty-four pages of rulings, this and other motions for dismissal, including Gubitchev's claim of diplomatic immunity, were denied. Ironically, in making his final determination to go to trial, the judge acknowledged the deciding factor—William Foley's disputed testimony.

"The government has shown to my satisfaction that it does have proof obtained independently of telephone and microphone interceptions. Though much of this independent proof depends on the credibility of the witness Foley, the court cannot and will not now determine that his testimony is not worthy of belief."

Trial was set to begin Tuesday, January 24, one day short of the anniversary of the placement of a microphone in Judith Coplon's office at the Department of Justice—the microphone that failed to work for a few critical minutes the morning of March 4 , the microphone that could have proved, or disproved, William Foley's testimony.

Judge Ryan made reference to the electronic misadventures that had caused such turmoil in the proceedings, rebuking the FBI for wiretapping, an act the judge acknowledged as illegal. His acknowledgment, which may have seemed unhelpful at the time, would later lend support to appellate arguments.

For the defense, it was the bitter, although not unexpected, result of a valiant effort to show government wrongdoing and to escape trial. For Judith, it was particularly devastating. She would need to go through the angst and daily misery of another trial and face the terrifying possibility of being sentenced to additional years in prison. The media's darling star was, for now, lost in clouds of despair.

As for Judy's somber codefendant, he continued to remain in the shadows. On the one hand, there is the evidence that a secret deal already had been worked out to ensure that he would never serve another day behind U.S. bars, which for now put him in a much more comfortable position than Judith. On the other, however, Gubitchev well understood that his future, as a Russian "failed spy," could be in far greater jeopardy than hers.

Finally, as for the Bureau, it suffered an ugly coat of tarnish from what was considered, by now, a fatal "legal smashup." The entire case brought enormous embarrassment to the FBI and, both professionally and personally, to its director. A leader who demanded perfection, Hoover's outrage over what he considered to be a bungled case stayed with him for years afterward. He would never forgive Judith Coplon. Although Howard Fletcher, Lamphere's boss at the time, was not exiled to Butte, Montana (a favorite Hoover punishment), he found himself in chilling disfavor and assigned to a lesser job. Lamphere says today that he was blessedly fortunate Hoover's fury had not been directed toward him. "He never liked the case from the beginning," Lamphere notes. "We talked him into it."

More than fifty years after the Coplon case reached the off-Broadway stage at Foley Square, the FBI was suffering what many considered an unprecedented image tarnishing. Waco. Ruby Ridge. Robert Hanssen. The McVeigh documents. Even those who believed J. Edgar Hoover to have been an egomaniacal tyrant grudgingly were insisting that "these things never would have happened under Hoover." A testy Congress, convinced that the Bureau had "too much power and too little oversight," was calling for extensive hearings and even, on the part of some, a breakup of the agency. Few seemed to recall that it happened before.

It was during these tempestuous New York pretrial hearings that the enormity of the government's miscalculations was becoming apparent, even with the Washington conviction. First, there had been the decision to go ahead with a trial when the legality of the arrest was in question and without firm evidence that Judith Coplon had passed secrets to the enemy; second, there was the decision to continue with the Washington trial once Judge Reeves had decided that the Bureau's raw files would be made public; and third, there was the decision to have government witnesses lie on the stand about wiretapping and destroy wiretapping evidence.

Underlying all of these was the unfortunate decision to try an alleged spy when it was impossible to tell the world, and the court, the real identity of the "confidential informant" responsible for leading the Bureau to Judith Coplon. By now, nearly everyone believed the mysterious tattletale to have been a wiretap.

It was not.

The Final Act

The prosecution ended its case twenty-three days into the nation's second Cold War trial; the defense ended its case exactly one hour later. The unexpected conclusion was no more outrageous than much of the rest of the trial, which on occasion was reduced to screaming and name calling within the courtroom and a physical scuffle outside. Unlike the pretrial hearings, the New York trial had present from beginning to surprising end all of its main characters—Archie the attorney-clown; Kelley, the steely chief prosecutor; his colleague Whearty, the former boss, friend, and admirer of one of the defendants; Abraham Pomerantz, the highly distinguished new member of the team; the same supporting cast of FBI supervisors, agents, and "illegal wiretappers"; and, finally, the stars—Judith Coplon, America's typical girl next door and convicted spy, and Valentin Gubitchev, Russian engineer and accused spy. Missing, to no one's surprise, was Harold Shapiro.

Those who had expected yet another spectacle filled with fire and drama, which was essentially everyone, were not disappointed. If they had expected the same flammable ingredients, however, they were wrong.

In anticipation of the trial, differing media views of what had happened thus far in the yearlong espionage drama and what was likely to transpire in the days ahead were offered to the public in abundance, all according to the

political position of the newspaper. The far-left-wing press ran huge headlines and biting articles filled with vituperation for the FBI, the attorney general, and the entire government of the United States. Its tone pictured
American law as a jaundiced jurisprudence, a system diseased by democracy
and practiced by the unconscionable.

The *People's World* wrote, under the bold headline FBI TAPS PHONES OF UN
OFFICIALS, that revelations coming from the just-concluded pretrial hearings
"created a sensation in the field of foreign relations." It cited tales of the
United States snatching and opening diplomatic mail, searching trash cans,
and tapping telephones. Complaining that the metropolitan press ignored
much of this unethical behavior, and in order to right this wrong, the newspaper published excerpts of agents' reports of intercepted diplomatic messages.
"Francis W. Zangle, special FBI agent, reported Nov. 22, 1948, on a secret
investigation of Georgi Dimitrov Sotirov, Bulgarian official attached to the
Immigration Section of the Department of Social Affairs at the UN." Zangle's
report indicated that his confidential informant was "T-3," a wiretapper. There
were many more details about Zangle and the work of his colleagues.

Prosecutor Raymond P. Whearty was "clinging tenaciously to tattered
scraps of manufactured evidence" in preparing for trial, the *Daily Worker*
informed its readers. A few days later, the newspaper would be saddened to
report that the jury was composed of six men and six women, "from which
all working men and women have been excluded." Panel demographics did
not agree with the *Worker.*

The mainstream press was content to rehash the essentials of the hearings,
repeat the story of the arrests and the Washington trial, set the stage for the
upcoming trial, and review, once again, details of the enormous battle over
wiretapping. However, even here there was concern over what the country
had just learned in Foley Square. In an editorial appearing the day before the
trial opened, the *Hartford Courant,* hardly left wing, took issue with
McGrath's position. "Mr. McGrath would do well to take his desire for
power to tap wires to Congress." In another, the *World Telegram* wrote, "This
stern insistence of a federal judge on the federal illegality of wiretapping
should stir Congress to stiffen the Federal Communications Act in ways to
make it less easy for the FBI to go on deliberately and notoriously violating
this law."

On opening day, Archie Palmer and his client arrived together, or rather in close proximity, he stomping ahead carrying two briefcases and some papers, she scurrying along behind carrying his oversized hat along with her handbag and her own case. Gubitchev, eyes looking neither to the right or left, arrived alone. Once again studiously avoiding acknowledging each other, the defendants settled into their seats; Pomerantz arrived moments later. The press, watching every move, would report the following day that Judy's demeanor was different than it had been.

"The flashing smile and merry eyes, which enhanced her sultry attractiveness at the Washington trial, were displayed only at rare intervals yesterday," the *Washington Star* observed. It was true, at least until examination of prospective jurors took place. Until then, she sat quietly listening, head slightly bowed; not inattentive, as she had been on other occasions in court.

With the principal players present, Ryan began the proceedings by announcing that defending attorneys would be cited for contempt if either mentioned Miss Coplon's Washington conviction in the presence of the jury about to be selected. Palmer objected.

"No juror in the world, even if he were a lunatic, could sit here unprejudiced after all the newspaper noise about the Washington trial!" he insisted.

The judge was equally insistent.

Archie had another objection, this time about the courtroom. The trial was being held on the same premises, in the very *room*, where eleven top Communists were recently tried and convicted. This unfortunate circumstance certainly would influence the proceedings and create an atmosphere unfair to his client. Regardless, the judge sighed, the trial would take place where scheduled. Perhaps, then, Archie offered, the judge might be good enough to ask prospective jurors certain questions to help alleviate the prejudicial ambience created by the ghosts of convicted Communists and the "Washington noise." For example, would His Honor ask if they were ever subjected to Red-baiting loyalty oaths? No, His Honor most decidedly would not. The judge was more receptive to the question Pomerantz posed, which clearly indicated the dapper, urbane attorney's intention to play the sex card during the trial:

"Would the fact that Mr. Gubitchev, a married man, had been meeting Miss Coplon, an unmarried girl, influence your judgment?"

They all said it would not, whereupon Ryan, in each instance, would say, "The defendants are not charged with immorality—they are charged with a more serious crime." Whereupon, Archie, in each instance, would bounce to his feet and insist that the judge add that Judy thought Gubitchev to be unmarried during their relationship.

Judge Ryan was obvious in his intent to provide the defense with a fair trial, honoring nearly every defense jury challenge for "cause." He raised the issue of Gubitchev's nationality, asking, "If it is shown that one of the defendants was an important officer of the Soviet Union and as such was a member of the Communist Party, would that influence your judgment?" One prospective juror, a veteran of two world wars, felt it most likely would.

"That's the kind of honest answer I like to hear," the judge said.

An immediate, personal metamorphosis took place in defendant Coplon once jury selection began. She brightened, took up a notepad and pencil, and began making copious notes. As they had in Washington nine months earlier, Judy and Archie put their heads together and whispered about each candidate who would, or would not, be called upon to decide her fate.

The court moved quickly and deftly past Archie's inevitable interventions, and six men and six women were selected to serve on the jury. All of the women were housewives. The men were a stock clerk, an employee of the Travelers' Aid Society, an assistant hotel manager, two painting contractors, and a salesman. All were white.

Late in the day, after jury members had been seated, the defendants were called to stand before them. Side by side but miles apart, Judy and Gubitchev stood, neither humbly nor defiantly, in federal court facing their twelve judges. No one blinked.

It took exactly one day for the defense team to fall apart and the courtroom fireworks to begin. The morning after the jury was impaneled, Pomerantz furiously protested, outside its hearing, to Palmer's planned opening remarks, scheduled for delivery the following day. It was Archie's intention, approved by Judge Ryan, to tell the jury, in great detail, about the Washington trial—except, of course, about the conviction.

Pomerantz said Archie's remarks would seriously prejudice the jury against his Russian client, and told the court he would seek a mistrial if there were any references to the Washington trial. Kelley and Whearty strongly agreed with this position; in fact, it was Kelley who made the initial motion to exclude any information about Judith's trial in the nation's capital.

On his feet, whirling to glare first at an old enemy and then at a new adversary, Archie yelled that he would be "straitjacketed" if he were unable to tell the jury the facts, as he saw them, about Judy's lengthy trial in Washington.

Seething, Pomerantz told Ryan in heroic understatement, "This is not the first instance of differences between Mr. Palmer and myself. The fact is, we don't see eye to eye on a number of questions."

Miffed, Archie muttered and fussed until the judge determined it was a prudent moment for chastisement. "Remember," he cautioned, "you are an officer of the court."

A Tattered Curtain Rises

Continued dispute between the defense attorneys delayed the trial's official opening, but only for a day. Like opposing litigants settling their disagreement on the courthouse steps, the pair resolved the issue moments before the trial began. In this case, Pomerantz won. Archie, with something less than graceful acquiescence, agreed to slap a hairy paw over his mouth and not mention the Washington trial.

Thus, on January 26, the curtain, already torn by dispute, rose on the second heated Cold War trial. Raymond Whearty, as before, opened for the government, with first Abraham Pomerantz and then Archie Palmer opening for the defense. As the proceedings got under way, jury members sat at full attention in an atmosphere not of prejudice, as Archie had predicted, but of undisguised fascination.

The prosecutor got as far as, "May it please the court, ladies, and gentlemen . . ." before Judge Ryan was compelled to interrupt with, "Excuse me, Mr. Whearty," then, pointing, "Stay where you are, Mr. Palmer, stay at the counsel table; stay away from the jurybox!" With a clearly annoyed glance in Archie's direction, Whearty approached the jury. He began with a careful explanation of the four charges of the indictment. The first, against both defendants, alleged acts of conspiracy based on the Espionage Act and having to do with the transmittal of information, removal of documents, and defrauding the United States of the "fair and impartial" services of Judith Coplon. The other counts, he said, charged *attempted*, not committed, espionage. The second count, against Judith alone, charged her with attempting to remove information for the purpose of giving it to an unauthorized person; and the third charged Gubitchev with being that person. The fourth count, against Judith alone, charged her with attempting to commit espionage.

It sounded a lot like Washington, except for the inclusion of Gubitchev and all the attempting to do something that didn't happen.

"I find that it is generally a little better not to say the government will show this and attempt to prove that, but, rather to give to the jury a statement of the facts in running order as the government expects the proof will establish them to be," Whearty told the jury, who wondered exactly how this would work. In a very brief summary, he told them who Judy was and where she was working at the time she was placed under surveillance, an action taken based on information coming to the Bureau "to the effect that Judith Coplon might be engaged in espionage activities."

Raymond Whearty must have learned something from the Washington reaction to his mind-deadening recital on the ancient geological underpinnings of Manhattan Island. This irrelevant, although scholarly, information was now missing. Unfortunately, he had learned nothing from a similar reaction to his minute detailing of the subway system that ultimately pierced through the various strata now left unmentioned.

"You all know that St. Nicholas Avenue is up high and the subway is a considerable distance under the street level. If you are going up to St. Nicholas Avenue you take that elevator. . . ." At different points during his recitation, Whearty described entrances and exits, tunnels and elevators, at tedious length. "There is a tunnel which leads to the Eighth Avenue subway, and it is a rather long tunnel, and it leads in at about track level."

He also spoke of buses and trains. "Coming back to the 18th of February, Judith Coplon did not come to New York on the one o'clock train that day. She came on the two o'clock train. . . . They got on a bus, and the door slammed, and the lights changed, and the bus went south on Ninth Avenue."

On one night underground, the defendant did something that seemed peculiar to Whearty. "But Judith Coplon got off and she took the elevator to the street level. Before she took the elevator to the street level, the evidence will show, she stopped to powder her nose at a little gum machine or something on the station level." Humm, mused Whearty, "that ordinarily—well, I should not comment at all on that."

Finally, after reciting Judith's and Gubitchev's step-by-step evasive meandering through New York City on three occasions (which agent after agent would later repeat), he finally got to the arrest on March 4. Briefly, and taking very little time to do so, he described the contents of Judith's purse, noting that one of the documents mentioned "geophones to measure blast pressures at the Alamogordo tests," a rather limited description of the instrument.

In concluding, Whearty said, "With respect to Mr. Gubitchev . . . he carried certain papers that identified him . . . and a little diary and had $125 in cash in a white envelope and another four dollars in his pocket, and some cents." He smiled at the jury. "Now, I think I have covered practically all of the facts that the government intends to prove, and upon those facts we feel confident that you will see the clear guilt of the defendants."

To do so, one might observe, would require an extraordinary clarity of vision. The facts the government would present, if one relied on Whearty's presentation, were that the defendants had traveled from point A to point Z by going through the entire alphabet, and that Judy had carried specific documents with her. He spoke of neither intent nor attempt.

Significantly, he spoke not a word about romance.

Abraham Pomerantz did. It would be the emotional conclusion to his presentation.

After identifying his client and providing a brief résumé of his life and work, Gubitchev's attorney said that there was "going to be very little difference on the facts" presented by Whearty. The facts, as set out by opposition counsel, were essentially correct insofar as Pomerantz, speaking only for Gubitchev, was concerned.

He immediately came to the point. "We are going to show you here that in spite of one of the most intensive and extensive investigations ever conducted by the FBI, in spite of the fact that the defendants were trailed by as many as 30 or 40 agents, in spite of surveillances of these defendants, their persons, their mail and other kinds of surveillances, legal and illegal . . . you will find that Mr. Gubitchev never received a single piece of paper from Coplon that related to the United States of America. You will not find that Gubitchev ever had on his person a single piece of paper at any time which belonged to our government or related to our government."

Referring to the night of the arrest, Pomerantz noted that the alleged conspirators had "upwards of two and a half hours" in which to "pass trunks full of Government archives," but nothing had exchanged hands. Still, the FBI, having found no evidence at all on his person, charged the Russian with an *attempt* to receive government documents and held him in jail. "And then, in addition, the indictment has a count of a conspiracy to receive and attempt to receive government documents." This, all of this, is "why we are here today."

Pomerantz, speaking directly and clearly, appeared to be scoring with the jury. The courtroom was deathly silent, with everyone, not just the jury, eager to hear about Gubitchev. Everyone, it seemed, except the defendant Coplon, who remained frozen, eyes fixed on Pomerantz until she turned away, looked at the wall, and rubbed a hand across her forehead.

Until now, the public knew very little about the Russian and absolutely nothing about his feelings for Judy. She had claimed love; he had claimed nothing. She might have been on Venus. All that was publicly known about her codefendant (called the "cospy" by the *Washington Post*) came from reports of his angry tirades about the impudence of the U.S. government in planning to put him on trial.

Pomerantz claimed his only dispute with Whearty's description of the defendants' surreptitious actions was his calling their meeting places "isolated and deserted." They were not that at all, he said, suggesting that traffic signals and bus stops and shops showed the opposite to be true. As to why Judith and Gubitchev took such circuitous routes to their assignations, Pomerantz spoke of his client's being a foreign national, a Russian to boot, with a girlfriend employed in a sensitive area of the U.S. government. Of course they had to be careful meeting. "It was deemed discreet that these meetings not be held in Times Square." Judith could lose her job, or worse. Further, Miss Coplon "is an unmarried girl, and Gubitchev's wife was living right here in Manhattan."

The attorney hastened to raise the issue of marital infidelity. "I am not here to defend the morals or the virtue of Mr. Gubitchev. The impropriety

. . . of what he did in meeting up with an unmarried girl is no part of the very serious crime charged here."

The scene in the Dyckman Street restaurant the night of January 14 was called to the jurors' attention. "You will note," the attorney said, "some rather extraordinary behavior for two secret conspirators in espionage." Once out on the street, Pomerantz continued, "right out on Broadway, and in the presence of an audience, if you wish, Miss Coplon hauled off and struck at Gubitchev several times—not once, but several times. Mind you, they didn't yet know they were being trailed."

When they came to their deliberations, Pomerantz wanted the jury "to use your common sense . . . to determine whether fisticuffs is the manner of spies, whether two Russian spies haul off and sock each other in the middle of Broadway . . . or whether this is fantastically inconsistent with any such inference."

After the confrontation that night, the defendants went home by way of "some subway in the environs." Pomerantz placed his hands on the jury rail and smiled broadly. "I don't know which one it is; Mr. Whearty seems to pay quite a lot of attention to entrances and exits of subways. I don't think you will find that relevant."

As for the night of March 4, what made Gubitchev run? Why did he cling to Miss Coplon for two and half hours instead of doing one of two things—either achieving a mission of espionage or, given the surveillance, abandoning that mission and going his own way, and Judith hers?

Pomerantz had the answers. Gubitchev ran because he was "engaging in that horrible neurotic conflict of a man who desperately wanted to be with a girl whom he shouldn't have been with . . . and yet was scared to death of being seen with her, scared of his wife, scared of his compatriots, scared of the effect it might have on the job of Miss Coplon, scared of everything in the world." Gubitchev was crazy in love and behaving crazily.

It was the government, not the defense, charged with burden of proof, the distinguished attorney reminded his audience, adding, "I am, nevertheless, making this bold assertion to you. You will find that none but lunatic spies, and I don't understand the government to contend that these two people are lunatics, none but musical comedy spies would have done what these two people did."

Closing his remarks, Pomerantz implored the jury to make its decision "free of any prejudice growing out of nationality, free of all this atmosphere of Cold War which, unfortunately, suffuses everything nowadays."

Pomerantz returned to sit beside his client, whose expression changed not at all during the presentation made in his defense. For a man once "crazy in love," he seemed unmoved by references to his lost romance or, given his demeanor, one who was hardly capable of such madness in the first place.

The court took a deep breath as Archie approached the jury. Those who had witnessed earlier performances either were anticipating an entertaining bit of showmanship or bemoaning the certainty of florid hyperbole and rambling rhetoric.

Affably, as if addressing interesting new friends, Archie approached the jury suggesting they get to know each other since they, the jurors, and he, the attorney, would "be with each other for a while to come." Everyone should get to know one another, especially Archie and Judy and the jury.

Ryan snorted. "No, Mr. Palmer that is not proper. You are here in the capacity of attorney for the defendant Coplon."

"I am," Archie agreed.

"Please make your statement of what you intend to prove. I do not want to interrupt you, but follow along as Mr. Pomerantz did and nobody will interrupt you."

Archie frowned. He wanted to get friendship into the picture; it was not enough to be present "in the capacity of an attorney" for Judy. He was not a hired stranger. Archie turned again to the jury. "I am the attorney for Judith Coplon, and have known her for years."

"Mr. Palmer!" the judge scolded. "You are directly defying the order of the Court."

A brief argument followed, with Archie finally saying, "Very good." He would begin by telling the grinning jurors that he would prove "not only is the girl blameless but upon whom the blame shall fall for this situation, and the future will hold its own passage as to who is to blame for this situation." He was off to a great start.

Judith's background and schooling, her patriotic "antecedents" and family life, her work and her loyalty were all brought to the attention of the jury. He would prove that "the bugaboo of communism does not exist here; that she never was a Communist." She was friendly by nature, "friendly with every-body." A devoted daughter, she normally traveled to New York once every three weeks to visit her ailing parents.

"You can tell by her manners and by her very atmosphere . . . her five feet of height, her appearance, her smile and the balance—almost of the little kitten-type that loved to go around and have the sunlight of people's approval." The kitten-type at the defense table lowered her head and covered her mouth. Her shoulders shook.

Judith labored long and diligently at the Department of Justice, receiving "encomium upon encomium" from her supervisors, including from the man now prosecuting her, Raymond Whearty. When she was not working, Judy loved to write. Still, something was lacking in her life—job security. At the time of her arrest, she was hoping to achieve permanent civil service status and was taking steps to prepare for the examinations required for appointment.

Archie wandered among plots and irrelevancies and "mosaic puzzles" until the judge was forced to interrupt with, "Mr. Palmer, don't you think that you could confine remarks to what you expect to prove?"

"Your Honor," Archie responded, "I intend to prove this." What, the audience wondered, was "this"?

Switching mental gears, Archie turned to wiretapping and illegal surveil-lance, making certain the jury understood that the government had acted outside the law. FBI agents continually had followed Judy "like the little lamb followed Mary . . . they found out what she was doing, whether she was washing her hair or powdering her nose . . . they watched her day and night." Nothing they found out, Archie asserted, had anything to do with national security. "Here is a girl twenty-seven years of age, and the mother's heart is always broken to think that the child is not married." If the jury had difficulty connecting national security with marital status, so did the judge.

"Mr. Palmer, I don't like to interrupt you . . ."

"Did I say anything?" Archie inquired.

"It seems to me you are going very, very far afield." And then, pleading, "Come on! Just state what you intend to prove."

Archie, although it was difficult to determine from his discourse, intended to prove that Judy had done nothing illegal, and that surveillance testimony to be given through "the lips of the agents who followed her" would do just that. He said that of all of his client's trips to New York, on only three did she meet the Russian. And she met the Russian because she loved him . . . a man who "might not care for his wife and wanted to get rid of her, as very often people do want to get rid of their wives, at least in this country of ours. . . .

"We will prove to you," Archie said, "that up to March 4th, at no time did she ever meet Mr. Gubitchev or . . . anybody of any kind or character who had anything to do with national security, which is the subject matter of this case." Neither, he contended, was anything relating to national security ever overheard in any electronic eavesdropping.

Archie talked to the jury about the decoy memorandum, its origin, and how it ended up in Judy's purse. He told them as well about classified documents lying about the FARS office and placed in unlocked desks and cabinets. Later testimony would indicate that this security lapse existed. The missing conversation was described, and the suspicious circumstances surrounding its nonexistence.

After several additional admonishments from Sylvester Ryan, Archie picked up his pace somewhat and spoke about the arrest and indications that it was planned all along, including the otherwise inexplicable appearance of Raymond Whearty in New York's FBI headquarters the night of March 4. "Whearty said he was officially connected with this case for the first time on March 4th at 1 P.M., and that at about 2 P.M., he, together with Mr. Foley, took the train to New York.

"So we have a situation where no one knows the girl is going to be arrested . . ." and yet, Whearty and Foley had hurried to New York to be a part of an action no one had planned. And following the arrest, Archie claimed, Agent Scott Miller knew exactly where in Judith's purse he would find the tightly folded note on the decoy memorandum, reaching not into the body of the purse but instead into a "flap" in which she had put the note. Allegedly put there in the presence of William Foley during the missing conversation.

Finally, with his audience exhausted, Archie approached his closing comments. Evidence that could prove Judith Coplon's innocence had been deliberately destroyed by FBI agents. "Where are we?" he asked the jury. "In what particular kind of country?"

From the evidence to be produced, jurors would need to determine whether the "odyssey of this girl's travail from March 4th, 1949 is a tragically innocent situation, or whether it was built up and carried on because the people behind it did not have enough guts to admit to the Unactivities [*sic*] Committee they had made a mistake."

It was a dramatic, bombastic ending, with Archie puffing his way back to Judith through an enormous cloud of sighed relief on the part of his listeners.

Ryan promptly announced a recess for everyone "to take a walk and get the air." He immediately followed his announcement with a statement that could be considered a reflection of the times. To the six women jurors he said, "Tomorrow, being Friday, some of you ladies have a little shopping. Instead of sitting until half past four, we will adjourn at four o'clock."

Even with Archie's convoluted and confusing soliloquy and Whearty's failure to extricate his case from the Manhattan transportation system and get to the point, jurors should have had a fair idea of the events to follow and the magnitude of their responsibility. Appropriately predictive in nature and prejudicial in content, the opening statements nevertheless proved to be misleading in the end, at least in terms of predictability. It was the jurors' expectation that, in orderly fashion, they would see Whearty and Kelley making the government's case, Palmer and Pomerantz defending Coplon and Gubitchev, and that, once both sides were presented, they would receive clear instructions from the bench and retire to decide what, in their minds, was what. How exquisitely naive.

Could it possibly happen once again? Could such reasonable expectations slip so inexorably away so early on? They could, and did. After the Washington circus, after the contentious New York pretrial hearings, the case should have completed its run of outrageous sideshows and surprises and settled into something akin to routine jurisprudence. That it failed to do so can be attributed not to new and revealing bits of testimony or startling new evidence, but rather to the unique and strategically incompatible characteristics of its characters.

If some aspects of the new trial were familiar, others were not. At times, the usual cast of characters read lines heard before, supported by the same evidentiary props. The same agents walked the same streets and witnessed the same suspicious acts on the parts of the defendants, albeit with new insight, more precise recall, or helpful coaching tweaking some of their testimonies. Defending attorneys would again counter agents' views of the defendants' acts and behaviors, challenging them with the incontrovertible fact that no one *really* saw either defendant do anything wrong. William Foley would sing his same old theme song, which, while never having been recorded, still reached the top of the government's Hit Parade. Old lies were repeated, joined by new. As for the wiretapping agents, some had come clean in the pretrial hearings, thus making a reconciliation of sorts with the court, if not with the public. In the end, certain witnesses were caught in the unseemly position of having given essentially three different versions of testimony—one in Washington, another at the pretrial hearings, and still another in this second trial—leaving doubt as to what was the truth, the whole truth, and nothing but.

What proved to be different, and thus both incredible and entertaining for the national audience, was far more than having Gubitchev in the production and a new theme of conspiracy; it was the way in which the trial made its way to its unlikely finale. Beginning as the expected reenactment of everything that had gone before, the trial soon took on a life of its own, a high drama that eventually went wildly askew. In the legal miasma that remained, defendant Coplon was, in essence, left defenseless.

Highlights of the truncated, boisterous five-week trial follow.

Week One: Friday and Saturday, January 27–28

It began with the night of January 14 and one critically significant word. Did Judith Coplon *gesticulate* at Gubitchev, as the prosecution held, or did she *strike* him, as the defense insisted? On the first day of testimony, Agent Richard Hradsky, armed once again with pointer and huge charts, marked a trail of surreptitious meandering by the defendants. His pointer landed at the De Luxe restaurant on Dyckman Street, where Judith and Gubitchev had had dinner, scene of the controversial confrontation between the two alleged spies. Defendant Coplon had "gesticulated" toward Mr. Gubitchev with a newspaper, Hradsky testified. He was immediately challenged by Archie Palmer over a variance between his current testimony and a written surveillance log.

"Is your written statement false?" Palmer demanded.

It was a matter of definition, observation, and interpretation, and it could make the difference in some minds between guilt and innocence, between romance and espionage. In the meanwhile, the critically signficant word at the center of the debate would make headlines. The word was *strike*. As Pomerantz had noted in his opening, spies don't get physical with each other in public during secret missions. It was now crucial for the prosecution to demonstrate to this new jury that Judy only gesticulated, and for the defense to show that she struck.

Pomerantz followed Archie and further challenged Hradsky about the surveillance log. Written immediately after the incident, it noted that Judy had struck the Russian not just once, but several times. But Hradsky explained today that he had not written the entry, had only "put my initials there to show I was present when the incident occurred. I would not have used those words to describe the incident."

The issue had not received significant attention during the course of the first trial, where agents' testimony could have been taken either way. In fact, in Washington Archie had said to Judy, "Agents have testified and the reports are in evidence now that . . . you beat him [Gubitchev] with your fist."

No one had objected.

With conspiratorial acts the basis for the present indictment, relevance of the issue was so profound that any such remark by the defense would have raised an immediate objection by the prosecution. While a profession of love had been essential to Judith's Washington defense, so had other strategies, such as writing a book, taking work home, and preparing for a civil service examination. It was different here, this business of two people meeting clandestinely for some specific reason, a reason that had to be explained away. It took two to tango, and it took two to conspire. They were doing one or the other—a conflicted dance of romance, or a brazen act of espionage.

Richard Brennan supported Hradsky's testimony, saying, "They stopped and faced each other and she was gesturing right at him."

As the noon recess ended on the first day of trial, a short, stocky man attempted to enter the courtroom without a pass. Blocked by security guards and turned away, the man said cheerfully, "All right, I go home." Fortunately,

Pomerantz learned of the incident and rushed to collect his client for the afternoon session. Going home would no doubt have been preferable for Gubitchev, who spent the rest of the day sitting sullenly, arms folded across his chest.

Throughout the opening day's continued wrangling over surveillance specifics, with tempers flaring and the defending counsel struggling to achieve a workable level of compatibility, the spotlight shone brightly on that pesky word. When the gavel finally sounded and the courtroom emptied, Archie told a group of reporters that he was calling a press conference for tomorrow, to provide Rebecca Coplon with an opportunity to make a public statement about her absence from the court's proceedings. They were delighted and promised to show up in force, rightly figuring the session would prove to be much more than announced.

"Certainly I hit him," Judy told reporters Saturday morning, before all the screaming and tears began. "I don't know why they say I 'gesticulated.' He had just told me for the first time that he was a married man and I lost all control of myself. I had been trying to get him to come home and meet my folks."

Mrs. Coplon believed. Desperate, saddened, she insisted that she had never lost faith in the innocence of her beloved daughter. She explained that her absence from the courtroom was because of failing health. It was clear she was telling the truth in both instances. Reporters, respecting her frailty and her tears, mercifully asked few questions.

Judith was another matter.

Was the still-circulating rumor true? Had she and an unnamed boyfriend smashed a photographer's camera during a late-hour nightclub adventure? She laughed, denying once again the tale of camera smashing. "There is absolutely nothing to it."

What about boyfriends and dates, now that the second trial was finally under way? Judy acknowledged that she was dating and dining and dancing, although there was no one special in her life. Old friends in New York were including her in their parties, and at times she could go out in a group without attracting attention. All of which appears to represent a paradigm switch from the earlier months of her ordeal. Sometimes, she said, she was amused on subway rides when "people all around me are reading tabloids with my picture on the front page," but were too engrossed to notice her.

As for Harold Shapiro, any interest—romantic or otherwise—on the part of the betrayed for the betrayer was long gone. And love for the love of her life, the Russian, vanished with the knowledge that he was a married man.

Reporters were having a splendid time talking about romance and dates and the men in her life. James Cullinane of the *Washington Star* noted, "The strain of two trials shown on the face of Miss Coplon but her trim figure still evokes wolf whistles," adding that she "still smiles at the slightest provocation."

When asked if she thought Gubitchev was a spy, Judy's whispered comment was inaudible to the reporters. Would she repeat? But before she could respond, Archie whipped toward her, his face flushed a sudden, angry red.

"That's a sarcastic answer," he snapped. "Don't get sarcastic with these men."

"But I didn't answer!" she protested.

"I heard you. It was a sarcastic, ridiculous statement."

"Well, not exactly," she countered.

Furious, Archie shook his finger in her face. "Don't argue with me. Say it was ridiculous! *Say it was ridiculous!*"

"All right, it was ridiculous."

Not satisfied to let the matter drop, her attorney roared at Judith, "I always told you you were a damned fool at times." Reporters, now furious themselves, insisted that Palmer leave the room and he stalked out, slamming the door. He was soon followed by a frightened Mrs. Coplon, led from the room by her daughter. Moments later, Judy, badly shaken, returned to face sympathetic journalists. It was not long before Archie returned to argue with what Judy had to say, to interrupt, to shout and chastise before stomping out once again. The distressing scene was repeated over and over again, turning the conference into what one writer called "a rout." On one occasion, Archie, with a smile this time, returned with a box of ballpoint pens, insisting that each reporter take three. A bankrupt client had paid his bill with a large supply of pens.

During a quiet moment, with Archie verbally constrained by complaining journalists, the subject of romance was reopened. "What about the man in Rochester?" one queried. "There is no man from Rochester," she told him. What about plans for marriage—with anyone?

"When? With a ten-year sentence in Washington and 35 years hanging over me here, I'll ask you, when?"

No one had an answer.

Week Two: Monday, January 30–Friday, February 3

The weekend, what was left of it, was devoted to calming pursuits, with Judy and her family avoiding the press and, it seems, Archie Palmer. On Monday, the strike/gesticulate dispute began with a particularly entertaining show.

Six-foot-tall FBI Special Agent Daniel Garde, who, it turned out, had been the author of the surveillance log entry reporting that Judith Coplon had landed blows on her codefendant, was asked to step down from the witness stand to impersonate Gubitchev. Palmer had been trying to hoist Garde on his own petard—his own words as they appeared in the log. Archie insisted that the agent demonstrate exactly what happened.

"Now, you're Gubitchev," Archie told Garde, hustling him over to stand on an imaginary mark drawn by the attorney.

"No," Garde stubbornly insisted. "I'm Garde."

"Well, you be Miss Coplon and *I'll* be Gubitchev," Archie decided. "Now, don't worry about hitting me."

The casting was entirely too unorthodox for Judge Ryan. "Stop, Mr. Palmer!" Looking frantically around the room, he asked, "Is there a US marshal present?" There was, much to the dismay of the marshal, who reluctantly went center stage to become Valentin Gubitchev. Spectators, including Judith but excluding Gubitchev, were smiling broadly. It was all so entertaining. Members of the jury were unsuccessful in trying not to laugh.

Garde waved a rolled report in the direction, and past the face of, the marshal—missing him completely. No, no, the stage director insisted. This was all wrong. Archie would further demonstrate. Grabbing a folded paper he flailed away at the startled agent, demanding, "Isn't that the way you strike a person?"

Icily, Garde eyed the rambunctious lawyer. "That may be the way you strike a person, but that's not what I saw."

Joining Garde to testify about surveillance and the contested behavior of the defendants the night of January 14 were Agents Brennan, Gauthier, and McAndrews. Each supported the other. Judy gesticulated.

Newspapers headlined the debate over "one little word" that succeeded in bringing to a halt the colorful proceedings in the main-floor courtroom in Foley Square. One began its trial story quoting *Webster's New International Dictionary:* "Strike—To touch or hit with some force, either with the hand or an instrument, to smite, to give a blow to . . ."

On Tuesday, with the strike/gesticulate issue still simmering, the prosecution moved to what had been planned as the Washington trial's Chapter Two, the defendants' meeting on February 18. Sappho Manos and Agent Thomas McAndrews told the jury about following Judy and Gubitchev that night, how she had broken the strap of her shoe, how frantic she had been about being late for an appointment. A spy on the run.

The never-identified piece of onion skin paper Scott Miller had seen during a brief moment that night when Judith, standing beside him on the subway, opened her purse seemed patently suspect, according to the prosecution. Most likely, it contained government secrets destined for Gubitchev's pocket during a five-second encounter on a New York street, a contact observed by Miller and three others.

On the stand, testifying for the prosecution, Miller said that as Judy crossed the street, she shifted her bag from the right side to the left, the bag holding the piece of onion skin paper he thought had "typewriting" on it.

"Within a few minutes, Gubitchev pulled alongside Miss Coplon," Miller said. "As he came alongside, he leaned over and extended his right arm across his body toward Miss Coplon's body." Walking at night some thirty to forty feet behind the couple, Miller was unable to see if anything passed between the two.

The defense would return to the paper, the purse, and the possibility—or probability—of a criminal act before the week was out. For now, Archie Palmer called Miller's attention to the defense attorney's most favored topic—the sinful business of wiretapping. The veteran agent admitted having seen, prior to March 4, recording discs he knew contained Coplon conversations. He now insisted, despite the Tiger Memorandum, that destruction of the discs had been a "routine procedure."

Judge Ryan, never comfortable with what he had declared to be "illegal" wiretapping, was compelled to ask before this jury if Miller, as a member of the bar, had not felt honor-bound to tell the prosecution about the wiretap operation early on.

"I did not so feel, Your Honor," Miller firmly answered. Perhaps the agent was splitting semantic hairs. Perhaps he had told Whearty and Kelley in his daily meetings, meetings that took place week after week, but not because he felt it was necessary "as a member of the bar."

On Wednesday, Archie Palmer said the P word in open court.

"Do you know the meaning of the word perjury?" he yelled at Scott Miller, shocking the jury and nearly everyone within earshot. Palmer read aloud from Miller's Washington testimony, where he said he did not "know" Judith's wires had been tapped. Now he demanded, *"Do you know the meaning of the word, perjury?"* Miller, still cool, unfazed, was saved by the judge, who ordered Palmer to avoid asking such prejudicial questions, like the one left hanging in the air.

The left-wing press had a glorious time with the P word, and their followers were led to strong inferences that the agents had been not simply deceptive, but in fact designedly diabolical. Fortunately for Mr. Hoover's state of mind concerning this now-chronic erupting sore, this unwanted espionage case, the mainstream press did not follow suit.

To no avail, Pomerantz tried to elicit information from Miller concerning how the Russian was first identified as a suspect, information he believed would lead to the reason his client was in this unfortunate legal morass. A testy exchange between Pomerantz and Ryan made it clear that the court intended to remain firm on this issue. The defending attorney was not going to have his question answered. Now, or ever. Pomerantz asked permission to argue his position in open court, with the jury absent, but the judge quickly denied the request.

At one point during the day, Archie Palmer attempted to introduce a new piece of evidence, a menu from the Italian De Luxe restaurant. Just why was beyond anyone's comprehension.

"What in God's name is the importance of the menu of an Italian café?" Ryan fussed. "Is it to show it is a spaghetti or chow mein . . ."

"It is to show that it is an ordinary eating place and not a de luxe establishment," Archie interrupted. Ryan lost his patience, and a protracted and thoroughly silly argument between the bench and the attorney ensued.

Watching gloomily from the defense table, Valentin Gubitchev was clearly disgusted. Is this, he must have questioned, Justice as it is practiced in America? No wonder the country was doomed and ripe for a Communist takeover. Yuri Novikov, acting as a representative of the Soviet embassy, sat daily with Gubitchev to help translate difficult legal arguments and pronouncements.

At the time, one could only imagine what was said in the whispered Russian that passed between the two foreigners.

Enter, on Thursday, the onion skin paper, the purse, and the possible conspiracy introduced on Tuesday. What no one saw happen, not Scott Miller nor Roger Robinson nor any of the other agents, became a fiery issue resulting in two heated demands for a mistrial by the defense, and a charge that the judge was behaving in a manner "highly inflammatory and prejudicial to the defense." At issue was the government's emphasis on the impossible-to-prove possibility that Judith had passed secret information to Gubitchev the night of February 18.

Pomerantz, joined by Palmer, insisted that the jury be transported to the scene of the nonhappening at the same time of night it didn't happen. Ryan disagreed. He said the jury had sufficient information about the setting through photographs. A visit was absolutely needed, Pomerantz argued, observing that evidentiary photos failed to represent the darkness affecting observation of the defendants. Not so, said the judge. Pomerantz was furious.

"Mr. Pomerantz," Ryan flared, "you have an unfortunate habit of assuming an air of injured innocence or of justice outraged, or amazement at the stupidity of the court in not ruling in your favor. I don't think it should continue. Call your next witness."

Ashen, a mortified Pomerantz asked for a few minutes to compose himself; in response, the judge called a five-minute recess. As the jury left the courtroom, Pomerantz returned to the defense table and muttered to Novikov that his treatment by the judge was "a new experience." Ryan overheard.

"I don't like the comment you just made," the judge snarled.

Pomerantz shot back that this was the first time in all of his twenty-five years in practice he had been treated so rudely by a judge. Well, offered the judge, he certainly hoped this was the first time Pomerantz deserved it. From all appearances, intellectual pride and perceived political differences could be considered as responsible as judicial rulings for this increasingly fractious relationship.

After the recess, in a calmer, more controlled atmosphere, Roger Robinson took the stand and said he had noticed that defendant Coplon's purse was open when she joined Gubitchev the night of February 18. The agent admitted, however, that his detailed handwritten notes of the scene, made immediately after the encounter, had no mention of an open purse. The official, typewritten notes prepared three days later, did.

Motions for a mistrial came in the afternoon, with Pomerantz complaining that, at one point, the judge had characterized Robinson as "a very truthful witness" in the presence of the jury. This and other such "colloquies," which he need not detail, compelled the attorney to seek a mistrial.

The second issue leading to a motion to dismiss was the prosecution's focus on a purported criminal act of attempt not charged in the indictment. The indictment was based on an attempt to pass information relevant to national security *only* on the night of March 4. February 18 was not March 4.

Both motions were denied. Throughout the day, the building tension between the judge and Gubitchev's attorney became even more apparent, with their body language, as well as their words, revealing an ever-deepening enmity.

At the end of the day, a clearly wearied and irritated Judge Ryan cautioned jurors to stay away from the troublesome February 18 meeting spot. Alone, or as a group.

On Friday, it was revealed that an on-the-record conference had taken place in Judge Ryan's chambers with prosecuting and defending attorneys in which Pomerantz argued his position with regard to the source of his client's identification as a suspected spy, and asked, again, to speak in open court. In the stormy session to follow, Archie Palmer reportedly leaped to his feet and agreed with Judge Ryan, defying Pomerantz. Later, Ryan took the opportunity to issue a warning to Pomerantz: The Coplon-Gubitchev trial would not become a "sounding board for Soviet propaganda," a tool for communistic diatribe. Curiously, the judge determined that the record of the conference in his chambers would not be made available to the press, and thus to the public. The on-the-record conference thus was determined to be off limits; a crafty *Washington Star* reporter managed to secure a copy, however, and the conference became public.

In public view, another round of the battle over what Judith Coplon did with her fists and her newspaper the night of January 14, and defense efforts to picture Judy and Gubitchev as "boy and girl" on a date, resulted in mixed reviews. More cat-and-mice episodes were related on the stand, with Agent John F. Malley testifying that he saw Gubitchev enter a supermarket on the night of February 18 and come out carrying a closed package. Gubitchev, at last amused at something in this trial, sent word to reporters about the bag's secret contents. "Herring, brown bread, and baloney."

At the end of the trial's second week, the jury still had not a clue as to the nature of the attack in front of the restaurant, and no one, save for perhaps the defendants, believed they had behaved like a couple in love.

Week Three: February 6–10

Much like an enticing theatrical announcement of a coming attraction, the prosecution had let the world know it would lead off this week's testimony with its star witness, William Foley. The supervisor of the Foreign Agents Registration Section deserved the billing, spending much of Monday and Tuesday testifying, under both direct and cross-examination. His would be the most compelling testimony of all.

Foley told the court that Judith Coplon had tried on three separate occasions to get her hands on a top-secret document, the same document Archie had unsuccessfully tried to place in evidence in Washington, the same document the prosecution insisted was the subject of the Michael Memorandum. Foley had managed to keep Judy from seeing the report, although, he admitted, he had later given Judith the so-called decoy memorandum authored by Robert Lamphere. It was the same old story, now told to a new and clearly captivated audience. As for Foley's long-standing contention that he didn't know the report was meant to tempt Judy alone, Lamphere would later tell the jury, "it was to be placed *in the hands of Judith Coplon* to see if it would fall into Russian hands." The hand-changing was clear.

Under questioning by Pomerantz, Foley, for the first time, admitted that he might have had a wee bit of doubt about the decoy memo.

"Did it look suspiciously like a plant?" demanded the attorney.

"You might say it that way," Foley said nervously, hastily adding that there was a definite distinction between "knowledge and suspicion."

"Entrapment!" Archie wailed.

Elusive actions of the defendants were repeatedly detailed until the jury most likely could have retraced their steps blindfolded. Interspersed, on Thursday, was the welcome, tension-relieving testimony of Margaret McKinny, a FARS secretary whose southern accent and sudden bursts of giggles thoroughly entertained the court. Settling into the witness box and surveying the courtroom, she broke into a wide smile. Margaret, it was obvious, intended to enjoy herself.

Judith Coplon had asked her for keys to a cabinet containing security documents, Margaret said, adding that Judy told her she often worked late and needed access to the cabinet. Margaret remembered the incident because she thought it was odd.

"Why odd?" Pomerantz asked.

"I don't know—it's just one of those things," Margaret said, then burst into uproarious giggles.

A surprise witness, Margaret admitted under cross-examination that she had been told by Foley to "keep the incident in mind," presumably to testify against Judy. Now, Archie wanted to know, did Margaret hate Judy?

"I don't know Miss Coplon very well," she drawled in her lovely southern way. "I thought very highly of her. I just feel sorry for her."

"Did you ever take offense at anything she did or said to you?" Judge Ryan asked the merry witness.

Well, yes, on one occasion. "I went into her office . . . and she told me I was too fat!" Margaret said, once again breaking into hysterical, hiccuping giggles.

Judith, sitting at the defense table, put her head down and laughed, along with the jury and the rest of Margaret's appreciative audience.

It was an amusing day all around. At one point, while examining Agent Malley, Archie asked, "What time did you see Mr. Tunnel going through the Gubitchev?" The courtroom was again filled with laughter, this time at Archie's unintended humor. The rest of the day, it was intended, to the point where Judge Ryan told him to keep his witticisms out of the courtroom and share them with the judge in private. "Come up and see me sometime," he told Archie in Mae West parlance.

Friday's events garnering major headlines were as irrelevant to the serious business of the trial as were Margaret's giggles and Archie's antics. It began with Agent Martin Carey testifying about surveilling the defendants. Enough, thought Pomerantz, who decided that listening to another dozen or more agents recounting the same story, an *uncontested* story, was nonsensical.

In the interest of saving time and getting on with this farcical trial,

Pomerantz said he was willing to concede the "points of cumulative evidence" agents were giving in the stultifying, repetitive testimony thus far. "I can see no useful purpose in this piling on of evidence. . . . There is no dispute as far as I'm concerned and as far as Mr. Gubitchev is concerned over the fact that the agents who followed the defendants on the night of March 4th are telling the truth."

The bomb he unintentionally exploded was Archie Palmer, utterly, horrendously shocked by Pomerantz's disloyal sabotaging of the defense position.

"Just why did he become the good Samaritan coming down from Jerusalem to bind up wounds?" he yelled. "I'm not going to bind up any wounds. I want the jury to hear all the testimony." Pomerantz argued the unreasonableness of continuing as they were. Twenty-six agents followed the defendants, Pomerantz stormed, and, in addition to those who already had testified, at least a dozen more would be called.

"I'll concede nothing," Archie raged. "Mr Pomerantz's generosity is not appreciated." His colleague, Archie complained, simply wanted to shorten the trial because of the inadequate fee being paid him. Archie, however, saw payment for defending the accused from a more altruistic view. "I'm not getting anything but the love of the family."

The jury left, and the fight continued.

"The more witnesses there are the more ridiculous this case gets," fumed Pomerantz. Few, other than cocounsel, would disagree with him.

"I challenge that!" Archie spluttered, carrying on his argument until Judge Ryan, shaking his head, left the bench and headed for the door.

Chameleon Archie turned to the departing judge and said, sweetly, "I hope Your Honor has a pleasant weekend and forgets all about me." He did not, he added, have any ill feeling toward his friend, Mr. Pomerantz.

"No, God, no!" growled Pomerantz. "God save me from my friends."

After Ryan had left the room, Archie turned back to his "friend," declaring, "Abe, I want to see you before the judge in his chambers!"

"I don't want to see you anywhere," Pomerantz snapped back.

The fight continued, with Pomerantz saying he didn't like to see Archie make such an "ass of himself." In return, Palmer assured his opponent in this verbal altercation that as far as he was concerned, "you are the front and the rear." Further, if Pomerantz wanted Archie to share stenographic minutes of the court's proceedings, tough luck. He had them and would not relinquish his copies. Oh, yes he would, Pomerantz yelled. The judge said so.

"Please stop!" Judy cried. "Will you please stop this. It's so stupid."

Gubitchev got to his feet, put on his hat and coat, and grabbed Pomerantz's arm. "Let's get out of here."

Week Four: February 13–17

With electronic eavesdropping gear long gone, one can only imagine what was being said in the Coplon family residence on Ocean Parkway this weekend. Archie Palmer was becoming totally impossible—if, in fact, he ever had been otherwise. The trial had lost all sense of dignity, with the defending attorneys mired in a crippling miasma of ill feeling, the judge furiously berating the defense, and the press lampooning both sides. There was nothing linear or logical about the course of the proceedings, which had spun off in various directions at various times. Too, references to Pomerantz's past representation of "left causes" and suggestions of Communist sympathies, which were creeping more and more into daily news reports, did nothing to help Judith's defense in a fearful, anti-Red national climate. In all, it was a nightmare.

Clearly, something had to be done. Plans for doing that something undoubtedly began to take shape on Ocean Parkway during the weekend recess.

Testimony, in a visibly strained atmosphere, returned on Monday to the subject the defense counsel had fought over—surveillance, step-by-step descriptions of suspicious movements. It also included hearing from Special Agent Robert Wirth, who admitted to having destroyed written summaries of FBI wiretaps.

"Didn't you think it improper, especially since you are a lawyer, to destroy material gotten over Mr. Gubitchev's wire?" Pomerantz asked.

"I did not consider it," Wirth answered.

If the going for the defense had been rough before, it was the proverbial ant-infested picnic compared to what came next, the circumstance that effectively destroyed Judith Coplon's chance for a fair trial.

It began, for all practical purposes, Thursday morning, February 16, in Judge Ryan's chambers, when he met, at her request, with Judith Coplon and Archie Palmer. Judy quickly came to the point.

"I feel I can no longer continue with Mr. Palmer as my attorney."

Judge Ryan wanted to know if Judy had a replacement in mind, and she said she did not. "Well," he worried, "you're in the middle of a trial now . . . it is a serious matter to change attorneys, and while you have that right, I can't let the trial continue without your being represented by somebody." Time was of the essence. Too, the judge told Judy, it would be "an imposition" to assign an attorney and "thrust him in the middle" of the trial.

"This is a very serious matter to me," Judy insisted. "I cannot feel that my liberty should be entrusted to this man, or that I should be defended by this man . . . I can say generally that our relationship has deteriorated to the point where we are practically not speaking to each other."

"This is silly. It's *silly*," a dismayed Archie protested, but Judy was determined.

Ryan told Judy that she should discuss the matter with her older brother. To change attorneys would not work to her ultimate benefit, he cautioned; however, if she had someone to take her case at this point, that was her right. Still, he repeated, she could not continue unless represented by counsel.

On one point he was especially clear—he would not grant a mistrial based on Judy's request for a new attorney.

Complicating matters was that Judy had no money. The court would have to appoint—and pay—Archie's replacement.

"I don't know what is going to happen in this case in New York," Judy said. "I hope I am vindicated and I am acquitted, but I do know that I face ten years in Washington, and whatever is going to happen here I want to get over with as quickly as possible. I am not interested in any sort of delay of any kind, but all I know is I cannot continue with this man anymore—this man here. It is virtually impossible."

The day following, Judge Ryan made a final, futile attempt to "patch up" Judy's relationship with Archie before appointing three new lawyers as defense counsel. Each welcomed the appointment as he would a case of poison ivy. Their busy schedules precluded taking on a new case, particularly one of this magnitude. How could they possibly be expected to abandon existing commitments to the clients whose cases filled their calendars? That, assumed the judge, was the trio's problem. They were ordered to serve.

Named were Samuel Neuburger, who had unofficially advised the Coplons now and again; Leonard Boudin; and Sidney S. Berman. All had the reputation of representing left causes; left or right, however, all were excellent attorneys and eminently qualified to defend Judy. Ironically, this was the team the prosecution had expected to face in Washington.

After the announcement of new counsel, Archie, turning gallant, told the mob of waiting reporters that a woman has a right to change her mind. "Judith Coplon, being a very sweet, lovable, personable woman should have the same right as any other member of her sex."

Judith Coplon, sweet, lovable, and personable, exercised that right. Archie Palmer was history.

Week Five: February 20–24, In Recess

NEW COPLON LAWYERS CHARGE PALMER HUNG ONE ON CLIENT, *Washington Post* headlines read this Monday morning. Samuel Neuburger, now officially Judith's chief counsel, made the charge before Judge Ryan that Archie had slapped his client. Ryan was amazed, saying that Palmer "denied this strenuously," and that he, the judge, believed Palmer had "a fatherly affection" for the accused.

Archie saw the allegation as a means of getting the trial adjourned. "They're trying to make up a cat-and-dog fight." It was "stupid business" to him, "a strange concoction of junk." He observed that Judy's three new attorneys were "associated with the Leftist groups in the CIO," which was widely reported.

Neuburger, with ample justification, requested a sixty-day delay to prepare a defense. To be reviewed were more than eight thousand pages of testimony from the Washington trial, over four thousand pages of significant New York pretrial testimony, and, as of this day, some three thousand pages of the current trial. There were hundreds of documents, motions, petitions, and appellate arguments as well. Three attorneys, even in sixty days, would have a monumental task in plowing through everything just to catch up with the past. In addition, there was the future to consider, a defense strategy to be planned. Neuburger's document, one of the most interesting in the Coplon court records, makes an unquestionably compelling case.

Ryan gave the new team exactly one week to prepare to defend Judith Coplon.

Impossible, Neuburger said, requesting dismissal for himself and his two colleagues. Turning away from the bench, he prepared to pack up his briefcase and leave. He didn't make it to the door. Forced to serve, he would do so, but on his own terms.

Court was recessed for the week, during which time Judy's new lawyers faced the impossible task set before them, the dragon-slaying exercise devised by Sylvester Ryan.

Week Six: February 27–March 3

In this, the last week of arguments, attention was directed to items in Judy's purse the night she was arrested. John Kelley attempted to introduce those items into evidence, but Pomerantz protested. For one thing, the "character sketches" had nothing to do with national defense and had no relevance to the charges against either defendant. Kelley argued the point. As for Mr. Neuburger, he contributed exactly what he would contribute throughout the day's formal proceedings. Nothing. He made no move to argue or to defend, sitting in stubborn silence beside his devastated, frightened client. Judge Ryan was outraged.

Neuburger explained his bizarre behavior by telling Judge Ryan, "Being half prepared is more dangerous to the defendant than not being prepared at all."

Irate, patience long lost, Ryan, seeing Neuburger pass a note to Pomerantz, said, "Let the record show that Mr.Neuburger is passing a note to Mr. Pomerantz."

Both attorneys moved for a mistrial. "The plain innuendo in your remark . . ." Pomerantz began, but Ryan cut him off sharply with, "There was no innuendo in that remark. It is plain distortion to read into an innocent remark any innuendo."

Angry confrontations and rancor were the order of the day. At one point,

Pomerantz charged that "Your Honor has done violence to the cause of the defendants," and His Honor, vainly trying to maintain some semblance of order, said the court would take into consideration the "heat in this case" before determining whether the attorney's remarks were "contemptuous."

Later, Ryan would call Judy's decision to change lawyers "not in good faith" and responsible for disrupting the "orderly progression of the trial." There was a shared wonder among the jurors, those present in the Foley Square courtroom, and the American public following the story in their daily newspapers. At what point *was* there orderly progression? Had they missed something?

Valentin Gubitchev, as involved in this case as the doorstop, had had his fill. There were hurried conversations, head shaking, and, finally, decisions. He wanted a mistrial because of the "chaotic situation that has arisen." The climate of the trial, given this latest mess, was not conducive for a fair defense for the Russian. He begged the court to try him alone.

"Where the Government has seen fit to put two defendants in one boat, the rights of one depend heavily on the other," Pomerantz argued. Gubitchev could be tried in three calm and orderly days, instead of being caught in the Coplon milieu. Unfortunately for passenger Gubitchev, there would be no disembarking from the government's boat. Both of the accused would remain there, however rough the seas, until the vessel reached the shore.

Amazingly, Judge Ryan first launched into a defense of the constantly censured Archie Palmer, who, he now said, had properly represented Miss Coplon, and then went on to express confidence in her new attorneys. Neuburger, with whom he had been continually sparring, and his able colleagues were quite capable of representing Miss Coplon for the rest of the trial. Implied were proceedings that would move in an orderly, harmonious fashion. Undoubtedly, there was additional cause for bewilderment among the extended audience. Hadn't Ryan been sitting on the bench all along? Had *he* missed something?

On Tuesday, the government succeeded in introducing into evidence the seized contents of Judith's purse. Judging by the reaction of the press, one would think the American public had seen none of it before; in fact, they had seen none of it as now presented. Newspapers devoted unprecedented amounts of space to actual photographs and reproductions of the evidence. Every word, in pen or typewritten, all of it constituting a display unequaled in media trial coverage. Later, David Greenglass's sketches of an atomic bomb mechanism would not receive nearly the detailed attention given Judith's handwritten note about geophones. In all, it was a new and unique thrill for the public's Red-tinged, obsessive fears. They could touch espionage.

Pomerantz, unexpectedly alone, was left to present any arguments to be made about the evidence, repeating defense themes presented in Washington—a book, a civil service exam, homework. In the end, to some, the argument seemed futile and the advocate exhausted. In any event, the jury was reminded that the papers Judith Coplon placed in her purse remained there until they were removed by FBI agents. Not one, not a single piece, was found on his client. Only an envelope containing $125 in cash, hardly incriminating, given that Friday, March 4, was payday.

On the twenty-third day of the trial, the prosecution rested.

The defense opened immediately, and closed one hour later. In the cyclonic interim, Pomerantz established that the FBI destroyed critical trial evidence; that the documents found in Judy's purse were displayed at times in her office, with no attempt to keep them secret; that Judy openly had a Justice Department secretary typing data slips, exactly like those found in her possession March 4; and, finally, that Raymond Whearty, when he was Judy's supervisor, routinely asked her to take work home at night. When he finished, the attorney walked back to the defense table, turned to Judge Ryan, and announced, "My client rests."

Neuburger jumped to his feet. "Miss Coplon rests," he said.

Gasps were heard throughout the courtroom, and the heat of Judge Ryan's displeasure sizzled. There would be no defense for accused conspirator Judith Coplon, no opportunity to tell the jury her side of the story, no witness to testify on her behalf. Filled with despair, Judith sat immobilized, spiritually and truly alone.

For the prosecution, the love card that had played so well in the Washington trial remained in the deck. Neither defendant had appeared on the stand to claim a romance with the other.

The Final Week: March 6–10

Monday was summation day, during which the art of dissembling was practiced so masterfully as to render rational minds less capable of rational thinking. It began with the eloquence of Abraham Pomerantz, who made quite good sense noting that the government truly had proved nothing, and ended with John Kelley insisting Mr. Pomerantz had made no sense at all. In a flight of subjective fancy, Pomerantz saw the government's witnesses as a cabal of lying jingoists, and Kelley, in a similar flight, saw Pomerantz as a lying snake in the national grass.

Pomerantz went first, suggesting that the Cold War, a rather hot cold war, had "whipped up" a terrific sentiment and passion, creating an environment in which both prejudice and suspicion had reached a frightening and intimidating proportion. Jurors needed to beware, lest either of these two evils influence their collective decision. The government, he suggested, had been influenced by this polluted environment and had built its case on suspicion, rather than on criminal activity.

"Where the government lacks evidence, they give you a double dose of suspicion, distortion and exaggeration. The hope is that in this poisoned atmosphere, you are going to add up two and two and get five."

The conspiracy indictment, Gubitchev's attorney reiterated, was "based on what happened, or perhaps I should say almost happened on March 4th." And *only* on March 4. Still, behavior of the defendants at the time of the two earlier meetings, January 14 and February 18, had become suspect. Pomerantz would address both, explaining that he agreed with the government's own evidence and testimony about these dates "100 percent," with two significant exceptions. One was the "so-called striking episode" on January 14, and the other was the "open pocketbook evidence," or lack thereof, on February 18.

"This in a sense is a very peculiar criminal case. In the ordinary case the question is, did a man do a certain act or didn't he? Did he pull a trigger or didn't he? . . . in other words, there is a crucial issue of fact between the government and the defense." Not so here, Pomerantz said. "We are in virtual agreement." The difference between the two sides is not what the defendants *did* but why they did it.

Gubtichev's behavior was "fantastically inconsistent with his being a spy," and the testimony not only "disproves it but denies the possibility." A Russian spy would not openly meet a "prominent" American "girl" working so close to the FBI to do the business of espionage; he would make other arrangements. He would not meet on public streets, dine in a lighted, public establishment, have a scuffle with a fellow spy in full view of the public, or execute obviously evasive movements if he thought the FBI was after him. No, he would "go home and live to pass another day." As for what Judy Coplon carried in her purse when arrested, information Gubitchev was allegedly attempting to receive, "everybody has secret stuff who is working for the government." Nothing she carried was out of the ordinary. Gubitchev, it should be remembered, carried not a single item of information belonging to, or related to, the government of the United States.

Various agents, including Miller, Robinson, and Bedford, were a part of a lying cabal. But Foley was the key to the whole business. Foley's testimony deserved meticulous scrutiny; it was inconsistent, devious, and ingenuous, even, at times, contradicted by fellow prosecution witnesses. Pomerantz played the Foley card as the ace up his sleeve, recounting and shredding the key witness's story. In all, it proved "nothing in the world except that she was being framed by Foley." Her supervisor knew what was in Judy's bag before she left for New York on March 4 because he saw her put it there. Of course the missing conversation would have proven Foley's deception, but it was, by design, forever lost.

The defending attorney's bottom line was that the government's own evidence proved, clearly and unquestionably, beyond a shadow of a doubt, that his client was innocent. He was guilty only of being a tragic romantic.

Kelley, in his summation, defended Foley and ridiculed Pomerantz's depiction of the FARS chief as a framer of the innocent.

"In connection with his assertion that Mr. Foley deliberately undertook to frame this defendant and thus these defendants, I suggested to you that Mr. Foley . . . was acting under instructions and orders from his superiors." Everything Foley did he was told to do—meet with Peyton Ford and Whearty, deliver the decoy to Judy—whatever, and all in a manner "not to arouse her suspicions."

"Now, Mr. Pomerantz suggests that . . . we have a perjurer in Mr. Foley." Those maligned by opposing counsel included not only Judith's former supervisor, but also others. "He suggested fantastic statements, impossible, and thus false statements on the part of Mr. Miller . . . as well as Mr. Robinson." The chief prosecutor, with consummate disdain directed toward Pomerantz, said, "He tells you that you must believe Bedford is also lying to us." Bedford, whose microphone had inexplicably quit working at such an importune time.

Pomerantz, Kelley advised, had attempted to "explain innocently that the evidence adduced here by the government was ultimately based on his assertion that the witness had lied to you." The government's witnesses had not lied. Their evidence, which Kelley painstakingly reviewed, was truthful and, by the way, come by through honest means. "Each of you know that there has not been one item of evidence introduced on this witness stand that wasn't the evidence of an eye witness to an actual event taking place in his presence," Kelley assured. "I suggest we have brought no evidence to you from a wiretap. Every word of their testimony," he continued, "has been from an eye witness, who either observed what was done, actually done by these defendants, or as to conversations actually had with one of them."

The prosecuting attorney's bottom line was that the government's evidence proved, clearly and unquestionably, beyond a shadow of a doubt, that Gubitchev and Coplon were Soviet spies, not tragic romantics. "There is no evidence before you, not one scintilla, that either of these defendants was in love," he declared.

Kelley went back to the night of the arrest, when Gubitchev was asked at the time, "Who is that girl?" meaning Judith Coplon.

"What girl?" Kelley quoted Gubitchev as responding.

Would an innocent man, a man in love, answer this way? Kelley asked jurors.

Kelley closed his remarks with feeling "secure in the knowledge" that the ladies and gentlemen of the jury would render a verdict based on evidence rather than on passion or prejudice or sympathy, and would find Gubitchev and his coconspirator, Miss Coplon, guilty. Guilty of espionage, not an illicit romance.

Mr. Pomerantz zealously had presented a case for his Russian client; Mr. Kelley had spoken extremely well for the government. That there were untruths and half-truths on both sides was not an issue. They did and said what was appropriate, and they did it skillfully.

It was Judith's turn, but no one rose to speak for her. Even now, at this critical juncture, no one wearing her colors stood before the court on her behalf; not Samuel Neuburger, or Leonard Boudin, or Sidney Berman.

Also missing, even from the courtroom, was a monumentally disappointed Archie Palmer and his audacious, unorthodox, and even rude behavior. He would have loved to have been there, wearing colors and verbal boxing gloves, "throwing punches" the whole way.

Jurors received the case at 4:34 on this same afternoon. It was one year and two days after the defendants' arrest on a street corner not that far away. Solemnly, those who would decide Judith's and Gubitchev's fate left the room, after hearing Judge Ryan review the charges and the evidence. Most significantly, he explained that although the government had failed to produce *direct* evidence of conspiracy, "a conspiracy may be proved by *circumstantial* evidence." Ryan carefully set out the content of proof required of the government to substantiate all four charges in the indictment. Jurors knew precisely what they had to do. At least, they thought they knew.

To understand what happened later, it is essential to struggle through the essentials of the complex four-count indictment with its interrelated charges:

> **Count 1** charged that Judith Coplon and Valentin Gubitchev
> unlawfully, willfully and knowingly, did . . . conspire . . . to vio-
> late the provisions of Sections 793, 794, and 371, Title 18 US
> Code; and to defraud the US (1) by impairing . . . the lawful
> functions of the Department of Justice and the FBI, and (2) to
> defraud the US of and concerning its right to the honest . . .
> and faithful services of the defendant Judith Coplon.

It was a part of the conspiracy, the indictment read, that Judith Coplon would obtain information to be used to the injury of the United States . . . and, for the same purpose, that Valentin Gubitchev would "receive and obtain" information "taken and made" by Miss Coplon. Further, she would willfully communicate and transmit and attempt to communicate and transmit the same to persons not entitled to receive them; further, she would attempt to deliver and transmit the same to, specifically, Valentin A.

Gubitchev. Finally, as a part of the conspiracy, Judith Coplon would willfully and unlawfully remove and conceal documents belonging to the Department of Justice, aided and abetted by Gubitchev. Both defendants were charged in this first count.

Overt acts cited in support of Count 1 conspiracy charges were the meetings that were the subject of the trial, occasions during which they "did meet and confer." Counts 2, 3, and 4 addressed the same criminal acts, but made them specific and charged independently to one or the other of the defendants.

> **Count 2** charged that on or about March 4, 1949 . . . Judith Coplin [alone] . . . lawfully having possession of . . . documents, writings, and notes containing intelligence reports relating to espionage and counter-espionage activities in the US, did willfully attempt to communicate and transmit said documents . . . to Valentin Gubitchev, who was . . . not entitled to receive the same.

> **Count 3** charged that on or about March 4, 1949, Valentin A. Gubitchev [alone], for the purpose of obtaining information respecting the national defense, did unlawfully attempt to receive and obtain from Judith Coplon documents, writing and notes . . . . relating to espionage and counter-espionage activities in the US containing intelligence reports.

> **Count 4** charged that on or about March 4, 1949 . . . Judith Coplon with . . . reason to believe they would be used to the injury of the US and to the advantage of a foreign nation, did attempt to communicate, deliver, and transmit to Valentin Gubitchev, a subject and citizen of the USSR, directly and indirectly documents, writings, notes and information relating to the national defense . . . containing intelligence reports relating to espionage and counter-espionage activities in the US.

Counts 2 and 4 against Judy and were essentially the same. Count 4 had her performing the same illegal act on the same date as Count 2, but doing so with reason to believe the act would injure the United States. Also,

Gubitchev was identified as a Soviet citizen in Count 4. With this as background, attention turns to what happened with the jury.

One hour and five minutes after receiving the case, jurors returned to the courtroom to review a portion of evidence before taking a brief break for dinner. At 6 P.M., they were once again back in the courtroom, asking that William Foley's testimony be read to them. They also asked to review Judy's handwritten notes on the decoy memorandum, the Michael Memorandum, and certain of the data slips. Deliberations were resumed at eight forty-five.

Shortly before 11 P.M., a marshal delivered a note from the jury to Judge Ryan:

"Sir: The jury wishes to know whether in Count 2 of the indictment the word appearing on line 3 should be 'lawfully' or 'unlawfully.'" It was signed by jury foreman J. Hopfer.

At 11:05 P.M., Hopfer and his fellow jurors were back in the jury box. Judge Ryan observed that the mimeographed copy of the espionage indictment given to jurors read, ". . . Judith Coplon, herein named as defendant, unlawfully having possession of . . ." Ryan, examining the copy, noted that there was a penciled correction changing the word in question to read "lawfully." Ryan next read aloud the original grand jury indictment, on which the defendants should have been tried, with the language, "the defendant, lawfully having possession . . ."

Regardless, the judge explained, legality of possession was not the issue. Reading from Section 793, he quoted, "Whoever, lawfully or unlawfully having possession of documents . . . ," attempts to transmit the same in violation of the law has committed a crime. This, Ryan believed, should settle the matter. The jury slowly left the room. It is uncertain whether they were convinced.

At 12:45 A.M., the jury returned to tell Judge Ryan that, for the second time, members found they were unable to reach a decision; however, if the judge wished, they were willing to keep trying. He fervently wished they would, and sent them to a hotel for the rest of the night.

At 10:35 Tuesday morning, with the jury back at work, Leonard Boudin appeared before Judge Ryan. Present were Boudin's partners, along with the government's attorneys. Boudin promptly moved for a mistrial based on the fact that virtually every part of the case against his client was "directed to unlawful possession of certain papers." The documents "purporting to be an indictment upon which the defendant Coplon was tried" indicated unlawful possession.

Ryan responded that he had told jurors in his charge that "Coplon was in possession, had access to, and was intrusted with certain documents, writings and notes by reason of her employment as a political analyst in the Department of Justice, Foreign Agents Registration Section." In any event, he reiterated, the statute "makes it immaterial as to how a person comes into possession of these documents." Whether they are stolen or legally acquired, the "unlawful intent required by the statute comes *after* possession has been acquired."

The fact that "one word was typographically set forth erroneously," Ryan determined, "did not work to the detriment or interfere with the proper presentation of the case in any respect." One might argue that it might have done so—might have swayed the thinking of the jury member or members who held out for acquittal until shortly before noon, when the jury delivered a verdict in direct conflict with itself.

"Mr. Foreman," Judge Ryan asked, "have you agreed on a verdict?"

"We have."

"How say you?" asked the clerk.

"On Count 1 of the indictment, we find both defendants guilty." Count 1, wherein the defendants were jointly charged with various conspiratorial acts as specified in Sections 793, 794, and 371 of Title 18, the U.S. Code.

"On Count 2, we find the defendant not guilty." Count 2, wherein Judith Coplon was charged alone with obtaining information with the intent and purpose to transmit documents to an unauthorized person.

"On Count 3, we find the defendant guilty as charged." Count 3, wherein Gubitchev was charged with being the unauthorized person attempting to receive documents from Coplon.

"On Count 4, we find the defendant guilty as charged." Count 4, wherein Coplon was charged with attempting to transmit secrets to Valentin Gubitchev, a Soviet citizen, and doing so with the belief they would be used to injure the United States.

Jaws dropped. If Judy was found not guilty of transmitting, or attempting to transmit, specific documents to Gubitchev on a specific date, how could he be found guilty of receiving, or attempting to receive the very same documents on that same date? Even more mind boggling was finding Judith guilty on Count 4 and not guilty on Count 2. If she was guilty on Count 4, which included the act charged in Count 2, she *had* to be guilty on both counts. And if she was not guilty of trying to transmit papers he was attempting to receive, did this affect their conspiratorial secret passing as charged in Count 1? Had they failed to conspire?

Later, jurors would admit to some confusion in their minds; defending attorneys admitted to confusion immediately after the verdict was read.

"I can't figure this damn thing out," Abraham Pomerantz complained.

"If you can explain this, then you're better than I," observed Samuel Neuburger.

If it is a tendency of the human genius to make rational that which appears not, attempts to do so would confound more minds today than those of the defense attorneys. Chief prosecutor John Kelley, whose mind apparently was not confounded, had no problem with the verdict. It would help make the country aware of "vicious elements" out to impugn "this great organization," the Federal Bureau of Investigation.

Judy Coplon paled but neither wept nor cried out at the verdict. Gubitchev's face flushed in the heat of the moment. Moving quickly, marshals approached the convicted spies. With a soft cry, Judy hugged her brother and sister-in-law tightly before she was led away to the Women's House of Detention. Gubitchev, expressionless, was placed in a federal detention house van with several other prisonors. Among them, according to the *Washington Post* that day, was John David Provoo, charged with treason. The sensibilities of Valentin Gubitchev, so profoundly offended by possible "income tax evaders" as jail mates earlier on, must have been more so in the presence of such an unseemly character.

Crime and Punishment

Nearly three dozen reporters surrounded a painfully subdued Judith Coplon the moment she stepped down from a house of detention van following its arrival in the federal courthouse garage. Calls of "Judy!" "Judy, turn this way!" failed to elicit the expected response, failed to bring the familiar quick

smile and cheerful wave. The stiff-upper-lip spirit, which Judy had maintained throughout so much of her ordeal, had left her. She was wan and
thinner now, seeming lost in a long black coat. Judy barely noticed the swarm
of eager reporters. Mercifully, and uncharacteristically, they quieted and
moved aside, allowing the twice-convicted spy and an escorting matron to
pass by. But their cameras flashed, had been flashing since the van came
within view.

Valentin Gubitchev, who would be sentenced first this crisp March 9
morning, arrived with little attention five minutes after Judy had disappeared
into the building.

The courtroom was packed, spectators jammed together and straining to
get a clear view of the country's newest spy celebrities. Once inside, Judy
went quickly to her brother and hugged him fiercely, in a poignant moment
of visibly shared pain. She turned away and went to her assigned seat, eyes
downcast. As the court came to order, attorneys speaking for both defendants
made motions to set aside the verdict, to arrest judgment, and to order a new
trial. This routine procedure seemed less so, given the confusing and conflicted verdict rendered in this case. The response, however, was routine.
Motions immediately were denied, and the process of pronouncing punishment for crimes committed began.

Called before the bench, a scowling thirty-three-year-old Valentin
Gubitchev did not have the look of either passionate lover or convicted spy.
He seemed disappointingly ordinary and nondescript. His counsel, Abraham
Pomerantz, asked permission for Gubitchev to make a statement before sentencing. With Judge Ryan's permission to speak, the Soviet spy began an
angry tirade, insisting that he was not guilty of any wrongdoing against the
United States of America. Everything that had happened to him over the
past year and five days was a violation of international law. The FBI had
framed him, for whatever unknown, insidious reasons. His voice was threatening, filled with fury and rancor. Spectators thoroughly enjoyed the
drama—it seemed so fitting for the occasion. And Mr. Gubitchev had taken
on the persona of a proper spy, especially because he was speaking rapid,
clipped Russian, and, to most, simply being Russian was suspect.

Unmoved and unimpressed, Ryan told Gubitchev, "You have been convicted by a verdict of a jury after a fair, impartial and public trial. You have

had the protection of the laws of this country and you have enjoyed and had the benefit of privileges afforded to those accused of crime in few countries of the world." Gubitchev, also unmoved and unimpressed, stood motionless while Ryan continued. "You came here as an emissary of peace; you were acceptable among us in the role of a friend; you violated your oath of office to the Secretariat of the United Nations of the world."

There was more, including destroying the hopes of millions of people searching for worldwide comity and peace. By now, a slight smile played across Gubitchev's lips. He well knew what would happen next. Five years in prison upon Count 1, and ten upon Count 2, to be served consecutively and not concurrently. In truth, not to be served at all.

Based on the recommendation of the attorney general and the secretary of state, Judge Ryan announced, sentence would be suspended and Valentin Gubitchev would be sent back to Russia. The judge, strongly disagreeing with the recommendation, was nonetheless compelled to comply.

Nervously, Judith sat listening intently, watching, studying. Gubitchev, whom she once knew as "Val," would be free to go about his life, at home, with his family and daughter. It seemed so very wrong.

"If arrangements are made for your immediate deportation," the judge said, "I shall suspend sentence on the day you are about to leave this country, provided that a marshal accompany you to the ship upon which you are to depart and keep you in custody until the ship shall leave our shores. Never to return."

Attorney Pomerantz said the recommendation had come to him "as a surprise."

This was the surprise conceived almost exactly a year earlier, when Attorney General Tom Clark wrote his secret memorandum to the president objecting to the State Department's recommendation that Gubitchev be deported, suggesting that he stand trial and then be sent home. Thus, for the past fifty-one weeks the government had well known the ending, as well as the beginning and the middle of this aspect of the Coplon-Gubitchev story.

With the matter of her coconspirator settled, Judith Coplon now stood before Judge Ryan flanked by her attorneys, who asked for leniency. She already had been sentenced in Washington for essentially the same offenses, and pleading for leniency seemed appropriate. It did not seem so to Judge Ryan, whose scathing denunciation and tough sentencing would make his feelings clear. Standing ramrod straight, arms at her sides, she answered, "Not at this time, Your Honor," when Ryan asked if she had anything to say.

"Judith Coplon, it is now my duty to pronounce sentence upon you," he began. "You have brought dishonor upon the name you bear; you have brought disgrace and even tragedy upon your family. You have been disloyal to the country which has nourished you, helped you acquire an education and placed in you high trust and confidence.

"Your country looks upon you with sorrow. You have proved yourself an ungrateful daughter." Ominously, the judge added, "My observation of you during the trial and my knowledge of the facts convince me that the seeds of disloyalty still find root within you.

"Your country does not seek vengeance, but you must, in justice, receive substantial punishment, not only for your treacherous acts, but as a warning to others of your kind, in whom we have placed trust. . . ."

Judith was sentenced to five years in prison for Count 1, and fifteen for Count 4, to be served concurrently. However, Ryan stipulated, these fifteen years could not be served concurrently with her Washington sentence. Twenty-five consecutive years, all together, given the ten in Washington.

Stunned, Judy stood unmoving for a second then wavered, but only slightly, as her attorneys reached out with steadying hands. A marshal rushed forward to take her arm, then hurried her from the courtroom. Someone picked up Judy's purse and coat and ran after her. The room was completely silent, the only movement Bertram Coplon's heading for the door. He caught up with his sister in the anteroom and was allowed a moment with her. Pulling her close, he kissed her, smoothed her hair. "I love you," he told her.

Lillian McLaughlin, deputy U.S. marshal, was happy to talk about the moment with a reporter, saying, "She doesn't react to things like a normal woman." Judy was "the coldest, most unemotional, enigmatic woman I've handled in fourteen years. At first, I thought she was just sullen. She isn't. She has actually mellowed since I first saw her last year."

As a Washington matron had complained a year earlier, Judy did not cry, as women *normally* do when tragic or terrifying events occur. Now, McLaughlin observed, "There wasn't a tear, when most women prisoners break down completely." McLaughlin compared Judy with other, more easily understood, prisoners assigned to her.

"Judy was the exact opposite of Lucille Mallin, the white-slaver queen who entered prison in a mink coat. She was friendly, nice, beautiful. Judy used only lipstick, there wasn't even a mirror in her purse." Prisoner Coplon, however, worried that her stockings were "too big and sloppy" on her way to court for sentencing.

Judy also "was not like Minnie the Moocher Leeder, the department store wizard." Minnie, it seems, in addition to having a penchant for snitching from stores, was gracious enough to entertain Deputy McLaughlin with stories of shopping misadventures. One was about a friend of Minnie's, who told her, "I just saw the nicest purse in a store up the street," and Minnie had offered, "Wait five minutes and I'll get it for you."

Judy had no stories to share. She was said to be uncommunicative; conversation with her keepers and van drivers was limited. Uncomplaining, Judy was cooperative behind bars and helped with the routine searches prisoners experienced when leaving or entering the detention facility.

Today, as in other horrific days of this year and four days, Judith Coplon was keeping her pain to herself. Some called it abnormal. Others might have called it courageous.

Pomp and Circumstance

Circumstance was the keystone in the arch of the New York conviction of Judith Coplon.

No direct evidence was presented in court to support the architectural structure of guilt, not a single, solid, evidentiary building block. Evidence was inescapably *suggestive*, but not concretely *conclusive*. Constructing the edifice of conviction would have been a much cleaner and simpler task if the accused had been caught in the act, or if they had admitted guilt, or both— had been like a Robert Hanssen apprehended after making a dead drop, or a Harry Gold immediately admitting guilt when confronted with a lone piece of circumstantial evidence.

In New York, as opposed to Washington, the case revolved around conspiracy, around two people working together to commit, or attempting to commit, a crime. As Judge Ryan told the jury on March 6, "a conspiracy may be proved by circumstantial evidence." Ironically, the only *directly* provable lawbreaking in New York was the government's wiretapping, declared illegal by the court, with evidence of specific illegal acts being the FBI agents' signed affidavits and courtroom testimonies.

In Washington, there was direct evidence to support charges of Judith's having specific kinds of materials in her possession. The indictment made possession wrongful based on her alleged intention to use them in a manner detrimental to the United States, an allegation by its nature— mental determination—incapable of proof by direct evidence. In New York, in those last few hours of the trial, it was made clear that Judy had *lawful* possession of the information she carried. Intent was the basis, in both cases, for arguments and questions left unsettled for half a century. Valentin Gubitchev, representing intent, was only a possibility in the trial on Constitution Avenue; he became the reality, the incarnation, at Foley Square.

Ultimately, varying and conflicting interpretations of both circumstantial and direct evidence by two juries, two district courts, and two U.S. courts of appeals—as well as the Supreme Court's decision, yet to come—made final, legal determination of guilt a Hydra-headed judicial exercise.

Had those juries and courts had certain information hidden away in Arlington, Virginia, it would have been a different matter entirely. Evidentiary questions would have become moot, and the FBI would have been perceived as hero rather than villain.

From the scathing tone of his sentencing remarks, Judge Ryan was pleased with the jury's decision, but most likely would have preferred that Judy had been found guilty on all three of the counts charged against her. If, in the ethical and moral sense, he believed what he said about the country's not seeking to extract vengeance, his actions seemed to suggest that its legal system wanted precisely that. The ceremonious way in which his oratory was delivered, the pageantry of the setting, all spoke of *pomp* as much as it did of law, of vengeance as much as punishment.

Immediately after Judy was taken from the courtroom, her attorneys requested, and were denied, release on bond pending appeal.

Leonard Boudin hurriedly filed a petition with the U.S. District Court of Appeals for the Second Circuit asking for an order admitting Judy to twenty thousand dollars' bail pending appeal. It raised all of the principal issues of the case, including lack of representation based on Ryan's refusal to grant new counsel sufficient time to prepare; unlawful wiretapping, including intercepted conversations between her and counsel; the questioned legality of the arrest; double jeopardy; the conflict between the originally worded indictment and that which was subsequently the basis for the trial; and the conflicting jury decisions involving Counts 2 and 4. Judge Thomas Swan heard arguments for and against bail. On March 13, Swan granted bail in the amount of forty thousand dollars.

It was time to go home.

PART FOUR

At **Home** in **Brooklyn**

It was a quiet homecoming. The family, relieved to be together again, was drained and exhausted. Friends and neighbors, still firmly believing in Judy's innocence, were circumspect in their greetings, yet enthusiastic in expressing their personal assurances of that belief. They were supported by knowledge that, for them, there had been no substantive proof of treachery. Judy, the young woman they knew, some better than others, was the hideously wronged Innocent. Framed, they believed, and lied about by a government they had trusted. With the ordeal of two trials finally over, there was a sense of completion, if not of closure; closure could come only after the appeals process had run its course.

Remarkably, even then the story would not be over. There were more surprises to come. Unmasking the elusive confidential informant, for one.

One thing was certain. Judge Ryan ultimately would be proved wrong; they were not "seeds of disloyalty," but of courage and determination that remained within young Judith Coplon when she returned home. Capitulation and surrender were not in her nature.

If family and friends believed in Judy's innocence, it appeared as if most of the rest of the world did not, assuming that the press reflected prevailing thought about the matter. And if *madness* can be defined as a state of fury as well as a condition of frenzied activity, it also can define the media's vibrantly enthusiastic response to Judge Ryan's tongue-lashing and tough sentencing. Considered the beautiful, brilliant, malicious, and twice-confirmed Soviet spy next door, she was irresistible to both editors and readers. Santa's daughter, patriot's daughter, American Red, she deserved her sentence. Judith Coplon was real-life confirmation that strong concern about spies and Communist plots was justified, and that equally strong concern about a growing national "hysteria" was not. Within two months, atomic spy Harry Gold's confession would confirm the truth of the former; and, not all that long afterward, Joseph McCarthy's obsession would put the lie to the latter.

Among the various editorial observations made during those first few days in Brooklyn was one clearly reflecting on the Coplon case, one noting that the country's problems with Communist subversion would not have been so serious if "arrogant young intellectuals" understood that espionage and betrayal of one's country are "crimes of deadly seriousness." Nearly all supported Ryan's sentence, declaring that Judy got exactly what she deserved, which excluded both mercy and sympathy. But leave it to acerbic journalist Robert Ruark to get to the point in typical style:

"We don't jail our own traitors, and we turn loose other people's spies," he complained. "Instead of shooting the Russian, or socking him away in the freezer, we let him trickle back to the Soviet with a basket of bon voyage fruit." As for Gubitchev's convicted coconspirator, "from a standpoint of high moral indignation, we might justifiably have shot little Judy."

"Little Judy" was seen differently now than she was a year earlier, when she had been a "gay, good looking girl," said one writer. She was now "a frightened wight miserable in a self-made tragedy." Her appearance was misleading, observed another, with her being "the sort of girl whom no one would take for a criminal and who would instantly appeal to the protective impulses of any man." Yet the man who wrote this last comment hurried on to assure his readers that Judy was unquestionably guilty, apparently over-coming instant appeal.

While the press ruminated and commented about the two historic trials held this past year and the criminal behavior defined by Judy's convictions, she had her own thoughts about it all.

Reflections on the "Year of Hell"

Eschatological debate about Hell, among and between believers and nonbe-lievers, has tantalized the intellect for centuries. Did it exist or did it not; and, if so, in what sort of earthly or supernatural context? Judith Coplon thought she knew, and offered her intensely personal answer: Hell existed, on earth, for a finite period of time—the period from March 4, 1949, to March 13, 1950. Two espionage trials, paparazzi, rumors, and smoldering hatred toward her defined the characteristics of Hell's inferno.

One week following her release from the Women's Detention Center and return to Brooklyn, Judy told New York journalist Fern Marja, "I feel like a patient who has been strapped down on an operating table—whose body has been opened. I have the feeling of being dissected for everyone to see. I've lost weight. I've lost my appetite." Friends would note that she had "aged ten years."

"How do you think a person feels when her wire is tapped, her mail checked, her friends investigated, her movements followed, and when everyone stares?" She answered her own question. "You feel exactly like the fly under glass. It took me quite a while to get adjusted to it. Finally you get indif-ferent. Not because you're hard, but because there's nothing else you can do."

Particularly hurtful were comments like those of her "handlers" when she was incarcerated in Washington and New York, comments that pictured an enigmatic ice-water-veined woman, an abnormal woman. Or the obverse, a woman who, when she smiled, was not taking her predicament seriously, when, "I'm seen as frivolous or callous." She was neither. "I've only to look at my mother to see how it has affected her. It tears my heart to look at her.

"Cry? Of course I cry!" And she smiled, in an effort to boost her mother's spirits as well as her own.

As for being distant and unfriendly, she showed Marja a four-leaf-clover bracelet on her wrist. It was a gift from a fellow prisoner. For good luck.

It was impossible to forget, during any waking moments, that she twice had been convicted for espionage. "When you see yourself in a newspaper, you get butterflies in your stomach. When I look at the pictures of me, I can't identify myself with them. It seems to me I'm a different person." How very much she wished to fade into obscurity, to be able to go for a walk without the stares, to pick up a newspaper without seeing her photograph and her name in headlines. The wish would be only partly granted, and not for some time to come.

One night while having dinner, her date looked around the restaurant and exclaimed, "You're spotted! Everyone here recognizes you!" He "meant well," she realized, but his remark and the unwanted attention ruined the evening. In truth, fame—or infamy—had changed her life forever. No matter how many men or women later would be apprehended for espionage, she always would carry the stigma of being America's first convicted Cold War spy. It was a heavy mantle for such small shoulders.

Judy had agreed to the interview in Samuel Neuburger's office, where she sat behind a lawyer's desk nearly lost in a large leather chair, nervously swiveling back and forth as she spoke. At twenty-eight, Judy ached to lead a normal life—to get married and raise a family. Also, "I want to do some creative kind of work," she said. Standing in the way of her longing for the kind of life people take for granted were the events of this hellish year. "The most horrible part is that I'm absolutely innocent."

There was enormous sadness about Judy, until the inevitable love-life questions surfaced. She had been dating, seeing men. Were there any marriage plans?

Her answer came not in words but in a sudden change in body language— the familiar smile returned, a hunched figure lifted, a sense of spiritual lifting as well. So different from when the same question was asked during Archie's wild press conference on January 28, when Judy had answered, "When? With a ten-year sentence in Washington and 35 years hanging over me here, I'll ask you, when?"

On this day, the questioner had to be satisfied with an unspoken answer. Judy revealed nothing about the new someone in her life, a handsome young lawyer with Samuel Neuburger's firm, whom she had met in January. But only since her change in counsel, some three weeks earlier, had she gotten to know him. Albert Socolov was the one wonderful thing that happened to her during this nightmare of a year.

Five days after Judy spoke about her year of Hell, U.S. Attorney Irving S. Saypol wrote to Judge Sylvester Ryan, "Pursuant to your directions, the defendant Valentin A. Gubitchev was delivered in the custody of US Marshal Daniel J. McCartan and his deputies to the liner, MS Batory at Pier 88, North River, prior to its departure at noon today." Thereafter, Mr. Gubitchev would be under the supervision of a customs officer and a member of the Immigration and Naturalization Service. The Russian was escorted to stateroom 102.

"Present in the stateroom were Mrs. Gubitchev, two border patrolmen, Lev S. Tolokonnikov, and Yuri V. Novikov." Accompanying the party on board, and to the stateroom, were Raymond Whearty and an unnamed FBI agent. Gubitchev was last seen, from the dock, standing at the *Batory*'s railing with his wife, waving to those who had escorted him to the ship.

To make certain that nothing went wrong, the ship was followed by two launches of the police department and a Coast Guard cutter. The cutter, in fact, would follow the *Batory* some fifty miles out to sea. Additionally, Coast Guard planes would follow the ship for several miles, a rather amazing precautionary exercise for one five-foot-three Russian on his way home.

"This concluded the assignment delegated to me and closes the case," Saypol wrote. There was one minor matter Saypol didn't mention. Gubitchev sent a message to Judith Coplon. He wished her luck.

Her response was simply, "I welcome good luck wishes from anyone." Whether they had ever been lovers, whether they were solely Soviet intelligence officer and agent, the finality of Gubitchev's leaving had to have created a certain poignancy in Judy. After all, she was not, as pictured, a cold, unemotional woman. She had a bracelet to prove it.

Albert and Judy

Nothing else, no one else, could have infused the miracle of belief into Judith's life as did young Albert Socolov. In the process of changing her life,

Albert daily demonstrated his confidence in a future of freedom. His belief in an innocent Judy was both passionate and eternal, as was his love. Albert was convincing; Judith would not go to prison, despite worldwide opinion to the contrary. Even after seemingly irrefutable revelations condemning Judy came to light half a century after the fact, Albert still believed in his beloved wife. Had J. Edgar Hoover, reincarnated, flanked on either side by retired KGB officers Oleg Kalugin and Oleg Tsarev, come to accuse her of espionage, Albert would have confidently confronted them with his unshaken trust. What had happened to his beloved was not the result of wrongdoing, but of anti-Red fervor, unchecked and out of control.

The couple's romance was never one-sided, its inherent strength never belonging solely to Albert. The favorable characteristics that had so circumscribed the child and the young woman would sustain Judith for the rest of her life and make for Albert the only woman he wanted.

Albert, twenty-nine, had been with the firm of Neuburger, Shapiro, Rabinowitz, and Boudin only a short time when two of its members, Neuburger and Boudin, were assigned the Coplon case. A 1942 graduate of Ohio State University, he earned his law degree at the New York University Law School. Well educated, intellectual, interested in the arts and cultural pursuits, tall, handsome Albert was the ideal man for Judith. Anyone criticizing his relationship with Judy had to admit that Albert possessed demonstrable patriotism, evidenced by valiant service in World War II as a fighting man, a survivor of the historic battle on Normandy beach.

On May 16, two months after Judith's second conviction, the couple called a press conference to announce their engagement. By now, Judy was free on sixty thousand dollars' bond, an extraordinary sum in 1950, and was facing twenty-five years in prison. Seated in her mother's home, glowing with love and excitement, none of this seemed to matter. They were in love and would be married. Albert had given Judy his late mother's diamond.

"I'm very much in love and, as a lawyer and someone who loves Judy, I feel confident about the outcome of the appeal. I think we have every chance for a happy married life," he told reporters. He was certain of his love for Judy in March, and, "I proposed in April, on the last Sunday in April, in Prospect Park. We were sitting under an oak tree near the lake." All of March and April they had been dating, going together to theaters, museums, movies.

They went to dinner, went dancing, went to the movies, behaving like any other young couple in love.

Judy was asked about having children. "Yes, I'd like to have children, and so would he," she smiled. "I would like to have a family," he agreed, taking her hand.

Their unmistakable, absolute confidence in the future must have given reporters pause. How could this fairy-tale romance be confirmed before their very eyes? How could two highly intelligent people in such untenable circumstances, with such frightening possibilities for the future, be sitting together, smiling, speaking of having children, of living a "normal, ordinary life," of excitement about moving into a three-room apartment? Didn't they understand that she might be moving into something much smaller, with bars instead of lace curtains at the window, and that their only time together might be on opposite sides of a glass wall?

"I have a great deal of faith and confidence in Judy," Albert said. "I feel sure that we'll come out all right in the courts." The thought of imprisonment, he made clear, never entered into their decision. Their future would be bright, their only hope that they would have a measure of privacy and a chance to "work out our own lives."

"I am very hopeful, very happy," Judy said. "I'm very much in love."

Ten days later, Albert and Judy were among 110 people securing marriage licenses at Borough Hall in Brooklyn.

Nothing marked the conclusion of the year of Hell with such convincing finality as the wedding, held May 28 at Rebecca's Brooklyn apartment, with fifty relatives and friends in attendance.

Even given the uniqueness of the circumstances surrounding the bridal couple, some of the newspapers covering the event offered the kind of traditional coverage granted the typical girl next door who marries her typical boyfriend.

"The bride, whose eyes were misty, wore a dress of beige organza over rose taupe crepe. The full-skirted, ankle-length dress was cinched in with a rose twist at the waist and had a tight decollete bodice. Mrs. Socolov wore a single strand of pearls, a hat covered with a veil in back and decorated with pearls, and carried a small bouquet of lilies-of-the-valley and brown and yellow orchids.

"Mr. Socolov's brother was the best man, while Mrs. Shirley Bertram Coplon, sister-in-law of the bride, was matron of honor."

Before the wedding, Judy and Albert met briefly with eleven reporters camped outside the door. Photographers wanted a kiss. "We'll save that for after the wedding," Albert said, but gave in after reporters insisted. One asked, "How does the bride look to you?"

"She looks beautiful," Albert grinned.

"He looks handsome and wonderful," Judy laughed. "I love him because he's handsome and wonderful."

Rabbi Max Felshin performed the double-ring Orthodox ceremony under a wine-colored brocade huppah. Lohengrin's wedding march began the ceremony, and Albert stepped on a wineglass with his heel, breaking it on the first try. At the end of the service he held his bride tenderly. "I love you," he told her. There was not a dry eye in the room.

While the wedding itself was traditional, the rabbi's comments were hardly that.

"We who believe in your innocence have admired the calm courage and dignity with which you bore your ordeal," Felshin told the bride. "Let us hope that truth will eventually triumph and your loyalty to our beloved country will be thoroughly vindicated." The case against her had resulted from "contemporary witch-hunting" and "mass hysteria."

"But beyond mere conjecture, there is neither proof nor certainty as to any act of disloyalty on your part. No one has testified to having actually seen or heard you divulge state secrets."

Reporters were not present at the wedding, but the rabbi's remarks were provided to the press following the ceremony.

The couple's honeymoon, by car, was limited geographically by court-imposed constraints on the bride's movements. She was confined to the southern and eastern districts of New York.

The wedding was the occasion for great joy among Judy's friends and relatives, but quite the contrary for some of the public—and some of the media—who were outraged by the audacity of "a convicted spy" falling in love, marrying, and starting out on a honeymoon, bright-eyed and full of joy, just like an ordinary, normal woman.

Twin Appeals

If it was during the New York pretrial hearings that the enormity of the government's many Coplon case miscalculations became apparent, it was during the appeals process that it became profound. The government's trials of Judith Coplon in Washington and New York were cantankerous twins, not identically but fraternally related, both seriously afflicted by the same flawed decisions that could prove fatal. There was another critical influence involved—Archie Palmer's, whose persistence in certain matters would prove vital to how the cases ended. Perhaps, after all, Archie Palmer's mysterious mountain had labored and given birth.

Appeal of the Washington conviction to the U.S. Court of Appeals for the First Circuit was filed before the FBI's wiretap operation was made public, and therefore did not address the issue of "tainted evidence." To solve the problem, Judy's lawyers asked that the appeal process be put on hold until action could be taken by the lower court on a motion for a new trial in Washington based on the wiretap revelations. Arguments on the motion were finally heard in June 1950, more than a year after the trial's end and three months after a decision in the New York trial. Judge Albert Reeves, seventy-five, who had presided with a demonstrably shaky and unskilled hand over Judith's first trial, heard arguments on the motion in the same courtroom that had been packed with spectators during the Washington trial. On this day, the courtroom was nearly empty, the public likely sated by now with Coplon courtroom drama; besides, the star would not be present. Mrs. Albert Socolov was at home in Brooklyn.

Leonard Boudin told the court that "rankest perjury" marked FBI testimony. The government engaged in the "grossest misconduct" not only before but also during her trial, and even afterward. Arguing against the motion was John Kelley, who insisted that "none of the government's case could possibly have consisted of evidence obtained from wiretapping."

On June 26, Reeves issued a brief, 250-word opinion saying that while the FBI action may have violated the Federal Communications Act and agents may have committed an "ethical" wrong, Judy was not entitled to a new trial. Not unless someone could prove to him that evidence obtained through the ethically incorrect wiretapping was used in her trial, and no one had done so.

"I find that the evidence upon which plaintiff was convicted did not stem from, nor was it traceable to, wiretapping, and being untainted, said motion should be overruled." Certainly, ruled the judge, there was no tainted evidence as suggested, "and counsel does not point out a line or even a scintilla of testimony procured in this way." Judy's attorneys immediately announced their intention to appeal Reeves's decision. Now the Washington appellate court had two Coplon cases to consider—appeal of conviction, Case 10339, and appeal of Reeves's failure to grant a new trial based on newly discovered evidence, Case 10801.

John Kelley was highly irritated by Judith Coplon's temerity in carrying her case any farther. There had been no wiretap evidence used against Judy, who had been convicted twice of Red-inspired, traitorous criminality. Continued court appearances only bolstered the cause of the Soviets. It was "high time to put an end to the practice of using our Federal courts as sounding boards," as a means of creating propaganda for Soviet use "in undermining this Nation's position abroad," he told the press.

Meanwhile, preparation of Judith's appeal of her New York conviction was under way. It would become Case 21790 of the U.S. Court of Appeals for the Second Circuit. The whole business was becoming more and more complex, for both sides. Richard Hradsky, armed with his pointer and a chart tracking the multitude of supportive filings for the cases, now three, might well have been a welcomed addition to the frenetic scene.

Boudin and company were not moving fast enough for Irving Saypol, the U.S. attorney who had bade Gubitchev a less-than-fond farewell. On August 12, he asked that the New York appellate court immediately end Judith's appeal process and put her, just as immediately, behind bars. Twice now she had missed her filing date. It was time to send her away. The court declined to take any such drastic reaction and, instead, extended her filing date to October 2, with arguments scheduled November 2, and decided that Judy would remain free under the terms of her bail agreement.

Back in Washington, Judith's appeal of her conviction based on numerous errors would be argued on November 30. In those precomputer days, typewriters were tapping incessantly and mimeograph machines whirling night and day. Paper was everywhere.

Points included in the New York appeal included two related to wiretapping: one, that leads were developed from tapping and records subsequently destroyed, and two, that the appellant was denied her right to effective assistance of counsel because of interception of attorney-client conversations. Two related to the arrest and seizure without warrant. The conflict between the verdicts on Counts 2 and 4, and the failure of the government to prove Judith "knew" Gubitchev to be a spy as required in Count 4, as well as the inapplicability of the conspiracy charge, also were points supporting the appeal.

The appellate battle was launched in New York on November 2, with attorney Fred Strine defending the legality of the March 4 arrest before the three-judge panel. The distinguished jurist Learned Hand said that Judith Coplon's conviction would not stand if the court determined her arrest had been illegal. Strine answered that he believed the FBI had the same power to arrest afforded "ordinary citizens."

"The FBI has less power than an ordinary policeman or an ordinary citizen," Hand declared. The history and power of arrest by Bureau agents consumed page upon page in every brief, response, and judgment involved with this case. On this day, Strine found himself in an untenable position, arguing a point upon which even appellate judges would disagree.

"Why on earth should you not have been able to get a warrant here or in Washington?" Hand demanded, but before Strine could answer, the judge wanted to know about the possibility that Gubitchev might flee. Was there "any indication that the jig was up?" he asked. Even so, that could justify the Russian's arrest, but not hers.

Destruction of wiretap data also raised the judge's ire. When Strine defended the action, saying that there had been no deliberate or wanton destruction, Hand replied with, "Could there have been anything more wanton and deliberate?" The two also clashed over "security reasons" offered to excuse the wholesale destruction of evidence, an issue of special import to Hand. "You can point a finger at any person and say 'for security reasons,'" he snorted.

In all, the day had been far more comfortable for Boudin than for Strine. At home, Judith and Albert held their breath and waited, daring to hope. In various New York and Washington offices of the Department of Justice, various officials also held their breath and were deeply concerned about Judge

Learned Hand. There was so much at stake here. If anything went wrong, the Supreme Court was all that was left, and who knew if they would even hear the case?

Washington came next, before any word from New York.

Appellant Coplon's Washington appeal of her conviction cited errors with regard to composition of the jury; denial of her motion for return of papers and property seized on March 4 with a focus on the illegality of her arrest without a warrant and the subsequent seizure; failure of the government to provide sufficient evidence to sustain the jury's verdict; and errors in the jury's charge. Two errors dealt with prosecutorial behavior, one citing misconduct and the other noting "highly inflammatory" statements made in summation, including prejudicial "unfounded statements" violating the defendant's rights. The court also would consider her appeal based on the wiretap issues.

On November 30, 1950, Leonard Boudin told the appeals court that the FBI tapped Judith Coplon's calls to her attorney, including one discussing the advisability of her taking the witness stand. Oh, responded Fred Strine, undoubtedly still smarting from the scene in New York, this was of no consequence because the information was not used as evidence. Judge Barrett Prettyman was not pleased with Strine's words.

"I'd like to have it explained to me," the judge said testily, "how any appellant can have a fair trial if conversations between him and his counsel are intercepted. . . . Suppose I was on trial, and you were hearing secretly what I and my counsel are saying. Is that allowed under the Constitution?" Over the course of the heated and extended argument about wiretapping, Judge Prettyman frequently interrupted to assure Strine that the government had not established justification for its illicit operation. Strine, red faced, suffered even greater discomfort after acknowledging that wiretap records were destroyed by the government.

"Do you mean that wiretap data was destroyed while cases involving the defendant were on appeal in two courts?" a seemingly incredulous Prettyman inquired, knowing full well that such was the case. The legality of the arrest was argued as well, the same issues and same arguments confronted in New York. The egregious mistake in deciding to have two cases and two trials for alleged criminal violations stemming from the same act was becoming more and more apparent.

Boudin would not have his answer from Washington's First Circuit for another six months. He had his answer, however, from New York's Second Circuit only five days after the Washington argument was concluded.

The court's highly unusual decision, announced December 5, was the first cause for celebration in the Coplon camp in nearly two years. Judy and Al, who had been awaiting word in his downtown office, were photographed as they left the building. A smiling, elated Al was tightly holding his wife's arm. Judy, in a long coat and cloche hat, looked thoughtful.

The opinion written by Judge Hand, with Judges Jerome N. Frank and Thomas L. Swan concurring, held that Judith's "guilt was plain," but suggested that the government was guilty as well. Her arrest without a warrant was determined to be illegal; therefore the search and seizure were illegal as well. Failure of the government to allow Judy access to wiretap records was wrong. "Few weapons in the arsenal of freedom are more useful than the power to compel a government to disclose the evidence on which it seeks to forfeit the liberty of its citizens," Hand wrote. Whether or not the defendant could have demonstrated that certain "leads" in the case came from wiretaps, she should have had an opportunity to try. And, elsewhere in the court's opinion, discussing the troublesome issue of national security versus introduction of otherwise privileged documents, he said the prosecution "must decide whether the public prejudice of allowing the crime to go unpunished was greater than the disclosure of such 'state secrets' to the defense." The very same argument raised prior to release of the FBI's raw data files. The same never-resolved argument of individual rights versus "national security" or "state secret" exigencies.

Judy's conviction was overturned; however, the indictment was not dismissed. Someday, another trial, if it were to take place, *might* have more evidence supporting an arrest without a warrant, the prosecution *might* decide to divulge the contents of the wiretaps, and examination *might* confirm that the confidential informant was not a wiretapper, speculated Hand.

As condemning as was Hand's the "guilt is plain" statement to the defendant, excoriation was worse for a government—in this case, particularly for an attorney general—failing to obey its own laws. "Where the head of the same department of a government which has charge of the prosecution has directed the unlawful acquisition of the information, this is the only tolerable result."

For the government, the result was hardly tolerable. A retrial of the New York case was unthinkable. With the arrest and search found illegal, all of the evidence had vanished. The government would go to the Supreme Court. It was imperative that the appellate court be overturned. Otherwise, their only hope was the Washington decision.

Also intolerable to the government on this landmark day was a statement given to the press by Archibald Palmer:

"In my opinion, this case can never be won by the government. I feel now, as I said all along in Washington and New York, that Judy was innocent. I'm no prophet, but I believe that the conviction against her in Washington must be reversed also." It was a kind and gentlemanly thing for Archie to say.

Huge, two- and three-inch headlines announced to the world that Coplon's conviction had been overturned. Across the United States, there was a widespread campaign to write new laws permitting the FBI broader powers to arrest.

By now, the national commentary was of little consequence to the Socolovs. It was old hat, just a new style. Judith continued to work with the three attorneys representing her, but most closely with a junior member of the firm, her husband. Except for the remarkable strength and resiliency of the couple, the stress of eating, sleeping, and working with the case constantly in mind could well have been all-consuming. As it was, they constructed for themselves an amazingly ordinary life under supremely extraordinary circumstances. According to Al, all they have ever wanted was a "normal, ordinary" life, doing ordinary, normal things. One must observe that their lives may at times have been normal, but they have never been, and never will be "ordinary."

On December 20, Supreme Court justice Robert H. Jackson gave the government until February 3 to appeal the New York court's decision. It responded nearly two months later, when Solicitor General Phillip Perlman, speaking for the government, asked the Supreme Court to set aside the second circuit court's decision that the arrest was illegal and that wiretap data should have been made available to the defendant. Broader issues concerned the underlying issue of protecting "secrets."

Two items of interest concerning Judith Coplon appeared in the news on the same day some four months later. One was far more important than the other, which was merely titillating.

June 1, 1951, in Dorothy Kilgallen's *Times Herald* column:

"Harold Shapiro, the Department of Justice lawyer who 'loved and told' in the Judy Coplon spy case, is furnishing Washington with its most exciting cocktail hour conversations. The gossips are gabbing over the uncanny resemblance between his new bride and Judy—and the bride also is a government girl."

June 1, 1951, from the U.S. Court of Appeals for the First Circuit, a long-awaited decision.

The court of appeals, with circuit judge Wilbur K. Miller writing the opinion, upheld the lower court. The arrest was legal, the evidence was sufficient to sustain the conviction. Other alleged errors had been considered; Judith's conviction was upheld. Case 10339 was affirmed. Joining in the affirmation were Judges Barrett Prettyman and James M. Proctor.

The government was not home free. In its second action, the court disagreed with the district court's holding that interception of telephone messages between the defendant and her counsel before and during her trial, *if* it occurred, was nothing more than a serious breach of ethics. *If* the interception took place, the defendant had been denied the effective aid and assistance of counsel. The appellate court could not sanction this denial of basic rights, and Reeves's order denying motion for a new trial was set aside. The case was remanded for a hearing to determine whether the alleged interceptions actually occurred. If so, Judith Coplon was to be given a new trial. Judge Prettyman concurred with Miller's opinion, but Proctor disagreed, which changed nothing.

If the interceptions took place. In New York, the government's own witnesses testified that they had intercepted at least fourteen conversations between the defendant and counsel. Their testimonies were on record and irrefutable. Now the government had to decide whether it wanted to get back into this convoluted, miserable mess with yet another Coplon trial. To do so was about as appealing as being poked in the eye with a sharp stick.

The result of all of this was that the Washington indictment was not vacated and Judith remained convicted, technically awaiting a trial that common sense suggested never would take place. One appellate court had found her arrest legal, another found it illegal; two had made the unusual decision not to vacate her indictments while overturning and remanding. Evidence against her was "tainted" in one court and pure in another.

The combined decisions added monumental confusion to the country's most bizarre espionage case. Judith Coplon would remain free on bail until a new trial occurred, if ever.

The only solution to the legal conundrum now bewildering not only the public, but also the more esoteric world of American jurisprudence, was the Supreme Court. And it was to its wisdom that both sides were appealing. Not only did the government petition the country's highest court, but Judith also was a petitioner, asking that the Washington appellate court's decision finding her arrest legal be modified. Referring to the list of cases before the 162nd term of the Supreme Court, the *Washington Star*'s John Gerrity wrote, "Of those [cases] listed for hearing perhaps the most outstanding from the aspect of notoriety is that of Judith Coplon, former Justice Department employee."

The holiday season this year was filled with anticipation for the Socolovs. Judy was expecting their first child and was happily looking forward to becoming a mother. Albert was equally delighted. There was, of course, enormous anticipation involving another coming event—the Supreme Court's decision.

It came, again with huge headlines on January 28, 1952, in the largest media barrage since Judy's arrest three years earlier. COPLON WINS IN HIGH COURT; JUDY COPLON MAY GO FREE; JUDY COPLON WINS ROUND IN HIGH COURT; U.S. MAY DROP JUDY!

Writ of certiorari, the decision to hear the case, was denied for both the government and for Judy, which was seen as a major victory for her. Although the Washington conviction stood, she could at least have a new trial if she wished—or would have if the government wished—but the New York reversal also stood, which declared her arrest illegal. She was in a far better place than was the opposition.

Refusal to hear the government's appeal left it in a very difficult position, legally, politically, and publicly. The series of court rulings was now widely seen as having created an impossible legal tangle. The Department of Justice had to either abandon its efforts to put Judy behind bars or construct an entirely new case, knowing that a new court and a new jury might well find its evidence tainted and Judy's arrest illegal. And even if they won, there would be another appeal.

For the FBI, failure of the court to grant certiorari was seen as a disaster. Robert Lamphere, Howard Fletcher, Scott Miller—all were heartsick. They feared the woman would go free, a walking embarrassment for the agency that had devoted so much time and so many resources to putting her where they fervently believed she belonged. As for Mr. Hoover, his seething rage steamed throughout the Bureau's halls. Lamphere blamed Judge Hand for bringing the government to this miserable juncture. "He was a hero of mine, an excellent judge. But he couldn't have been more wrong," Lamphere says.

A copy of the High Court's official denial of certiorari has a typewritten note at the bottom. "Mr. Justice Clark took no part in the consideration or decision of this application." Mr. Tom Clark, now a member of the U.S. Supreme Court, who had made the decision to continue Judy's Washington trial at the critical intersection between release of secret files and the rights of a defendant.

The Legal Aftermath

On February 5, in the week following the Supreme Court's decision to look the other way, the Department of Justice sent out word via an unnamed "high department source" that it had new evidence and would retry "the Mata Hari in Bobby Sox." No clue as to the nature or origin of the new evidence was revealed, most likely because it did not exist. Solicitously, the Justice Department spokesperson noted that because Judith Coplon Socolov was expecting a child within weeks, her trial would be delayed until late spring or early summer.

The unidentified source acknowledged that it would be "useless" to retry Judy in New York, because although the evidence against her was declared legal in Washington, it was found to be illegal in New York. This left Washington as the venue of necessity.

On this same day, a Senate Internal Security Committee blamed Judy for being at least partly responsible for "tons of foreign propaganda inimical to the US" which was "fanning out over the nation every month." The accusation was based on failure of the *State* Department to "require propagandists in the embassies and legations to label their literature as required by the Foreign Agents Registration Act." Further, Judy, who worked for the *Justice* Department, was present at a conference where "regulations for the Four Continent Book Corporation were eased."

What heroic capabilities this young woman had, creating such widespread havoc by doing all that fanning out and, with others, attending a government conference. This sort of irrational pronouncement made it clear that Judith had become the poster girl for subversive activity in the nation's capital. In commenting on Judy's remarkable level of achievement in this regard, another unnamed Justice Department spokesman (who apparently had not discussed his statement with his colleague) said, "The government has no intention of allowing her to go free by default," although "no new evidence has been uncovered."

From this point on, the government had enormous difficulty in developing and conveying a consistent Coplon-case rhetoric. Its "official" position varied from day to day, from year to year, and from source to source. Still, unofficially, insiders were doubtful that the case would ever be retried. With good reason; the absolutely last place the government wanted to be, short of square in the middle J. Edgar Hoover's carpet, was in a courtroom with Judith Coplon and company.

On November 19, 1952, the Justice Department announced that it was "still" trying to decide what to do about the tangled case of Judith Coplon.

In April of the following year, the new Eisenhower administration, inheritor of the Coplon conundrum, began clearing the way for a new trial in Washington. Meanwhile, of course, the accused/convicted Judy was still out on a total of sixty thousand dollars' bond and still confined to two districts in New York.

Eisenhower's attorney general, Herbert Brownell, planned to ask Congress for legislation permitting the use of wiretap evidence in cases approved by the attorney general—any attorney general, whenever. (This, of course, was the authority McGrath had insisted was his.) The intention was to provide the mechanism for retroactively transforming illegal evidence taken from Judith Coplon's purse to legal status. At the same time, Senator Alexander Wiley of Wisconsin introduced a bill permitting legal use of wiretap evidence under the authorization of a federal judge. Brownell hoped to amend Wiley's measure by changing authorization responsibility to attorney general; otherwise, his plans to resuscitate the Coplon evidence would be lost.

A month later, in May 1953, the administration refused to commit itself on whether it would, in fact, use the proposed legislation to launder the papers found in Judith's purse; still, in the person of Deputy Attorney General William P. Rogers, it urged that the law apply retroactively, thereby allowing the government to "re-examine certain cases." In particular, Rogers said, such a law was necessary in cases affecting national security.

Not a soul wondered which "certain case" affecting national security he had in mind.

By late November, word was out that the Justice Department would "definitely" retry Judy—if authorizing legislation passed.

"At the present time, information received by tapping wires cannot be used as evidence in the Federal courts," Brownell said. "There are cases of espionage presently in the Justice Department, but since some of the important evidence was obtained by wire-tapping, the cases cannot be proved. . . ."

Another official, not Brownell, promised, "We will definitely try her in one of the cities [New York or Washington], maybe in both."

As the argument grew like a prairie wildfire, few seemed to take notice of the fact that proof existed, in the public record, that agents wiretapped conversations between Judy and her attorney. No new legislation was likely to snatch back so sacred a constitutional gift as the rights of defendant and counsel to private conversation. As Judge Wilbur K. Miller had written in the Coplon appellate decision rendered in Washington:

> The Fifth Amendment enjoins that no person be deprived of life, liberty or property without due process of law. Such due process includes the right of one accused of crime to have the effective and substantial aid of counsel. Moreover, the Sixth Amendment provides that "In all criminal prosecutions, the

accused shall enjoy the right. . . . to have the assistance of counsel for his defense."

In 1954, with the issue still not resolved legislatively, someone finally did take notice, but apparently not at the Department of Justice. J. Woodbury, writing in the *New York Post* on January 19, cautioned against making statements claiming Judy's convictions were set aside "because part of the vital testimony came from wiretaps." Not so, said the writer. They were set aside because, in New York, the arrest was declared illegal and, in Washington, because her right to counsel was violated.

Where was the rest of the world on this issue? Even with the now-suppressed evidence made clean, and even if lower courts convicted, appellate courts would still have to deal with the issues of the arrest and violation of rights to counsel. The likelihood of making a conviction stick was almost nil.

Unquestionably, this constant wolf-crying harassment was intended to make life as uncomfortable and frightening as possible for Judith Coplon. Some associated with the case in the early 1950s admit today that once the Supreme Court failed to grant certiorari, the die was cast. Threats of new trials and suggestions of newly discovered evidence were a means of mentally punishing the legally untouchable.

Assistant Attorney General Warren Olney III, in testifying before the House Appropriations Committee during February 1954 budget hearings, reported on the status of the Coplon case:

"[It] is in a state of suspended animation. It is not a case that has been closed out. It is only a matter of whether sufficient legal usable evidence can be presented to the court . . . to date, we have not been satisfied it is a wise thing for us to proceed with that case at the present time." Implied was that more money might help solve the problem.

Judy had become a budgetary issue. On more than occasion, her case would be brought into congressional arguments by branches of government seeking budget increases. Another poster assignment for the young woman from Brooklyn.

In April 1954, Representative Kenneth Keating of New York spoke before the House of Representatives in a different kind of hearing:

"We should not delude ourselves any longer, that in the interest of this so-called privacy we should continue to shackle our law-enforcement agents with outmoded and outdated legal principles." He made clear that passage of yet another proposed new law "may very well permit the conviction of Judith Coplon." Here was the stuff of an issue more profound than that of money: the right to privacy versus the government's right to eavesdrop, one right violating the other.

Amazingly, while the Department of Justice would not let go, neither would the press, with editorials periodically appearing asking the government to retry and get around to serving Judy her just desserts. A *New York World Telegram* editorial said punishment of Judith is "sure to be a first question of Americans outraged by the continued complete freedom . . . of a twice-convicted spy. . . ." Most likely, Americans, by this time, had other issues as "first questions."

During the following year, 1955, the government was determined to secure a legislative resolution to the nagging wiretap-versus-individual-rights issue. Judith's name was in the news daily, seen as both cause and effect of what was happening on Capitol Hill, with regard to both new legislation and monetary needs of the cause of Justice.

On February 28, Brownell worried members of the House Appropriations Committee with the news that 230 alien subversives were running around the country, "at liberty" in the United States because their Communist countries would not repatriate them. He caused further worry by suggesting that Judith Coplon might not be retried. Irritated committee members challenged him about not finding and prosecuting Communists in his "own bailiwick."

"None has turned up since Judy Coplon," he responded, almost seven years ago. This looked bad for Brownell, one of the members observed, adding testily, "Then that means you haven't found any Communists! Judy Coplon was indicted and convicted by the previous administration, not you."

Three days later, Representative John Rooney, debating a $4.5-million appropriation for the Departments of State and Justice, the U.S. Information Service, and the federal courts, demanded, "What have they done about Judy Coplon?" Money wasn't the issue, it was noted; new legislation was. Whereupon Representative John Robison of Kentucky observed that it would be a "sorry day" when Congress must pass special legislation in order to permit the Justice Department, "with all of its resources, to prosecute a defendant successfully." Rooney added that he believed the Justice Department could "successfully re-prosecute Judith Coplon on spy charges even without a wiretap law, if all the facts in the case were brought out." While many were curious, Rooney did not reveal what facts he had in mind.

Could there be more? Yes, indeed. The Senate Internal Security Committee began to "pry open the case of Judy Coplon" in July 1956. "We are attempting to discover how Miss Coplon got her job; what duties were assigned to her; and the identity of her associates."

An intriguing letter to the editor was published in the February 18, 1957, *New York Daily News*. Different from the multitude of others demanding prison for Judy, Frances Dreyer's letter asked, "Did it ever occur to anyone that the reason she hasn't been imprisoned is she may have been an FBI plant?" An FBI file copy of the news clipping has a handwritten note with a line drawn to Ms. Dreyer's name: "No identification in the indices." Copies of the letter went, among others, to Deputy Director Clyde Tolson. The Bureau still was being careful about who was saying what about Judy.

In April of that same year, Attorney General Brownell said the case of Judith Coplon "is dead." The same day, Assistant Attorney General W. F. Tompkins, in charge of the Justice Department's Internal Security Division, said her case was still pending. "I would not say it's dead," he said firmly. It should be noted that both statements were made during hearings before the House Appropriations Committee, when members were considering the department's funding request.

Representative Francis Walter, chair of the House Committee on Un-American Activities, wrote a special article for the March 6, 1958, *Philadelphia Inquirer*, chronicling details of the entire Coplon case. Just in the event anyone had forgotten. No one had, and by 1961, Judith was still News. The *Washington Evening Star* reported that Judy and her husband, with their four children, lived in a 130-year-old redbrick building in downtown Brooklyn. The neighborhood was "mixed," and the house had no mailbox. The Socolovs' telephone was unlisted. "Remember Judith Coplon?" was the article's lead. It continued this way, with feature stories and articles rehashing the case, the protagonist, and her family. Fading into obscurity was the persistent, impossible goal for the family.

An eager young Kennedy administration and Attorney General Robert

Kennedy inherited and struggled with the contentious issue and, in the end, did nothing different from their predecessors. The case remained in painful limbo until 1967, when everything changed.

A new attorney general, Ramsey Clark—ironically the son of former attorney general Tom Clark, who had presided over the case at its inception—was appalled to find the seventeen-year-old Coplon case "still pending. I thought it had been settled years ago," he told author Tom Mitchell. "I was shocked that a case this old would still be pending. It did not seem right that something like this should be held over a person's head for so long."

On Friday, January 6, 1967, exactly eighteen years after the Department of Justice first installed a wiretap on Judith Coplon's telephone, that same department sent out a press release announcing that it was moving for dismissal of the two spy cases against her.

"The government said it had concluded, because of the lapse of many years and after reviewing available evidence, that it could not successfully retry the cases," read the release.

Although its author was an unidentified public information specialist, its ghostly coauthor was a squat, bombastic, madcap, and undeniably persistent bankruptcy attorney. It had to have been a glorious day for Archie, now eighty-two. He would live another two years, until his death following a short illness. His passing was noted by the press, in lengthy, colorful articles about his more-than-fifteen minutes of fame as the "aggressive, flamboyant" attorney for Judith Coplon, an eccentric whose behavior infuriated judges.

It seems appropriate to note that the monumental national debate over the legality of wiretapping versus individual rights, launched those many years ago by Archie Palmer, had a new and horrific launching on September 11, 2001. Words and arguments remained the same, whether offered on Capitol Hill or in private homes and businesses. Only the names changed, most particularly, *John Ashcroft* replacing *Herbert Brownell*. At what point, Americans asked once again, does concern over national safety take precedence over individual rights guaranteed by the Constitution?

Those who hold that "everything changed" following the horrific terrorist attack that cruel September morning are wrong. The argument is the argument of old, and goes well beyond placing taps on telephones and sifting through trash cans.

The Personal Aftermath

In the midst of the first few weeks of the legal wrangling and ominous threats that followed the Supreme Court's historic undecision, a child was born.

At ten o'clock on the morning of February 18, 1952, Judith Coplon Socolov gave birth to a daughter in Manhattan General Hospital; news reports said the birth was "normal" and both mother and child were in "very good condition." Reporters scrambled for details, but found that mother and child were "off limits" at the hospital. Albert said all that would be said about the birth of his only daughter:

"We feel we are just ordinary parents and don't want to make anything special out of this." An Associated Press photo of the couple leaving the hospital with their week-old child shows extraordinarily happy parents, the father holding a blanket-wrapped bundle.

The next few months were relatively quiet for the young Socolov family, who desperately hoped to stay out of the public eye. The hope was futile, at least where the country's editorial writers were concerned; Judy remained firmly fixed in their eyes and their creative psyches. Albert has told the authors that a key to the family's normalcy over the years has been a refusal to read what has been written about Judy and the case.

It had been the authors' intention, at the outset, to write in detail about Judith's "afterlife," but compelling reasons have caused not only a change of mind but also a change of heart. A picture painted below, hopefully complete enough, conveys the image of Judy's life since the ending of her legal case, without unduly imposing on that part of her life that no longer makes headlines. Granted, her name appears on the Internet, where she has been referred to as "an American spy for the Soviets," and, since publication of the Venona documents, she is once again in the public eye. People are curious about her. Nevertheless, the authors chose to limit information about her personal aftermath to what follows.

For those who have complained over the years that she was not "punished for her crime," the authors suggest that she was severely punished by seventeen years of breath-holding anxiety, years of waking every day wondering if that day would be the last of freedom. It has been argued that she "remained free," able to live as she chose during those years. In return, the authors would argue that fear-generated confinement of the mind and spirit can be every bit as punishing as confinement of the body. Particularly so when the mind is so agile and the spirit so full.

The threats to retry and jail Judy, recounted above, were constantly with the family, especially since Albert was a member of the law firm representing her. For all of those years under an ever-present cloud of uncertainty, they kept their sanity and their stability through an unfailing devotion to each other, and a tenacious determination to achieve the physical and mental nirvana they so desperately desired.

As the years went on, neighbors either were not aware of, or paid little attention to, Judy's legal history. The Socolovs bought a larger home, which Judy skillfully decorated. She played the multifaceted role of housewife and mother, neighbor and friend, with enormous success and seeming contentment. Three sons were born, in 1954, 1956, and 1960. Always in the background of this apparently "typical middle-class" life was the specter, at least during those seventeen years, of a prison cell. Too, there was the problem of Judy's movements being restricted geographically. Al says that during those years, when the family went traveling, Judy was forced to remain at home.

Judy anguished over the problem of keeping her legal history from her young children. She dreaded their reaching the point where they could read. When a news team attempted to interview her on her fortieth birthday, she unceremoniously sent them packing. She wanted no "at home" stories or photos about Mrs. Socolov as Judy Coplon. A child might see them, or a child's friend. Ultimately, of course, the children would know. And not all that long thereafter.

When the news of the historic 1967 decision finally freeing Judy came, she and Al were out to dinner, and their daughter was at home with the boys. Although she had been taught not to open the door when only the children were home, she did so that night, greeting waiting reporters with a dignity beyond her fourteen years. "I'm very proud of my mother for what she went through," she said firmly, "and that also goes for all my little brothers." Albert's face beams when he tells the story. Judy's only comment came through her husband, who said at the time that she was "very, very happy."

Judy, who had been in the process of getting a master's degree when she was arrested, returned to postgraduate work, performed brilliantly (as always), and achieved her goal. She was a teacher, and a marketing manager for a major book company. For a number of years, she and her husband owned a popular New York restaurant, where, Albert notes, all of the children worked at one time or another.

In 1981, the law briefly, although frighteningly, once again entered their private space—this time, when charges were brought against Al based on his having handled investments for a client whose source of income turned out to be drug related. It seems as if the world came out in his support, including lawyers and judges, along with other prominent citizens who well knew he was innocent of any wrongdoing. He was acquitted, but the press duly noted that his wife, who had been convicted of espionage, was present at the trial.

As was true for all of her life, Judy continued a strong and knowledgeable interest in cultural affairs, in music and in the visual and performing arts, one enthusiastically shared by her husband. Judy's love of literature and interest in writing has been constant. As a volunteer, she has taught creative writing to women on parole.

Judy has traveled extensively with Albert in the years since restrictions on her movements were lifted. Their trips are not simply sight-seeing adventures, but intellectual pursuits of historic and cultural significance.

When their daughter was born, Albert spoke of being "ordinary parents"; it must be observed that they have been more than that. This first child is on her way to becoming a successful writer, with one excellent novel already published and another on the way. The sons also are successful and a source of pride to their parents. The Coplon brood is well educated, through advanced university degrees, talented, and accomplished. As of this writing, there are three grandchildren. At some point, they will learn a fascinating bit of family history as yet unknown to them.

The "Universal" Aftermath—Brief Observations

"Brief," because proper consideration of ethics, principles, morals, and related conceptual exercises with implications for this case would require volumes and a team of learned scholars into the bargain.

Suffice it to say that the plethora of moral and ethical questions that followed legal closure of the Coplon espionage case remain unanswered. No wonder, for they are the same that have occupied, and stymied, the intellect for centuries. Her case simply added new fuel to an old fire of the mind.

If Judith Coplon *was* guilty as charged, if she made a conscious decision to spy, one wonders about the ethical and moral precepts involved in that decision, given her superior intelligence and patriotic upbringing. For insight, one might look to Lawrence Kohlberg's theory of moral development, which begins with moral decision making based on the concept of punishment and obedience. A child makes a decision whether to snitch a cookie from the jar according to the likelihood of getting the snitching hand slapped. Obedience and punishment.

Mature, thoughtful adults make their decisions based on more advanced, more sophisticated conceptual data increasing in sophistication and complexity to Kohlberg's culminating point of universal, ethical principles. Universal principles affect all of humankind, all of the life experience, and are neither exclusive nor finite in nature. Kohlberg notes, "When laws violate these principles, one acts in accordance with the principle."

Judith Coplon's scholastic achievements, youthful exposure to a politically accepted pro-Communist mentality, deep concern for economic and political assistance for Russia, and strong interest in human rights could well add up to a reason for decisions made. One might conclude that there was a compelling sense of "rightness" involved. Thus, were her acts, those with which she was charged, immoral in a realistic and legal sense, and ethical in another sense?

Ends justifying means?

Some of these same questions also must be raised with regard to the government that prosecuted Judy. Addled old Judge Reeves was on target when he observed that, if a defendant's rights to evidence against her imperiled the government, "the government ought not to be here." Was the government "right" in presenting a case that was, in part, false? In having Bureau agents lie under oath? In bringing a case wherein a defendant could not challenge, or even identify, her accuser? Yet in bringing the case, the government believed it was taking a spy out of service and likely preventing serious harm to its counterespionage activities, perhaps even saving its agents' lives. It did so during a period of America's history when a persuasive Red fear colored a great many decisions in Washington. In a sense, the government believed it was doing far more than prosecuting an accused spy. It was fighting for survival of this country's way of life.

Ends justifying means?

In any case, the rightness and/or wrongness on both sides led to what is still considered to be one of the government's most entangled, confounding, and hopelessly doomed legal cases. The concept of right or wrong—sometimes unclear, undefined, elusive—plagued both sides in the Coplon case from the very beginning, but never managed to define it.

In the tricorn aftermath, Judith Coplon lived life as a model citizen, raising a family of decent, law-abiding children, and serving her community; the government set about to clean up its act, as it were, and avoided falling into another Coplon-case legal morass; and the country, for many years, debated about crime and undelivered punishment in its sometimes fevered contemplation of right and wrong.

PART FIVE

To **Moscow**

Putting the Puzzle Together

A night in December 1994, from Marcia Mitchell's journal:

"The secret 'confidential informant' was a wiretap," Al Socolov, Judy's husband, insisted. Bewildered, I said, "No, Al, it was not. It was Soviet message traffic."

We were walking arm in arm along Fifth Avenue on the most beautifully crisp and fresh Manhattan night I had ever seen. Christmas was two short weeks away, silvery lights sparkling brilliantly through a gentle darkness, carols sounding now and then from one building or another. The air was exquisitely fresh, invigorating. Tom, my daughter Kristin, and her husband Peter were walking ahead of us, gaining distance as Al and I, deep in conversation, increasingly slowed our pace.

Al stopped suddenly and turned to face me. "What," he asked, "are you saying?"

My God, I thought. Surely he must know! In his book *The KGB-FBI War*, Robert Lamphere had a few years before identified the "confidential informant" kept secret for decades. Surely Al had read it. I asked if he had.

"I don't read these things about her," he answered. "Now, tell me what you're talking about."

Over dinner, Al had made it clear that he still believed in Judith's innocence, still believed she was the victim of an elaborate government frame-up. Perhaps he really had not read Lamphere.

"Soviet message traffic identified her in 1944, when she was going from New York to Washington," I told him.

We hadn't moved, either of us. We stood rooted to the sidewalk, face to face. "By name?" he asked.

"No," I conceded. "Not by name."

"So it's the FBI's word. It's their identification. It could be more of the same . . ."

It could, I conceded awkwardly. Actually, I thought, it really could. In a telephone interview with an FBI official I was told to "take Lamphere's book with a grain of salt. Just because he says something doesn't mean it's true. Or false, either." An ambiguous, curious comment. And the only reference we had found thus far to decoded KGB messages was Lamphere's. For several years, we had sought corroboration from the government, waging a futile Freedom of Information and Privacy Act battle.

Now, on this chilly Manhattan street corner, forty-five years after Judith's arrest on a corner not that far away, I saw shock and disbelief in her husband's eyes. Was he dissembling; was this an act for my benefit? And then I reminded myself that I truly believed in Al's honesty. If so, what was left?

Left was the realization that he might well have been deceived by his wife, from the very beginning. That, as he insisted, he truly believed her innocent, believed all of these years that she was the victim, the scapegoat in an elaborate, self-serving government scheme. Daughter not only of the Santa of the Adirondacks, but also of the Red Menace.

Or, that Lamphere was wrong. A grain of salt.

"Soviet message traffic," he said softly. "My God. You know so much about this case, and I was her lawyer . . ."

Having reached an accommodation of sorts, we continued our stroll this frosty night, ending up at Rockefeller Center, where we watched colorfully clad skaters skimming across the ice, where we stood admiring the center's festive Christmas tree. Our thoughts went to Santa and children in the mountains, to the young Judith and Bertram, to Rebecca. Other Christmases, so long ago.

Al had asked, "What are you saying?" The "what" was the critical piece to the Coplon puzzle, to the construct begun that rainy 1988 afternoon. The piece was at hand, but not yet confirmed, not yet ready to be placed in the picture. The government not only refused to provide information about the contents of the Soviet message traffic, it would not even confirm its existence. FOIPA requests had resulted in a file of form letters and denials, and, after one successful appeal, nothing. At the time of Al's question, there was only that single source of information, Lamphere's book. The puzzle still had gaping holes.

The Key to Arlington Hall

It was Robert Lamphere who provided the information, two years after Al's question, that the project known as Venona was being made public. Located at Arlington Hall in northern Virginia, Venona was the storehouse of the Cold War's most remarkable secret. Beginning in 1995, the National Security Administration and the Central Intelligence Agency began opening the door, releasing the Venona files segment by segment, including the message traffic Lamphere had said existed. By 1997, critical information was in the authors' hands, including Venona material not yet made available to the public, thanks to Lamphere's assistance and to the NSA's Robert Louis Benson, the man behind release of the files.

The Venona files changed everything. They brought the KGB and its activity in Washington, D.C., and New York to life after half a century of silence.

By way of background, it is helpful to note that although the Soviets' security and intelligence function remained essentially the same over many decades, its nomenclature did not. From *Cheka* in 1917 to *KGB* in 1991, it went through a series of name changes and reincorporations, but never a true reincarnation. Commonly, *KGB* is used to describe the security and intelligence operation of the whole Soviet era (as is done here), as well as for the period after 1954, which is more accurate. During the "Coplon era," the civilian Soviet intelligence operation was commonly called the NKVD and, later, the KGB. The Venona message traffic involved both the civilian (NKVD, KGB) and military (GRU) operations of the Soviet intelligence system.

Throughout World War II and immediately thereafter, KGB and GRU agents operating in the United States made regular use of commercial telegraph lines to communicate with Moscow via enciphered messages. In 1939, with world war threatening, the U.S. Army began collecting encrypted Soviet diplomatic messages by the thousands, and in June 1942 it was determined that the army's Signals Security Agency (SSA), forerunner of the National Security Agency, would have full responsibility for their analysis.

Launched on February 1, 1943, the Venona project began its study of encrypted messages by sorting those on hand for years, along with all new messages collected. Earlier, SSA analysts had examined Soviet message traffic in an effort to determine whether it was readable. Others in the army and navy from time to time had made the same effort with little success. Finally, cryptanalysts working in Finland were able to determine characteristics for sorting the secret Soviet communications.

Under the guidance of a former Virginia schoolteacher, Gene Grabeel, and helped by the work of the Finns, Arlington Hall analysts now were able to identify five separate cryptographic systems used by five different "subscribers." These were trade representatives, diplomats, the KGB, the GRU's Soviet army intelligence staff, and, separately, its naval intelligence staff. It was not until 1946, however, that Arlington Hall was able to recognize the difference between standard diplomatic communications and those of the

KGB, which were double-encrypted and extremely difficult to penetrate.

Thus began the incredibly difficult, grueling effort that would lead to the eventual deciphering, in whole or in part, of more than twenty-nine hundred secret spy messages, the total comprising only a fraction of the volume of messages sent and received. Eventually Venona would supply critical information to United States' counterintelligence activities and would expose Soviet agents operating throughout this country. Among them would be a young woman of intense interest to the authors.

From the Venona Files

On July 20, 1944, a year after Judith Coplon's graduation from Barnard, KGB officer Stepan Apresyan, chief of the Soviets' New York Residency, sought permission from Moscow to "put through the recruitment" of a potential spy, a woman code-named SIMA.

In his secret message, Apresyan said the woman worked in the Economic Section of the Military Department of the Ministry of Justice—not quite an accurate description of Judith Coplon's workplace, but close enough. "If we are interested in the materials of her office, it is necessary to put through her recruitment," he wrote. His message also speaks of a preliminary investigation of the potential recruit's background prior to requesting "sanction for her recruitment." He asked that Moscow telegraph a decision.

All KGB residencies abroad came under the Soviets' First Chief Directorate (Foreign Intelligence) of Moscow Centre. Head of the directorate was Lieutenant General P. M. Fitin, code name VIKTOR. It was to VIKTOR that Apresyan's message was sent.

Apresyan was a relative newcomer to the New York Soviet espionage scene, taking over his high-level role in 1944. His youth and inexperience led Apresyan's residency colleague, Vladimir Sergaevich Pravdin, to complain to Moscow about his appointment. Only twenty-eight years old, Apresyan, as the New York Resident, operated under a legitimate vice consul cover.

At the time Apresyan sent his message to headquarters, Flora Don Wovschin, code name ZORA, Judith's friend from college, already was working on espionage matters with SIMA, whom she undoubtedly had recruited. Flora Don was messianic about enlisting others to the cause, to the degree where her Soviet controllers sent word to Moscow on March 28, 1945, that she had been forbidden "to recruit all her acquaintances one after the other." They had more potential agents than they could handle in the last days of World War II.

Wovschin was the daughter of a Russian-born woman who, with Flora Don's stepfather, was active in the Communist movement in Wisconsin. Flora Don was employed by the Office of War Information in 1943 and moved to the Department of State on February 20, 1945, her twenty-second birthday. Credited by the FBI with having recruited Marion Davis Berdecio as well as Judith Coplon, Flora Don was for a time a valuable, if hyperenergetic, Soviet asset. By the time of Judith's Washington trial, however, she had renounced her American citizenship, moved to Russia, and married an engineer.

On July 26, Apresyan wrote back to Moscow, saying he had put both ZORA and SIMA temporarily "on ice," as requested by headquarters. "Recently you telegraphed that we were to put probationers of the colony on ice until the arrival of a special worker, but by post you ask whom we can nominate for this work," he wrote. Further, "Does it mean that in spite of the seriousness of the situation you do not intend to send anybody?" Apresyan had responsibility for having a "full complement" of personnel in the office. "What are the prospects of getting this issue resolved?" he wanted to know. "One hopes that in the sphere of personnel," the resident concluded, "one will not have to employ oneself in squaring the circle."

To be "put on ice" was to be deactivated. A "probationer" was an agent.

By October of this same year, 1944, Apresyan had a new concern. Fearing possible "unpleasantness" on the part of the FBI, SIMA and ZORA were to avoid further meetings. After two meetings, "as a consequence of the tailing," the two should not be seen together, he wrote. The Bureau, of course, had not put Judith under surveillance until December 1948, which raises a question as to who was tailing whom in this instance. No answer is available.

The Soviet agent's personnel problems continued. In November, he wrote to General Fitin that ZORA's transfer to a still-unidentified controller code-named URAL had been delayed, and it was "absolutely necessary" that someone at a high level have a conversation with her. "Her morale is extremely unsatisfactory," he wrote. Her apartment was full of materials waiting to be turned over to the Soviets, but she had not had the opportunity to make the transfer. Further, she was still asking for "additional instructions" to guide her and SIMA's conduct in relation to their work and "personal connections."

A month later, the conversation had taken place, and the Soviets were reassured about Wovschin, noting that "despite her youth" she was extremely serious, well developed, and understood her task. "Skilled leadership is all the more important now that through ZORA we are processing . . . and counting on drawing into active work SIMA and Marion Davis (henceforth 'LOU')," Apresyan wrote to Fitin. "The time is ripe for signing on SIMA, after careful preparation through NAZAR. . . ." NAZAR, either an agent or officer operating in New York, was Stepan Nikolaevich Shundenko. To be explored was the question of a direct liaison between SIMA and Moscow, bypassing ZORA.

The Soviets were clearly pleased to learn about a change in SIMA's employment within the Department of Justice: She would be leaving the Economic Section of the War Department in New York and transferring to a Department of Justice office in Washington, D.C. On the thirty-first of December, Wovschin advised VIKTOR that "SIMA had got work in the Registration of Foreign Agents Branch of the War Office Division of the Department of Justice."

Pravdin, the senior-level operative at the New York Residency who earlier had complained about Apresyan, met with SIMA on January 4, 1945, about her new role in Washington. Reporting on the meeting to Fitin, he wrote on January 8 that on the basis of "preliminary information there is reason to assume that in her new job SIMA will be able to carry out very important work for us in throwing light on the activities of the KhATA [the FBI]." He added a caveat: "Although SIMA gives the impression of being a serious person who is politically well developed," with a "sincere desire to help us," it should be remembered that she "from an operational point of view is quite undeveloped and she will need time to learn conspiracy and to correctly gain in understanding of the questions which interest us."

A final decision on the question of "direction and liaison" would be made only after SIMA had moved to Washington, when specifics about her new job could be ascertained. The work of the new spy apparently was under way.

On June 26, 1945, Fitin was notified that SIMA would "refrain from removing documents until she was quite sure that she was trusted." Further, the message read, "As you were advised earlier, on the advice of her superiors, SIMA is studying the Russian language." From the balance of the decrypted portion of the message, it seems likely that this study was with regard to a Department of Justice unit "which is investigating the actions of the USSR and the Communists." SIMA, the message reported, was given the task of "studying the Club, its methods of work, the way in which documents are kept." The Club is presumed to be the Department of Justice.

Judith Coplon earned the trust and respect of her superiors in short order. Her first employment review at FARS noted that she had "superior talent," and that her judgment "had a scope and dependability not usually found in persons of equal age and experience." Then, in 1946, her supervisor at the time, Jesse MacKnight, wrote to let her know that she had become "an able and valuable colleague." And, of course, there was Attorney General Clark's congratulatory note sent to her in 1948.

Judith began her work with FARS on the same date that SIMA arrived there. In all, the unit had a staff of two lawyers and two secretaries who had been with the section for some time, and the newcomer, Judith Coplon, a political analyst. A second political analyst was no longer with FARS. From these messages, the FBI identified Judith Coplon as SIMA late in 1948, almost four years after she began her work in Washington. Immediately after making the connection, the Bureau placed Judith under surveillance.

Venona proved to be another entity named "confidential informant."

Richard Rhodes, writing in *Dark Sun: The Making of the Hydrogen Bomb*, speculated that Judith Coplon might have been one of the Soviet agents active "around the Manhattan Project" in late 1944. Given the Venona material, this hardly seems likely. More likely is a different connection. A 1952 HUAC report, *The Shameful Years*, says that in 1948, "Highly confidential investigative reports being conducted by the FBI concerning Soviet and Russian satellite diplomats were finding their way back to these individuals . . . someone having access to FBI files was channeling the information to Moscow." SIMA knew the names of the Russian diplomats who most interested the FBI.

Venona's history and that of Judith Coplon were inextricably entwined. Not only did Venona lead to the identification of Judith Coplon, but it also made the young political analyst, as the first to be arrested and tried, a "star" among the more than two hundred named or code-named Soviet assets or contacts identified through the project's tireless efforts.

Judith Coplon's fate was sealed not only by the success of the Venona project, but also by the fact that the FBI's Robert Lamphere in 1948 joined Venona's principal translator, Meredith Gardner, at Arlington Hall. Lamphere's assignment was to serve as the Bureau's liaison and case supervisor for espionage information coming from the Venona decrypts. It was Lamphere who read the SIMA messages and subsequently identified Judith Coplon; it was he who determined that she would be caught. It also was Lamphere who would later identify master atomic spy Klaus Fuchs from a lead in a Venona message.

"In 1948," the FBI agent later wrote, "some newly deciphered messages struck me quite forcefully. A woman who had been working in the Department of Justice in New York had been a KGB agent." As of a specific date, the woman had been transferred to a specific job in Washington. "There can't be any doubt," concluded Lamphere. "Her name is Judith Coplon." Very few in the intelligence community would be told of the discovery; among these few was Robert McQueen, the FBI's Soviet embassy case agent.

Judith was in notable company. Venona disclosed activities of Julius and Ethel Rosenberg, Harry Gold, and David and Ruth Greenglass—all cases on which author Tom Mitchell worked. It also verified Elizabeth Bentley's inflammatory and controversial accusations, which so many said were figments of her imagination (they were not), and proved that Whittaker Chambers's accusations against Alger Hiss were true.

Often it would be years after the fact that espionage activities were uncovered at Arlington Hall. Nothing happened in "real time." It was between 1947 and 1952 that most of the "breakable" 1944 and 1945 KGB messages between Moscow and its New York and Washington Residencies were broken. Yet when the project was terminated in 1980, its work still had not been completed. Its "customers," the FBI, CIA, and "appropriate allied services," supported the project for thirty-seven years, even though the Venona material was from such a limited time frame. Investigations of espionage activity based on the material continued for years after the Soviet information pipeline had shut down. By 1980, however, it was apparent there was little likelihood that new and productive spycatching leads would come from further work.

The Soviets knew that the United States was working on deciphering their messages. Moscow learned the secret of Venona in 1947, when a Soviet agent working in SSA, William Weisband, gave them the news. Weisband is said to have been peering over Meredith Gardner's shoulder at the time Gardner was "producing one of his first important decrypts," a December 1944 NKVD message regarding Soviet spying at Los Alamos. As early as 1945, Soviet agent Elizabeth Bentley had told the FBI that Russia had information about an effort to break the code, but as with almost everything Bentley attempted to reveal, there was no evidence to support her story.

In the fall of 1949 Britain's SIS appointed Kim Philby, the infamous and remarkably successful Soviet spy, as its station commander in Washington. Before he arrived in the nation's capital, Philby was thoroughly briefed on Venona by the Soviets. Once in Washington, he had no difficulty in gaining access to Arlington Hall and the Venona decrypts. A year following Philby's arrival in Washington, and thus on the Venona scene, the Soviets lost the services of Weisband, who was arrested and sent to prison.

Until Weisband's confirmation of Venona's success, and despite earlier hints that the United States was working on breaking their code, the Soviets believed the West would have enormous difficulty in unlocking their encryptions. Soviet messages, already in code, were enciphered by "additive," number groups taken from a one-time pad of random numbers. Correct use of one-time pads makes a message impervious to decryption. In the case of the Venona breakthrough, a manufacturing error resulted in the Soviets using duplicate pads, which made the encrypted messages vulnerable, although not totally recoverable. There are Venona messages and portions of messages that still keep their secrets.

It is ironic that Kim Philby knew the Venona story five years before the CIA, and that President Harry Truman never knew. General Omar Bradley knew the secret and, as Louis Benson told the authors, Bradley insisted, "If someone has to tell the President, *I'll* be the one to do it." This was no assignment for a sissy. Thus, while army intelligence (G-2), the FBI, British intelligence, and the Soviets were brought into the picture, the president of the United States, who called threats of espionage in government "red herrings," who would never believe spies might be operating in his White House, was not.

Although an illegal wiretap was widely considered to be the mysterious Coplon informant, over the years there were other suggestions and claims. The most inventive may have come from retired FBI counterspy Matt Cvetic, who posed as a Communist for many years. Cvetic claimed credit for "blowing the whistle" on Coplon after getting a tip from a "not too clever female Communist agent." The woman, boasting about female Communists, supposedly told Cvetic that Judith Coplon was one of the Soviets' best agents. The incident may have happened, but it was not Cvetic's blowing a whistle that led to Judy.

Another story widely circulated was that the "original tip" leading to Judy came from an FBI "plant" on board the Polish steamship *Batory*—ironically the same ship Gubitchev took back to Russia after his conviction. Supposedly, the undercover agent reported overhearing Judith's name, and a routine check followed. Speculation ran wild, with version after version duly reported to the public.

As for the government trying Coplon based on the decrypts, it could not; the world could not know the manner in which Judith was identified as a spy. To do so would have compromised the invaluable, sacrosanct Venona project. This meant that a "confidential informant" had to be manufactured, and a case built upon circumstantial evidence, on suggestions, suspicions, and an illicit love affair. Had the government been able to use the Soviet decrypts at trial, the case would have been brought to a quick and decisive end. As it was, for all but those few insiders who knew about Venona, it ended only with the release of the secret message traffic nearly half a century later.

Venona, then, had given answers to specific key questions, putting in place critical pieces of the puzzle. Venona said Judith Coplon was SIMA. As SIMA, she would not have been, as John Kelley assumed, "a full fledged agent" when she graduated from Barnard. She would have been recruited by Wovschin in 1944, and not by Gubitchev years later. The Soviets wanted information from the FBI files to which Judith had access, especially concerning the Bureau's interst in specific individuals. The woman who was SIMA had expressed her interest in helping Russia, but not, it seems, because of "hatred for the United States," a theme of the government that prosecuted her.

Missing was perhaps the most significant question of all. Did SIMA accomplish her mission? *Did she actually pass information to the Soviets?* Venona set the scene with its background information on recruitment, personal identification, and intended espionage activity, but it did not write the ending. The final, and ultimately most significant puzzle piece would have to come from Moscow, from the KGB. To be convincing, not just from one source, but at least two.

In 1992, the authors had written to former KGB general Oleg Kalugin, at a time when he had become a public critic of the KGB and its operations. He answered questions about Valentin Gubitchev and Judith Coplon. Of Gubitchev, Kalugin said he did not know whether the former Soviet officer was alive or dead, observing that "Russian intelligence officers seldom live long." Four years after Gubitchev's deportation, Soviet defector Yuri Rastorov had told of being in Russia when Gubitchev returned. Rastorov, who would later be targeted for assassination by the Soviets, said, "I saw him when he came from this country after an unsuccessful operation against Coplon. . . . He was recalled and later fired from the service." One assumes, given other evidence, that a language problem was the reason for Rastorov's use of "against Coplon"; that he'd meant "with" Coplon. Had Gubitchev been working against Judith, his mission would have been considered successful. According to Rostorov, Gubitchev had been a captain in the GRU's overseas intelligence branch, and, after losing his rank, was arrested and apparently sent into a chilly exile.

About Judy, Kalugin's reply was succinct: Yes, Judith Coplon was a spy; yes, she gave information to the Soviets; and yes, Valentin Gubitchev was Judith's controller. Still wishing to have at least two sources for this information, the authors were haunted by the need, at some point, to go to Moscow.

To Moscow

In March 1997, an item in the *Grapevine*, a publication of the Society of Former Agents of the FBI, carried an announcement of special interest to the Mitchells. Daniel J. Mulvenna, former head of the Soviet Desk at Royal

Canadian Mounted Police headquarters, would lead a trip to Moscow, offering opportunities to meet former KGB officers. Here was the chance to search for a confirming KGB source, to fit the truly critical piece of the puzzle.

Mulvenna's group was an eclectic collection of former intelligence officers and prestigious writers about espionage, along with Francis Gary Powers Jr. (son of the U2 pilot shot down over Russia, imprisoned, and eventually exchanged for Rudolph Abel), and the widow and daughter of a former U.S. news bureau chief in Moscow. Fifteen, in all.

KGB hosts were Lev Koshliakov and Oleg Tsarev; special guests at dinners included Lieutenant General S. Kondrashov, Colonel V. Barkovsky, General V. Fedorov, Lieutenant General V. Kirpichenko, General V. Dozhalev,and Colonel A. Maximov—all intelligence experts. The ambience, the people, and the place were alive with excitement and anticipation.

On Wednesday, June 4, the authors privately asked the ultimate Judith Coplon question. At first there was a refusal to reveal this sort of information, even after so many KGB files had been shared with the West. Finally, however, it was reluctantly, very reluctantly, answered. Yes, she had passed information from the FBI files to her controllers. Yes, she had spied for the Soviets, sending lists of names via her controllers. Tsarev told of one recently declassified document in his possession, which he said was a message from Coplon naming individuals in the United States suspected of working for the Soviets. Could the authors secure a copy? Perhaps, perhaps not. On the final day in Moscow, in the process of leaving their hotel for the airport, they were handed a manila envelope, sent by Tsarev. Inside was the document. Names had been blacked out, except for one: Poyntz, dead many years. A note in Russian on the bottom of the page was someone's response. Those listed were not working for the KGB. They may, however, have been working for the GRU.

A final Russian word: In 1998, at a Washington, D.C., gathering, Oleg Kalugin spoke with the authors' daughter about Judith Coplon. "She was an ideological spy rather than a mercenary," he said, unlike the spies of today. "She was in it for her beliefs, like the Rosenbergs."

There remained two questions to be answered: Was Harold Shapiro, regardless of his testimony to the contrary, a plant? Was his relationship with Judy

Coplon a setup? "No," former agent Lamphere insisted in 2001, during an interview in Arizona. Shapiro, badly shaken, had gone to the Department of Justice frightened and distressed after the arrest. He would not, at the beginning, provide details about the relationship. In short order, Lamphere says, the issue was put to the young lawyer in very simple terms. Tell all, or face the consequences, including losing his job with the government. Threatened and coerced, he finally capitulated. Although he had not set out to trap her, in the end it was his revelation about her "unconventional" behavior that helped convict her of espionage.

The last remaining question was whether Granville and his team *knew* Judith Coplon carried something "special" in her purse March 4. Granville's answer, also given in 2001, must be considered as affirmative. "Well, yes, we *suspected* that she did, something to do with national security." Only *this* night, the night of the full-court press, and not on two other nights when it was known she would be meeting Gubitchev. The answer has implications for Foley's testimony, on which was based Ryan's decision to proceed to trial in New York, and for the "missing conversation."

It was over. The puzzle was completed, insofar as possible, given the abundant surveillance information still locked away in the Hoover Building.

In truth, in the final analysis, there really has not been finality. In addition to exploration of unanswerable questions about right and wrong, there remains another related issue deserving purposeful contemplation—the concept of "innocence" juxtaposed to the context of "guilt," a compelling issue raised here and left with readers.

EPILOGUE

Views from a Common Window

In the beginning, she said:

There was something terribly wrong about the case. FBI agents lied in court, one after another committing perjury . . . A young government lawyer who would later be a part of the prosecution team was the defendant's lover . . . There was not a single shred of evidence presented in either of her trials that proved she had spied against her country. . . . In the beginning, I thought she was innocent.

And he said:

In my mind, Judith was unquestionably guilty of espionage, a Soviet agent who escaped federal prison through the antics of a zany attorney. There was never a doubt in my mind. I was there . . . My belief in her guilt was based on the suspicious nature of her behavior . . . and on the evidence found in her purse the night of March 4. And because, one night two weeks later, I heard the voice of guilt.

How disparate were these views! In the first case, author Marcia Mitchell could see only the wrong of a government taking a suspect to trial with its briefcase filled not with evidence but only with suspicion and innuendo, with *might haves* and *attempts*. Author Tom Mitchell could see only the correctness of what the government did, never considering Bureau agents' false testimonies as "lies," but only "evasions"; seeing the papers in Judith's purse and her clandestine meetings with Gubitchev as absolute proof of espionage.

What happened to both views between the prologue and the epilogue was not so much a sudden, recognizable paradigm switch as it was a slow change of cerebral direction. At some point along the way, the authors found themselves on parallel paths, not quite certain how they had gotten there or precisely when.

Now, she says:

I was right about some of it. At the time.

But this is another time, and I understand Tom's thinking and have an understanding of, if not an unqualified appreciation for, the government's behavior in this case. The Bureau was determined to stanch the flow of secret information to Moscow Centre, choosing to do so at whatever cost the tourniquet. The Bomb was a terrifying possibility, and the ghosts of Hiroshima and Nagasaki haunted a troubled world community. Espionage was the international exercise of the time, and our government, apparently, considered the elimination of one of the opposition's players more important than adhering to the law. The Red Menace was threatening the spirit; the government would save the body.

The government knew at the time what none of us, save a select few, would learn until fifty years after the fact. Judith Coplon had been identified as the Soviet agent SIMA. It was SIMA who had to be prosecuted.

There remain serious, compelling questions about a government breaking its own laws to accomplish its goals, however vital. Throughout this writing, we have attempted to raise certain of these issues, not to propose answers, but to stimulate thoughts about governmental power versus individual rights.

Suffice it to say, in looking back at more than a decade of researching this story, I have moved from my formerly intractable position of feeling that Judith Coplon was, completely and wrongly, a victim of an arrogant, lawbreaking government. Perhaps not a totally innocent victim, but a victim nevertheless.

There were other questions that made me suspicious of the government's motives and kept me fixed in that position for so long. For one, I pictured a grandstanding, posturing government constructing an Archie mountain from a tiny molehill, all for the sake of appearing effective in crushing Soviet espionage. If Judith Coplon had been a "significant" spy, a *real* spy, I wondered, why was she missing from our history books? Why didn't her name come as easily to the mind as, say, that of Rosenberg or Fuchs, or Philby? Even in books written on Cold War espionage, some do not even mention her name.

In all, from information available a little more than a decade ago—in the multitude of court records and documents, in certain interviews—it seemed then as if there was little to condemn Judith Coplon and much to suggest that she might unwittingly have been made the Cold War espionage poster girl. The unprecedented extent of press coverage suggested this possibility.

Where was the *proof* of guilt? Not guilt of having an illicit affair with Shapiro, for the government presented proof of *that*, but of espionage? I saw no solid evidence that material had changed hands, no absolutely irrefutable evidence that Judith was about to give secrets to the Russians. I saw a case based on what was found to be (in one court or another) illegal wiretapping and an illegal arrest.

At the end of the story, I still believe that Judith never should have been tried when the government could not present an honest case against her. I still believe she was convicted in Washington, D.C., because the jury found it impossible to believe that a young woman could be in love with one man while having an affair with another; and in New York because she was denied a proper defense. And I still believe Judith was held in judicial limbo for eighteen years because J. Edgar Hoover and company wanted to make life as miserable as possible for her.

But I also believe, now, that the government had solid evidence of guilt, as did the KGB. If a poster child was created, the creation was of her own making.

To those who complain that Judith Coplon was never punished, we have suggested that she was. She suffered through two terrifying trials; through those stultifying, threatening eighteen years of "neighborhood" confinement and fear of prison; and continues to suffer through a lifetime of inescapable notoriety.

It is no longer Judith who troubles me; it is SIMA. She, young, ideologically misdirected, was the guilty party. Not the wife and mother and good citizen who has taken her place these past fifty years.

MARCIA MITCHELL

And he says:

I did not doubt my belief in Judith Coplon's guilt because, in fact, I *was* there at the time—not in Washington, but in New York. I kept in close touch with the case and its stormy progress from the night of March 4 through the

Supreme Court's decision—and its fascinating aftermath as well. I had some involvement in the invesigation, an involvement that created a long-standing interest in the case I considered to be the strangest in modern history. Throughout, even during the toughest moments for the Bureau, I had full confidence in friends and colleagues more closely associated with the case than I was. These included Bob Granville, Dick Hradsky, Scotty Miller, Roger Robinson, and Bob Wirth. I should point out that my belief in Judith's guilt was not based on knowledge of the identity of the highly secret "confidential informant." I think it's safe to say none of the above knew any more about the informant than I did. Ironically, most of us would not learn that identity until Bob Lamphere would reveal it so many years later and Venona would confirm it.

I would never have believed, then, that decades later I would be poring through thousands of pages of Coplon case material, calling on some of these old friends and writing the story that began in 1949, with Judith's arrest. Actually it began a second time, in 1988, when I told my wife about Archie and Judith, her Russian friend, and Harold Shapiro.

In looking back, there was something other than confidence in Bureau colleagues that supported my belief in Judith's guilt. Although I was not assigned to monitor her telephone, I was present when my colleague overheard and recorded her desperate attempts to speak with Kelley or Whearty the night of March 18; and, that night, I heard the panic, and, I was certain, the guilt in her voice.

With regard to the wiretap issue, I knew my friends had been assured that their monitoring activity, concerning national security, *if* approved by the attorney general, was "legal." I knew they had been told it was safe to claim "no knowledge" of the operation unless they had witnessed the actual installation of specific taps.

As we progressed through our research, through old trial records and case documents, and conducting interviews with key players, I differed with my coauthor on her use of such words as *entrapment, frame-up, perjury, lies,* and other expressions of that ilk. The government, I felt, would not be a party to actions related to these terms.

My feelings and convictions changed as we delved deeper into old files and records. At first, change came gradually, as I studied original court transcripts and tap records, including the highly questionable tap log with its conveniently missing conversation the morning of March 4. Change became complete as my wife handed me the original Tiger Memorandum. All of the protestations under oath about "routine" destruction were false.

At this point of revelation, my negative feelings were not directed toward Bureau agents, but toward the prosecution and its dallying with the truth. The government well knew, for example, that the attorney general could not then legally authorize wiretapping. Individual agents, loyal to The Cause, believed what they were told and read the lines given them—to a point, at which they would go no farther.

In no way do I join in telling this story to criticize their behavior, and I remain essentially firm in this regard where individual agents are concerned. I must admit, however, having read the infamous Tiger document and certain of the tap logs, my steadfast loyalty, with regard to higher levels, remains severely shaken.

In summary, I still believe Judith Coplon was guilty of espionage. But I also believe mismanagement by the prosecution, successful and skillful manipulation of witnesses by Archie Palmer, and the wisdom of the federal appeals courts justify the final decision—the ultimate vacating of the indictments, and her freedom.

As poor old Judge Reeves insisted, if the government could not have presented an honest case, it should not have been in the courtroom.

TOM MITCHELL

TIMELINE

March 4, 1949

Judith Coplon is arrested in Manhattan with Soviet engineer Valentin A. Gubitchev and charged with espionage.

March 21, 1949

Judith, alone, is arrested and arraigned in Washington on new espionage charges related to the New York charges.

April 25 to June 29, 1949

Judith's high-profile espionage trial in Washington takes on a circus astmosphere, some of the FBI's most colorful and intriguing secret files are made public, and rumors are rampant that J. Edgar Hoover will resign over the Bureau's embarrassment.

June 30, July 1, 1949

Judith is convicted of espionage; her sentence, forty months to ten years.

November 14, 1949 to January 17, 1950

Contentious pretrial hearings in New York reveal the fact of FBI wiretapping and false testimony by agents during the Washington trial.

January 24 to March 7, 1950

A second bizarre trial, with Gubitchev, has Judith firing Archie Palmer midstream. She is left without a defense, but the trial continues.

March 7, 9, 1950

In a conflicted and confusing verdict, the jury finds Judith and Gubitchev guilty of conspiracy charges, but finds her not guilty of attempting to give him documents he is found guilty of trying to receive from her. She is sentenced to fifteen years in prison; Gubitchev is given a suspended sentence and ordered deported to Russia.

December 5, 1950

The U.S. Court of Appeals for the Second Circuit in New York sets aside Judith's conviction although "her guilt is plain." The court finds Judith's arrest and subsequent search illegal. Further, questions are raised about illegal wiretapping.

June 1, 1951

The U.S. Court of Appeals for the First Circuit in Washington upholds the lower court, finding the arrest legal and the evidence sufficient to sustain the conviction. (A view opposite that of the New York appellate court.) However, it determined that Judith could have a new trial if communications between her and counsel were compromised by electronic surveillance.

January 28, 1952

The U.S. Supreme Court, petitioned by both Coplon and the government, refuses to grant certiorari. Its refusal to hear the case is considered a major win for Coplon.

January 6, 1967

After years of threatening to retry Coplon while she has been free on $60,000 bond, the Department of Justice finally ends the case and dismisses the indictments.

SOURCES

Federal Records

Federal Bureau of Investigation, Hoover Building, Washington, D.C.
Bentley, Elizabeth T. 134-435, Vol. 4, Sec. 4, Serials 134–153
Coplon, Judith. 65-58365 (Media, Sub. A, Sections 1–13)
Gillars, Mildred. 100-232559, Part 2 of 2
Rosenberg, Ethel. 94-3-4-317, Serial 348, pp. 3–43
Rosenberg, Julius and Ethel. 65-56402, Vol. 25, Sub. Silvermaster
Rosenberg, Julius et al. 134–182, Vol. 1, Serials 3–66, Sub. Bentley

National Archives and Records Administration, Northeast Region. 201 Varick Street, New York, NY
Coplon, Judith: C125-158. Court dockets, filings, hearings and judgments; evidence entered; trial transcript, pages 1–4012a; pretrial transcripts, pages 1–4247; memoranda and related materials. Appellate Case #21790. Filings, judgment. (See also "Selected Wiretaps and Recordings.")

Washington National Records Center, Suitland, MD.
Coplon, Judith: CR381-49. Court dockets, filings, hearings and judgments; evidence entered; trial transcript, pages 1–8504; memoranda and related materials. Appellate Cases 10339 and 10801. Filings, judgments.

KGB (Central Intelligence Service, Moscow)

Report said to be from SIMA, November 16, 1945

Publications

Albright, Joseph and Marcia Kunstel. *Bombshell: The Secret Story of America's Unknown Atomic Spy Conspiracy*. New York. Random House, 1997.

Andrew, Christopher and Vasili Mitrokhin. *The Mitrokhin Archive*. London. Allen Lane, The Penguin Press, 1999.

Benson, Robert Louis and Michael Warner, Eds. *Venona, Soviet Espionage and The American Response, 1939-1957*. Washington, D.C. National Security Agency and Central Intelligence Agency, 1996.

Benson, Robert Louis. *Introductory History of Venona and Guide to the Translations.* Venona Historical Monograph #1. Fort George G. Meade, MD. National Security Agency, 1995.

Benson, Robert Louis. *The 1944-45 New York and Washigton-Moscow KGB Messages.* Venona Historical Monograph #3. Fort George G. Meade, MD. National Security Agency, 1996.

Benson, Robert Louis. *The KGB in San Francisco and Mexico City, The GRU in New York and Washington.* Venona Historical Monograph #4. Washington, D.C. National Security Agency, 1966.

Bentley, Elizabeth. *Out of Bondage.* New York. The Devlin-Adair Co., 1951.

Considine, Bob. *How Russia Stole America's Atomic Secrets.* University of California Radiation Laboratory. (Reprinted collection of a series.) International News Service, 1951.

deGramont, Sanche. *The Secret War: The Story of International Espionage Since World War II.* London. Andre Deutsch, 1962.

DeLoach, Cartha "Deke." *Hoover's FBI.* Washington. D.C. Regnery Publishing, Inc. 1995.

DeMause, Lloyd, Ed. *Foundations of Psychohistory.* New York. Creative Roots, 1982.

Gentry, Curt. *J. Edgar Hoover, the Man and the Secrets.* New York. Norton, 1991.

Hoover, J. Edgar. *Masters of Deceit.* New York. Henry Holt and Co., 1958.

Klehr, Harvey. *The Heyday of American Communism: The Depression Decade.* New York. Basic Books, 1984.

Klehr, Harvey, John Hayes, and Fridrikh Igorevich Firsov. *The Secret World of American Communism.* New Haven. Yale University Press, 1995.

Knightly, Phillip. *The Second Oldest Profession: Spies and Spying in the Twentieth Century.* New York. Penguin Press, 1987.

Kohlberg, Lawrence. *The Philosophy of Moral Development.* New York. Harper and Row, 1981.

Lamphere, Robert J. and Tom Schactman. *The FBI-KGB War.* New York. Random House, 1986.

Mitford, Jessica, Hon. *A Fine Old Conflict.* New York. Knopf, 1977.

Pells, Richard H. *Radical Vision and American Dreams: Culture and Social Thought in the Depression Years.* Middletown, CT. Wesleyan University Press, 1985.

Pells, Richard H. *The Liberal Mind in a Conservative Age: Intellectuals in the 1940s and 1950s.* New York. Harper and Row, 1983.

Pincher, Chapman. *Traitors.* New York. Penguin Books, 1987.

Rhodes, Richard. *Dark Sun: The Making of the Hydrogen Bomb.* New York. Simon and Schuster, 1995.

Romerstein, Herbert and Stanislav Levchenco. *The KGB Against the Main Enemy: How the Soviet Intelligence Service Operates Against the United States.* Lexington, MA. Lexington Books, 1989.

Romerstein, Herbert and Eric Breindel. *The Venona Secrets.* Washington, D.C. Regnery Publishing, Inc., 2000.

Whitehead, Don. *The FBI Story.* New York. Random House, 1956.

Selected Periodicals

Antics for Judy. *Newsweek* 34:22, November 28, 1949.

Conspirators or Lovers? *Newsweek* 35:21, Feburary 13, 1950.

Day of Judgment. *Time* 55:17, March 20, 1950.

FBI's Security Watch. *Newsweek* 35:20, January 30, 1950.

Guilty. *Time* 54:18, July 11, 1949.

It Was Love. *Time* 53:19, June 27, 1949.

Judy at Bat. *Newsweek* 33:24, June 27, 1949.

Judy's Night Life. *Newsweek* 34:16, July 4, 1949.

Judy's Windup. *Newsweeek* 35:24, March 13, 1950.

Jug for Judy. *Newsweek* 34:22, July 11, 1949/35:23, March 20, 1950.

Let Justice Be Done. *Newsweek* 33:18, June 20, 1949.

Love Story. *Time* 53:27, May 9, 1949.

Tragedy of Inexperience. F. Downing, *Commonweal* 50:364, July 22, 1949.

Trial of Miss Giggles. *Newsweek* 33:25, May 9, 1949.

Your Witness, Mr. Kelley. *Time* 54:15, July 4, 1949.

Youth and Talent Wasted. *New Republic* 121:15, July 25, 1949.

Interviews

Benson, Robert Louis

Bowers, Hollis

Clark, Former Attorney General Ramsey

Granville, Robert

Kalugin, Gen. Oleg

Koshliakov, Lev

Lamphere, Phyllis

Lamphere, Robert

McQueen, Robert

Mendenhall, Thomas

Perrine, Donald

Tsarev, Oleg

Internet

Center for Research Libraries
wwwcrl.uchicago.edu

Centre for Counterintelligence and Security Studies
www.cicentre.com

The Cold War Museum
www.coldwar.org

National Security Agency
www.nsa.gov

WITNESS TESTIMONY

Numbers below indicate the beginning page numbers for uninterrupted testimony and are taken from the stenographic notes.

Name	Washington	NY Pretrial	New York
Ascherl, Vincent		1829	
Avignone, Arthur		3574	
Bedford, Lynn		1757, 3800	3678
Belmont, Alan		1044, 1388, 1427, 4077, 4150	
Bianchi, Mario		2048	
Boguslav, Anatole		2010	
Braune, Edward		3683	
Brennan, Richard	477, 678	1284, 2362	515, 628
Broderick, Robert		2037	
Brodsky, William	8026		
Carey, Martin	2456		2431, 2437
Chamblis, John	7974		
Christiansen, John		2110	
Condon, Catherine	1582		2046, 2059
Condon, E.U.	6571	1338*	
Condon, Emilie	6583		
Coplon, Judith	6907		
Coplon, Bertram			3571

Name	Washington	NY Pretrial	New York
Cuddy, Teresa		3785	
Daley, John	2617, 2669		
deGuinzbourg		56	
Delavigne, Kenneth	6552	1691, 3258	
Dyer, Dale		2460, 2500, 2762	
Dyer, Johnnie		2056	
Eilers, Edwin		2083	
Ferentz, Anthony		2091	
Filmer, William		2120	
Fletcher, Howard	6641, 6766	950, 2709, 3145, 4186	3698
Foley, William	213, 6379	438, 1491, 306	1637, 1710, 1849
Fox, William		2118	
Franke, Nathan	193		378
Fusco, Bernard		2124	
Gallaher, Lester		2098	
Garde, Daniel	3433, 3642	369, 1268	716, 3283
Gauthier, Leo	602, 1439, 1459, 4348, 4355, 4381	4065	795
Granville, Robert	3, 4046	91, 1083	3343, 3431, 3492
Gunn, Daniel		1703	
Hendricks, William		1852	
Hottel, Guy	6385, 6539		
Hradsky, Richard	435, 808, 1367	389, 437, 1603	
Ickes, Harold	6566		
Jones, Courtland	4903		3557, 3590, 3620
Kearns, Roland		2129	
Kelley, John	6589	878, 1753	
Koffsky, Harold	8067		
Lamphere, Robert	4946, 4976, 6213	255, 4015	1656, 3493, 3540
Laughlin, Leo		1483	

Name	Washington	NY Pretrial	New York
Lenvin, Nathan		8040	
Leonard, Michael		2065	
Leonard, Robert		2684	
Lynch, James		1720	
Mackenzie, Fred		2147	
Malley, John	508, 2314		1453, 1526, 2346
Manos, Sappho	944	222	908
Martin, William		2140	
McAndrews, T.J.	806, 893	1316, 4246	802, 855, 3468
McCarthy, Edward	126, 4151, 4234	234, 389	3324
McCarthy, John		2158	
McKinney, Margaret			2097
McNulty, Joseph		2161	
McShane, Thomas		2165	
Mendenhall, Thomas	50, 6481	235, 1428, 1579, 1600	
Meyerson, Jack		2806	
Miller, T. Scott	27, 86, 1020, 1053, 2074, 2873, 3074, 4417, 4380, 4787, 5439, 7959	272, 1233, 1295, 1863, 1907, 3955	953, 1059, 3346, 3410, 3465
Mugavin, Robert		2516	
Murphy, John	3289	364	2795, 2817, 2922
Murtagh, John		2169	
Oberndorf, Ludwig			3606
O'Shaughnessy, John		1807	
Palmer, Clive		1458	
Patton, Daniel		2176	
Payne, Dudley		3357	

Name	Washington	NY Pretrial	New York
Peck, Charles		1788	
Pote, Gerard		2211	
Robinson, Roger	558, 1210, 1255	1183	1181, 1261
Rodman, Roy		2583	
Rossen, Ruth	408		2016
Rust, Allen		2230	
Saliba, Sophie		3481, 3556, 3756	
Schedler, Dean		412	
Shapiro, Harold		3916	
Shimkin, Arthur	7980		
Shindoler, John		2248	
Solby, Robert		2813	
Sweeney, William		2269	
Taylor, Etta			3660
Taylor, Oscar		3655	
Walsh, John		2291	
Ward, John			3302
Ware, John	3748, 3847	3524	
Webb, Frederick	8088		3612
Whearty, Raymond	6681, 6752, 6773	422, 910, 1233, 1295, 1320, 1863, 1907, 1949, 1999	3672
Wilson, Brewer	1608, 1641, 1867, 2261	1697	2165, 2245
Wirth, Robert	2904	1300, 2309, 4020, 4055	2624
Wolf, Alexander	7954		
Zoeller, Thomas	3123, 3247	2727	

*This page number may be incorrectly recorded in the files.

Trial Transcript Location

Washington, D.C. transcripts: Federal Records Center, Suitland, Maryland. CR 381-49, WNRC Location 16-80-8-4, Boxes 1470,1471.

New York pretrial hearings and trial: National Archives and Records

Administration, Northeast Region, New York. Pretrial: C129-158, Boxes 3,4,5,7,8. Full trial, Box 15.

Note: Reorganization of old files taking place in New York meant that pages of testimony appeared in more than one box and not always in sequence in the files, some of which had not been touched in many years. The effort of going back to decades-old materials and refiling is an enormous task not yet completed by the archives' excellent staff.

SELECTED WIRETAPS AND RECORDINGS

The following is an example of the type and extent of information the Bureau learned about Judith Coplon's personal and professional life through electronic surveillance. Most significant, from the first log, wiretaps provided information about her trips to New York City, information the government contended was learned through sources independent of listening devices. From the second, in the context of a tragic family scenario, the government learned other information critical to its case. All are from 1949, just prior to and following Judith's arrest.

Later electronic surveillance covered more detailed and critical communications between the subject and her attorney. The authors were unable to locate those records, if, in fact, any have survived. *Note: The reports listed below are a part of the public record.*

DR LOG: Listening devices at Coplon's Department of Justice office.

Date and subject of communication:

January 26
Coplon to Shapiro about dining at the Kitcheteria, after which she will go shopping at Garfinckels.
Coplon to Shapiro regarding a movie date.
Shapiro to Coplon, will leave the office for an hour to see Shapiro's landlord.

January 27
Coplon from Shapiro, going home together.

January 28
Coplon to Shapiro, discussing a movie date.
Coplon to unidentified man saying she would be in New York Feb. 18–19.
(Agent indicated this in-room message was "important.")

February 4
Coplon tells someone (probably Foley) that she put confidential material in her desk.

February 11
Coplon and unidentified man discuss loyalty board and specific incident.

February 14
Lenvin invites Shapiro and Koski for cards.
Coplon to Foley regarding not seeing communist reports lately.

February 16
Coplon requests that a civil service exam be mailed to her.

February 17
Coplon to female regarding change in reading of reports.
Room conversation between Coplon and Foley regarding trip the next day to New York; she would leave Washington at 2 P.M.
Coplon to Ext. 500 asking for a specific file.

February 18
Coplon meeting with Foley, "unpleasant," she wishes for a new job.
Coplon to "Henry" saying she was taking the train to New York.

March 2
Coplon to Bernie Morris, saying she will be leaving for New York March 4.

March 3 (the day before the arrest)

Coplon heard moving about the room.

Room conversation. Coplon tells Foley her plans for New York tomorrow. (Agent notes the call is not recorded.)

Bernie Morris to Coplon regarding his getting "it" to her; her plans for the lunch hour.

Room conversation with Foley regarding March 4 trip to New York.

Sid Brodie to Coplon asking her to lunch with him and Shapiro.

Annis to Coplon, discussing Italian and Netherlands information.

Coplon to Ext. 500, asking for new sections of a file.

Coplon to Shapiro at home; he has a cold.

March 4

Coplon heard in room.

Shapiro, leaving word.

Shapiro to Coplon, with her telling Shapiro she would take the 1 P.M. train.

Room conversation. Coplon tells Shapiro that she will call Saturday.

Coplon to Bernie Morris and his return call regarding filing an application.

March 7–9

Calls and conversations relating to the arrest and reactions to it.

REB:MTL Log, General Activities of Judith Coplon
Wiretap at the Brooklyn family residence

This log is more detailed; its full entries provide information on the Coplon family's feelings, reactions, and activities in the period February 27 to March 23. The surveillance also allowed the government to keep track of the Coplons' thinking and planning with regard to legal counsel for Judith, as well as listening in on conversations with counsel.

Date and subject of comunication:

February 27

Bertram Coplon to his mother saying Judith had tried to reach her.

Judith Coplon to her mother giving plans for her March 4 trip to New York.

March 5

Reporter to Mrs. Coplon advising of Judith's arrest and the charges.

Bertram Coplon to his mother regarding the arrest.

Bertram Coplon to his wife discussing the charge against his sister.

Bernie Morris to Bertram Coplon expressing concern and offering help.

Bertram Coplon talks with his wife and her father; his father-in-law suggests getting in touch with Archie Palmer.

Bertram Coplon to his mother saying he had gone to retrieve Judith's bag left at Penn Station; further, predicts Judith would be out on bail on Monday.

Bertram Coplon to the wife of the family physician regarding thoughts about whether his sister was a Communist.

Bertram Coplon to his wife, a tense conversation about Judith's arrest.

March 6

Bertram's call to a business friend regarding the question of Judith's guilt.

Sidney Berman to Mrs. Coplon discussing his friendship with Judith.

Bertram Coplon (several calls) to business associate Mel Rodgers; Rodgers offers a loan of $10,000 for bail.

Al Rosen to Bertram Coplon offering to inquire at the U.S. Attorney's office regarding competent counsel.

March 7

Bertram Coplon to his aunt regarding counsel for Judith.

Bertram Coplon to his wife saying he would live with his sister for the time being.

March 8

Bertram Coplon in discussion with parents and Aunt Rose on his visit to Judith and further discussion on counsel.

March 9

Discussion between Bertram Coplon and Mel Rodgers concerning bail situation and Coplon's claim of securing "the biggest attorney in the U.S."

March 11

Harry Rogue to Mrs. Coplon; he is "extremely anxious" to find Bertram Coplon.

Bertram Coplon makes frequent unsuccessful calls to a cousin in New Jersey.

Bertram Coplon to attorney Bertram Adams, saying he was changing the telephone number and that he was seeking a "peaceful" place for Judith when she was freed.

March 12

Bertram Coplon calls his wife and aunt advising they call friends to tell them the new unlisted telephone number.

Judith Coplon to union official Arthur Kinoy asking for advice on securing an attorney.

March 13

Bertram Kaye (cousin) and attorney Adams discuss Judith's refusal to discuss the "facts of this case" even with her family, noting that she was "very emotional."

March 14

Judith Coplon and Anna Wolin, who adivsed that Archie Palmer wished to see Judith.

Bertram Coplon to Judith confirming a meeting with Palmer.

Judith Coplon to her sister-in-law saying the situation was intolerable and that she was about ready to shoot herself.

March 15

Bertram Coplon to his sister reporting on attorneys recommended by his father-in-law, banker J.A. Seidman, noting the confidentiality of the conversation.

Mrs. Coplon to her sister cautioning against visits to the family home for reasons of safety, also discussing Judith's safety.

March 16

Bertram Coplon in conversation with his lawyer Adams regarding a $5,000 exclusive interview with a news service.

Bertram Coplon to new lawyer Archie Palmer, wherein Palmer first raises the question of possible tapping of the family's telephones.

Bertram Coplon and attorney Bertram Adams discuss Judith's second arrest in Washington, including Coplon's concerns about making bail.

Judith and Bertram Coplon discuss strategy with one of her attorneys, Sam Neuburger.

Bertram Coplon to his wife, who relays messages from attorney Archie Palmer.

March 17

Bertram Coplon and his wife discuss Palmer's representation; Coplon expresses concern about Judith's being left alone with their elderly parents.

March 18

Judith and Bertram Coplon discuss her being distraught; he becomes alarmed when she says she is going to take some pills and near hysteria results.

Judith and Bertram in highly emotional exchanges with accusations hurled back and forth.

March 19

Bertram Coplon tells Archie Palmer details about bail raised for Judith.

March 20

Bertram Coplon to his wife, advising that Palmer would accompany Judith to Washington for her second arrest, more on family finances.

March 22

Attorney Neuburger to Judith Coplon regarding various issues and setting a meeting date at his home.

Judith Coplon to Anna Volin concerning returning to her Washington apartment to get clothes and belongings.

Archie Palmer to Judith Coplon scolding her for remarks made to the press and discussing work to be done.

Bertram Coplon to Paul Lazarus regarding serious financial problems and rumors that Coplon was a Communist.

March 23

Judith Coplon to her mother discussing meetings with Archie Palmer.

Bertram Coplon and Archie Palmer on financial matters.

Judith Coplon to Sylvan Wolin regarding her belongings left in Washington.

Tap Log Location

DR Log: National Archives and Records Administration, Northeast Division, C129-158. Box 1, folder 3. Court Exhibit 57, U.S. District Court, Second District of New York, Feb. 7, 1950. Pages 8, 76–80, 97, 138–150.

REB:MTL Log, National Archives and Records Administration, Northeast Division, NY65-14932. Box 1, folder 1. Court Exhibit 46b12 U.S. District Court for the Second District of New York, January 16, 1950. Pages 120–130.

VENONA DOCUMENTS RELATED TO SIMA

From: *Venona, Soviet Espionage and The American Response* 1939–1957. Also from private sources.

1944

Date	To	From	No.	Subject
20 July	MOSCOW	NY (MAJ)[1]	1014	SIMA's[2] New York workplace; request for her recruitment as agent
26 July	VIKTOR[3]	NY (MAJ)	1050	Putting SIMA "on ice"
1 October	VIKTOR	NY (MAJ)	1385	SIMA temporarily avoiding ZORA[4]
12 November	VIKTOR	NY	1587	SIMA disappointed about not having an anticipated "personal talk," and ZORA's needing instructions for their work
5 December	VIKTOR	NY (MAJ)	1714	Counting on making SIMA active
31 December	VIKTOR	NY (MAJ & BORIS)[5]	1845	SIMA goes to FARS in Washington. From Boris: Destroy p.7, pad 5/219

1945

Date	To	From	No.	Subject
8 January	VIKTOR	NY (MAJ)	27	SERGEJ's[6] meeting with SIMA
15 January	VIKTOR	NY (MAJ)	55	Re: detailed report of above meeting
17 January	VIKTOR	NY (MAJ)	76	Unclear on SIMA identification, but assumes "she" was satisfied with it.
24 March	NEW YORK	MOSCOW	268	Change in technical liaison for SIMA
28 March	NEW YORK	MOSCOW	286&284	Re: ZORA's reports.
26 June	MOSCOW	NY	992	SIMA should refrain from taking documents "until she is trusted"
5 July	VIKTOR	ANTON[7]	1053	Re: liaison with SIMA

1949

Date	To	From	No.	Subject
16 March	President Truman	Clark	V.24	Deportation of Valentin Gubitchev
9 May	Gardner	Lamphere	V.25	Flora Don Wovschin (ZORA)

[1] MAJ: Stepan Apresyan
[2] SIMA: Identified as Judith Coplon
[3] VIKTOR: Lt. Gen. P.M. Fitin
[4] ZORA: Flora Don Wovschin
[5] BORIS: Aleksandr Pavlovich Saprykin
[6] SERGEJ: Vladimir Sergeavich Pravdin
[7] ANTON: Leonid Romanovich Kvasnikov

ACKNOWLEDGMENTS

Heartfelt thanks go to former FBI special agents connected with this case who offered support and information to the authors throughout the project. While recognizing that the Bureau made critical errors during America's first arrest and trial of a Cold War spy, they, like Tom Mitchell, remain steadfast in their dedication to the Bureau and proud of its exemplary work over the years. Special thanks go to Robert Lamphere, who was nothing short of phenomenal, providing meticulous detail, continued inspiration, and treasured friendship. Robert Granville, like Lamphere, is a hero to the authors, a fine man who revealed much about that historic night of March 4, 1949, and its tumultuous aftermath. Hollis Bowers not only shared his story of working on the case, but also prepared a fabulous feast for us. Robert McQueen, a wellspring of information, admits to being the "only surveillance agent who lost Judy three times in one day"—in a beauty salon, a department store, and finally on the dance floor of the Mayflower Hotel. Also speaking with us was Thomas Mendenhall, who was on the Coplon surveillance squad and who rode with her on the train to New York that fateful afternoon of March 4, 1949. Bureau colleague and carpooling friend from the past, Donald Perrine, a neighbor of the accused early on, knew her in the days before her arrest and provided insight about the young woman considered the typical, the ideal "girl next door."

At Bureau headquarters, the J. Edgar Hoover Building in Washington, Bobbi Oliveri and Charlie Miller were gracious and helpful during the early days of research, and Linda Colton was extremely kind and supportive years later as research was ending.

Not of the FBI, the sister-in-law of former agent Lamphere, Phyllis

Lamphere, was good enough to talk with us about college days when she and Judith were at Barnard. Martha Lamphere, Harriet "Peg" McQueen, and Patricia Perrine were most gracious about our lengthy conversations with their husbands.

One cannot say enough about Robert Louis "Lou" Benson of the National Security Agency and his willingness to be of help. He was a key to the NSA-CIA release of the Venona files, and thus is a hero not only to us, but also to every writer and historian interested in World War II and Cold War espionage.

Appreciation extends halfway around the globe, to Moscow and two very special people, Oleg Tsarev and Lev Koshliakov. Former KGB officers, they were superb hosts and instructors—and in the end, it was Oleg who put into place the most vital piece of the Coplon puzzle. We are grateful for their words: "First we were adversaries, then colleagues; now we are friends." Very special thanks to Oleg Kalugin, former KGB Major General and chief of KGB worldwide counterintelligence. Internationally known commentator on counterintelligence and intelligence isues, author of *The First Chief Directorate*, this remarkable man provided us with our first real clue about the guilt or innocence in this complex case. We are deeply grateful for his candid and thoughtful response to our questions.

A great many hours were spent in the Federal Archives in Manhattan, and at the Federal Records Center in Suitland, Maryland. We are especially grateful to Richard Gelbke in New York, whose generosity with his time and talent made our days among thousands of pages easier than they otherwise would have been, and to Joseph Majid Jr., who was especially helpful during our last trip there. The Maryland staff was also helpful, as were staffs at the federal courthouses in Washington and in New York.

Invisible Cities Press senior editors Rowan Jacobsen and Joel Bernstein deserve very special thanks for their enthusiasm and guidance, for caring about this project, and for bringing it to fruition. Thanks to the ICP team of copyeditor Laura Jorstad, designer Peter Holm, and proofreader Janet Jesso for their superb work on this project. To Frankie Ross, in Ireland, who offered editorial comment, we say *go raibh maith agat*. To a fine writer, daughter and author Kristin Donnan, thanks for emotional and invaluable editorial support.

Other family members watched the project over a decade, offering unfailing encouragement and understanding—sons Jay and Alan and their families.

Finally, deep and loving thanks to someone who wants none, someone who hoped this story would stay buried, while surely understanding that it could not. The gracious someone who spoke to us candidly and openly, that one person we hope will understand why we believed the storytellers *had* to be us, and no one else.

INDEX